Java 9 Concurrency Cookbook

Second Edition

D1477041

Master the art of fast, effective Java development with the power of concurrent and parallel programming

Javier Fernández González

Packt>

BIRMINGHAM - MUMBAI

Java 9 Concurrency Cookbook

Second Edition

First published: October 2012

Second edition: April 2017

Production reference: 1170417

Published by Packt Publishing Ltd.
Livery Place
35 Livery Street
Birmingham
B32PB, UK.
ISBN 978-1-78712-441-7

www.packtpub.com

Credits

Author

Javier Fernández González

Reviewer

Piotr Bzdyl

Commissioning Editor

Kunal Parikh

Acquisition Editor

Denim Pinto

Content Development Editor

Nikhil Borkar

Technical Editor

Subhalaxmi Nadar

Copy Editor

Gladson Monteiro

Project Coordinator

Vaidehi Sawant

Proofreader

Safis Editing

Indexer

Tejal Daruwale Soni

Graphics

Abhinash Sahu

Production Coordinator

Melwyn Dsa

About the Author

Javier Fernández González is a software architect with almost 15 years of experience in Java technologies. He has worked as a teacher, researcher, programmer, analyst, and writer, and he now works as an architect in all types of projects related to Java, especially J2EE. As a teacher, has taken over 1,000 hours of training in basic Java, J2EE, and the Struts framework. As a researcher, he has worked in the field of information retrieval, developing applications for processing large amounts of data in Java, and has participated as a coauthor in several journal articles and conference presentations. Recently, he worked on developing J2EE web applications for various clients from different sectors (public administration, insurance, healthcare, transportation, and so on). Currently, he works as a software architect. He is the author of the book, *Java 7 Concurrency Cookbook* and *Mastering Concurrency Programming with Java 8* by Packt.

About the Reviewer

Piotr Bzdyl is focused on Java concurrency topics, including other JVM languages and their libraries, aimed at helping in creating highly concurrent applications (async IO, non-blocking APIs, Scala, Akka, and Clojure). He has been helping teams with JVM tuning and troubleshooting.

He has also created a training course for Java concurrency topics, covering core JDK multithreading concepts as well as those from external libraries and languages (actors, STM, parallel collections, and functional languages).

You can connect with Piotr on LinkedIn at `https://www.linkedin.com/in/piotrbzdyl` and on GitHub at `https://github.com/pbzdyl`. You can follow him on Stack Overflow at `http://stackoverflow.com/cv/piotrekbzdyl`.

www.PacktPub.com

For support files and downloads related to your book, please visit www.PacktPub.com.

Did you know that Packt offers eBook versions of every book published, with PDF and ePub files available? You can upgrade to the eBook version at www.PacktPub.com and as a print book customer, you are entitled to a discount on the eBook copy. Get in touch with us at service@packtpub.com for more details.

At www.PacktPub.com, you can also read a collection of free technical articles, sign up for a range of free newsletters and receive exclusive discounts and offers on Packt books and eBooks.

https://www.packtpub.com/mapt

Get the most in-demand software skills with Mapt. Mapt gives you full access to all Packt books and video courses, as well as industry-leading tools to help you plan your personal development and advance your career.

Why subscribe?

- Fully searchable across every book published by Packt
- Copy and paste, print, and bookmark content
- On demand and accessible via a web browser

Customer Feedback

Thanks for purchasing this Packt book. At Packt, quality is at the heart of our editorial process. To help us improve, please leave us an honest review on this book's Amazon page at https://www.amazon.com/dp/178712441X.

If you'd like to join our team of regular reviewers, you can e-mail us at customerreviews@packtpub.com. We award our regular reviewers with free eBooks and videos in exchange for their valuable feedback. Help us be relentless in improving our products!

To Nuria, Paula, and Pelayo, for you infinite love and patience

Table of Contents

Preface

When you work with a computer, you can do several things at once. You can listen to music while you edit a document in a word processor and read your e-mails. This can be done because your operating system allows the concurrency of tasks. Concurrent programming is about the elements and mechanisms a platform offers to have multiple tasks or programs running at once and communicating with each other, to exchange data or to synchronize with each other. Java is a concurrent platform, and it offers a lot of classes to execute concurrent tasks inside a Java program. With each version, Java increases the functionalities offered to programmers to facilitate the development of concurrent programs. This book covers the most important and useful mechanisms included in version 9 of the Java concurrency API, so you will be able to use them directly in your applications. The mechanisms are as follows:

- Basic thread management
- Thread synchronization mechanisms
- Thread creation and management delegation with executors
- Fork/Join framework to enhance the performance of your application
- Parallel streams to process big sets of data in a parallel way, including the new Java 9 reactive streams
- Data structures for concurrent programs
- Adapting the default behavior of some concurrency classes to your needs
- Testing Java concurrency applications

What this book covers

Chapter 1, *Thread Management*, teaches you how to make basic operations with threads. The creation, execution, and status management of threads are explained through basic examples.

Chapter 2, *Basic Thread Synchronization*, covers how to use low-level Java mechanisms to synchronize code. Locks and the synchronized keyword are explained in detail.

Chapter 3, *Thread Synchronization Utilities*, teaches how to use the high-level utilities of Java to manage the synchronization between threads in Java. It includes an explanation of how to use the Phaser class to synchronize tasks divided into phases.

Chapter 4, *Thread Executors*, explores the delegation of thread management to executors. They allow running, managing, and getting the results of concurrent tasks.

Chapter 5, *Fork/Join Framework*, covers the use of the Fork/Join framework. It's a special kind of executor oriented to execute tasks that will be divided into smaller ones using the divide and conquer technique.

Chapter 6, *Parallel and Reactive Streams*, teaches you how to create streams and use all its intermediate and terminal operations to process big collections of data in a parallel and functional way. Streams were introduced in Java 8. Java 9 has included some new interfaces to implement reactive streams.

Chapter 7, *Concurrent Collections*, explains how to use some concurrent data structures provided by the Java language. These data structures must be used in concurrent programs to avoid the use of synchronized blocks of code in their implementation.

Chapter 8, *Customizing Concurrency Classes*, teaches you how to adapt some of the most useful classes of the Java concurrency API to your needs.

Chapter 9, *Testing Concurrent Applications*, covers how to obtain information about the status of some of the most useful structures of the Java 7 concurrency API. You will also learn how to use some free tools to debug concurrent applications, such as the Eclipse, NetBeans IDE, or FindBugs applications to detect possible bugs in your applications.

Chapter 10, *Additional Information*, explores the notions of synchronization, the executor, the Fork/Join framework, concurrent data structures, and the monitoring of concurrent objects, which were not included in the respective chapters.

Chapter 11, *Concurrent Programming Design*, provides some tips that every programmer should consider when they develop a concurrent application.

What you need for this book

To follow this book, you need some basic knowledge of the Java programming language. You should know how to use an IDE, such as Eclipse or NetBeans, but this is not a necessary prerequisite.

Who this book is for

If you are a Java developer interested in enhancing your knowledge of concurrent programming and multithreading further, as well as discovering the new concurrency features of Java 8 and Java 9, then the *Java 9 Concurrency Cookbook* is for you. You should already be comfortable with general Java development practices, and a basic grasp of threads would be an advantage.

Sections

In this book, you will find several headings that appear frequently (Getting ready, How to do it, How it works, There's more, and See also).

To give clear instructions on how to complete a recipe, we use these sections as follows:

Getting ready

This section tells you what to expect in the recipe, and describes how to set up any software or any preliminary settings required for the recipe.

How to do it...

This section contains the steps required to follow the recipe.

How it works...

This section usually consists of a detailed explanation of what happened in the previous section.

There's more...

This section consists of additional information about the recipe in order to make the reader more knowledgeable about the recipe.

See also

This section provides helpful links to other useful information for the recipe.

Conventions

In this book, you will find a number of text styles that distinguish between different kinds of information. Here are some examples of these styles and an explanation of their meaning.

Code words in text, database table names, folder names, filenames, file extensions, pathnames, dummy URLs, user input, and Twitter handles are shown as follows: "The one that executes the `main()` method."

A block of code is set as follows:

```
Thread task=new PrimeGenerator();
task.start();
```

New terms and **important words** are shown in bold. Words that you see on the screen, for example, in menus or dialog boxes, appear in the text like this: "Create a new project by clicking on the **New Project** option under the **File** menu"

Warnings or important notes appear in a box like this.

Tips and tricks appear like this.

Reader feedback

Feedback from our readers is always welcome. Let us know what you think about this book-what you liked or disliked. Reader feedback is important for us as it helps us develop titles that you will really get the most out of.

To send us general feedback, simply e-mail `feedback@packtpub.com`, and mention the book's title in the subject of your message.

If there is a topic that you have expertise in and you are interested in either writing or contributing to a book, see our author guide at `www.packtpub.com/authors`.

Customer support

Now that you are the proud owner of a Packt book, we have a number of things to help you to get the most from your purchase.

Downloading the example code

You can download the example code files for this book from your account at `http://www.p acktpub.com`. If you purchased this book elsewhere, you can visit `http://www.packtpub.c om/support` and register to have the files e-mailed directly to you.

You can download the code files by following these steps:

1. Log in or register to our website using your e-mail address and password.
2. Hover the mouse pointer on the **SUPPORT** tab at the top.
3. Click on **Code Downloads & Errata**.
4. Enter the name of the book in the **Search** box.
5. Select the book for which you're looking to download the code files.
6. Choose from the drop-down menu where you purchased this book from.
7. Click on **Code Download**.

You can also download the code files by clicking on the **Code Files** button on the book's webpage at the Packt Publishing website. This page can be accessed by entering the book's name in the **Search** box. Please note that you need to be logged in to your Packt account.

Once the file is downloaded, please make sure that you unzip or extract the folder using the latest version of:

- WinRAR / 7-Zip for Windows
- Zipeg / iZip / UnRarX for Mac
- 7-Zip / PeaZip for Linux

The code bundle for the book is also hosted on GitHub at `https://github.com/PacktPublishing/Java-9-Concurrency-Cookbook-Second-Edition`. We also have other code bundles from our rich catalog of books and videos available at `htt ps://github.com/PacktPublishing/`. Check them out!

Errata

Although we have taken every care to ensure the accuracy of our content, mistakes do happen. If you find a mistake in one of our books-maybe a mistake in the text or the code-we would be grateful if you could report this to us. By doing so, you can save other readers from frustration and help us improve subsequent versions of this book. If you find any errata, please report them by visiting http://www.packtpub.com/submit-errata, selecting your book, clicking on the **Errata Submission Form** link, and entering the details of your errata. Once your errata are verified, your submission will be accepted and the errata will be uploaded to our website or added to any list of existing errata under the Errata section of that title.

To view the previously submitted errata, go to https://www.packtpub.com/books/content/support and enter the name of the book in the search field. The required information will appear under the **Errata** section.

Piracy

Piracy of copyrighted material on the Internet is an ongoing problem across all media. At Packt, we take the protection of our copyright and licenses very seriously. If you come across any illegal copies of our works in any form on the Internet, please provide us with the location address or website name immediately so that we can pursue a remedy.

Please contact us at copyright@packtpub.com with a link to the suspected pirated material.

We appreciate your help in protecting our authors and our ability to bring you valuable content.

Questions

If you have a problem with any aspect of this book, you can contact us at questions@packtpub.com, and we will do our best to address the problem.

1
Thread Management

In this chapter, we will cover the following topics:

- Creating, running, and setting the characteristics of a thread
- Interrupting a thread
- Controlling the interruption of a thread
- Sleeping and resuming a thread
- Waiting for the finalization of a thread
- Creating and running a daemon thread
- Processing uncontrolled exceptions in a thread
- Using thread local variables
- Grouping threads and processing uncontrolled exceptions in a group of threads
- Creating threads through a factory

Introduction

In the computer world, when we talk about concurrency, we refer to a series of independent and unrelated tasks that run simultaneously on a computer. This simultaneity can be real if the computer has more than one processor or a multi-core processor, or it can be apparent if the computer has only one core processor.

All modern operating systems allow the execution of concurrent tasks. You can read your e-mails while listening to music or reading news on a web page. We can say this is process-level concurrency. But inside a process, we can also have various simultaneous tasks. Concurrent tasks that run inside a process are called **threads**. Another concept related to concurrency is parallelism. There are different definitions and relations with the concurrency concept. Some authors talk about concurrency when you execute your application with multiple threads in a single-core processor. With this, you can see when your program execution is apparent. They talk about parallelism when you execute your application with multiple threads in a multi-core processor or in a computer with more than one processor, so this case is real as well. Other authors talk about concurrency when the threads of an application are executed without a predefined order, and they discuss parallelism when all these threads are executed in an ordered way.

This chapter presents a number of recipes that will show you how to perform basic operations with threads, using the Java 9 API. You will see how to create and run threads in a Java program, how to control their execution, process exceptions thrown by them, and how to group some threads to manipulate them as a unit.

Creating, running, and setting the characteristics of a thread

In this recipe, we will learn how to do basic operations over a thread using the Java API. As with every element in the Java language, threads are objects. We have two ways of creating a thread in Java:

- Extending the `Thread` class and overriding the `run()` method.
- Building a class that implements the `Runnable` interface and the `run()` method and then creating an object of the `Thread` class by passing the `Runnable` object as a parameter--this is the preferred approach and it gives you more flexibility.

In this recipe, we will use the second approach to create threads. Then, we will learn how to change some attributes of the threads. The Thread class saves some information attributes that can help us identify a thread, know its status, or control its priority. These attributes are:

- **ID**: This attribute stores a unique identifier for each thread.
- **Name**: This attribute stores the name of the thread.
- **Priority**: This attribute stores the priority of the Thread objects. In Java 9, threads can have priority between 1 and 10, where 1 is the lowest priority and 10 is the highest. It's not recommended that you change the priority of the threads. It's only a hint to the underlying operating system and it doesn't guarantee anything, but it's a possibility that you can use if you want.
- **Status**: This attribute stores the status of a thread. In Java, a thread can be present in one of the six states defined in the Thread.State enumeration: NEW, RUNNABLE, BLOCKED, WAITING, TIMED_WAITING, or TERMINATED. The following is a list specifying what each of these states means:
    - NEW: The thread has been created and it has not yet started
    - RUNNABLE: The thread is being executed in the JVM
    - BLOCKED: The thread is blocked and it is waiting for a monitor
    - WAITING: The thread is waiting for another thread
    - TIMED_WAITING: The thread is waiting for another thread with a specified waiting time
    - TERMINATED: The thread has finished its execution

In this recipe, we will implement an example that will create and run 10 threads that would calculate the prime numbers within the first 20,000 numbers.

Getting ready

The example for this recipe has been implemented using the Eclipse IDE. If you use Eclipse or a different IDE, such as NetBeans, open it and create a new Java project.

How to do it...

Follow these steps to implement the example:

1. Create a class named `Calculator` that implements the `Runnable` interface:

   ```
   public class Calculator implements Runnable {
   ```

2. Implement the `run()` method. This method will execute the instructions of the thread we are creating, so this method will calculate the prime numbers within the first 20000 numbers:

   ```
   @Override
   public void run() {
       long current = 1L;
       long max = 20000L;
       long numPrimes = 0L;

       System.out.printf("Thread '%s': START\n",
                         Thread.currentThread().getName());
       while (current <= max) {
         if (isPrime(current)) {
           numPrimes++;
         }
         current++;
       }
       System.out.printf("Thread '%s': END. Number of Primes: %d\n",
                       Thread.currentThread().getName(), numPrimes);
   }
   ```

3. Then, implement the *auxiliar* `isPrime()` method. This method determines whether a number is a prime number or not:

   ```
   private boolean isPrime(long number) {
       if (number <= 2) {
         return true;
       }
       for (long i = 2; i < number; i++) {
         if ((number % i) == 0) {
           return false;
         }
       }
       return true;
   }
   ```

4. Now implement the main class of the application. Create a class named `Main` that contains the `main()` method:

```
public class Main {
        public static void main(String[] args) {
```

5. First, write some information regarding the values of the maximum, minimum, and default priority of the threads:

```
System.out.printf("Minimum Priority: %s\n",
                Thread.MIN_PRIORITY);
System.out.printf("Normal Priority: %s\n",
                Thread.NORM_PRIORITY);
System.out.printf("Maximun Priority: %s\n",
                Thread.MAX_PRIORITY);
```

6. Then create 10 `Thread` objects to execute 10 `Calculator` tasks. Also, create two arrays to store the `Thread` objects and their statuses. We will use this information later to check the finalization of the threads. Execute five threads (the even ones) with maximum priority and the other five with minimum priority:

```
Thread threads[];
Thread.State status[];
threads = new Thread[10];
status = new Thread.State[10];
for (int i = 0; i < 10; i++) {
threads[i] = new Thread(new Calculator());
  if ((i % 2) == 0) {
    threads[i].setPriority(Thread.MAX_PRIORITY);
  } else {
    threads[i].setPriority(Thread.MIN_PRIORITY);
  }
    threads[i].setName("My Thread " + i);
}
```

7. We are going to write information in a text file, so create a try-with-resources statement to manage the file. Inside this block of code, write the status of the threads in the file before you launch them. Then, launch the threads:

```
try (FileWriter file = new FileWriter(".\\data\\log.txt");
PrintWriter pw = new PrintWriter(file);) {

  for (int i = 0; i < 10; i++) {
    pw.println("Main : Status of Thread " + i + " : " +
                threads[i].getState());
    status[i] = threads[i].getState();
```

```
    }
    for (int i = 0; i < 10; i++) {
      threads[i].start();
    }
```

8. After this, wait for the finalization of the threads. As we will learn in the *Waiting for the finalization of a thread* recipe of this chapter, we can use the `join()` method to wait for this to happen. In this case, we want to write information about the threads when their statuses change, so we can't use this method. We use this block of code:

```
boolean finish = false;
while (!finish) {
  for (int i = 0; i < 10; i++) {
    if (threads[i].getState() != status[i]) {
      writeThreadInfo(pw, threads[i], status[i]);
      status[i] = threads[i].getState();
    }
  }

  finish = true;
  for (int i = 0; i < 10; i++) {
    finish = finish && (threads[i].getState() ==
                    State.TERMINATED);
  }
}

} catch (IOException e) {
  e.printStackTrace();
}
}
```

9. In the previous block of code, we called the `writeThreadInfo()` method to write information about the status of a thread in the file. This is the code for this method:

```
private static void writeThreadInfo(PrintWriter pw,
                                Thread thread,
                                State state) {
  pw.printf("Main : Id %d - %s\n", thread.getId(),
            thread.getName());
  pw.printf("Main : Priority: %d\n", thread.getPriority());
  pw.printf("Main : Old State: %s\n", state);
  pw.printf("Main : New State: %s\n", thread.getState());
  pw.printf("Main : ************************************\n");
}
```

10. Run the program and see how the different threads work in parallel.

How it works...

The following screenshot shows the console part of the output of the program. We can see that all the threads we have created run in parallel to do their respective jobs:

```
Problems  @ Javadoc  Declaration  Search  Console ⊠  Err
<terminated> Main (1) [Java Application] C:\Program Files\Java\jdk-9\bin\j
Minimum Priority: 1
Normal Priority: 5
Maximun Priority: 10
Thread 'My Thread 0': START
Thread 'My Thread 3': START
Thread 'My Thread 2': START
Thread 'My Thread 8': START
Thread 'My Thread 6': START
Thread 'My Thread 8': END. Number of Primes: 2263
Thread 'My Thread 0': END. Number of Primes: 2263
Thread 'My Thread 1': START
Thread 'My Thread 4': START
Thread 'My Thread 5': START
Thread 'My Thread 9': START
Thread 'My Thread 4': END. Number of Primes: 2263
Thread 'My Thread 6': END. Number of Primes: 2263
Thread 'My Thread 2': END. Number of Primes: 2263
Thread 'My Thread 9': END. Number of Primes: 2263
Thread 'My Thread 5': END. Number of Primes: 2263
Thread 'My Thread 7': START
Thread 'My Thread 3': END. Number of Primes: 2263
Thread 'My Thread 1': END. Number of Primes: 2263
Thread 'My Thread 7': END. Number of Primes: 2263
```

In this screenshot, you can see how threads are created and how the ones with an even number are executed first, as they have the highest priority, and the others executed later, as they have minimum priority. The following screenshot shows part of the output of the `log.txt` file where we write information about the status of the threads:

```
 6 Main : Status of Thread 5 : NEW
 7 Main : Status of Thread 6 : NEW
 8 Main : Status of Thread 7 : NEW
 9 Main : Status of Thread 8 : NEW
10 Main : Status of Thread 9 : NEW
11 Main : Id 13 - My Thread 0
12 Main : Priority: 10
13 Main : Old State: NEW
14 Main : New State: RUNNABLE
15 Main : ***********************************
16 Main : Id 14 - My Thread 1
17 Main : Priority: 1
18 Main : Old State: NEW
19 Main : New State: BLOCKED
20 Main : ***********************************
21 Main : Id 15 - My Thread 2
22 Main : Priority: 10
23 Main : Old State: NEW
24 Main : New State: RUNNABLE
25 Main : ***********************************
```

Every Java program has at least one execution thread. When you run the program, JVM runs the execution thread that calls the `main()` method of the program.

When we call the `start()` method of a Thread object, we are creating another execution thread. Our program will have as many execution threads as the number of calls made to the `start()` method.

The `Thread` class has attributes to store all of the information of a thread. The OS scheduler uses the priority of threads to select the one that uses the CPU at each moment and actualizes the status of every thread according to its situation.

If you don't specify a name for a thread, JVM automatically assigns it one in this format: Thread-XX, where XX is a number. You can't modify the ID or status of a thread. The `Thread` class doesn't implement the `setId()` and `setStatus()` methods as these methods introduce modifications in the code.

A Java program ends when all its threads finish (more specifically, when all its non-daemon threads finish). If the initial thread (the one that executes the main() method) ends, the rest of the threads will continue with their execution until they finish. If one of the threads uses the System.exit() instruction to end the execution of the program, all the threads will end their respective execution.

Creating an object of the Thread class doesn't create a new execution thread. Also, calling the run() method of a class that implements the Runnable interface doesn't create a new execution thread. Only when you call the start() method, a new execution thread is created.

There's more...

As mentioned in the introduction of this recipe, there is another way of creating a new execution thread. You can implement a class that extends the Thread class and overrides the run() method of this class. Then, you can create an object of this class and call the start() method to have a new execution thread.

You can use the static method currentThread() of the Thread class to access the thread object that is running the current object.

You have to take into account that the setPriority() method can throw an IllegalArgumentException exception if you try to establish priority that isn't between 1 and 10.

See also

- The *Creating threads through a factory* recipe of this chapter

Interrupting a thread

A Java program with more than one execution thread only finishes when the execution of all of its threads end (more specifically, when all its non-daemon threads end their execution or when one of the threads uses the `System.exit()` method). Sometimes, you may need to finish a thread because you want to terminate a program or when a user of the program wants to cancel the tasks that a thread object is doing.

Java provides an interruption mechanism that indicates to a thread that you want to finish it. One peculiarity of this mechanism is that thread objects have to check whether they have been interrupted or not, and they can decide whether they respond to the finalization request or not. A thread object can ignore it and continue with its execution.

In this recipe, we will develop a program that creates a thread and forces its finalization after 5 seconds, using the interruption mechanism.

Getting ready

The example for this recipe has been implemented using the Eclipse IDE. If you use Eclipse or a different IDE, such as NetBeans, open it and create a new Java project.

How to do it...

Follow these steps to implement the example:

1. Create a class called `PrimeGenerator` that extends the `Thread` class:

   ```
   public class PrimeGenerator extends Thread{
   ```

2. Override the `run()` method including a loop that will run indefinitely. In this loop, process consecutive numbers beginning from one. For each number, calculate whether it's a prime number; if yes, as in this case, write it to the console:

   ```
   @Override
   public void run() {
     long number=1L;
     while (true) {
       if (isPrime(number)) {
         System.out.printf("Number %d is Prime\n",number);
       }
   ```

3. After processing a number, check whether the thread has been interrupted by calling the `isInterrupted()` method. If this method returns `true`, the thread has been interrupted. In this case, we write a message in the console and end the execution of the thread:

```
if (isInterrupted()) {
  System.out.printf("The Prime Generator has been
                   Interrupted");
  return;
}
number++;
  }
}
```

4. Implement the `isPrime()` method. You can get its code from the *Creating, running, and setting information of a thread* recipe of this chapter.

5. Now implement the main class of the example by implementing a class called `Main` and the `main()` method:

```
public class Main {
  public static void main(String[] args) {
```

6. Create and start an object of the `PrimeGenerator` class:

```
Thread task=new PrimeGenerator();
task.start();
```

7. Wait for 5 seconds and interrupt the `PrimeGenerator` thread:

```
try {
  Thread.sleep(5000);
} catch (InterruptedException e) {
  e.printStackTrace();
}
task.interrupt();
```

8. Then, write information related to the status of the interrupted thread. The output of this piece of code will depend on whether the thread ends its execution before or after:

```
System.out.printf("Main: Status of the Thread: %s\n",
                   task.getState());
System.out.printf("Main: isInterrupted: %s\n",
                   task.isInterrupted());
System.out.printf("Main: isAlive: %s\n", task.isAlive());
}
```

9. Run the example and see the results.

How it works...

The following screenshot shows the result of the execution of the previous example. We can see how the PrimeGenerator thread writes the message and ends its execution when it detects that it has been interrupted. Refer to the following screenshot:

```
Javadoc   Declaration   Search   Console ⊠   Problems
<terminated> Main (21) [Java Application] C:\Program Files\Java\jdk-9\b
Number 82721 is Prime
Number 82723 is Prime
Number 82727 is Prime
Number 82729 is Prime
Main: Status of the Thread: RUNNABLE
Main: isInterrupted: true
Main: isAlive: true
Number 82757 is Prime
The Prime Generator has been Interrupted
```

The Thread class has an attribute that stores a boolean value indicating whether the thread has been interrupted or not. When you call the interrupt() method of a thread, you set that attribute to true. The isInterrupted() method only returns the value of that attribute.

The main() method writes information about the status of the interrupted thread. In this case, as this code is executed before the thread has finished its execution, the status is RUNNABLE, the return value of the isInterrupted() method is true, and the return value of the isAlive() method is true as well. If the interrupted Thread finishes its execution before the execution of this block of code (you can, for example, sleep the main thread for a second), the methods isInterrupted() and isAlive() will return a false value.

There's more...

The `Thread` class has another method to check whether a thread has been interrupted or not. It's the static method, `interrupted()`, that checks whether the current thread has been interrupted or not.

 There is an important difference between the `isInterrupted()` and `interrupted()` methods. The first one doesn't change the value of the interrupted attribute, but the second one sets it to `false`.

As mentioned earlier, a thread object can ignore its interruption, but this is not the expected behavior.

Controlling the interruption of a thread

In the previous recipe, you learned how you can interrupt the execution of a thread and what you have to do to control this interruption in the thread object. The mechanism shown in the previous example can be used if the thread that can be interrupted is simple. But if the thread implements a complex algorithm divided into some methods or it has methods with recursive calls, we will need to use a better mechanism to control the interruption of the thread. Java provides the `InterruptedException` exception for this purpose. You can throw this exception when you detect the interruption of a thread and catch it in the `run()` method.

In this recipe, we will implement a task that will look for files with a determined name in a folder and in all its subfolders. This is to show how you can use the `InterruptedException` exception to control the interruption of a thread.

Getting ready

The example for this recipe has been implemented using the Eclipse IDE. If you use Eclipse or a different IDE, such as NetBeans, open it and create a new Java project.

How to do it...

Follow these steps to implement the example:

1. Create a class called `FileSearch` and specify that it implements the `Runnable` interface:

   ```
   public class FileSearch implements Runnable {
   ```

2. Declare two private attributes: one for the name of the file we are going to search for and one for the initial folder. Implement the constructor of the class, which initializes these attributes:

   ```
   private String initPath;
   private String fileName;
   public FileSearch(String initPath, String fileName) {
      this.initPath = initPath;
      this.fileName = fileName;
   }
   ```

3. Implement the `run()` method of the `FileSearch` class. It checks whether the attribute `fileName` is a directory; if it is, it calls the `directoryProcess()` method. This method can throw an `InterruptedException` exception, so we have to catch them:

   ```
   @Override
   public void run() {
      File file = new File(initPath);
      if (file.isDirectory()) {
         try {
            directoryProcess(file);
         } catch (InterruptedException e) {
            System.out.printf("%s: The search has been interrupted",
                        Thread.currentThread().getName());
         }
      }
   }
   ```

4. Implement the `directoryProcess()` method. This method will obtain the files and subfolders in a folder and process them. For each directory, the method will make a recursive call, passing the directory as a parameter. For each file, the method will call the `fileProcess()` method. After processing all files and folders, the method checks whether the thread has been interrupted; if yes, as in this case, it will throw an `InterruptedException` exception:

```
private void directoryProcess(File file) throws
                        InterruptedException {
  File list[] = file.listFiles();
  if (list != null) {
    for (int i = 0; i < list.length; i++) {
      if (list[i].isDirectory()) {
        directoryProcess(list[i]);
      } else {
        fileProcess(list[i]);
      }
    }
  }
  if (Thread.interrupted()) {
    throw new InterruptedException();
  }
}
```

5. Implement the `fileProcess()` method. This method will compare the name of the file it's processing with the name we are searching for. If the names are equal, we will write a message in the console. After this comparison, the thread will check whether it has been interrupted; if yes, as in this case, it will throw an `InterruptedException` exception:

```
private void fileProcess(File file) throws
                        InterruptedException {
  if (file.getName().equals(fileName)) {
    System.out.printf("%s : %s\n",
                Thread.currentThread().getName(),
                file.getAbsolutePath());
  }
  if (Thread.interrupted()) {
    throw new InterruptedException();
  }
}
```

6. Now let's implement the main class of the example. Implement a class called `Main` that contains the `main()` method:

```
public class Main {
    public static void main(String[] args) {
```

7. Create and initialize an object of the `FileSearch` class and thread to execute its task. Then start executing the thread. I have used a Windows operating system route. If you work with other operating systems, such as Linux or iOS, change the route to the one that exists on your operating system:

```
FileSearch searcher = new FileSearch("C:\\Windows",
                                     "explorer.exe");
Thread thread=new Thread(searcher);
thread.start();
```

8. Wait for 10 seconds and interrupt the thread:

```
try {
    TimeUnit.SECONDS.sleep(10);
} catch (InterruptedException e) {
    e.printStackTrace();
}
thread.interrupt();
}
```

9. Run the example and see the results.

How it works...

The following screenshot shows the result of an execution of this example. You can see how the `FileSearch` object ends its execution when it detects that it has been interrupted.

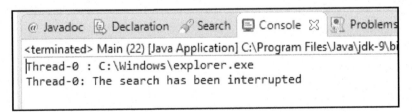

In this example, we use Java exceptions to control the interruption of a thread. When you run the example, the program starts going through folders by checking whether they have the file or not. For example, if you enter in the \b\c\d folder, the program will have three recursive calls to the `directoryProcess()` method. When it detects that it has been interrupted, it throws an `InterruptedException` exception and continues the execution in the `run()` method, no matter how many recursive calls have been made.

There's more...

The `InterruptedException` exception is thrown by some Java methods related to a concurrency API, such as `sleep()`. In this case, this exception is thrown if the thread is interrupted (with the `interrupt()` method) when it's sleeping.

See also

- The *Interrupting a thread* recipe of this chapter

Sleeping and resuming a thread

Sometimes, you may be interested in pausing the execution of a thread during a determined period of time. For example, a thread in a program checks the sensor state once per minute. The rest of the time, it does nothing. During this time, the thread doesn't use any resources of the computer. After this period is over, the thread will be ready to continue with its execution when the operating system scheduler chooses it to be executed. You can use the `sleep()` method of the `Thread` class for this purpose. This method receives a long number as a parameter that indicates the number of milliseconds during which the thread will suspend its execution. After that time, the thread continues with its execution in the next instruction to the `sleep()` one when the JVM assigns it CPU time.

Another possibility is to use the `sleep()` method of an element of the `TimeUnit` enumeration. This method uses the `sleep()` method of the `Thread` class to put the current thread to sleep, but it receives the parameter in the unit that it represents and converts it into milliseconds.

In this recipe, we will develop a program that uses the `sleep()` method to write the actual date every second.

Getting ready

The example for this recipe has been implemented using the Eclipse IDE. If you use Eclipse or a different IDE, such as NetBeans, open it and create a new Java project.

How to do it...

Follow these steps to implement the example:

1. Create a class called `ConsoleClock` and specify that it implements the `Runnable` interface:

```
public class ConsoleClock implements Runnable {
```

2. Implement the `run()` method:

```
@Override
public void run() {
```

3. Write a loop with 10 iterations. In each iteration, create a `Date` object, write it to the console, and call the `sleep()` method of the `SECONDS` attribute of the `TimeUnit` class to suspend the execution of the thread for 1 second. With this value, the thread will be sleeping for approximately 1 second. As the `sleep()` method can throw an `InterruptedException` exception, we have to include some code to catch it. It's good practice to include code that frees or closes the resources the thread is using when it's interrupted:

```
for (int i = 0; i < 10; i++) {
  System.out.printf("%s\n", new Date());
  try {
    TimeUnit.SECONDS.sleep(1);
  } catch (InterruptedException e) {
    System.out.printf("The FileClock has been interrupted");
  }
}
}
```

4. We have implemented the thread. Now let's implement the main class of the example. Create a class called `Main` that contains the `main()` method:

```
public class Main {
  public static void main(String[] args) {
```

5. Create an object of the `FileClock` class and a `thread` to execute it. Then, start executing a thread:

```
FileClock clock=new FileClock();
Thread thread=new Thread(clock);
thread.start();
```

6. Call the `sleep()` method of the `SECONDS` attribute of the `TimeUnit` class in the main thread to wait for 5 seconds:

```
try {
  TimeUnit.SECONDS.sleep(5);
} catch (InterruptedException e) {
  e.printStackTrace();
};
```

7. Interrupt the `FileClock` thread:

```
thread.interrupt();
```

8. Run the example and see the results.

How it works...

When you run the example, you would see how the program writes a `Date` object per second and also the message indicating that the `FileClock` thread has been interrupted.

When you call the `sleep()` method, the thread leaves the CPU and stops its execution for a period of time. During this time, it's not consuming CPU time, so the CPU could be executing other tasks.

When the thread is sleeping and is interrupted, the method throws an `InterruptedException` exception immediately and doesn't wait until the sleeping time is finished.

There's more...

The Java concurrency API has another method that makes a thread object leave the CPU. It's the `yield()` method, which indicates to the JVM that the thread object can leave the CPU for other tasks. The JVM does not guarantee that it will comply with this request. Normally, it's only used for debugging purposes.

Waiting for the finalization of a thread

In some situations, we will have to wait for the end of the execution of a thread (the `run()` method ends its execution). For example, we may have a program that will begin initializing the resources it needs before proceeding with the rest of the execution. We can run initialization tasks as threads and wait for their finalization before continuing with the rest of the program.

For this purpose, we can use the `join()` method of the `Thread` class. When we call this method using a thread object, it suspends the execution of the calling thread until the object that is called finishes its execution.

In this recipe, we will learn the use of this method with an initialization example.

Getting ready

The example for this recipe has been implemented using the Eclipse IDE. If you use Eclipse or a different IDE, such as NetBeans, open it and create a new Java project.

How to do it...

Follow these steps to implement the example:

1. Create a class called `DataSourcesLoader` and specify that it implements the `Runnable` interface:

   ```
   public class DataSourcesLoader implements Runnable {
   ```

2. Implement the `run()` method. It writes a message to indicate that it starts its execution, sleeps for 4 seconds, and writes another message to indicate that it ends its execution:

   ```
   @Override
   public void run() {
     System.out.printf("Beginning data sources loading: %s\n",
                     new Date());
     try {
       TimeUnit.SECONDS.sleep(4);
     } catch (InterruptedException e) {
       e.printStackTrace();
     }
   ```

```
System.out.printf("Data sources loading has finished: %s\n",
                new Date());
    }
```

3. Create a class called `NetworkConnectionsLoader` and specify that it implements the `Runnable` interface. Implement the `run()` method. It will be equal to the `run()` method of the `DataSourcesLoader` class, but it will sleep for 6 seconds.

4. Now, create a class called `Main` that contains the `main()` method:

```
public class Main {
    public static void main(String[] args) {
```

5. Create an object of the `DataSourcesLoader` class and a thread to run it:

```
DataSourcesLoader dsLoader = new DataSourcesLoader();
Thread thread1 = new Thread(dsLoader,"DataSourceThread");
```

6. Create an object of the `NetworkConnectionsLoader` class and a thread to run it:

```
NetworkConnectionsLoader ncLoader = new NetworkConnectionsLoader();
Thread thread2 = new Thread(ncLoader,"NetworkConnectionLoader");
```

7. Call the `start()` method of both the thread objects:

```
thread1.start();
thread2.start();
```

8. Wait for the finalization of both the threads using the `join()` method. This method can throw an `InterruptedException` exception, so we have to include the code to catch it:

```
try {
    thread1.join();
    thread2.join();
} catch (InterruptedException e) {
    e.printStackTrace();
}
```

9. Write a message to indicate the end of the program:

```
System.out.printf("Main: Configuration has been loaded: %s\n",
                new Date());
```

10. Run the program and see the results.

How it works...

When you run this program, you would understand how both the thread objects start their execution. First, the `DataSourcesLoader` thread finishes its execution. Then, the `NetworkConnectionsLoader` class finishes its execution. At this moment, the `main` thread object continues its execution and writes the final message.

There's more...

Java provides two additional forms of the `join()` method:

- `join (long milliseconds)`
- `join (long milliseconds, long nanos)`

In the first version of the `join()` method, instead of indefinitely waiting for the finalization of the thread called, the calling thread waits for the milliseconds specified as the parameter of the method. For example, if the object `thread1` has `thread2.join(1000)`, `thread1` suspends its execution until one of these two conditions are met:

- `thread2` has finished its execution
- 1,000 milliseconds have passed

When one of these two conditions is `true`, the `join()` method returns. You can check the status of the thread to know whether the `join()` method was returned because it finished its execution or because the specified time had passed.

The second version of the `join()` method is similar to the first one, but it receives the number of milliseconds and nanoseconds as parameters.

Creating and running a daemon thread

Java has a special kind of thread called **daemon** thread. When daemon threads are the only threads running in a program, the JVM ends the program after finishing these threads.

With these characteristics, daemon threads are normally used as service providers for normal (also called **user**) threads running in the same program. They usually have an infinite loop that waits for the service request or performs the tasks of a thread. A typical example of these kinds of threads is the Java garbage collector.

In this recipe, we will learn how to create a daemon thread by developing an example with two threads: one user thread that would write events on a queue and a daemon thread that would clean the queue, removing the events that were generated more than 10 seconds ago.

Getting ready

The example for this recipe has been implemented using the Eclipse IDE. If you use Eclipse or a different IDE, such as NetBeans, open it and create a new Java project.

How to do it...

Follow these steps to implement the example:

1. Create the `Event` class. This class only stores information about the events our program will work with. Declare two private attributes: one called the date of the `java.util.Date` type and the other called the event of the `String` type. Generate the methods to write and read their values.

2. Create the `WriterTask` class and specify that it implements the `Runnable` interface:

```
public class WriterTask implements Runnable {
```

3. Declare the queue that stores the events and implement the constructor of the class that initializes this queue:

```
private Deque<Event> deque;
public WriterTask (Deque<Event> deque){
  this.deque=deque;
}
```

4. Implement the `run()` method of this task. This method will have a loop with 100 iterations. In each iteration, we create a new event, save it in the queue, and sleep for 1 second:

```
@Override
public void run() {
  for (int i=1; i<100; i++) {
    Event event=new Event();
    event.setDate(new Date());
    event.setEvent(String.format("The thread %s has generated
                   an event", Thread.currentThread().getId()));
    deque.addFirst(event);
```

```
    try {
        TimeUnit.SECONDS.sleep(1);
    } catch (InterruptedException e) {
        e.printStackTrace();
    }
  }
}
```

5. Create the `CleanerTask` class and specify that it extends the `Thread` class:

```
public class CleanerTask extends Thread {
```

6. Declare the queue that stores the events and implement the constructor of the class that initializes this queue. In the constructor, mark this thread as a daemon thread with the `setDaemon()` method:

```
private Deque<Event> deque;
public CleanerTask(Deque<Event> deque) {
    this.deque = deque;
    setDaemon(true);
}
```

7. Implement the `run()` method. It has an infinite loop that gets the actual date and calls the `clean()` method:

```
@Override
public void run() {
    while (true) {
        Date date = new Date();
        clean(date);
    }
}
```

8. Implement the `clean()` method. It gets the last event, and if it was created more than 10 seconds ago, it deletes it and checks the next event. If an event is deleted, it writes the message of the event and the new size of the queue so you can see its evolution:

```
private void clean(Date date) {
    long difference;
    boolean delete;

    if (deque.size()==0) {
     return;
    }
    delete=false;
    do {
```

```
      Event e = deque.getLast();
      difference = date.getTime() - e.getDate().getTime();
      if (difference > 10000) {
        System.out.printf("Cleaner: %s\n",e.getEvent());
        deque.removeLast();
        delete=true;
      }
    } while (difference > 10000);
    if (delete){
      System.out.printf("Cleaner: Size of the queue: %d\n",
                        deque.size());
    }
  }
```

9. Now implement the `main` class. Create a class called `Main` with a `main()` method:

```
public class Main {
  public static void main(String[] args) {
```

10. Create the queue to store the events using the `Deque` class:

```
Deque<Event> deque=new ConcurrentLinkedDeque<Event>();
```

11. Create and start as many `WriterTask` threads as available processors have the JVM and one `CleanerTask` method:

```
WriterTask writer=new WriterTask(deque);
for (int i=0; i< Runtime.getRuntime().availableProcessors();
     i++){
  Thread thread=new Thread(writer);
  thread.start();
}
CleanerTask cleaner=new CleanerTask(deque);
cleaner.start();
```

12. Run the program and see the results.

How it works...

If you analyze the output of one execution of the program, you would see how the queue begins to grow until it has a size of, in our case, 40 events. Then, its size will vary around 40 events it has grown up to until the end of the execution. This size may depend on the number of cores of your machine. I have executed the code in a four-core processor, so we launch four `WriterTask` tasks.

The program starts with four `WriterTask` threads. Each thread writes an event and sleeps for 1 second. After the first 10 seconds, we have 40 events in the queue. During these 10 seconds, `CleanerTask` are executed whereas the four `WriterTask` threads sleep; however, but it doesn't delete any event because all of them were generated less than 10 seconds ago. During the rest of the execution, `CleanerTask` deletes four events every second and the four `WriterTask` threads write another four; therefore, the size of the queue varies around 40 events it has grown up to. Remember that the execution of this example depends on the number of available cores to the JVM of your computer. Normally, this number is equal to the number of cores of your CPU.

You can play with time until the `WriterTask` threads are sleeping. If you use a smaller value, you will see that `CleanerTask` has less CPU time and the size of the queue will increase because `CleanerTask` doesn't delete any event.

There's more...

You only can call the `setDaemon()` method before you call the `start()` method. Once the thread is running, you can't modify its daemon status calling the `setDaemon()` method. If you call it, you will get an `IllegalThreadStateException` exception.

You can use the `isDaemon()` method to check whether a thread is a daemon thread (the method returns `true`) or a non-daemon thread (the method returns `false`).

Processing uncontrolled exceptions in a thread

A very important aspect in every programming language is the mechanism that helps you manage error situations in your application. The Java programming language, as almost all modern programming languages, implements an exception-based mechanism to manage error situations. These exceptions are thrown by Java classes when an error situation is detected. You can also use these exceptions or implement your own exceptions to manage the errors produced in your classes.

Java also provides a mechanism to capture and process these exceptions. There are exceptions that must be captured or re-thrown using the `throws` clause of a method. These exceptions are called checked exceptions. There are exceptions that don't have to be specified or caught. These are unchecked exceptions:

- **Checked exceptions**: These must be specified in the `throws` clause of a method or caught inside them, for example, `IOException` or `ClassNotFoundException`.
- **Unchecked exceptions**: These don't need to be specified or caught, for example, `NumberFormatException`.

When a checked exception is thrown inside the `run()` method of a thread object, we have to catch and treat them because the `run()` method doesn't accept a `throws` clause. When an unchecked exception is thrown inside the `run()` method of a thread object, the default behavior is to write the stack trace in the console and exit the program.

Fortunately, Java provides us with a mechanism to catch and treat unchecked exceptions thrown in a thread object to avoid ending the program.

In this recipe, we will learn this mechanism using an example.

Getting ready

The example for this recipe has been implemented using the Eclipse IDE. If you use Eclipse or a different IDE, such as NetBeans, open it and create a new Java project.

How to do it...

Follow these steps to implement the example:

1. First of all, we have to implement a class to treat unchecked exceptions. This class must implement the `UncaughtExceptionHandler` interface and implement the `uncaughtException()` method declared in this interface. It's an interface enclosed in the `Thread` class. In our case, let's call this class `ExceptionHandler` and create a method to write information about `Exception` and `Thread` that threw it. The following is the code:

```
public class ExceptionHandler implements UncaughtExceptionHandler {
  @Override
  public void uncaughtException(Thread t, Throwable e) {
```

```
System.out.printf("An exception has been captured\n");
System.out.printf("Thread: %s\n",t.getId());
System.out.printf("Exception: %s: %s\n",
                        e.getClass().getName(),e.getMessage());
System.out.printf("Stack Trace: \n");
e.printStackTrace(System.out);
System.out.printf("Thread status: %s\n",t.getState());
    }
  }
```

2. Now implement a class that throws an unchecked exception. Call this class `Task`, specify that it implements the `Runnable` interface, implement the `run()` method, and force the exception; for example, try to convert a `String` value into an `int` value:

```
public class Task implements Runnable {
  @Override
  public void run() {
    int numero=Integer.parseInt("TTT");
  }
}
```

3. Now implement the main class of the example. Implement a class called `Main` with its `main()` method:

```
public class Main {
  public static void main(String[] args) {
```

4. Create a `Task` object and `Thread` to run it. Set the unchecked exception handler using the `setUncaughtExceptionHandler()` method and start executing the thread:

```
Task task=new Task();
Thread thread=new Thread(task);
thread.setUncaughtExceptionHandler(new ExceptionHandler());
thread.start();
    }
  }
```

5. Run the example and see the results.

How it works...

In the following screenshot, you can see the results of the execution of the example. The exception is thrown and captured by the handler that writes the information about Exception and Thread that threw it. This information is presented in the console:

```
<terminated> Main (3) [Java Application] C:\Program Files\Java\jdk-9\bin\javaw.exe (26 mar. 2017 3:07:07)
An exception has been captured
Thread: 13
Exception: java.lang.NumberFormatException: For input string: "TTT"
Stack Trace:
java.lang.NumberFormatException: For input string: "TTT"
        at java.lang.NumberFormatException.forInputString(java.base@9-ea/NumberFormatException.java:65)
        at java.lang.Integer.parseInt(java.base@9-ea/Integer.java:695)
        at java.lang.Integer.parseInt(java.base@9-ea/Integer.java:813)
        at com.packtpub.java9.concurrency.cookbook.chapter01.recipe07.task.Task.run(Task.java:15)
        at java.lang.Thread.run(java.base@9-ea/Thread.java:843)
Thread status: RUNNABLE
Thread has finished
```

When an exception is thrown in a thread and remains uncaught (it has to be an unchecked exception), the JVM checks whether the thread has an uncaught exception handler set by the corresponding method. If it does, the JVM invokes this method with the Thread object and Exception as arguments.

If the thread doesn't have an uncaught exception handler, the JVM prints the stack trace in the console and ends the execution of the thread that had thrown the exception.

There's more...

The Thread class has another method related to the process of uncaught exceptions. It's the static method setDefaultUncaughtExceptionHandler() that establishes an exception handler for all the thread objects in the application.

When an uncaught exception is thrown in the thread, the JVM looks for three possible handlers for this exception.

First it looks for the uncaught exception handler of the thread objects, as we learned in this recipe. If this handler doesn't exist, the JVM looks for the uncaught exception handler of `ThreadGroup` as explained in the *Grouping threads and processing uncontrolled exceptions in a group of threads* recipe. If this method doesn't exist, the JVM looks for the default uncaught exception handler, as we learned in this recipe.

If none of the handlers exits, the JVM writes the stack trace of the exception in the console and ends the execution of the Thread that had thrown the exception.

See also

- The *Grouping threads and processing uncontrolled exceptions in a group of threads* recipe of this chapter

Using thread local variables

One of the most critical aspects of a concurrent application is shared data. This has special importance in objects that extend the `Thread` class or implement the `Runnable` interface and in objects that are shared between two or more threads.

If you create an object of a class that implements the `Runnable` interface and then start various thread objects using the same `Runnable` object, all the threads would share the same attributes. This means that if you change an attribute in a thread, all the threads will be affected by this change.

Sometimes, you will be interested in having an attribute that won't be shared among all the threads that run the same object. The Java Concurrency API provides a clean mechanism called **thread-local variables** with very good performance. They have some disadvantages as well. They retain their value while the thread is alive. This can be problematic in situations where threads are reused.

In this recipe, we will develop two programs: one that would expose the problem in the first paragraph and another that would solve this problem using the thread-local variables mechanism.

Getting ready

The example for this recipe has been implemented using the Eclipse IDE. If you use Eclipse or a different IDE, such as NetBeans, open it and create a new Java project.

How to do it...

Follow these steps to implement the example:

1. First, implement a program that has the problem exposed previously. Create a class called UnsafeTask and specify that it implements the Runnable interface. Declare a private java.util.Date attribute:

```
public class UnsafeTask implements Runnable{
  private Date startDate;
```

2. Implement the run() method of the UnsafeTask object. This method will initialize the startDate attribute, write its value to the console, sleep for a random period of time, and again write the value of the startDate attribute:

```
@Override
public void run() {
  startDate=new Date();
  System.out.printf("Starting Thread: %s : %s\n",
                    Thread.currentThread().getId(),startDate);
  try {
    TimeUnit.SECONDS.sleep( (int)Math.rint(Math.random()*10));
  } catch (InterruptedException e) {
    e.printStackTrace();
  }
  System.out.printf("Thread Finished: %s : %s\n",
                    Thread.currentThread().getId(),startDate);
}
```

3. Now, implement the main class of this problematic application. Create a class called `Main` with a `main()` method. This method will create an object of the `UnsafeTask` class and start 10 threads using this object, sleeping for 2 seconds between each thread:

```
public class Main {
    public static void main(String[] args) {
        UnsafeTask task=new UnsafeTask();
        for (int i=0; i<10; i++){
            Thread thread=new Thread(task);
            thread.start();
            try {
                TimeUnit.SECONDS.sleep(2);
            } catch (InterruptedException e) {
                e.printStackTrace();
            }
        }
    }
}
```

4. In the following screenshot, you can see the results of this program's execution. Each thread has a different start time, but when they finish, there is a change in the value of the attribute. So they are writing a bad value. For example, check out the thread with the ID 13:

```
<terminated> Main (4) [Java Application] C:\Program Files\Java\jdk-9\bin\javaw.exe
Starting Thread: 13 : Sun Mar 26 03:12:42 CEST 2017
Starting Thread: 14 : Sun Mar 26 03:12:44 CEST 2017
Starting Thread: 15 : Sun Mar 26 03:12:46 CEST 2017
Thread Finished: 14 : Sun Mar 26 03:12:46 CEST 2017
Thread Finished: 13 : Sun Mar 26 03:12:46 CEST 2017
Thread Finished: 15 : Sun Mar 26 03:12:46 CEST 2017
```

5. As mentioned earlier, we are going to use the thread-local variables mechanism to solve this problem.

6. Create a class called `SafeTask` and specify that it implements the `Runnable` interface:

```
public class SafeTask implements Runnable {
```

7. Declare an object of the `ThreadLocal<Date>` class. This object will have an implicit implementation that would include the `initialValue()` method. This method will return the actual date:

```
private static ThreadLocal<Date> startDate=new
                                       ThreadLocal<Date>(){
protected Date initialValue(){
  return new Date();
}
};
```

8. Implement the `run()` method. It has the same functionality as the `run()` method of `UnsafeTask class`, but it changes the way it accesses the `startDate` attribute. Now we will use the `get()` method of the `startDate` object:

```
@Override
public void run() {
  System.out.printf("Starting Thread: %s : %s\n",
              Thread.currentThread().getId(),startDate.get());
  try {
    TimeUnit.SECONDS.sleep((int)Math.rint(Math.random()*10));
  } catch (InterruptedException e) {
    e.printStackTrace();
  }
  System.out.printf("Thread Finished: %s : %s\n",
              Thread.currentThread().getId(),startDate.get());
}
```

9. The `Main` class of this example is the same as the unsafe example. The only difference is that it changes the name of the `Runnable` class.

10. Run the example and analyze the difference.

How it works...

In the following screenshot, you can see the results of the execution of the safe sample. The ten `Thread` objects have their own value of the `startDate` attribute:

```
<terminated> SafeMain [Java Application] C:\Program Files\Java\jdk-9\b
Starting Thread: 13 : Sun Mar 26 03:15:17 CEST 2017
Starting Thread: 14 : Sun Mar 26 03:15:19 CEST 2017
Starting Thread: 15 : Sun Mar 26 03:15:21 CEST 2017
Thread Finished: 15 : Sun Mar 26 03:15:21 CEST 2017
Thread Finished: 13 : Sun Mar 26 03:15:17 CEST 2017
Thread Finished: 14 : Sun Mar 26 03:15:19 CEST 2017
```

The thread-local variables mechanism stores a value of an attribute for each thread that uses one of these variables. You can read the value using the `get()` method and change the value using the `set()` method. The first time you access the value of a thread-local variable, if it has no value for the thread object that it is calling, the thread-local variable will call the `initialValue()` method to assign a value for that thread and return the initial value.

There's more...

The thread-local class also provides the `remove()` method that deletes the value stored in a thread-local variable for the thread that it's calling.

The Java Concurrency API includes the `InheritableThreadLocal` class that provides inheritance of values for threads created from a thread. If thread A has a value in a thread-local variable and it creates another thread B, then thread B will have the same value as thread A in the thread-local variable. You can override the `childValue()` method that is called to initialize the value of the child thread in the thread-local variable. It receives the value of the parent thread as a parameter in the thread-local variable.

Grouping threads and processing uncontrolled exceptions in a group of threads

An interesting functionality offered by the concurrency API of Java is the ability to group threads. This allows us to treat the threads of a group as a single unit and provide access to the thread objects that belong to a group in order to do an operation with them. For example, you have some threads doing the same task and you want to control them. You can, for example, interrupt all the threads of the group with a single call.

Java provides the `ThreadGroup` class to work with a groups of threads. A `ThreadGroup` object can be formed by thread objects and another `ThreadGroup` object, generating a tree structure of threads.

In the *Controlling the interruption of a thread* recipe, you learned how to use a generic method to process all the uncaught exceptions that are thrown in a thread object. In the *Processing uncontrolled exceptions in a thread* recipe, we wrote a handler to process the uncaught exceptions thrown by a thread. We can use a similar mechanism to process the uncaught exceptions thrown by a thread or a group of threads.

In this recipe, we will learn to work with `ThreadGroup` objects and how to implement and set the handler that would process uncaught exceptions in a group of threads. We'll do this using an example.

Getting ready

The example for this recipe has been implemented using the Eclipse IDE. If you use Eclipse or a different IDE, such as NetBeans, open it and create a new Java project.

How to do it...

Follow these steps to implement the example:

1. First, extend the `ThreadGroup` class by creating a class called `MyThreadGroup` that would be extended from `ThreadGroup`. You have to declare a constructor with one parameter because the `ThreadGroup` class doesn't have a constructor without it. Extend the `ThreadGroup` class to override the `uncaughtException()` method in order to process the exceptions thrown by the threads of the group:

```
public class MyThreadGroup extends ThreadGroup {
  public MyThreadGroup(String name) {
    super(name);
  }
}
```

2. Override the `uncaughtException()` method. This method is called when an exception is thrown in one of the threads of the `ThreadGroup` class. In this case, the method will write information about the exception and the thread that throws it; it will present this information in the console. Also, note that this method will interrupt the rest of the threads in the `ThreadGroup` class:

```
@Override
public void uncaughtException(Thread t, Throwable e) {
  System.out.printf("The thread %s has thrown an Exception\n",
                    t.getId());
  e.printStackTrace(System.out);
  System.out.printf("Terminating the rest of the Threads\n");
  interrupt();
}
```

3. Create a class called `Task` and specify that it implements the `Runnable` interface:

```
public class Task implements Runnable {
```

4. Implement the `run()` method. In this case, we will provoke an `AritmethicException` exception. For this, we will divide 1,000 with random numbers until the random generator generates zero to throw the exception:

```
@Override
public void run() {
  int result;
  Random random=new Random(Thread.currentThread().getId());
  while (true) {
    result=1000/((int)(random.nextDouble()*1000000000));
```

```
            if (Thread.currentThread().isInterrupted()) {
              System.out.printf("%d : Interrupted\n",
                                Thread.currentThread().getId());
              return;
            }
          }
        }
```

5. Now, implement the main class of the example by creating a class called `Main` and implement the `main()` method:

```
public class Main {
  public static void main(String[] args) {
```

6. First, calculate the number of threads you are going to launch. We use the `availableProcessors()` method of the `Runtime` class (we obtain the runtime object associated with the current Java application with the static method, called `getRuntime()`, of that class). This method returns the number of processors available to the JVM, which is normally equal to the number of cores of the computer that run the application:

```
int numberOfThreads = 2 * Runtime.getRuntime()
                              .availableProcessors();
```

7. Create an object of the `MyThreadGroup` class:

```
MyThreadGroup threadGroup=new MyThreadGroup("MyThreadGroup");
```

8. Create an object of the `Task` class:

```
Task task=new Task();
```

9. Create the calculated number of `Thread` objects with this `Task` class and start them:

```
for (int i = 0; i < numberOfThreads; i++) {
  Thread t = new Thread(threadGroup, task);
  t.start();
}
```

10. Then, write information about `ThreadGroup` in the console:

```
System.out.printf("Number of Threads: %d\n",
                  threadGroup.activeCount());
System.out.printf("Information about the Thread Group\n");
threadGroup.list();
```

11. Finally, write the status of the threads that form the group:

```
Thread[] threads = new Thread[threadGroup.activeCount()];
threadGroup.enumerate(threads);
for (int i = 0; i < threadGroup.activeCount(); i++) {
  System.out.printf("Thread %s: %s\n", threads[i].getName(),
                    threads[i].getState());
  }
 }
}
```

12. Run the example and see the results.

How it works...

In the following screenshot, you can see the output of the `list()` method of the `ThreadGroup` class and the output generated when we write the status of each `Thread` object:

```
 Problems  Javadoc  Declaration  Search  Console     Error Log
<terminated> Main (6) [Java Application] C:\Program Files\Java\jdk-9\bin\javaw.exe (23 ago. 2016 23:01:12)
Number of Threads: 8
Information about the Thread Group
com.packtpub.java9.concurrency.cookbook.chapter01.recipe09.group.MyThreadGroup[name=MyThreadGroup,maxpri=10]
    Thread[Thread-0,5,MyThreadGroup]
    Thread[Thread-1,5,MyThreadGroup]
    Thread[Thread-2,5,MyThreadGroup]
    Thread[Thread-3,5,MyThreadGroup]
    Thread[Thread-4,5,MyThreadGroup]
    Thread[Thread-5,5,MyThreadGroup]
    Thread[Thread-6,5,MyThreadGroup]
    Thread[Thread-7,5,MyThreadGroup]
Thread Thread-0: RUNNABLE
Thread Thread-1: RUNNABLE
Thread Thread-2: RUNNABLE
Thread Thread-3: RUNNABLE
Thread Thread-4: RUNNABLE
Thread Thread-5: RUNNABLE
Thread Thread-6: RUNNABLE
Thread Thread-7: RUNNABLE
```

The `ThreadGroup` class stores thread objects and other `ThreadGroup` objects associated with it so it can access all of their information (status, for example) and perform operations over all its members (interrupt, for example).

Check out how one of the thread objects threw the exception that interrupted the other objects:

```
The thread 18 has thrown an Exception
java.lang.ArithmeticException: / by zero
        at com.packtpub.java9.concurrency.cookbook.chapter01.recipe09.task.Task.run(Task.java:18)
        at java.lang.Thread.run(java.base@9-ea/Thread.java:843)
Terminating the rest of the Threads
19 : Interrupted
14 : Interrupted
15 : Interrupted
13 : Interrupted
20 : Interrupted
17 : Interrupted
16 : Interrupted
```

When an uncaught exception is thrown in a `Thread` object, the JVM looks for three possible handlers for this exception.

First, it looks for the uncaught exception handler of the thread, as explained in the *Processing uncontrolled exceptions in a thread* recipe. If this handler doesn't exist, then the JVM looks for the uncaught exception handler of the `ThreadGroup` class of the thread, as learned in this recipe. If this method doesn't exist, the JVM looks for the default uncaught exception handler, as explained in the *Processing uncontrolled exceptions in a thread* recipe.

If none of the handlers exists, the JVM writes the stack trace of the exception in the console and ends the execution of the thread that had thrown the exception.

See also

- The *Processing uncontrolled exceptions in a thread* recipe

Creating threads through a factory

The factory pattern is one of the most used design patterns in the object-oriented programming world. It is a creational pattern, and its objective is to develop an object whose mission should be this: creating other objects of one or several classes. With this, if you want to create an object of one of these classes, you could just use the factory instead of using a new operator.

With this factory, we centralize the creation of objects with some advantages:

- It's easy to change the class of the objects created or the way you'd create them.
- It's easy to limit the creation of objects for limited resources; for example, we can only have *n* objects of a given type.
- It's easy to generate statistical data about the creation of objects.

Java provides an interface, the `ThreadFactory` interface, to implement a thread object factory. Some advanced utilities of the Java concurrency API use thread factories to create threads.

In this recipe, you will learn how to implement a `ThreadFactory` interface to create thread objects with a personalized name while saving the statistics of the thread objects created.

Getting ready

The example for this recipe has been implemented using the Eclipse IDE. If you use Eclipse or a different IDE, such as NetBeans, open it and create a new Java project.

How to do it...

Follow these steps to implement the example:

1. Create a class called `MyThreadFactory` and specify that it implements the `ThreadFactory` interface:

   ```
   public class MyThreadFactory implements ThreadFactory {
   ```

2. Declare three attributes: an integer number called counter, which we will use to store the number of thread objects created, a string called name with the base name of every thread created, and a list of string objects called stats to save statistical data about the thread objects created. Also, implement the constructor of the class that initializes these attributes:

   ```
   private int counter;
   private String name;
   private List<String> stats;

   public MyThreadFactory(String name){
     counter=0;
     this.name=name;
   ```

```
stats=new ArrayList<String>();
}
```

3. Implement the `newThread()` method. This method will receive a `Runnable` interface and return a thread object for this `Runnable` interface. In our case, we generate the name of the thread object, create the new thread object, and save the statistics:

```
@Override
public Thread newThread(Runnable r) {
  Thread t=new Thread(r,name+"-Thread_"+counter);
  counter++;
  stats.add(String.format("Created thread %d with name %s on %s\n",
                          t.getId(),t.getName(),new Date()));
  return t;
}
```

4. Implement the `getStatistics()` method; it returns a `String` object with the statistical data of all the thread objects created:

```
public String getStats(){
  StringBuffer buffer=new StringBuffer();
  Iterator<String> it=stats.iterator();

  while (it.hasNext()) {
    buffer.append(it.next());
    buffer.append("\n");
  }

  return buffer.toString();
}
```

5. Create a class called `Task` and specify that it implements the `Runnable` interface. In this example, these tasks are going to do nothing apart from sleeping for 1 second:

```
public class Task implements Runnable {
  @Override
  public void run() {
    try {
      TimeUnit.SECONDS.sleep(1);
    } catch (InterruptedException e) {
      e.printStackTrace();
    }
  }
}
```

6. Create the main class of the example. Create a class called `Main` and implement the `main()` method:

```
public class Main {
  public static void main(String[] args) {
```

7. Create a `MyThreadFactory` object and a `Task` object:

```
MyThreadFactory factory=new MyThreadFactory("MyThreadFactory");
Task task=new Task();
```

8. Create 10 `Thread` objects using the `MyThreadFactory` object and start them:

```
Thread thread;
System.out.printf("Starting the Threads\n");
for (int i=0; i<10; i++){
   thread=factory.newThread(task);
  thread.start();
}
```

9. Write the statistics of the thread factory in the console:

```
System.out.printf("Factory stats:\n");
System.out.printf("%s\n",factory.getStats());
```

10. Run the example and see the results.

How it works...

The `ThreadFactory` interface has only one method, called `newThread()`. It receives a `Runnable` object as a parameter and returns a `Thread` object. When you implement a `ThreadFactory` interface, you have to implement it and override the `newThread` method. The most basic `ThreadFactory` has only one line:

```
return new Thread(r);
```

You can improve this implementation by adding some variants, as follows:

- Creating personalized threads, as in the example, using a special format for the name or even creating your own `Thread` class that would inherit the Java `Thread` class
- Saving thread creation statistics, as shown in the previous example
- Limiting the number of threads created
- Validating the creation of the threads

You can add anything else you can imagine to the preceding list. The use of the factory design pattern is a good programming practice, but if you implement a `ThreadFactory` interface to centralize the creation of threads, you will have to review the code to guarantee that all the threads are created using the same factory.

See also

- The *Implementing the ThreadFactory interface to generate custom threads* and *Using our ThreadFactory in an Executor object* recipes in `Chapter 8`, *Customizing Concurrency Classes*

2
Basic Thread Synchronization

In this chapter, we will cover the following topics:

- Synchronizing a method
- Using conditions in synchronized code
- Synchronizing a block of code with a lock
- Synchronizing data access with read/write locks
- Using multiple conditions in a lock
- Advanced locking with the StampedLock class

Introduction

One of the most common situations in concurrent programming occurs when more than one execution thread shares a resource. In a concurrent application, it is normal for multiple threads to read or write the same data structure or have access to the same file or database connection. These shared resources can provoke error situations or data inconsistency, and we have to implement mechanisms to avoid these errors. These situations are called **race conditions** and they occur when different threads have access to the same shared resource at the same time. Therefore, the final result depends on the order of the execution of threads, and most of the time, it is incorrect. You can also have problems with change visibility. So if a thread changes the value of a shared variable, the changes would only be written in the local cache of that thread; other threads will not have access to the change (they will only be able to see the old value).

The solution for these problems lies in the concept of **critical section**. A critical section is a block of code that accesses a shared resource and can't be executed by more than one thread at the same time.

To help programmers implement critical sections, Java (and almost all programming languages) offers synchronization mechanisms. When a thread wants access to a critical section, it uses one of these synchronization mechanisms to find out whether there is any other thread executing the critical section. If not, the thread enters the critical section. If yes, the thread is suspended by the synchronization mechanism until the thread that is currently executing the critical section ends it. When more than one thread is waiting for a thread to finish the execution of a critical section, JVM chooses one of them and the rest wait for their turn. This chapter presents a number of recipes that will teach you how to use the two basic synchronization mechanisms offered by the Java language:

- The `synchronized` keyword
- The `Lock` interface and its implementations

Synchronizing a method

In this recipe, you will learn how to use one of the most basic methods of synchronization in Java, that is, the use of the `synchronized` keyword to control concurrent access to a method or a block of code. All the `synchronized` sentences (used on methods or blocks of code) use an object reference. Only one thread can execute a method or block of code protected by the same object reference.

When you use the `synchronized` keyword with a method, the object reference is implicit. When you use the `synchronized` keyword in one or more methods of an object, only one execution thread will have access to all these methods. If another thread tries to access any method declared with the `synchronized` keyword of the same object, it will be suspended until the first thread finishes the execution of the method. In other words, every method declared with the `synchronized` keyword is a critical section, and Java only allows the execution of one of the critical sections of an object at a time. In this case, the object reference used is the own object, represented by the `this` keyword. Static methods have a different behavior. Only one execution thread will have access to one of the static methods declared with the `synchronized` keyword, but a different thread can access other non-static methods of an object of that class. You have to be very careful with this point because two threads can access two different `synchronized` methods if one is static and the other is not. If both methods change the same data, you can have data inconsistency errors. In this case, the object reference used is the class object.

When you use the `synchronized` keyword to protect a block of code, you must pass an object reference as a parameter. Normally, you will use the `this` keyword to reference the object that executes the method, but you can use other object references as well. Normally, these objects will be created exclusively for this purpose. You should keep the objects used for synchronization private. For example, if you have two independent attributes in a class shared by multiple threads, you must synchronize access to each variable; however, it wouldn't be a problem if one thread is accessing one of the attributes and the other accessing a different attribute at the same time. Take into account that if you use the `own` object (represented by the `this` keyword), you might interfere with other synchronized code (as mentioned before, the `this` object is used to synchronize the methods marked with the `synchronized` keyword).

In this recipe, you will learn how to use the `synchronized` keyword to implement an application simulating a parking area, with sensors that detect the following: when a car or a motorcycle enters or goes out of the parking area, an object to store the statistics of the vehicles being parked, and a mechanism to control cash flow. We will implement two versions: one without any synchronization mechanisms, where we will see how we obtain incorrect results, and one that works correctly as it uses the two variants of the `synchronized` keyword.

Getting ready

The example of this recipe has been implemented using the Eclipse IDE. If you use Eclipse or a different IDE, such as NetBeans, open it and create a new Java project.

How to do it...

Follow these steps to implement the example:

1. First, create the application without using any synchronization mechanism. Create a class named `ParkingCash` with an internal constant and an attribute to store the total amount of money earned by providing this parking service:

```
public class ParkingCash {
private static final int cost=2;
private long cash;

public ParkingCash() {
  cash=0;
}
```

2. Implement a method named `vehiclePay()` that will be called when a vehicle (a car or motorcycle) leaves the parking area. It will increase the cash attribute:

```
public void vehiclePay() {
  cash+=cost;
}
```

3. Finally, implement a method named `close()` that will write the value of the cash attribute in the console and reinitialize it to zero:

```
public void close() {
  System.out.printf("Closing accounting");
  long totalAmmount;
  totalAmmount=cash;
  cash=0;
  System.out.printf("The total amount is : %d",
                    totalAmmount);
  }
}
```

4. Create a class named `ParkingStats` with three private attributes and the constructor that will initialize them:

```
public class ParkingStats {
private long numberCars;
private long numberMotorcycles;
private ParkingCash cash;

public ParkingStats(ParkingCash cash) {
  numberCars = 0;
  numberMotorcycles = 0;
    this.cash = cash;
}
```

5. Then, implement the methods that will be executed when a car or motorcycle enters or leaves the parking area. When a vehicle leaves the parking area, cash should be incremented:

```
public void carComeIn() {
  numberCars++;
}

public void carGoOut() {
  numberCars--;
  cash.vehiclePay();
}
```

```
public void motoComeIn() {
  numberMotorcycles++;
}

public void motoGoOut() {
  numberMotorcycles--;
  cash.vehiclePay();
}
```

6. Finally, implement two methods to obtain the number of cars and motorcycles in the parking area, respectively.

7. Create a class named `Sensor` that will simulate the movement of vehicles in the parking area. It implements the `Runnable` interface and has a `ParkingStats` attribute, which will be initialized in the constructor:

```
public class Sensor implements Runnable {

  private ParkingStats stats;

  public Sensor(ParkingStats stats) {
    this.stats = stats;
  }
```

8. Implement the `run()` method. In this method, simulate that two cars and a motorcycle arrive in and then leave the parking area. Every sensor will perform this action 10 times:

```
@Override
public void run() {
  for (int i = 0; i< 10; i++) {
    stats.carComeIn();
    stats.carComeIn();
    try {
      TimeUnit.MILLISECONDS.sleep(50);
    } catch (InterruptedException e) {
      e.printStackTrace();
    }
    stats.motoComeIn();
    try {
      TimeUnit.MILLISECONDS.sleep(50);
    } catch (InterruptedException e) {
      e.printStackTrace();
    }
```

```
        stats.motoGoOut();
        stats.carGoOut();
        stats.carGoOut();
    }
}
```

9. Finally, implement the main method. Create a class named `Main` with the `main()` method. It needs `ParkingCash` and `ParkingStats` objects to manage parking:

```
public class Main {

  public static void main(String[] args) {

    ParkingCash cash = new ParkingCash();
    ParkingStats stats = new ParkingStats(cash);

    System.out.printf("Parking Simulator\n");
```

10. Then, create the `Sensor` tasks. Use the `availableProcessors()` method (that returns the number of available processors to the JVM, which normally is equal to the number of cores in the processor) to calculate the number of sensors our parking area will have. Create the corresponding `Thread` objects and store them in an array:

```
intnumberSensors=2 * Runtime.getRuntime()
                             .availableProcessors();
Thread threads[]=new Thread[numberSensors];
for (int i = 0; i<numberSensors; i++) {
  Sensor sensor=new Sensor(stats);
  Thread thread=new Thread(sensor);
  thread.start();
  threads[i]=thread;
}
```

11. Then wait for the finalization of the threads using the `join()` method:

```
for (int i=0; i<numberSensors; i++) {
  try {
    threads[i].join();
  } catch (InterruptedException e) {
    e.printStackTrace();
  }
}
```

12. Finally, write the statistics of `Parking`:

```
System.out.printf("Number of cars: %d\n",
                  stats.getNumberCars());
System.out.printf("Number of motorcycles: %d\n",
                  stats.getNumberMotorcycles());
cash.close();
    }
}
```

In our case, we executed the example in a four-core processor, so we will have eight `Sensor` tasks. Each task performs 10 iterations, and in each iteration, three vehicles enter the parking area and the same three vehicles go out. Therefore, each `Sensor` task will simulate 30 vehicles.

If everything goes well, the final stats will show the following:

- There are no cars in the parking area, which means that all the vehicles that came into the parking area have moved out
- Eight `Sensor` tasks were executed, where each task simulated 30 vehicles and each vehicle was charged 2 dollars each; therefore, the total amount of cash earned was 480 dollars

When you execute this example, each time you will obtain different results, and most of them will be incorrect. The following screenshot shows an example:

```
Problems  Javadoc  Declaration  Search  Console   Erro
<terminated> Main (8) [Java Application] C:\Program Files\Java\jdk-9\bin\ja
Parking Simulator
Number of cars: -3
Number of motorcycles: -3
Closing accountingThe total ammount is : 458
```

We had race conditions, and the different shared variables accessed by all the threads gave incorrect results. Let's modify the previous code using the synchronized keyword to solve these problems:

1. First, add the synchronized keyword to the `vehiclePay()` method of the `ParkingCash` class:

```
public synchronized void vehiclePay() {
  cash+=cost;
}
```

2. Then, add a `synchronized` block of code using the `this` keyword to the `close()` method:

```
public void close() {
  System.out.printf("Closing accounting");
  long totalAmmount;
  synchronized (this) {
    totalAmmount=cash;
    cash=0;
  }
  System.out.printf("The total amount is : %d",totalAmmount);
}
```

3. Now add two new attributes to the `ParkingStats` class and initialize them in the constructor of the class:

```
private final Object controlCars, controlMotorcycles;
public ParkingStats (ParkingCash cash) {
  numberCars=0;
  numberMotorcycles=0;
  controlCars=new Object();
  controlMotorcycles=new Object();
  this.cash=cash;
}
```

4. Finally, modify the methods that increment and decrement the number of cars and motorcycles, including the `synchronized` keyword. The `numberCars` attribute will be protected by the `controlCars` object, and the `numberMotorcycles` attribute will be protected by the `controlMotorcycles` object. You must also synchronize the `getNumberCars()` and `getNumberMotorcycles()` methods with the associated reference object:

```
public void carComeIn() {
  synchronized (controlCars) {
    numberCars++;
  }
}

public void carGoOut() {
  synchronized (controlCars) {
    numberCars--;
  }
  cash.vehiclePay();
}
```

```
public void motoComeIn() {
  synchronized (controlMotorcycles) {
    numberMotorcycles++;
  }
}

public void motoGoOut() {
  synchronized (controlMotorcycles) {
    numberMotorcycles--;
  }
  cash.vehiclePay();
}
```

5. Execute the example now and see the difference when compared to the previous version.

How it works...

The following screenshot shows the output of the new version of the example. No matter how many times you execute it, you will always obtain the correct result:

Let's see the different uses of the `synchronized` keyword in the example:

- First, we protected the `vehiclePay()` method. If two or more `Sensor` tasks call this method at the same time, only one will execute it and the rest will wait for their turn; therefore, the final amount will always be correct.
- We used two different objects to control access to the car and motorcycle counters. This way, one `Sensor` task can modify the `numberCars` attribute and another `Sensor` task can modify the `numberMotorcycles` attribute at the same time; however, no two `Sensor` tasks will be able to modify the same attribute at the same time, so the final value of the counters will always be correct.

Finally, we also synchronized the `getNumberCars()` and `getNumberMotorcycles()` methods. Using the `synchronized` keyword, we can guarantee correct access to shared data in concurrent applications.

As mentioned at the introduction of this recipe, only one thread can access the methods of an object that uses the `synchronized` keyword in their declaration. If thread (A) is executing a `synchronized` method and thread (B) wants to execute another `synchronized` method of the same object, it will be blocked until thread (A) is finished. But if thread (B) has access to different objects of the same class, none of them will be blocked.

When you use the `synchronized` keyword to protect a block of code, you use an object as a parameter. JVM guarantees that only one thread can have access to all the blocks of code protected with this object (note that we always talk about objects, not classes).

We used the `TimeUnit` class as well. The `TimeUnit` class is an enumeration with the following constants: DAYS, HOURS, MICROSECONDS, MILLISECONDS, MINUTES, NANOSECONDS, and SECONDS. These indicate the units of time we pass to the sleep method. In our case, we let the thread sleep for 50 milliseconds.

There's more...

The `synchronized` keyword penalizes the performance of the application, so you must only use it on methods that modify shared data in a concurrent environment. If you have multiple threads calling a `synchronized` method, only one will execute them at a time while the others will remain waiting. If the operation doesn't use the `synchronized` keyword, all the threads can execute the operation at the same time, reducing the total execution time. If you know that a method will not be called by more than one thread, don't use the `synchronized` keyword. Anyway, if the class is designed for multithreading access, it should always be correct. You must promote correctness over performance. Also, you should include documentation in methods and classes in relation to their thread safety.

You can use recursive calls with `synchronized` methods. As the thread has access to the `synchronized` methods of an object, you can call other `synchronized` methods of that object, including the method that is being executed. It won't have to get access to the `synchronized` methods again.

We can use the `synchronized` keyword to protect access to a block of code instead of an entire method. We should use the `synchronized` keyword in this way to protect access to shared data, leaving the rest of the operations out of this block and obtaining better performance of the application. The objective is to have the critical section (the block of code that can be accessed only by one thread at a time) as short as possible. Also, avoid calling blocking operations (for example, I/O operations) inside a critical section. We have used the `synchronized` keyword to protect access to the instruction that updates the number of persons in the building, leaving out the long operations of the block that don't use shared data. When you use the `synchronized` keyword in this way, you must pass an object reference as a parameter. Only one thread can access the `synchronized` code (blocks or methods) of this object. Normally, we will use the `this` keyword to reference the object that is executing the method:

```
synchronized (this) {
  // Java code
}
```

See also

- The *Using conditions in synchronized code* recipe in this chapter

Using conditions in synchronized code

A classic problem in concurrent programming is the producer-consumer problem. We have a data buffer, one or more producers of data that save it in the buffer, and one or more consumers of data that take it from the buffer.

As the buffer is a shared data structure, we have to control access to it using a synchronization mechanism, such as the `synchronized` keyword, but here we have more limitations. A producer can't save data in the buffer if it's full, and a consumer can't take data from the buffer if it's empty.

For these types of situations, Java provides the `wait()`, `notify()`, and `notifyAll()` methods implemented in the `Object` class. A thread can call the `wait()` method inside a `synchronized` block of code. If it calls the `wait()` method outside a `synchronized` block of code, JVM throws an `IllegalMonitorStateException` exception. When the thread calls the `wait()` method, JVM puts the thread to sleep and releases the object that controls the `synchronized` block of code that it's executing and allows other threads to execute other blocks of `synchronized` code protected by this object. To wake up the thread, you must call the `notify()` or `notifyAll()` methods inside a block of code protected by the same object.

In this recipe, you will learn how to implement the producer-consumer problem using the `synchronized` keyword and the `wait()`, `notify()`, and `notifyAll()` methods.

Getting ready

The example of this recipe has been implemented using the Eclipse IDE. If you use Eclipse or a different IDE, such as NetBeans, open it and create a new Java project.

How to do it...

Follow these steps to implement the example:

1. Create a class named `EventStorage`. It has two attributes, namely an `int` attribute called `maxSize` and a `List<Date>` attribute called `storage`:

   ```
   public class EventStorage {

       private int maxSize;
       private Queue<Date> storage;
   ```

2. Implement the constructor of the class that initializes the attributes of the class:

   ```
   public EventStorage(){
       maxSize=10;
       storage=new LinkedList<>();
   }
   ```

3. Implement the `synchronized` method `set()` to store an event in `storage`. First, check whether storage is full or not. If it's full, it calls the `wait()` method until it has empty space. At the end of the method, we call the `notify()` method to wake up all the threads that are sleeping in the `wait()` method. In this case, we will ignore `InterruptedException`. In a real implementation, you must think what treatment you must give to them. You can rethrow or transform them into a different type of exception of the application:

```
public synchronized void set(){
  while (storage.size()==maxSize){
    try {
      wait();
    } catch (InterruptedException e) {
      e.printStackTrace();
    }
  }
  storage.offer(new Date());
  System.out.printf("Set: %d",storage.size());
  notify();
}
```

4. Implement the `synchronized` method `get()` to get an event for storage purposes. First, check whether storage has events or not. If it has no events, it calls the `wait()` method until it is given some events. At the end of the method, we call the `notifyAll()` method to wake up all the threads that are sleeping in the `wait()` method. In this case, we will ignore `InterruptedException`. In a real implementation, you must think what treatment you must give to them. You can rethrow or transform them into a different type of exception of the application:

```
public synchronized void get(){
  while (storage.size()==0){
    try {
      wait();
    } catch (InterruptedException e) {
      e.printStackTrace();
    }
  }
  String element=storage.poll().toString();
  System.out.printf("Get: %d: %s\n",storage.size(),element);
  notify();

}
```

5. Create a class named `Producer` and specify that it implements the `Runnable` interface. It will implement the producer of the example:

```
public class Producer implements Runnable {
```

6. Declare an `EventStore` object and implement the constructor of the class that initializes this object:

```
private EventStorage storage;

public Producer(EventStorage storage){
   this.storage=storage;
}
```

7. Implement the `run()` method that calls the `set()` method of the `EventStorage` object 100 times:

```
@Override
public void run() {
   for (int i=0; i<100; i++){
     storage.set();
   }
}
```

8. Create a class named `Consumer` and specify that it implements the `Runnable` interface. It will implement the consumer of the example:

```
public class Consumer implements Runnable {
```

9. Declare an `EventStorage` object and implement the constructor of the class that initializes this object:

```
private EventStorage storage;

public Consumer(EventStorage storage){
   this.storage=storage;
}
```

10. Implement the `run()` method. It calls the `get()` method of the `EventStorage` object 100 times:

```
@Override
public void run() {
  for (int i=0; i<100; i++){
    storage.get();
  }
}
```

11. Create the main class of the example by implementing a class named `Main` and adding the `main()` method to it:

```
public class Main {

    public static void main(String[] args) {
```

12. Create an `EventStorage` object:

```
EventStorage storage=new EventStorage();
```

13. Create a `Producer` object and `Thread` to run it:

```
Producer producer=new Producer(storage);
Thread thread1=new Thread(producer);
```

14. Create a `Consumer` object and `Thread` to run it:

```
Consumer consumer=new Consumer(storage);
Thread thread2=new Thread(consumer);
```

15. Start both the threads:

```
thread2.start();
thread1.start();
```

How it works...

The key to this example is the `set()` and `get()` methods of the `EventStorage` class. First of all, the `set()` method checks whether there is free space in the storage attribute. If it's full, it calls the `wait()` method to wait for free space. When the other thread calls the `notify()` method, this thread wakes up and checks the condition again. The `notify()` method doesn't guarantee that the condition is met. This process is repeated until there is free space in storage and it can generate a new event and store it.

The behavior of the `get()` method is similar. First, it checks whether there are events on the storage attribute. If the `EventStorage` class is empty, it calls the `wait()` method to wait for events. When the other thread calls the `notify()` method, this thread wakes up and checks the condition again until there are some events in storage.

 You have to keep checking the conditions and calling the `wait()` method in a `while` loop. You will not be able to continue until the condition is `true`.

If you run this example, you will find that although the producer and consumer are setting and getting events, storage never has the capacity to include more than 10 events.

There's more...

There are other important uses of the `synchronized` keyword. See the *See also* section of this recipes that explain the use of this keyword.

See also

- The *Synchronizing a method* recipe in this chapter

Synchronizing a block of code with a lock

Java provides another mechanism for synchronizing blocks of code. It's a more powerful and flexible mechanism than the `synchronized` keyword. It's based on the `Lock` (of the `java.util.concurrent.locks` package) interface and classes that implement it (as `ReentrantLock`). This mechanism presents some advantages, which are as follows:

- It allows you to structure synchronized blocks in a more flexible way. With the `synchronized` keyword, you only have control over a synchronized block of code in a structured way. However, the `Lock` interface allows you to get more complex structures to implement your critical section.

- The `Lock` interface provides additional functionalities over the `synchronized` keyword. One of the new functionalities is implemented by the `tryLock()` method. This method tries to get control of the lock, and if it can't, because it's used by another thread, it returns `false`. With the `synchronized` keyword, if thread (A) tries to execute a synchronized block of code when thread (B) is executing it, thread (A) is suspended until thread (B) finishes the execution of the synchronized block. With lock, you can execute the `tryLock()` method. This method returns a `Boolean` value indicating whether there is another thread running the code protected by this lock.

- The `ReadWriteLock` interface allows a separation of read and write operations with multiple readers and only one modifier.

- The `Lock` interface offers better performance than the `synchronized` keyword.

The constructor of the `ReentrantLock` class admits a `boolean` parameter named `fair`; this parameter allows you to control its behavior. The `false` value is the default value and it's called the **non-fair mode**. In this mode, if some threads are waiting for a lock and the lock has to select one of these threads to get access to the critical section, it randomly selects anyone of them. The `true` value is called the **fair mode**. In this mode, if some threads are waiting for a lock and the lock has to select one to get access to a critical section, it selects the thread that has been waiting for the longest period of time. Take into account that the behavior explained previously is only used in the `lock()` and `unlock()` methods. As the `tryLock()` method doesn't put the thread to sleep if the `Lock` interface is used, the fair attribute doesn't affect its functionality.

In this recipe, you will learn how to use locks to synchronize a block of code and create a critical section using the `Lock` interface and the `ReentrantLock` class that implements it, implementing a program that simulates a print queue. You will also learn how the fair parameter affects the behavior of `Lock`.

Getting ready

The example in this recipe has been implemented using the Eclipse IDE. If you use Eclipse or a different IDE, such as NetBeans, open it and create a new Java project.

How to do it...

Follow these steps to implement the example:

1. Create a class named `PrintQueue` that will implement the print queue:

    ```
    public class PrintQueue {
    ```

2. Declare a `Lock` object and initialize it with a new object of the `ReentrantLock` class in the constructor. The constructor will receive a `Boolean` parameter we will use to specify the fair mode of the `Lock`:

    ```
    private Lock queueLock;
    public PrintQueue(booleanfairMode) {
      queueLock = new ReentrantLock(fairMode);
    }
    ```

3. Implement the `printJob()` method. It will receive `Object` as a parameter and it will not return any value:

    ```
    public void printJob(Object document){
    ```

4. Inside the `printJob()` method, get control of the `Lock` object by calling the `lock()` method:

    ```
    queueLock.lock();
    ```

5. Then, include the following code to simulate the process of printing a document:

    ```
    try {
      Long duration=(long)(Math.random()*10000);
      System.out.println(Thread.currentThread().getName()+ ":
                      PrintQueue: Printing a Job during "+
                      (duration/1000)+" seconds");
      Thread.sleep(duration);
    } catch (InterruptedException e) {
      e.printStackTrace();
    }
    ```

6. Finally, free the control of the `Lock` object with the `unlock()` method:

```
finally {
  queueLock.unlock();
}
```

7. Then, repeat the same process again. The `printJob()` method will help you get access to the lock and then free it twice. This strange behavior will allow us to see the difference between fair and non-fair mode in a better way. We include this piece of code in the `printJob()` method:

```
queueLock.lock();
try {
  Long duration = (long) (Math.random() * 10000);
  System.out.printf("%s: PrintQueue: Printing a Job during
                    %d seconds\n", Thread.currentThread()
                    .getName(), (duration / 1000));
  Thread.sleep(duration);
} catch (InterruptedException e) {
  e.printStackTrace();
} finally {
  queueLock.unlock();
}
```

8. Create a class named `Job` and specify that it implements the `Runnable` interface:

```
public class Job implements Runnable {
```

9. Declare an object of the `PrintQueue` class and implement the constructor of the class that initializes this object:

```
private PrintQueue printQueue;

public Job(PrintQueue printQueue){
  this.printQueue=printQueue;
}
```

10. Implement the `run()` method. It uses the `PrintQueue` object to send a job to print:

```
@Override
public void run() {
    System.out.printf("%s: Going to print a document\n",
                        Thread.currentThread().getName());
    printQueue.printJob(new Object());
    System.out.printf("%s: The document has been printed\n",
                        Thread.currentThread().getName());
}
```

11. Create the main class of the application by implementing a class named `Main` and adding the `main()` method to it:

```
public class Main {

    public static void main (String args[]){
```

12. We are going to test the `PrintQueue` class using a lock with the fair mode returning both `true` and `false`. We will use an auxiliary method to implement both the tests so the code of the `main()` method is simple:

```
System.out.printf("Running example with fair-mode =
                        false\n");
testPrintQueue(false);
System.out.printf("Running example with fair-mode = true\n");
testPrintQueue(true);
}
```

13. Create the `testPrintQueue()` method and create a shared `PrintQueue` object inside it:

```
private static void testPrintQueue(Boolean fairMode) {
    PrintQueue printQueue=new PrintQueue(fairMode);
```

14. Create 10 `Job` objects and 10 threads to run them:

```
Thread thread[]=new Thread[10];
for (int i=0; i<10; i++){
    thread[i]=new Thread(new Job(printQueue),"Thread "+ i);
}
```

15. Start the 10 threads:

```
for (int i=0; i<10; i++){
   thread[i].start();
}
```

16. Lastly, wait for the finalization of the 10 threads:

```
for (int i=0; i<10; i++) {
   try {
      thread[i].join();
   } catch (InterruptedException e) {
      e.printStackTrace();
   }
}
```

How it works...

In the following screenshot, you can see a part of the output of one execution of this example:

```
<terminated> Main (9) [Java Application] C:\Program Files\Java\jdk-9\bin\javaw.exe
Thread 9: Going to print a document
Thread 0: PrintQueue: Printing a Job during 7 seconds
Thread 0: The document has been printed
Thread 1: PrintQueue: Printing a Job during 6 seconds
Thread 1: PrintQueue: Printing a Job during 0 seconds
Thread 1: The document has been printed
Thread 2: PrintQueue: Printing a Job during 3 seconds
Thread 2: PrintQueue: Printing a Job during 4 seconds
Thread 2: The document has been printed
Thread 3: PrintQueue: Printing a Job during 4 seconds
Thread 3: PrintQueue: Printing a Job during 9 seconds
Thread 4: PrintQueue: Printing a Job during 2 seconds
```

The key to the example is in the printJob() method of the PrintQueue class. When we want to implement a critical section using locks and guarantee that only one execution thread will run a block of code, we have to create a ReentrantLock object. At the beginning of the critical section, we have to get control of the lock using the lock() method. When thread (A) calls this method, if no other thread has control of the lock, it gives thread (A) control of the lock and returns immediately to allow the thread to execute the critical section. Otherwise, if there is another, say thread (B), executing the critical section controlled by this lock, the lock() method puts thread (A) to sleep until thread (B) finishes the execution of the critical section.

At the end of the critical section, we have to use the `unlock()` method to free the control of the lock and allow other threads to run the critical section. If you don't call the `unlock()` method at the end of the critical section, other threads that are waiting for the block will wait forever, causing a deadlock situation. If you use try-catch blocks in your critical section, don't forget to put the sentence containing the `unlock()` method inside the `finally` section.

The other topic we tested in this example was fair mode. We had two critical sections in every job. In the previous screenshot, you saw how all the jobs execute the second part immediately after the first one. This is the usual case, but there are exceptions. This occurs when we have non-fair mode, that is to say, we pass a false value to the constructor of the `ReentrantLock` class.

On the contrary, when we establish fair mode by passing the true value to the constructor of the `Lock` class, the behavior is different. The first thread that requests control of the lock is `Thread 0`, then `Thread 1`, and so on. While `Thread 0` is running the first block of code protected by the lock, we have nine threads waiting to execute the same block of code. When `Thread 0` releases the lock, it immediately requests the lock again, so we have 10 threads trying to get the lock. As the fair mode is enabled, the `Lock` interface will choose `Thread 1`, as it's the thread that has been waiting for more time for the lock. Then, it chooses `Thread 2`, then `Thread 3`, and so on. Until all the threads have passed the first block protected by the lock, none of them will execute the second block protected by the lock. Once all the threads have executed the first block of code protected by the lock, then it will be the turn of `Thread 0` again, then `Thread 1`, and so on. The following screenshot shows the difference:

```
<terminated> Main (9) [Java Application] C:\Program Files\Java\jdk-9\bin\javaw.exe
Thread 9: Going to print a document
Thread 1: PrintQueue: Printing a Job during 4 seconds
Thread 2: PrintQueue: Printing a Job during 3 seconds
Thread 3: PrintQueue: Printing a Job during 3 seconds
Thread 4: PrintQueue: Printing a Job during 7 seconds
Thread 5: PrintQueue: Printing a Job during 6 seconds
Thread 6: PrintQueue: Printing a Job during 6 seconds
Thread 7: PrintQueue: Printing a Job during 2 seconds
Thread 8: PrintQueue: Printing a Job during 7 seconds
Thread 9: PrintQueue: Printing a Job during 5 seconds
Thread 0: PrintQueue: Printing a Job during 8 seconds
Thread 0: The document has been printed
Thread 1: PrintQueue: Printing a Job during 5 seconds
Thread 2: PrintQueue: Printing a Job during 9 seconds
Thread 1: The document has been printed
```

There's more...

The Lock interface (and the ReentrantLock class) includes another method to get control of the lock. It's the tryLock() method. The biggest difference with the lock() method is that this method, if the thread that uses it can't get control of the Lock interface, returns immediately and doesn't put the thread to sleep. It returns the boolean value true if the thread gets control of the lock and false if not. You can also pass a time value and a TimeUnit object to indicate the maximum amount of time the thread will wait to get the lock. If the time elapses and the thread doesn't get the lock, the method will return the false value. The TimeUnit class is an enumeration with the following constants: DAYS, HOURS, MICROSECONDS, MILLISECONDS, MINUTES, NANOSECONDS, and SECONDS; these indicate the units of time we pass to a method.

 Take into consideration that it is the responsibility of the programmer to take into account the result of this method and act accordingly. If the method returns false, it's apparent that your program is unable to execute the critical section. If it does, you probably will have wrong results in your application.

The ReentrantLock class also allows the use of recursive calls. When a thread has control of a lock and makes a recursive call, it continues with the control of the lock, so the calling to the lock() method will return immediately and the thread will continue with the execution of the recursive call. Moreover, we can also call other methods. You should call the unlock() method as many times as you called the lock() method in your code.

Avoiding deadlocks

You have to be very careful with the use of locks to avoid **deadlocks**. This situation occurs when two or more threads are blocked while waiting for locks that will never be unlocked. For example, thread (A) locks Lock (X) and thread (B) locks Lock (Y). Now, if thread (A) tries to lock Lock (Y) and thread (B) simultaneously tries to lock Lock (X), both the threads will be blocked indefinitely because they are waiting for locks that will never be liberated. Note that the problem occurs because both threads try to get the locks in the opposite order. The Appendix, *Concurrent Programming Design*, provides some good tips to design concurrent applications adequately and avoid these deadlock problems.

See also

- The *Synchronizing a method* and *Using multiple conditions in a lock* recipes in this chapter
- The *Monitoring a Lock interface* recipe in `Chapter 9`, *Testing Concurrent Applications*

Synchronizing data access with read/write locks

One of the most significant improvements offered by locks is the `ReadWriteLock` interface and the `ReentrantReadWriteLock` class, the unique class that implements that interface. This class has two locks: one for read operations and one for write operations. There can be more than one thread using read operations simultaneously, but only one thread can use write operations. If a thread is doing a write operation, other threads can't write or read.

In this recipe, you will learn how to use a `ReadWriteLock` interface by implementing a program that uses it to control access to an object that stores the prices of two products.

Getting ready...

You should read the *Synchronizing a block of code with a lock* recipe to better understand this recipe.

How to do it...

Follow these steps to implement the example:

1. Create a class named `PricesInfo` that stores information about the prices of two products:

   ```
   public class PricesInfo {
   ```

2. Declare two `double` attributes named `price1` and `price2`:

   ```
   private double price1;
   private double price2;
   ```

3. Declare a `ReadWriteLock` object called `lock`:

```
private ReadWriteLock lock;
```

4. Implement the constructor of the class that initializes the three attributes. For the `lock` attribute, create a new `ReentrantReadWriteLock` object:

```
public PricesInfo(){
    price1=1.0;
    price2=2.0;
    lock=new ReentrantReadWriteLock();
}
```

5. Implement the `getPrice1()` method that returns the value of the `price1` attribute. It uses the read lock to control access to the value of this attribute:

```
public double getPrice1() {
    lock.readLock().lock();
    double value=price1;
    lock.readLock().unlock();
    return value;
}
```

6. Implement the `getPrice2()` method that returns the value of the `price2` attribute. It uses the read lock to control access to the value of this attribute:

```
public double getPrice2() {
    lock.readLock().lock();
    double value=price2;
    lock.readLock().unlock();
    return value;
}
```

7. Implement the `setPrices()` method that establishes the values of two attributes. It uses the write lock to control access to them. We are going to make the thread sleep for 5 seconds. This shows that even though it has the write lock, there are no other threads getting the read lock:

```
public void setPrices(double price1, double price2) {
    lock.writeLock().lock();
    System.out.printf("%s: PricesInfo: Write Lock Adquired.\n",
                    new Date());
    try {
      TimeUnit.SECONDS.sleep(10);
    } catch (InterruptedException e) {
      e.printStackTrace();
```

```
        }
        this.price1=price1;
        this.price2=price2;
        System.out.printf("%s: PricesInfo: Write Lock Released.\n",
                          new Date());
        lock.writeLock().unlock();
    }
```

8. Create a class named `Reader` and specify that it implements the `Runnable` interface. This class implements a reader of the values of the `PricesInfo` class attribute:

```
public class Reader implements Runnable {
```

9. Declare a `PricesInfo` object and implement the constructor of the class that could initialize this object:

```
private PricesInfo pricesInfo;

public Reader (PricesInfo pricesInfo){
    this.pricesInfo=pricesInfo;
}
```

10. Implement the `run()` method for this class. It reads the value of the two prices 10 times:

```
@Override
public void run() {
    for (int i=0; i<20; i++){
        System.out.printf("%s: %s: Price 1: %f\n",new Date(),
                          Thread.currentThread().getName(),
                          pricesInfo.getPrice1());
        System.out.printf("%s: %s: Price 2: %f\n",new Date(),
                          Thread.currentThread().getName(),
                          pricesInfo.getPrice2());
    }
}
```

11. Create a class named `Writer` and specify that it implements the `Runnable` interface. This class implements a modifier of the values of the `PricesInfo` class attribute:

```
public class Writer implements Runnable {
```

12. Declare a `PricesInfo` object and implement the constructor of the class that could initialize this object:

```
private PricesInfo pricesInfo;

public Writer(PricesInfo pricesInfo){
  this.pricesInfo=pricesInfo;
}
```

13. Implement the `run()` method. It modifies the value of the two prices that are sleeping for 2 seconds between modifications three times:

```
@Override
public void run() {
  for (int i=0; i<3; i++) {
    System.out.printf("%s: Writer: Attempt to modify the
                        prices.\n", new Date());
    pricesInfo.setPrices(Math.random()*10, Math.random()*8);
    System.out.printf("%s: Writer: Prices have been
                        modified.\n", new Date());
    try {
      Thread.sleep(2);
    } catch (InterruptedException e) {
      e.printStackTrace();
    }
  }
}
```

14. Implement the main class of the example by creating a class named `Main` and adding the `main()` method to it:

```
public class Main {
  public static void main(String[] args) {
```

15. Create a `PricesInfo` object:

```
PricesInfo pricesInfo=new PricesInfo();
```

16. Create five `Reader` objects and five `Thread` objects to execute them:

```
Reader readers[]=new Reader[5];
Thread threadsReader[]=new Thread[5];

for (int i=0; i<5; i++){
  readers[i]=new Reader(pricesInfo);
  threadsReader[i]=new Thread(readers[i]);
}
```

17. Create a `Writer` object and `Thread` to execute it:

```
Writer writer=new Writer(pricesInfo);
Thread   threadWriter=new Thread(writer);
```

18. Start the threads:

```
for (int i=0; i<5; i++){
   threadsReader[i].start();
}
threadWriter.start();
```

How it works...

In the following screenshot, you can see a part of the output of one execution of this example:

```
Mon Aug 29 13:58:01 GMT+01:00 2016: Thread-0: Price 2: 2,000000
Mon Aug 29 13:58:01 GMT+01:00 2016: Thread-2: Price 1: 1,000000
Mon Aug 29 13:58:01 GMT+01:00 2016: Writer: Attempt to modify the prices.
Mon Aug 29 13:58:01 GMT+01:00 2016: Thread-4: Price 1: 1,000000
Mon Aug 29 13:58:01 GMT+01:00 2016: Thread-3: Price 1: 1,000000
Mon Aug 29 13:58:01 GMT+01:00 2016: Thread-1: Price 1: 1,000000
Mon Aug 29 13:58:01 GMT+01:00 2016: PricesInfo: Write Lock Acquired.
Mon Aug 29 13:58:01 GMT+01:00 2016: Thread-2: Price 2: 2,000000
Mon Aug 29 13:58:11 GMT+01:00 2016: PricesInfo: Write Lock Released.
Mon Aug 29 13:58:11 GMT+01:00 2016: Writer: Prices have been modified.
Mon Aug 29 13:58:01 GMT+01:00 2016: Thread-4: Price 2: 5,991554
Mon Aug 29 13:58:11 GMT+01:00 2016: Thread-4: Price 1: 2,259680
Mon Aug 29 13:58:11 GMT+01:00 2016: Thread-4: Price 2: 5,991554
Mon Aug 29 13:58:11 GMT+01:00 2016: Thread-4: Price 1: 2,259680
Mon Aug 29 13:58:11 GMT+01:00 2016: Thread-4: Price 2: 5,991554
Mon Aug 29 13:58:11 GMT+01:00 2016: Thread-4: Price 1: 2,259680
```

While the writer has acquired the write lock, none of the reader tasks can read the data. You can see some messages of the reader tasks after the `Write Lock Acquired` message, but they are instructions that were executed before and not shown yet in the console. Once the writer task has released the lock, reader tasks gain access to the prices information again and show the new prices.

As mentioned previously, the `ReentrantReadWriteLock` class has two locks: one for read operations and one for write operations. The lock used in read operations is obtained with the `readLock()` method declared in the `ReadWriteLock` interface. This lock is an object that implements the `Lock` interface, so we can use the `lock()`, `unlock()`, and `tryLock()` methods. The lock used in write operations is obtained with the `writeLock()` method declared in the `ReadWriteLock` interface. This lock is also an object that implements the `Lock` interface, so we can use the `lock()`, `unlock()`, and `tryLock()` methods. It is the responsibility of the programmer to ensure correct use of these locks, using them for the same purposes for which they were designed. When you get the read lock of a `Lock` interface, you can't modify the value of the variable. Otherwise, you probably will have data errors related to inconsistency.

See also

- The *Synchronizing a block of code with a lock* recipe in this chapter
- The *Monitoring a Lock interface* recipe in `Chapter 9`, *Testing Concurrent Applications*

Using multiple conditions in a lock

A lock may be associated with one or more conditions. These conditions are declared in the `Condition` interface. The purpose of these conditions is to allow threads to have control of a lock and check whether a condition is `true` or not. If it's `false`, the thread will be suspended until another thread wakes it up. The `Condition` interface provides the mechanisms to suspend a thread and wake up a suspended thread.

A classic problem in concurrent programming is the producer-consumer problem. We have a data buffer, one or more producers of data that save it in the buffer, and one or more consumers of data that take it from the buffer, as explained earlier in this chapter.

In this recipe, you will learn how to implement the producer-consumer problem using locks and conditions.

Getting ready

You should read the *Synchronizing a block of code with a lock* recipe to better understand this recipe.

How to do it...

Follow these steps to implement the example:

1. First, implement a class that will simulate a text file. Create a class named FileMock with two attributes: a String array named content and int named index. They will store the content of the file and the line of the simulated file that will be retrieved:

```
public class FileMock {

    private String[] content;
    private int index;
```

2. Implement the constructor of the class that initializes the content of the file with random characters:

```
public FileMock(int size, int length){
    content = new String[size];
    for (int i = 0; i< size; i++){
        StringBuilder buffer = new StringBuilder(length);
        for (int j = 0; j < length; j++){
            int randomCharacter= (int)Math.random()*255;
            buffer.append((char)randomCharacter);
        }
        content[i] = buffer.toString();
    }
    index=0;
}
```

3. Implement the hasMoreLines() method that returns true if the file has more lines to process or false if you have reached the end of the simulated file:

```
public boolean hasMoreLines(){
    return index <content.length;
}
```

4. Implement the `getLine()` method that returns the line determined by the index attribute and increases its value:

```
public String getLine(){
  if (this.hasMoreLines()) {
    System.out.println("Mock: " + (content.length-index));
    return content[index++];
  }
  return null;
}
```

5. Now implement a class named `Buffer` that will implement the buffer shared by both the producers and consumers:

```
public class Buffer {
```

6. This class has six attributes:

- A `LinkedList<String>` attribute named `buffer` that will store the shared data. For example:

  ```
  private final LinkedList<String> buffer;
  ```

- An `int` type named `maxSize` that will store the length of the buffer. For example:

  ```
  private final int maxSize;
  ```

- A `ReentrantLock` object called `lock` that will control access to the blocks of code that modify the buffer. For example:

  ```
  private final ReentrantLock lock;
  ```

- Two `Condition` attributes named `lines` and `space`. For example:

  ```
  private final Condition lines;
  ```

  ```
  private final Condition space;
  ```

- A `boolean` type called `pendingLines` that will indicate whether there are lines in the buffer. For example:

  ```
  private boolean pendingLines;
  ```

7. Implement the constructor of the class. It initializes all the attributes described previously:

```
public Buffer(int maxSize) {
    this.maxSize = maxSize;
    buffer = new LinkedList<>();
    lock = new ReentrantLock();
    lines = lock.newCondition();
    space = lock.newCondition();
    pendingLines =true;
}
```

8. Implement the `insert()` method. It receives `String` as a parameter and tries to store it in the buffer. First, it gets control of the lock. When it has this, it checks whether there is empty space in the buffer. If the buffer is full, it calls the `await()` method in the `space` condition to wait for free space. The thread will be woken up when another thread calls the `signal()` or `signalAll()` method in the `space` condition. When this happens, the thread stores the line in the buffer and calls the `signallAll()` method over the `lines` condition. As we'll see in a moment, this condition will wake up all the threads that are waiting for lines in the buffer. To make the code easier, we ignore the `InterruptedException` exception. In real cases, you will probably have to process it:

```
public void insert(String line) {
    lock.lock();
    try {
        while (buffer.size() == maxSize) {
            space.await();
        }
        buffer.offer(line);
        System.out.printf("%s: Inserted Line: %d\n",
                          Thread.currentThread().getName(),
                          buffer.size());
        lines.signalAll();
    } catch (InterruptedException e) {
        e.printStackTrace();
    } finally {
        lock.unlock();
    }
}
```

9. Implement the `get()` method. It returns the first string stored in the buffer. First, it gets control of the lock. When this is done, it checks whether there are lines in the buffer. If the buffer is empty, it calls the `await()` method in the `lines` condition to wait for lines in the buffer. This thread will be woken up when another thread calls the `signal()` or `signalAll()` method in the lines condition. When this happens, the method gets the first line in the buffer, calls the `signalAll()` method over the `space` condition, and returns `String`:

```
public String get() {
  String line = null;
  lock.lock();
  try {
    while ((buffer.size() == 0) && (hasPendingLines())) {
      lines.await();
    }

    if (hasPendingLines()) {
      line = buffer.poll();
      System.out.printf("%s: Line Readed: %d\n",
                        Thread.currentThread().getName(),
                        buffer.size());
      space.signalAll();
    }
  } catch (InterruptedException e) {
    e.printStackTrace();
  } finally {
    lock.unlock();
  }
  return line;
}
```

10. Implement the `setPendingLines()` method that establishes the value of the `pendingLines` attribute. It will be called by the producer when it has no more lines to produce:

```
public synchronized void setPendingLines(boolean pendingLines) {
  this.pendingLines = pendingLines;
}
```

11. Implement the `hasPendingLines()` method. It returns `true` if there are more lines to be processed or `false` otherwise:

```
public synchronized boolean hasPendingLines() {
  return pendingLines || buffer.size()>0;
}
```

12. Now it's the turn of the producer. Implement a class named `Producer` and specify that it implements the `Runnable` interface:

```
public class Producer implements Runnable {
```

13. Declare two attributes, namely an object of the `FileMock` class and an object of the `Buffer` class:

```
private FileMock mock;

private Buffer buffer;
```

14. Implement the constructor of the class that initializes both the attributes:

```
public Producer (FileMock mock, Buffer buffer){
    this.mock = mock;
    this.buffer = buffer;
}
```

15. Implement the `run()` method that reads all the lines created in the `FileMock` object and use the `insert()` method to store them in the buffer. Once this is done, use the `setPendingLines()` method to alert the buffer that it will not generate more lines:

```
@Override
public void run() {
    buffer.setPendingLines(true);
    while (mock.hasMoreLines()){
        String line = mock.getLine();
        buffer.insert(line);
    }
    buffer.setPendingLines(false);
}
```

16. Next is the consumer's turn. Implement a class named `Consumer` and specify that it implements the `Runnable` interface:

```
public class Consumer implements Runnable {
```

17. Declare a `Buffer` object and implement the constructor of the class that initializes it:

```
private Buffer buffer;

public Consumer (Buffer buffer) {
   this.buffer = buffer;
}
```

18. Implement the `run()` method. While the buffer has pending lines, it tries to get one line and process it:

```
@Override
public void run() {
   while (buffer.hasPendingLines()) {
      String line = buffer.get();
      processLine(line);
   }
}
```

19. Implement the auxiliary method `processLine()`. It only sleeps for 10 milliseconds to simulate some kind of processing with the line:

```
private void processLine(String line) {
   try {
      Random random = new Random();
      Thread.sleep(random.nextInt(100));
   } catch (InterruptedException e) {
      e.printStackTrace();
   }
}
```

20. Implement the main class of the example by creating a class named `Main` and adding the `main()` method to it.

```
public class Main {

   public static void main(String[] args) {
```

21. Create a `FileMock` object:

```
FileMock mock = new FileMock(100, 10);
```

22. Create a `Buffer` object:

```
Buffer buffer = new Buffer(20);
```

23. Create a `Producer` object and `Thread` to run it:

```
Producer producer = new Producer(mock, buffer);
Thread producerThread = new Thread(producer,"Producer");
```

24. Create three `Consumer` objects and three threads to run them:

```
Consumer consumers[] = new Consumer[3];
Thread consumersThreads[] = new Thread[3];

for (int i=0; i<3; i++){
  consumers[i] = new Consumer(buffer);
  consumersThreads[i] = new Thread(consumers[i],"Consumer "+i);
}
```

25. Start the producer and the three consumers:

```
producerThread.start();
for (int i = 0; i< 3; i++){
  consumersThreads[i].start();
}
```

How it works...

All the `Condition` objects are associated with a lock and are created using the `newCondition()` method declared in the `Lock` interface. Before we can do any operation with a condition, you have to have control of the lock associated with the condition. So operations with conditions must be done in a thread that holds the lock with a call to a `lock()` method of a `Lock` object and then frees it with an `unlock()` method of the same `Lock` object.

When a thread calls the `await()` method of a condition, it automatically frees the control of the lock so that another thread can get it and either begin the execution or another critical section protected by that lock.

When a thread calls the signal() or signallAll() methods of a condition, one or all of the threads that were waiting for that condition are woken up, but this doesn't guarantee that the condition that made them sleep is now true. So you must put the await() calls inside a while loop. You can't leave this loop until the condition is true. When the condition is false, you must call await() again.

You must be careful with the use of await() and signal(). If you call the await() method in a condition and never call the signal() method in the same condition, the thread will sleep forever.

A thread can be interrupted while it is sleeping, after a call to the await() method, so you have to process the InterruptedException exception.

There's more...

The Condition interface has other versions of the await() method, which are as follows:

- await(long time, TimeUnit unit): Here, the thread will sleep until:
  - It's interrupted
  - Another thread calls the signal() or signalAll() methods in the condition
  - The specified time passes
  - The TimeUnit class is an enumeration with the following constants: DAYS, HOURS, MICROSECONDS, MILLISECONDS, MINUTES, NANOSECONDS, and SECONDS

- awaitUninterruptibly(): The thread will sleep until another thread calls the signal() or signalAll() methods, which can't be interrupted
- awaitUntil(Date date): The thread will sleep until:
  - It's interrupted
  - Another thread calls the signal() or signalAll() methods in the condition
  - The specified date arrives

You can use conditions with the ReadLock and WriteLock locks of a read/write lock.

See also

- The *Synchronizing a block of code with a lock* and *Synchronizing data access with read/write locks* recipes in this chapter

Advanced locking with the StampedLock class

The StampedLock class provides a special kind of lock that is different from the ones provided by the Lock or ReadWriteLock interfaces. In fact, this class doesn't implement these interfaces, but the functionality it provides is very similar.

The first point to note about this kind of lock is that its main purpose is to be a helper class to implement thread-safe components, so its use will not be very common in normal applications.

The most important features of StampedLock locks are as follows:

- You can obtain control of the lock in three different modes:
    - **Write**: In this mode, you get exclusive access to the lock. No other thread can have control of the lock in this mode.
    - **Read**: In this mode, you have non-exclusive access to the lock. There can be other threads that have access to the lock in this mode or the Optimistic Read mode.
    - **Optimistic Read**: Here, the thread doesn't have control over the block. Other threads can get control of the lock in write mode. When you get a lock in the Optimistic Read mode and you want to access the shared data protected by it, you will have to check whether you can access them or not using the validate() method.
- The StampedLock class provides methods to:
    - Acquire control over the lock in one of the previous modes. If the methods (readLock(), writeLock(), readLockInterruptibly()) are unable to get control of the lock, the current thread is suspended until it gets the lock.

- Acquire control over the lock in one of the previous modes. If the methods (`tryOptimisticRead()`, `tryReadLock()`, `tryWriteLock()`) are unable to get control of the lock, they return a special value to indicate this circumstance.
- Convert one mode into another, if possible. If not, the methods (`asReadLock()`, `asWriteLock()`, `asReadWriteLock()`) return a special value.
- Release the lock.

- All these methods return a long value called stamp that we need to use to work with the lock. If a method returns zero, it means it tried to get a lock but it couldn't.
- A `StampedLock` lock is not a reentrant lock, such as the `Lock` and `ReadWriteLock` interfaces. If you call a method that tries to get the lock again, it may be blocked and you'll get a deadlock.
- It does not have the notion of ownership. They can be acquired by one thread and released by another.
- Finally, it doesn't have any policy about the next thread that will get control of the lock.

In this recipe, we will learn how to use the different modes of the `StampedLock` class to protect access to a shared data object. We will use a shared object between three concurrent tasks to test the three access modes with `StampedLock` (write, read, and Optimistic Read).

Getting ready

The example of this recipe has been implemented using the Eclipse IDE. If you use Eclipse or a different IDE, such as NetBeans, open it and create a new Java project.

How to do it...

Follow these steps to implement the example:

1. First, implement the shared data object. Create a class named `Position` with two integer attributes, namely `x` and `y`. You have to include the methods to get and set the values of the attributes. Its code is very simple so it is not included here.

2. Now let's implement the `Writer` task. It implements the `Runnable` interface and it will have two attributes: a `Position` object named `position` and `StampedLock` named `lock`. They will be initialized in the constructor:

```
public class Writer implements Runnable {

  private final Position position;
  private final StampedLock lock;

  public Writer (Position position, StampedLock lock) {
    this.position=position;
    this.lock=lock;
  }
```

3. Implement the `run()` method. In a loop that we will repeat 10 times, get the lock in write mode, change the value of the two attributes of the position object, suspend the execution of the thread for a second, release the lock (in the `finally` section of a `try...catch...finally` structure to release the lock in any circumstance), and suspend the thread for a second:

```
@Override
public void run() {

  for (int i=0; i<10; i++) {
    long stamp = lock.writeLock();

    try {
      System.out.printf("Writer: Lock acquired %d\n",stamp);
      position.setX(position.getX()+1);
      position.setY(position.getY()+1);
      TimeUnit.SECONDS.sleep(1);
    } catch (InterruptedException e) {
      e.printStackTrace();
    } finally {
      lock.unlockWrite(stamp);
      System.out.printf("Writer: Lock released %d\n",stamp);
    }

    try {
      TimeUnit.SECONDS.sleep(1);
    } catch (InterruptedException e) {
      e.printStackTrace();
    }
  }

}
```

4. Then, implement the `Reader` task to read the values of the shared object. Create a class named `Reader` that implements the `Runnable` interface. It will have two attributes: a `Position` object named `position` and a `StampedLock` object named `lock`. They will be initialized in the constructor of the class:

```
public class Reader implements Runnable {

    private final Position position;
    private final StampedLock lock;

    public Reader (Position position, StampedLock lock) {
        this.position=position;
        this.lock=lock;
    }
```

5. Now implement the `run()` method. In a loop that we will repeat 50 times, get control of the lock in read mode, write the values of the position object in the console, and suspend the thread for 200 milliseconds. Finally, release the lock using the `finally` block of a `try...catch...finally` structure:

```
@Override
public void run() {
    for (int i=0; i<50; i++) {
        long stamp=lock.readLock();
        try {
            System.out.printf("Reader: %d - (%d,%d)\n", stamp,
                              position.getX(), position.getY());
            TimeUnit.MILLISECONDS.sleep(200);
        } catch (InterruptedException e) {
            e.printStackTrace();
        } finally {
            lock.unlockRead(stamp);
            System.out.printf("Reader: %d - Lock released\n", stamp);
        }
    }
}
```

6. Then, implement the `OptimisticReader` task. The class `OptimisticReader` class implements the `Runnable` interface. It will have two attributes: a `Position` object named `position` and a `StampedLock` object named `lock`. They will be initialized in the constructor of the class:

```java
public class OptimisticReader implements Runnable {

    private final Position position;
    private final StampedLock lock;

    public OptimisticReader (Position position, StampedLock lock) {
        this.position=position;
        this.lock=lock;
    }
```

7. Now implement the `run()` method. First obtain the stamp of the lock in the optimistic read mode using the `tryOptimisticRead()` method. Then, repeat the loop `100` times. In the loop, validate whether you can access data using the `validate()` method. If this method returns true, write the values of the position object in the console. Otherwise, write a message in the console and get another stamp using the `tryOptimisticRead()` method again. Then, suspend the thread for `200` milliseconds:

```java
@Override
public void run() {
    long stamp;
    for (int i=0; i<100; i++) {
        try {
            stamp=lock.tryOptimisticRead();
            int x = position.getX();
            int y = position.getY();
            if (lock.validate(stamp)) {
                System.out.printf("OptmisticReader: %d - (%d,%d)\n",
                                   stamp,x, y);
            } else {
                System.out.printf("OptmisticReader: %d - Not Free\n",
                                   stamp);
            }
            TimeUnit.MILLISECONDS.sleep(200);
        } catch (InterruptedException e) {
            e.printStackTrace();
        }
    }
}
```

8. Finally, implement the `Main` class with the `main()` method. Create a `Position` and `StampedLock` object, create three threads--one for each task--start the threads, and wait for their finalization:

```java
public class Main {

    public static void main(String[] args) {

        Position position=new Position();
        StampedLock lock=new StampedLock();

        Thread threadWriter=new Thread(new Writer(position,lock));
        Thread threadReader=new Thread(new Reader(position, lock));
        Thread threadOptReader=new Thread(new OptimisticReader
                                        (position, lock));

        threadWriter.start();
        threadReader.start();
        threadOptReader.start();

        try {
            threadWriter.join();
            threadReader.join();
            threadOptReader.join();
        } catch (InterruptedException e) {
            e.printStackTrace();
        }
    }
}
```

How it works...

In this example, we tested the three modes you can use with a stamped lock. In the `Writer` task, we get the lock with the `writeLock()` method (that acquires the lock in write mode). In the `Reader` task, we get the lock with the `readLock()` method (that acquires the lock in read mode). Finally, in the `OptimisticRead` task, first we use `tryOptimisticRead()` and then we use the `validate()` method to check whether we can access data or not.

The first two methods, if they can get control of the lock, wait until they get the lock. The `tryOptimisticRead()` method always returns a value. It will be 0 if we are unable to use the lock and a value different from 0 if we can use it. Remember that in this case, we always need to use the `validate()` method to check whether we can really access the data.

The following screenshot shows part of the output of an execution of the program:

```
Problems  @ Javadoc  Declaration  Search  Console 

<terminated> Main (10) [Java Application] C:\Program Files\Java\jdk

Reader: 257 - (0,0)
OptmisticReader: 256 - (0,0)
OptmisticReader: 256 - (0,0)
Writer: Lock aquired 384
Reader: 257 - Lock released
OptmisticReader: 256 - Not Free
OptmisticReader: 0 - Not Free
OptmisticReader: 0 - Not Free
OptmisticReader: 0 - Not Free
Writer: Lock released 384
Reader: 513 - (1,1)
OptmisticReader: 0 - Not Free
Reader: 513 - Lock released
Reader: 513 - (1,1)
OptmisticReader: 512 - (1,1)
Reader: 513 - Lock released
Reader: 513 - (1,1)
```

While the `Writer` task has control of the lock, neither `Reader` nor `OptimisticReader` can access the values. The `Reader` task is suspended in the `readLock()` method, while in `OptimisticReader`, the call to the `validate()` method returns `false` and the call to the `tryOptimisticRead()` method returns 0 to indicate that the lock is controlled in write mode by another thread. When the `Writertask` releases the lock, both `Reader` and `OptimisticReader` tasks will be able to access the values of the shared object.

There's more...

The `StampedLock` class has other methods that you should know:

- `tryReadLock()` and `tryReadLock(long time, TimeUnit unit)`: These methods try to acquire the lock in read mode. If they can't, the first version is returned immediately and the second one waits for the amount of time specified in the parameter. These methods also return a stamp that must be checked (`stamp != 0`).

- `tryWriteLock()` and `tryWriteLock(long time, TimeUnit unit)`: These methods try to acquire the lock in write mode. If they can't, the first version is returned immediately and the second one waits for the amount of time specified in the parameter. These methods also return a stamp that must be checked (`stamp != 0`).
- `isReadLocked()` and `isWriteLocked()`: These methods are returned if the lock is currently held in read or write mode, respectively.
- `tryConvertToReadLock(long stamp)`, `tryConvertToWriteLock(long stamp)`, and `tryConvertToOptimisticRead(long stamp)`: These methods try to convert the stamp passed as a parameter to the mode indicated in the name of the method. If they can, they return a new stamp. If not, they return `0`.
- `unlock(long stamp)`: This releases the corresponding mode of the lock.

See also

- The *Synchronizing a block of code with a lock* recipe in this chapter

3

Thread Synchronization Utilities

In this chapter, we will cover the following topics:

- Controlling concurrent access to one or more copies of a resource
- Waiting for multiple concurrent events
- Synchronizing tasks at a common point
- Running concurrent-phased tasks
- Controlling phase change in concurrent-phased tasks
- Exchanging data between concurrent tasks
- Completing and linking tasks asynchronously

Introduction

In Chapter 2, *Basic Thread Synchronization*, you learned the concepts of synchronization and critical sections. Basically, we talk about synchronization when more than one concurrent task shares a resource, for example, an object or an attribute of an object. The blocks of code that access this shared resource are called critical sections.

If you don't use appropriate mechanisms, you might have incorrect results, data inconsistencies, or error conditions. Therefore, we have to adopt one of the synchronization mechanisms provided by the Java language to avoid these problems.

`Chapter 2`, *Basic Thread Synchronization,* taught you about the following basic synchronization mechanisms:

- The `synchronized` keyword
- The Lock interface and its implementation classes: `ReentrantLock`, `ReentrantReadWriteLock.ReadLock`, and `ReentrantReadWriteLock.WriteLock`
- The `StampedLock` class

In this chapter, you will learn how to use high-level mechanisms to synchronize multiple threads. These high-level mechanisms are as follows:

- **Semaphores**: A semaphore is a counter that controls access to one or more shared resources. This mechanism is one of the basic tools of concurrent programming and is provided by most programming languages.
- **CountDownLatch**: The `CountDownLatch` class is a mechanism provided by the Java language that allows a thread to wait for the finalization of multiple operations.
- **CyclicBarrier**: The `CyclicBarrier` class is another mechanism provided by the Java language that allows the synchronization of multiple threads at a common point.
- **Phaser**: The `Phaser` class is another mechanism provided by the Java language that controls the execution of concurrent tasks divided in phases. All the threads must finish one phase before they can continue with the next one.
- **Exchanger**: The `Exchanger` class is another mechanism provided by the Java language that provides a point of data interchange between two threads.
- **CompletableFuture**: The `CompletableFuture` class provides a mechanism where one or more tasks can wait for the finalization of another task that will be explicitly completed in an asynchronous way in future. This class was introduced in Java 8 and has introduced new methods in Java 9.

Semaphores are generic synchronization mechanisms that you can use to protect any critical section in any problem. Other mechanisms are thought to be used in applications with specific features, as described previously. Be sure to select the appropriate mechanism according to the characteristics of your application.

This chapter presents seven recipes that will show you how to use the mechanisms described.

Controlling concurrent access to one or more copies of a resource

In this recipe, you will learn how to use the semaphore mechanism provided by the Java language. A semaphore is a counter that protects access to one or more shared resources.

 The concept of a semaphore was introduced by Edsger Dijkstra in 1965 and was used for the first time in the THEOS operating system.

When a thread wants to access one of the shared resources, it must first acquire the semaphore. If the internal counter of the semaphore is greater than 0, the semaphore decrements the counter and allows access to the shared resource. A counter bigger than 0 implies that there are free resources that can be used, so the thread can access and use one of them.

Otherwise, if the counter is 0, the semaphore puts the thread to sleep until the counter is greater than 0. A value of 0 in the counter means all the shared resources are used by other threads, so the thread that wants to use one of them must wait until one is free.

When the thread has finished using the shared resource, it must release the semaphore so that another thread can access the resource. This operation increases the internal counter of the semaphore.

In this recipe, you will learn how to use the Semaphore class to protect more than one copy of a resource. You are going to implement an example, which has a print queue that could print documents in three different printers.

Getting ready

The example of this recipe has been implemented using the Eclipse IDE. If you use Eclipse or a different IDE, such as NetBeans, open it and create a new Java project.

How to do it...

Follow these steps to implement the example:

1. Create a class named `PrintQueue` that will implement the print queue:

```
public class PrintQueue {
```

2. This class will have three private attributes. A semaphore named `semaphore`, an array of Booleans named `freePrinters`, and a lock named `lockPrinters`, as shown in the following code snippet:

```
private final Semaphore semaphore;
private final boolean freePrinters[];
private final Lock lockPrinters;
```

3. Implement the constructor of the class. It initializes the three attributes of the class, as shown in the following code snippet:

```
public PrintQueue(){
    semaphore=new Semaphore(3);
    freePrinters=new boolean[3];
    for (int i=0; i<3; i++){
        freePrinters[i]=true;
    }
    lockPrinters=new ReentrantLock();
}
```

4. Implement the `printJob()` method that will simulate the printing of a document. It receives an object called `document` as a parameter:

```
public void printJob (Object document){
```

5. First of all, the `printJob()` method calls the `acquire()` method to acquire access to the semaphore. As this method can throw an `InterruptedException` exception, you must include the code to process it:

```
try {
    semaphore.acquire();
```

6. Then, get the number of the printers assigned to print this job, using the private method `getPrinter()`:

```
int assignedPrinter=getPrinter();
```

7. Then, implement the lines that simulate the printing of a document waiting for a random period of time:

```
long duration=(long) (Math.random()*10);
System.out.printf("%s - %s: PrintQueue: Printing a Job in
                Printer %d during %d seconds\n",
                new Date(), Thread.currentThread().getName(),
                assignedPrinter,duration);
TimeUnit.SECONDS.sleep(duration);
```

8. Finally, release the semaphore by calling the `release()` method and marking the printer used as free, and assign `true` to the corresponding index in the `freePrinters` array:

```
    freePrinters[assignedPrinter]=true;
} catch (InterruptedException e) {
    e.printStackTrace();
} finally {
    semaphore.release();
}
```

9. Next, implement the `getPrinter()` method. It's a private method that returns an `int` value and has no parameters:

```
private int getPrinter() {
```

10. First, declare an `int` variable to store the index of the printer:

```
int ret=-1;
```

11. Then, get access to the `lockPrinters` object:

```
try {
    lockPrinters.lock();
```

12. Post this, find the first true value in the `freePrinters` array and save its index in a variable. Modify this value to `false` because this printer will be busy:

```
for (int i=0; i<freePrinters.length; i++) {
    if (freePrinters[i]){
        ret=i;
        freePrinters[i]=false;
        break;
    }
}
```

13. Finally, free the `lockPrinters` object and return the index of the true value:

```
} catch (Exception e) {
    e.printStackTrace();
} finally {
    lockPrinters.unlock();
}
return ret;
```

14. Next, create a class called `Job` and specify that it implements the `Runnable` interface. This class implements the job that will send a document to the printer:

```
public class Job implements Runnable {
```

15. Declare a `PrintQueue` object. Call it `printQueue`:

```
private PrintQueue printQueue;
```

16. Implement the constructor of the class. It initializes the `PrintQueue` object declared in the class:

```
public Job(PrintQueue printQueue){
    this.printQueue=printQueue;
}
```

17. Implement the `run()` method:

```
@Override
    public void run() {
```

18. First, this method writes a message to the console that shows that the job has started its execution:

```
System.out.printf("%s: Going to print a job\n",
                Thread.currentThread().getName());
```

19. Then, it calls the `printJob()` method of the `PrintQueue` object:

```
printQueue.printJob(new Object());
```

20. Finally, the method writes a message to the console that shows that it has finished its execution:

```
System.out.printf("%s: The document has been printed\n",
                Thread.currentThread().getName());
}
```

21. Next, implement the main class of the example by creating a class named `Main` and implementing the `main()` method:

```
public class Main {
    public static void main (String args[]){
```

22. Create a `PrintQueue` object named `printQueue`:

```
PrintQueue printQueue=new PrintQueue();
```

23. Create 12 threads. Each one of these threads will execute a `Job` object that will send a document to the print queue:

```
Thread[] threads=new Thread[12];
for (int i=0; I < threads.length i++){
    thread[i]=new Thread(new Job(printQueue),"Thread"+i);
}
```

24. Finally, start the 12 threads:

```
for (int i=0; I < threads.length; i++){
    thread[i].start();
}
```

How it works...

The key to this example is the `printJob()` method of the `PrintQueue` class. This method shows three steps you must follow when you use a semaphore to implement a critical section and protect access to a shared resource:

1. First, you acquire the semaphore with the `acquire()` method.
2. Then, you do the necessary operations with the shared resource.
3. Finally, release the semaphore with the `release()` method.

Another important point in this example is the constructor of the `PrintQueue` class and the initialization of the `Semaphore` object. You pass the value 3 as the parameter of this constructor, so you are creating a semaphore that will protect three resources. The first three threads that call the `acquire()` method will get access to the critical section of this example, while the rest will be blocked. When a thread finishes a critical section and releases the semaphore, another thread will acquire it.

The following screenshot shows the output of an execution of this example:

```
Mon Sep 05 00:07:27 GMT+01:00 2016 - Thread 0: PrintQueue: Printing a Job in Printer 0 during 8 seconds
Thread 4: Going to print a job
Thread 3: Going to print a job
Thread 2: Going to print a job
Thread 1: Going to print a job
Mon Sep 05 00:07:27 GMT+01:00 2016 - Thread 8: PrintQueue: Printing a Job in Printer 2 during 6 seconds
Mon Sep 05 00:07:27 GMT+01:00 2016 - Thread 10: PrintQueue: Printing a Job in Printer 1 during 7 seconds
Thread 8: The document has been printed
Mon Sep 05 00:07:33 GMT+01:00 2016 - Thread 6: PrintQueue: Printing a Job in Printer 2 during 8 seconds
Thread 10: The document has been printed
Mon Sep 05 00:07:34 GMT+01:00 2016 - Thread 9: PrintQueue: Printing a Job in Printer 1 during 5 seconds
Thread 0: The document has been printed
Mon Sep 05 00:07:35 GMT+01:00 2016 - Thread 5: PrintQueue: Printing a Job in Printer 0 during 1 seconds
```

You can see how the first three print jobs start at the same time. Then, when one printer finishes its job, another one begins.

There's more...

The `Semaphore` class has three additional versions of the `acquire()` method:

- `acquireUninterruptibly()`: The `acquire()` method, when the internal counter of the semaphore is 0, blocks the thread until the semaphore is released. During this period, the thread may be interrupted; if this happens, the method will throw an `InterruptedException` exception. This version of the `acquire` operation ignores the interruption of the thread and doesn't throw any exceptions.

- `tryAcquire()`: This method tries to acquire the semaphore. If it can, it returns the `true` value. But if it can't, it returns `false` instead of being blocked and waits for the release of the semaphore. It's your responsibility to take correct action based on the return value.

- `tryAcquire(long timeout, TimeUnit unit)`: This method is equivalent to the previous one, but it waits for the semaphore for the period of time specified in the parameters. If the period of time ends and the method hasn't acquired the semaphore, it will return `false`.

The `acquire()`, `acquireUninterruptibly()`, `tryAcquire()`, and `release()` methods have an additional version, which has an `int` parameter. This parameter represents the number of permits the thread that uses them wants to acquire or release, in other words, the number of units that this thread wants to delete or add to the internal counter of the semaphore.

In the case of the `acquire()`, `acquireUninterruptibly()`, and `tryAcquire()` methods, if the value of the counter is less than the number passed as parameter value, the thread will be blocked until the counter gets the same value or a greater one.

Fairness in semaphores

The concept of fairness is used by the Java language in all classes that can have various threads blocked and are waiting for the release of a synchronization resource (for example, a semaphore). The default mode is called **non-fair mode**. In this mode, when the synchronization resource is released, one of the waiting threads is selected and is given this resource; however, it's selected without any criteria. Fair mode, on the other hand, changes this behavior and selects the thread that has been waiting for the longest period of time.

As it occurs with other classes, the `Semaphore` class admits a second parameter in its constructor. This parameter must take a Boolean value. If you give it a false value, you are creating a semaphore that will work in non-fair mode. You will get the same behavior if you don't use this parameter. If you give it a true value, you are creating a semaphore that will work in fair mode.

See also

- The *Monitoring a Lock interface* recipe in Chapter 9, *Testing Concurrent Applications*
- The *Synchronizing a block of code with a lock* recipe in Chapter 2, *Basic Thread Synchronization*

Waiting for multiple concurrent events

The Java concurrency API provides a class that allows one or more threads to wait until a set of operations are made. It's called the `CountDownLatch` class. This class is initialized with an integer number, which is the number of operations the threads are going to wait for. When a thread wants to wait for the execution of these operations, it uses the `await()` method. This method puts the thread to sleep until the operations are completed. When one of these operations finishes, it uses the `countDown()` method to decrement the internal counter of the `CountDownLatch` class. When the counter arrives at 0, the class wakes up all the threads that were sleeping in the `await()` method.

In this recipe, you will learn how to use the `CountDownLatch` class to implement a video conference system. The video conference system should wait for the arrival of all the participants before it begins.

Getting ready

The example of this recipe has been implemented using the Eclipse IDE. If you use Eclipse or a different IDE, such as NetBeans, open it and create a new Java project.

How to do it...

Follow these steps to implement the example:

1. Create a class named `Videoconference` and specify that it implements the `Runnable` interface. This class will implement the video conference system:

   ```
   public class Videoconference implements Runnable{
   ```

2. Declare a `CountDownLatch` object named controller:

   ```
   private final CountDownLatch controller;
   ```

3. Implement the constructor of the class that initializes the `CountDownLatch` attribute. The `Videoconference` class will wait for the arrival of the number of participants received as a parameter:

   ```
   public Videoconference(int number) {
     controller=new CountDownLatch(number);
   }
   ```

4. Implement the `arrive()` method. This method will be called each time a participant arrives for the video conference. It receives a `String` type named name as the parameter:

   ```
   public void arrive(String name){
   ```

5. First, it writes a message with the parameter it has received:

   ```
   System.out.printf("%s has arrived.",name);
   ```

6. Then, it calls the `countDown()` method of the `CountDownLatch` object:

```
controller.countDown();
```

7. Finally, it writes another message with the number of participants whose arrival is pending, using the `getCount()` method of the `CountDownLatch` object:

```
System.out.printf("VideoConference: Waiting for %d
                participants.\n",controller.getCount());
```

8. Next, implement the main method of the video conference system. It's the `run()` method that every `Runnable` object must have:

```
@Override
public void run() {
```

9. First, use the `getCount()` method to write a message with the number of participants in the video conference:

```
System.out.printf("VideoConference: Initialization: %d
                participants.\n",controller.getCount());
```

10. Then, use the `await()` method to wait for all the participants. As this method can throw an `InterruptedException` exception, you must include the code to process it:

```
try {
    controller.await();
```

11. Finally, write a message to indicate that all the participants have arrived:

```
System.out.printf("VideoConference: All the participants have
                come\n");
System.out.printf("VideoConference: Let's start...\n");
} catch (InterruptedException e) {
    e.printStackTrace();
}
```

12. Next, create the `Participant` class and specify that it implements the `Runnable` interface. This class represents each participant in the video conference:

```
public class Participant implements Runnable {
```

13. Declare a private `Videoconference` attribute named `conference`:

```
private Videoconference conference;
```

14. Declare a private `String` attribute named `name`:

```
private String name;
```

15. Implement the constructor of the class that initializes both the preceding attributes:

```
public Participant(Videoconference conference, String name) {
   this.conference=conference;
   this.name=name;
}
```

16. Implement the `run()` method of the participants:

```
@Override
public void run() {
```

17. First, put the thread to sleep for a random period of time:

```
long duration=(long)(Math.random()*10);
try {
   TimeUnit.SECONDS.sleep(duration);
} catch (InterruptedException e) {
   e.printStackTrace();
}
```

18. Then, use the `arrive()` method of the `Videoconference` object to indicate the arrival of this participant:

```
conference.arrive(name);
```

19. Finally, implement the main class of the example by creating a class named `Main` and adding the `main()` method to it:

```
public class Main {
   public static void main(String[] args) {
```

20. Next, create a `Videoconference` object named `conference` that waits for 10 participants:

```
Videoconference conference=new Videoconference(10);
```

21. Create `Thread` to run this `Videoconference` object and start it:

```
Thread threadConference=new Thread(conference);
threadConference.start();
```

22. Create 10 `Participant` objects, a `Thread` object to run each of them, and start all the threads:

```
for (int i=0; i<10; i++){
  Participant p=new Participant(conference, "Participant "+i);
  Thread t=new Thread(p);
  t.start();
}
```

How it works...

The `CountDownLatch` class has three basic elements:

- The initialization value that determines how many events the `CountDownLatch` object waits for
- The `await()` method, called by the threads that wait for the finalization of all the events
- The `countDown()` method, called by the events when they finish their execution

When you create a `CountDownLatch` object, it uses the constructor's parameter to initialize an internal counter. Every time a thread calls the `countDown()` method, the `CountDownLatch` object decrements the internal counter in one unit. When the internal counter reaches 0, the `CountDownLatch` object wakes up all the threads that were waiting in the `await()` method.

There's no way to re-initialize the internal counter of the `CountDownLatch` object or modify its value. Once the counter is initialized, the only method you can use to modify its value is the `countDown()` method explained earlier. When the counter reaches 0, all the calls to the `await()` method are returned immediately and all subsequent calls to the `countDown()` method have no effect.

However, there are some differences with respect to other synchronization methods, which are as follows:

- The `CountDownLatch` mechanism is not used to protect a shared resource or a critical section. It is used to synchronize one or more threads with the execution of various tasks.
- It only admits one use. As explained earlier, once the counter of `CountDownLatch` arrives at 0, all the calls to its methods have no effect. You have to create a new object if you want to do the same synchronization again.

The following screenshot shows the output of an execution of the example:

```
<terminated> Main (12) [Java Application] C:\Program Files\Java\jdk-9\bin\jav
Participant 4 has arrived.
VideoConference: Waiting for 4 participants.
Participant 5 has arrived.
VideoConference: Waiting for 3 participants.
Participant 1 has arrived.
VideoConference: Waiting for 2 participants.
Participant 6 has arrived.
VideoConference: Waiting for 1 participants.
Participant 3 has arrived.
VideoConference: All the participants have come
VideoConference: Let's start...
VideoConference: Waiting for 0 participants.
```

You can see how participants arrive, and once the internal counter arrives at 0, the
CountDownLatch object wakes up the Videoconference object that writes the messages
indicating that the video conference should start.

There's more...

The CountDownLatch class has another version of the await() method, which is as
follows:

- await(long time, TimeUnit unit): In this method, the thread will continue
  to sleep until it's interrupted, that is, either the internal counter of
  CountDownLatch arrives at 0 or the specified time passes. The TimeUnit class is
  an enumeration with the following constants: DAYS, HOURS, MICROSECONDS,
  MILLISECONDS, MINUTES, NANOSECONDS, and SECONDS.

Synchronizing tasks in a common point

The Java concurrency API provides a synchronizing utility that allows the synchronization
of two or more threads at a determined point. It's the CyclicBarrier class. This class is
similar to the CountDownLatch class explained in the *Waiting for multiple concurrent events*
recipe in this chapter, but it presents some differences that make it a more powerful class.

The `CyclicBarrier` class is initialized with an integer number, which is the number of threads that will be synchronized at a determined point. When one of these threads arrives at the determined point, it calls the `await()` method to wait for the other threads. When the thread calls this method, the `CyclicBarrier` class blocks the thread that is sleeping until the other threads arrive. When the last thread calls the `await()` method of the `CyclicBarrier` object, it wakes up all the threads that were waiting and continues with its job.

One interesting advantage of the `CyclicBarrier` class is that you can pass an additional `Runnable` object as an initialization parameter, and the `CyclicBarrier` class executes this object as a thread when all the threads arrive at the common point. This characteristic makes this class adequate for parallelization of tasks using the divide and conquer programming technique.

In this recipe, you will learn how to use the `CyclicBarrier` class to synchronize a set of threads at a determined point. You will also use a `Runnable` object that will be executed after all the threads arrive at this point. In the example, you will look for a number in a matrix of numbers. The matrix will be divided into subsets (using the divide and conquer technique), so each thread will look for the number in one subset. Once all the threads have finished their respective jobs, a final task will unify their results.

Getting ready

The example of this recipe has been implemented using the Eclipse IDE. If you use Eclipse or a different IDE, such as NetBeans, open it and create a new Java project.

How to do it...

Follow these steps to implement the example:

1. Start the example by implementing two auxiliary classes. First, create a class named `MatrixMock`. This class will generate a random matrix of numbers between one and 10, where the threads will look for a number:

   ```
   public class MatrixMock {
   ```

2. Declare a private `int` matrix named `data`:

   ```
   private final int data[][];
   ```

3. Implement the constructor of the class. This constructor will receive the number of rows of the matrix, the length of each row, and the number we are going to look for as parameters. All the three parameters are of the type `int`:

```
public MatrixMock(int size, int length, int number){
```

4. Initialize the variables and objects used in the constructor:

```
int counter=0;
data=new int[size][length];
Random random=new Random();
```

5. Fill the matrix with random numbers. Each time you generate a number, compare it with the number you are going to look for. If they are equal, increment the counter:

```
for (int i=0; i<size; i++) {
   for (int j=0; j<length; j++){
      data[i][j]=random.nextInt(10);
      if (data[i][j]==number){
         counter++;
      }
   }
}
```

6. Finally, print a message in the console, which shows the number of occurrences of the number you are going to look for in the generated matrix. This message will be used to check that the threads get the correct result:

```
System.out.printf("Mock: There are %d ocurrences of number in
                  generated data.\n",counter,number);
```

7. Implement the `getRow()` method. This method receives an `int` parameter with the number of a rows in the matrix; it returns the row if it exists and returns `null` if it doesn't:

```
public int[] getRow(int row){
   if ((row>=0) && (row<data.length)){
      return data[row];
   }
   return null;
}
```

8. Now implement a class named `Results`. This class will store, in an array, the number of occurrences of the searched number in each row of the matrix:

```
public class Results {
```

9. Declare a private `int` array named `data`:

```
private final int data[];
```

10. Implement the constructor of the class. This constructor receives an integer parameter with the number of elements of the array:

```
public Results(int size){
   data=new int[size];
}
```

11. Implement the `setData()` method. This method receives a position in the array and a value as a parameter, and it establishes the value of that position in the array:

```
public void  setData(int position,  int value){
   data[position]=value;
}
```

12. Implement the `getData()` method. This method returns the array with the array of the results:

```
public int[] getData(){
   return data;
}
```

13. Now that you have the auxiliary classes, it's time to implement threads. First, implement the `Searcher` class. This class will look for a number in the determined rows of the matrix of random numbers. Create a class named `Searcher` and specify that it implements the `Runnable` interface:

```
public class Searcher implements Runnable {
```

14. Declare two private `int` attributes, namely `firstRow` and `lastRow`. These two attributes will determine the subset of rows where this object will look for the number:

```
private final int firstRow;
private final int lastRow;
```

15. Declare a private `MatrixMock` attribute named `mock`:

```
private final MatrixMock mock;
```

16. Declare a private `Results` attribute named `results`:

```
private final Results results;
```

17. Declare a private `int` attribute named `number`, which will store the number we are going to look for:

```
private final int number;
```

18. Declare a `CyclicBarrier` object named `barrier`:

```
private final CyclicBarrier barrier;
```

19. Implement the constructor of the class that initializes all the attributes declared previously:

```
public Searcher(int firstRow, int lastRow, MatrixMock mock,
            Results results, int number, CyclicBarrier barrier){
    this.firstRow=firstRow;
    this.lastRow=lastRow;
    this.mock=mock;
    this.results=results;
    this.number=number;
    this.barrier=barrier;
}
```

20. Implement the `run()` method that will search for the number. It uses an internal variable called `counter` that will store the number of occurrences of the number in each row:

```
@Override
public void run() {
    int counter;
```

21. Print a message in the console with the rows assigned to this task:

```
System.out.printf("%s: Processing lines from %d to %d.\n",
            Thread.currentThread().getName(),
            firstRow,lastRow);
```

22. Process all the rows assigned to this thread. For each row, count the number of occurrences of the number you are searching for and store this number in the corresponding position of the `Results` object:

```
for (int i=firstRow; i<lastRow; i++){
  int row[]=mock.getRow(i);
  counter=0;
  for (int j=0; j<row.length; j++){
    if (row[j]==number){
      counter++;
    }
  }
  results.setData(i, counter);
}
```

23. Print a message in the console to indicate that this object has finished searching:

```
System.out.printf("%s: Lines processed.\n",
                  Thread.currentThread().getName());
```

24. Call the `await()` method of the `CyclicBarrier` object and add the necessary code to process the `InterruptedException` and `BrokenBarrierException` exceptions that this method can throw:

```
try {
  barrier.await();
} catch (InterruptedException e) {
  e.printStackTrace();
} catch (BrokenBarrierException e) {
  e.printStackTrace();
}
```

25. Now implement the class that calculates the total number of occurrences of the number in the matrix. This class uses the `Results` object that stores the number of appearances of the number in each row of the matrix to make the calculation. Create a class named `Grouper` and specify that it implements the `Runnable` interface:

```
public class Grouper implements Runnable {
```

26. Declare a private `Results` attribute named `results`:

```
private final Results results;
```

27. Implement the constructor of the class that initializes the `Results` attribute:

```
public Grouper(Results results){
   this.results=results;
}
```

28. Implement the `run()` method that will calculate the total number of occurrences of the number in the array of results:

```
@Override
public void run() {
```

29. Declare an `int` variable and write a message to the console to indicate the start of the process:

```
int finalResult=0;
System.out.printf("Grouper: Processing results...\n");
```

30. Get the number of occurrences of the number in each row using the `getData()` method of the `results` object. Then, process all the elements of the array and add their value to the `finalResult` variable:

```
int data[]=results.getData();
for (int number:data){
   finalResult+=number;
}
```

31. Print the result in the console:

```
System.out.printf("Grouper: Total result: %d.\n", finalResult);
```

32. Finally, implement the main class of the example by creating a class named `Main` and adding the `main()` method to it:

```
public class Main {
   public static void main(String[] args) {
```

33. Declare and initialize five constants to store the parameters of the application:

```
final int ROWS=10000;
final int NUMBERS=1000;
final int SEARCH=5;
final int PARTICIPANTS=5;
final int LINES_PARTICIPANT=2000;
```

34. Create a `MatrixMock` object named `mock`. It will have 10,000 rows of 1,000 elements. Now, you are going to search for the number five:

```
MatrixMock mock=new MatrixMock(ROWS, NUMBERS,SEARCH);
```

35. Create a `Results` object named `results`. It will have 10,000 elements:

```
Results results=new Results(ROWS);
```

36. Create a `Grouper` object named `grouper`:

```
Grouper grouper=new Grouper(results);
```

37. Create a `CyclicBarrier` object called `barrier`. This object will wait for five threads. When these five threads finish, it will execute the `Grouper` object created previously:

```
CyclicBarrier barrier=new CyclicBarrier(PARTICIPANTS,grouper);
```

38. Create five `Searcher` objects, five threads to execute them, and start the five threads:

```
Searcher searchers[]=new Searcher[PARTICIPANTS];
for (int i=0; i<PARTICIPANTS; i++){
  searchers[i]=new Searcher(i*LINES_PARTICIPANT,
                  (i*LINES_PARTICIPANT)+LINES_PARTICIPANT,
                 mock, results, 5,barrier);
  Thread thread=new Thread(searchers[i]);
  thread.start();
}
System.out.printf("Main: The main thread has finished.\n");
```

How it works...

The following screenshot shows the result of an execution of this example:

```
<terminated> Main (13) [Java Application] C:\Program Files\Java\jdk-9\bin\javaw.exe (28
Mock: There are 1000610 ocurrences of number in generated data.
Thread-0: Processing lines from 0 to 2000.
Thread-2: Processing lines from 4000 to 6000.
Thread-1: Processing lines from 2000 to 4000.
Main: The main thread has finished.
Thread-3: Processing lines from 6000 to 8000.
Thread-0: Lines processed.
Thread-1: Lines processed.
Thread-2: Lines processed.
Thread-4: Processing lines from 8000 to 10000.
Thread-3: Lines processed.
Thread-4: Lines processed.
Grouper: Processing results...
Grouper: Total result: 1000610.
```

The problem resolved in the example is simple. We have a big matrix of random integers, and you want to know the total number of occurrences of a number in this matrix. To get better performance, we used the divide and conquer technique. We divided the matrix into five subsets and used a thread to look for the number in each subset. These threads are objects of the Searcher class.

We used a CyclicBarrier object to synchronize the completion of the five threads and execute the Grouper task to process partial results and calculate the final one.

As mentioned earlier, the CyclicBarrier class has an internal counter to control how many threads need to arrive at the synchronization point. Each time a thread arrives at the synchronization point, it calls the await() method to notify the CyclicBarrier object that a thread has arrived at its synchronization point. CyclicBarrier puts the thread to sleep until all the threads reach the synchronization point.

When all the threads have arrived, the CyclicBarrier object wakes up all the threads that were waiting in the await() method. Optionally, it creates a new thread that executes a Runnable object passed as the parameter in the construction of CyclicBarrier (in our case, a Grouper object) to do additional tasks.

There's more...

The CyclicBarrier class has another version of the await() method:

- await(long time, TimeUnit unit): In this method, the thread will continue to sleep until it's interrupted, that is, either the internal counter of CyclicBarrier arrives at 0 or the specified time passes. The TimeUnit class is an enumeration with the following constants: DAYS, HOURS, MICROSECONDS, MILLISECONDS, MINUTES, NANOSECONDS, and SECONDS.

This class also provides the getNumberWaiting() method that returns the number of threads that are blocked in the await() method and the getParties() method that returns the number of tasks that are going to be synchronized with CyclicBarrier.

Resetting a CyclicBarrier object

The CyclicBarrier class has some points in common with the CountDownLatch class, but they also have some differences. One of the most important differences is that a CyclicBarrier object can be reset to its initial state, assigning to its internal counter the value with which it was initialized.

This reset operation can be done using the reset() method of the CyclicBarrier class. When this occurs, all the threads that were waiting in the await() method receive a BrokenBarrierException exception. This exception was processed in the example presented in this recipe by printing the stack trace; however, in a more complex application, it could perform some other operation, such as restarting the execution or recovering the operation at the point it was interrupted.

Broken CyclicBarrier objects

A CyclicBarrier object can be in a special state denoted by the broken state. When there are various threads waiting in the await() method and one of them is interrupted, the one that is interrupted receives an InterruptedException exception, but other threads receive a BrokenBarrierException exception; CyclicBarrier is placed in the broken state.

The CyclicBarrier class provides the isBroken() method. It returns true if the object is in the broken state; otherwise, it returns false.

See also

- The *Waiting for multiple concurrent events* recipe in this chapter

Running concurrent-phased tasks

One of the most complex and powerful functionalities offered by the Java concurrency API is the ability to execute concurrent-phased tasks using the Phaser class. This mechanism is useful when we have some concurrent tasks divided into steps. The Phaser class provides us with a mechanism to synchronize threads at the end of each step, so no thread will start with the second step until all the threads have finished the first one.

As with other synchronization utilities, we have to initialize the Phaser class with the number of tasks that participate in the synchronization operation, but we can dynamically modify this number by either increasing or decreasing it.

In this recipe, you will learn how to use the Phaser class to synchronize three concurrent tasks. The three tasks look for files with the extension .log modified in the last 24 hours in three different folders and their subfolders. This task is divided into three steps:

1. Get a list of the files with the extension .log in the assigned folder and its subfolders.
2. Filter the list created in the first step by deleting the files modified more than 24 hours ago.
3. Print the results in the console.

At the end of step 1 and step 2, we check whether the list has any elements or not. If it doesn't, the thread ends its execution and is eliminated from the Phaser class.

Getting ready

The example of this recipe has been implemented using the Eclipse IDE. If you use Eclipse or a different IDE, such as NetBeans, open it and create a new Java project.

How to do it...

Follow these steps to implement the example:

1. Create a class named `FileSearch` and specify that it implements the `Runnable` interface. This class implements the operation of searching for files with a determined extension modified in the last 24 hours in a folder and its subfolders:

   ```
   public class FileSearch implements Runnable {
   ```

2. Declare a private `String` attribute to store the folder in which the search operation will begin:

   ```
   private final String initPath;
   ```

3. Declare another private `String` attribute to store the extension of the files we are going to look for:

   ```
   private final String fileExtension
   ```

4. Declare a private `List` attribute to store the full path of the files we will find with the desired characteristics:

   ```
   private List<String> results;
   ```

5. Finally, declare a private `Phaser` attribute to control the synchronization of the different phases of the task:

   ```
   private Phaser phaser;
   ```

6. Next, implement the constructor of the class that will initialize the attributes of the class. It receives the full path of the initial folder as parameters, the extension of the files, and `phaser`:

   ```
   public FileSearch(String initPath, String fileExtension,
                     Phaser phaser) {
     this.initPath = initPath;
     this.fileExtension = fileExtension;
     this.phaser=phaser;
     results=new ArrayList<>();
   }
   ```

7. Now, implement some auxiliary methods that will be used by the run() method. The first one is the directoryProcess() method. It receives a File object as a parameter and it processes all its files and subfolders. For each folder, the method will make a recursive call while passing the folder as a parameter. For each file, the method will call the fileProcess() method:

```
private void directoryProcess(File file) {

  File list[] = file.listFiles();
  if (list != null) {
    for (int i = 0; i < list.length; i++) {
      if (list[i].isDirectory()) {
        directoryProcess(list[i]);
      } else {
        fileProcess(list[i]);
      }
    }
  }
}
```

8. Then, implement the fileProcess() method. It receives a File object as a parameter and checks whether its extension is equal to the one we are looking for. If they are equal, this method adds the absolute path of the file to the list of results:

```
private void fileProcess(File file) {
  if (file.getName().endsWith(fileExtension)) {
    results.add(file.getAbsolutePath());
  }
}
```

9. Now implement the filterResults() method. It doesn't receive any parameter and filters the list of files obtained in the first phase; it deletes files that were modified more than 24 hours ago. First, create a new empty list and get the actual date:

```
private void filterResults() {
  List<String> newResults=new ArrayList<>();
  long actualDate=new Date().getTime();
```

10. Then, go through all the elements of the results list. For each path in the list of results, create a File object for the file and get its last modified date:

```
for (int i=0; i<results.size(); i++){
  File file=new File(results.get(i));
```

```
long fileDate=file.lastModified();
```

11. Then, compare this date with the actual date, and if the difference is less than 1 day, add the full path of the file to the new list of results:

```
if (actualDate-fileDate< TimeUnit.MILLISECONDS
                        .convert(1,TimeUnit.DAYS)){
    newResults.add(results.get(i));
  }
}
```

12. Finally, change the old results list to the new ones:

```
results=newResults;
}
```

13. Next, implement the `checkResults()` method. This method will be called at the end of the first and second phase, and it will check whether the results list is empty or not. This method doesn't have any parameters:

```
private boolean checkResults() {
```

14. First, check the size of the results list. If it's 0, the object writes a message to the console indicating this. After this, it calls the `arriveAndDeregister()` method of the `Phaser` object to notify that this thread has finished the actual phase and it leaves the phased operation:

```
if (results.isEmpty()) {
  System.out.printf("%s: Phase %d: 0 results.\n",
                    Thread.currentThread().getName(),
                    phaser.getPhase());
  System.out.printf("%s: Phase %d: End.\n",
                    Thread.currentThread().getName(),
                    phaser.getPhase());
  phaser.arriveAndDeregister();
  return false;
```

15. If the results list has elements, the object writes a message to the console indicating this. Then, it calls the `arriveAndAwaitAdvance()` method of the `Phaser` object to notify that this thread has finished the actual phase and it wants to be blocked until all the participant threads in the phased operation finish the actual phase:

```
} else {
  System.out.printf("%s: Phase %d: %d results.\n",
                    Thread.currentThread().getName(),
```

```
                              phaser.getPhase(),results.size());
           phaser.arriveAndAwaitAdvance();
           return true;
       }
   }
```

16. The last auxiliary method is the `showInfo()` method that prints the elements of the results list to the console:

```
private void showInfo() {
    for (int i=0; i<results.size(); i++){
        File file=new File(results.get(i));
        System.out.printf("%s: %s\n",
                          Thread.currentThread().getName(),
                          file.getAbsolutePath());
    }
    phaser.arriveAndAwaitAdvance();
}
```

17. It's time to implement the `run()` method that executes the operation using the auxiliary methods described earlier. We'll also implement the `Phaser` object to control the change between phases. First, call the `arriveAndAwaitAdvance()` method of the `Phaser` object. The search won't begin until all the threads have been created:

```
@Override
public void run() {
    phaser.arriveAndAwaitAdvance();
```

18. Then, write a message to the console indicating the start of the search task:

```
System.out.printf("%s: Starting.\n",
                  Thread.currentThread().getName());
```

19. Check that the `initPath` attribute stores the name of a folder and use the `directoryProcess()` method to find the files with the specified extension in that folder and all its subfolders:

```
File file = new File(initPath);
if (file.isDirectory()) {
    directoryProcess(file);
}
```

20. Check whether there are any results using the `checkResults()` method. If there are no results, finish the execution of the thread with the `return` keyword:

```
if (!checkResults()){
    return;
}
```

21. Filter the list of results using the `filterResults()` method:

```
filterResults();
```

22. Check whether there are any results using the `checkResults()` method once again. If there are no results, finish the execution of the thread with the `return` keyword:

```
if (!checkResults()){
    return;
}
```

23. Print the final list of results to the console with the `showInfo()` method, deregister the thread, and print a message indicating the finalization of the thread:

```
showInfo();
phaser.arriveAndDeregister();
System.out.printf("%s: Work completed.\n",
                Thread.currentThread().getName());
```

24. Now, implement the main class of the example by creating a class named `Main` and adding the `main()` method to it:

```
public class Main {
    public static void main(String[] args) {
```

25. Create a `Phaser` object with three participants:

```
Phaser phaser=new Phaser(3);
```

26. Create three `FileSearch` objects with a different initial folder for each one. Look for the files with the `.log` extension:

```
FileSearch system=new FileSearch("C:\\Windows", "log", phaser);
FileSearch apps= new FileSearch("C:\\Program Files",
                        "log",phaser);
FileSearch documents= new FileSearch("C:\\Documents And Settings",
                        "log",phaser);
```

27. Create and start a thread to execute the first `FileSearch` object:

```
Thread systemThread=new Thread(system,"System");
systemThread.start();
```

28. Create and start a thread to execute the second `FileSearch` object:

```
Thread appsThread=new Thread(apps,"Apps");
appsThread.start();
```

29. Create and start a thread to execute the third `FileSearch` object:

```
Thread documentsThread=new Thread(documents, "Documents");
documentsThread.start();
```

30. Wait for the finalization of the three threads:

```
try {
  systemThread.join();
  appsThread.join();
  documentsThread.join();
} catch (InterruptedException e) {
  e.printStackTrace();
}
```

31. Write the value of the finalized flag of the `Phaser` object using the `isFinalized()` method:

```
System.out.println("Terminated: "+ phaser.isTerminated());
```

How it works...

The program starts creating a `Phaser` object that will control the synchronization of the threads at the end of each phase. The constructor of `Phaser` receives the number of participants as a parameter. In our case, `Phaser` has three participants. This number indicates `Phaser` the number of threads that need to execute the `arriveAndAwaitAdvance()` method before `Phaser` could change the phase and wake up the threads that have been sleeping.

Once `Phaser` has been created, we launch three threads that are executed using three different `FileSearch` objects.

In this example, we use paths of the Windows operating system. If you work with another operating system, modify the paths to adapt them to existing paths in your environment, such as /var/log, or similar.

The first instruction in the run() method of this FileSearch object is a call to the arriveAndAwaitAdvance() method of the Phaser object. As mentioned earlier, Phaser knows the number of threads that we want to synchronize. When a thread calls this method, Phaser decreases the number of threads that have to finalize the actual phase and puts this thread to sleep until all the remaining threads finish this phase. Calling this method at the beginning of the run() method ensures that none of the FileSearch threads begin their job until all the threads are created.

At the end of phase one and phase two, we check whether the phase has generated results and the list with the results has elements or the phase hasn't generated results and the list is empty. In the first case, the checkResults() method calls arriveAndAwaitAdvance() as explained earlier. In the second case, if the list is empty, there's no point in the thread continuing with its execution, so it ends its execution. But you have to notify the Phaser object that there will be one less participant. For this, we used arriveAndDeregister(). This notifies phaser that the thread has finished the actual phase, but it won't participate in future phases, therefore, phaser won't have to wait for it to continue.

At the end of the phase three implemented in the showInfo() method, there is a call to the arriveAndAwaitAdvance() method of phaser. With this call, we guarantee that all the threads finish at the same time. When this method ends its execution, there is a call to the arriveAndDeregister() method of phaser. With this call, we deregister the threads of phaser, as explained before, so when all the threads finish, phaser will have zero participants.

Finally, the main() method waits for the completion of the three threads and calls the isTerminated() method of phaser. When phaser has zero participants, it enters the so-called termination state, and this method returns true. As we deregister all the threads of phaser, it will be in the termination state, and this call will print true to the console.

A Phaser object can be in two states:

- **Active**: Phaser enters this state when it accepts the registration of new participants and its synchronization at the end of each phase. In this state, Phaser works as it has been explained in this recipe. This state is not mentioned in the Java concurrency API.

- **Termination**: By default, Phaser enters this state when all the participants in Phaser have been deregistered, which means it has zero participants. Further, Phaser is in the termination state when the method onAdvance() returns true. If you override this method, you can change the default behavior. When Phaser is in this state, the synchronization method arriveAndAwaitAdvance() returns immediately without doing any synchronization operation.

A notable feature of the Phaser class is that you haven't had to control any exception from the methods related to phaser. Unlike other synchronization utilities, threads that are sleeping in phaser don't respond to interruption events and don't throw an InterruptedException exception. There is only one exception, which is explained in the next section.

The following screenshot shows the results of one execution of the example:

```
<terminated> Main (15) [Java Application] C:\Program Files\Java\jdk-9\bin\javaw.exe
Documents: Starting.
System: Starting.
Apps: Starting.
Documents: Phase 1: 0 results.
Documents: Phase 1: End.
Apps: Phase 1: 9 results.
System: Phase 1: 271 results.
Apps: Phase 2: 0 results.
Apps: Phase 2: End.
System: Phase 2: 11 results.
System: C:\Windows\debug\mrt.log
System: C:\Windows\Logs\CBS\CBS.log
System: C:\Windows\Logs\CBS\FilterList.log
System: C:\Windows\Logs\DISM\dism.log
System: C:\Windows\Microsoft.NET\Framework\v4.0.30319\ngen.log
<
```

It shows the first two phases of the execution. You can see how the Apps thread finishes its execution in phase two because its results list is empty. When you execute the example, you will see how some threads finish a phase before the rest and how they wait until all have finished one phase before continuing with the rest.

There's more...

The Phaser class provides other methods related to the change of phase. These methods are as follows:

- arrive(): This method notifies the Phaser class that one participant has finished the actual phase but it should not wait for the rest of the participants to continue with their execution. Be careful with the utilization of this method because it doesn't synchronize with other threads.

- `awaitAdvance(int phase)`: This method puts the current thread to sleep until all the participants of the `phaser` parameter have finished the current phase, that is, if the number we pass as the parameter is equal to the actual phase of `phaser`. If the parameter and the actual phase of `phaser` aren't equal, the method ends its execution.
- `awaitAdvanceInterruptibly(int phaser)`: This method is equal to the method explained earlier, but it throws an `InterruptedException` exception if the thread that is sleeping in this method is interrupted.

Registering participants in Phaser

When you create a `Phaser` object, you indicate how many participants will have that `phaser`. But the `Phaser` class has two methods to increment the number of participants of `phaser`. These methods are as follows:

- `register()`: This method adds a new participant to `Phaser`. This new participant will be considered unarrived to the actual phase.
- `bulkRegister(int Parties)`: This method adds the specified number of participants to `phaser`. These new participants will be considered unarrived to the actual phase.

The only method provided by the `Phaser` class to decrement the number of participants is the `arriveAndDeregister()` method that notifies `phaser` that the thread has finished the actual phase and it doesn't want to continue with the phased operation.

Forcing the termination of Phaser

When `phaser` has zero participants, it enters a state denoted by termination. The `Phaser` class provides `forceTermination()` to change the status of `phaser` and makes it enter the termination state independently of the number of participants registered in `phaser`. This mechanism may be useful when one of the participants has an error situation, where the best thing to do would be to terminate `phaser`.

When `phaser` is in the termination state, the `awaitAdvance()` and `arriveAndAwaitAdvance()` methods immediately return a negative number, instead of a positive one that is returned normally. If you know that your `phaser` could be terminated, you should verify the return value of those methods (`awaitAdvance()` and `arriveAndAwaitAdvance()`) to know whether `phaser` has been terminated.

See also

- The *Monitoring a Phaser class* recipe in `Chapter 9`, *Testing Concurrent Applications*

Controlling phase change in concurrent-phased tasks

The `Phaser` class provides a method that is executed each time `phaser` changes the phase. It's the `onAdvance()` method. It receives two parameters: the number of the current phases and the number of registered participants. It returns a Boolean value `false` if `Phaser` continues its execution or the value `true` if `Phaser` has finished and has to enter the termination state.

The default implementation of this method returns `true` if the number of registered participants is zero, and `false` otherwise. But you can modify this behavior if you extend the `Phaser` class and override this method. Normally, you will be interested in doing this when you have to execute some actions when you advance from one phase to the next.

In this recipe, you will learn how to control phase change in a phaser that is implementing your own version of the `Phaser` class that overrides the `onAdvance()` method to execute some actions in every phase change. You are going to implement a simulation of an exam, where there will be some students who have to do three exercises. All the students have to finish one exercise before they proceed with the next one.

Getting ready

The example of this recipe has been implemented using the Eclipse IDE. If you use Eclipse or a different IDE, such as NetBeans, open it and create a new Java project.

How to do it...

Follow these steps to implement the example:

1. Create a class named `MyPhaser` and specify that it extends from the `Phaser` class:

```
public class MyPhaser extends Phaser {
```

2. Override the `onAdvance()` method. According to the value of the `phase` attribute, we call it a different auxiliary method. If the `phase` attribute is equal to zero, you have to call the `studentsArrived()` method. If the `phase` is equal to one, you have to call the `finishFirstExercise()` method. If the phase is equal to two, you have to call the `finishSecondExercise()` method. Finally, if the phase is equal to three, you have to call the `finishExam()` method. Otherwise, return the true value to indicate that `phaser` has terminated:

```
@Override
protected boolean onAdvance(int phase, int registeredParties) {
  switch (phase) {
    case 0:
      return studentsArrived();
    case 1:
      return finishFirstExercise();
    case 2:
      return finishSecondExercise();
    case 3:
      return finishExam();
    default:
      return true;
  }
}
```

3. Implement the auxiliary method `studentsArrived()`. It writes two log messages to the console and returns false to indicate that `phaser` is continuing with its execution:

```
private boolean studentsArrived() {
  System.out.printf("Phaser: The exam are going to start.
                    The students are ready.\n");
  System.out.printf("Phaser: We have %d students.\n",
                    getRegisteredParties());
  return false;
}
```

4. Implement the auxiliary method `finishFirstExercise()`. It writes two messages to the console and returns false to indicate that `phaser` is continuing with its execution:

```
private boolean finishFirstExercise() {
    System.out.printf("Phaser: All the students have finished the
                      first exercise.\n");
    System.out.printf("Phaser: It's time for the second one.\n");
    return false;
}
```

5. Implement the auxiliary method `finishSecondExercise()`. It writes two messages to the console and returns false to indicate that `phaser` is continuing with its execution:

```
private boolean finishSecondExercise() {
    System.out.printf("Phaser: All the students have finished the
                      second exercise.\n");
    System.out.printf("Phaser: It's time for the third one.\n");
    return false;
}
```

6. Implement the auxiliary method `finishExam()`. It writes two messages to the console and returns true to indicate that `phaser` has finished its work:

```
private boolean finishExam() {
    System.out.printf("Phaser: All the students have finished
                      the exam.\n");
    System.out.printf("Phaser: Thank you for your time.\n");
    return true;
}
```

7. Create a class named `Student` and specify that it implements the `Runnable` interface. This class will simulate the students of an exam:

```
public class Student implements Runnable {
```

8. Declare a `Phaser` object named `phaser`:

```
private Phaser phaser;
```

9. Implement the constructor of the class that initializes the `Phaser` object:

```
public Student(Phaser phaser) {
    this.phaser=phaser;
}
```

10. Implement the `run()` method that will simulate the realization of the exam:

```
@Override
public void run() {
```

11. First, the method writes a message in the console to indicate that a student has arrived at the exam hall and calls the `arriveAndAwaitAdvance()` method of `phaser` to wait for the rest of the threads:

```
System.out.printf("%s: Has arrived to do the exam. %s\n",
                Thread.currentThread().getName(),new Date());
phaser.arriveAndAwaitAdvance();
```

12. Then, write a message to the console and call the private `doExercise1()` method that simulates the realization of the first exercise of the exam. Post this, write another message to the console and the `arriveAndAwaitAdvance()` method of `phaser` to wait for the rest of the students to finish the first exercise:

```
System.out.printf("%s: Is going to do the first exercise.%s\n",
                Thread.currentThread().getName(),new Date());
doExercise1();
System.out.printf("%s: Has done the first exercise.%s\n",
                Thread.currentThread().getName(),new Date());
phaser.arriveAndAwaitAdvance();
```

13. Implement the same code for the second and third exercises:

```
System.out.printf("%s: Is going to do the second exercise.
                %s\n",Thread.currentThread().getName(),
                new Date());
doExercise2();
System.out.printf("%s: Has done the second exercise.%s\n",
                Thread.currentThread().getName(),new Date());
phaser.arriveAndAwaitAdvance();
System.out.printf("%s: Is going to do the third exercise.%s\n",
                Thread.currentThread().getName(),new Date());
doExercise3();
System.out.printf("%s: Has finished the exam.%s\n",
                Thread.currentThread().getName(),new Date());
phaser.arriveAndAwaitAdvance();
```

14. Implement the auxiliary method `doExercise1()`. This method puts the current thread or the thread that executes the method to sleep for a random period of time:

```
private void doExercise1() {
  try {
    long duration=(long)(Math.random()*10);
    TimeUnit.SECONDS.sleep(duration);
  } catch (InterruptedException e) {
    e.printStackTrace();
  }
}
```

15. Implement the auxiliary method `doExercise2()`. This method puts the current thread or the thread that executes the method to sleep for a random period of time:

```
private void doExercise2() {
  try {
    long duration=(long)(Math.random()*10);
    TimeUnit.SECONDS.sleep(duration);
  } catch (InterruptedException e) {
    e.printStackTrace();
  }
}
```

16. Implement the auxiliary method `doExercise3()`. This method puts the thread to sleep for a random period of time:

```
private void doExercise3() {
  try {
    long duration=(long)(Math.random()*10);
    TimeUnit.SECONDS.sleep(duration);
  } catch (InterruptedException e) {
    e.printStackTrace();
  }
}
```

17. Implement the main class of the example by creating a class named `Main` and adding the `main()` method to it:

```
public class Main {
  public static void main(String[] args) {
```

18. Create a `MyPhaser` object:

```
MyPhaser phaser=new MyPhaser();
```

19. Create five `Student` objects and register them in the `phaser` attribute using the `register()` method:

```
Student students[]=new Student[5];
for (int i=0; i<students.length; i++){
  students[i]=new Student(phaser);
  phaser.register();
}
```

20. Create five threads to run students and start them:

```
Thread threads[]=new Thread[students.length];
for (int i=0; i<students.length; i++){
  threads[i]=new Thread(students[i],"Student "+i);
  threads[i].start();
}
```

21. Wait for the finalization of the five threads:

```
for (int i=0; i<threads.length; i++){
  try {
    threads[i].join();
  } catch (InterruptedException e) {
    e.printStackTrace();
  }
}
```

22. Write a message to show that `phaser` is in the termination state, using the `isTerminated()` method:

```
System.out.printf("Main: The phaser has finished: %s.\n",
                  phaser.isTerminated());
```

How it works...

This exercise simulates the realization of an exam that has three exercises. All the students have to finish one exercise before they can start the next one. To implement this synchronization requirement, we use the `Phaser` class; however, in this case, you implemented your own `phaser`, extending the original class to override the `onAdvance()` method.

This method is called by `Phaser` before making a phase change and waking up all the threads that were sleeping in the `arriveAndAwaitAdvance()` method. The method is invoked by the last thread that finishes a phase as part of the code of the `arriveAndAwaitAdvance()` method. This method receives the number of the actual phase as parameters, where 0 is the number of the first phase and the number of registered participants. The most useful parameter is the actual phase. If you execute a different operation depending on the actual phase, you have to use an alternative structure (`if...else` or `switch`) to select the operation you want to execute. In the example, we used a `switch` structure to select a different method for each change of phase.

The `onAdvance()` method returns a Boolean value that indicates whether `phaser` has terminated or not. If `phaser` returns false, it indicates that it hasn't terminated; if this happens, the threads will continue with the execution of other phases. If `phaser` returns `true`, then `phaser` still wakes up the pending threads but moves `phaser` to the terminated state. With this, all future calls to any method of `phaser` will return immediately, and the `isTerminated()` method will return `true`.

In the `Main` class, when you created the `MyPhaser` object, you didn't specify the number of participants in the phaser. You made a call to the `register()` method for every `Student` object created to register a participant in `phaser`. This calling doesn't establish a relation between the `Student` object or the thread that executes it and `phaser`. Really, the number of participants in a phaser is only a number. There is no relationship between `phaser` and the participants.

The following screenshot shows the results of an execution of this example:

```
<terminated> Main (14) [Java Application] C:\Program Files\Java\jdk-9\bin\javaw.exe (28 mar. 2017 0:15:04)
Phaser: We have 5 students,
Student 3: Is going to do the first exercise. Tue Mar 28 00:15:05 CEST 2017
Student 2: Is going to do the first exercise. Tue Mar 28 00:15:05 CEST 2017
Student 4: Is going to do the first exercise. Tue Mar 28 00:15:05 CEST 2017
Student 0: Is going to do the first exercise. Tue Mar 28 00:15:05 CEST 2017
Student 1: Is going to do the first exercise. Tue Mar 28 00:15:05 CEST 2017
Student 1: Has done the first exercise. Tue Mar 28 00:15:05 CEST 2017
Student 3: Has done the first exercise. Tue Mar 28 00:15:06 CEST 2017
Student 0: Has done the first exercise. Tue Mar 28 00:15:10 CEST 2017
Student 2: Has done the first exercise. Tue Mar 28 00:15:12 CEST 2017
Student 4: Has done the first exercise. Tue Mar 28 00:15:14 CEST 2017
Phaser: All the students has finished the first exercise.
Phaser: It's turn for the second one.
Student 3: Is going to do the second exercise. Tue Mar 28 00:15:14 CEST 2017
Student 1: Is going to do the second exercise. Tue Mar 28 00:15:14 CEST 2017
```

You can see how the students finished the first exercise at different times. When all of them finish the first exercise, `phaser` calls the `onAdvance()` method that writes the log messages in the console, then all the students start the second exercise at the same time.

See also

- The *Running concurrent-phased tasks* recipe in this chapter
- The *Monitoring a Phaser class* recipe in `Chapter 9`, *Testing Concurrent Applications*

Exchanging data between concurrent tasks

The Java concurrency API provides a synchronization utility that allows interchange of data between two concurrent tasks. In more detail, the `Exchanger` class allows you to have a definition of a synchronization point between two threads. When the two threads arrive at this point, they interchange a data structure such that the data structure of the first thread goes to the second one and vice versa.

This class may be very useful in a situation similar to the producer-consumer problem. This is a classic concurrent problem where you have a common buffer of data, one or more producers of data, and one or more consumers of data. As the `Exchanger` class synchronizes only two threads, you can use it if you have a producer-consumer problem with one producer and one consumer.

In this recipe, you will learn how to use the `Exchanger` class to solve the producer-consumer problem with one producer and one consumer.

Getting ready

The example of this recipe has been implemented using the Eclipse IDE. If you use Eclipse or a different IDE, such as NetBeans, open it and create a new Java project.

How to do it...

Follow these steps to implement the example:

1. First, begin by implementing the producer. Create a class named `Producer` and specify that it implements the `Runnable` interface:

   ```
   public class Producer implements Runnable {
   ```

2. Declare a `List<String>` field named `buffer`. This will be the data structure that the producer will interchange with the consumer:

   ```
   private List<String> buffer;
   ```

3. Declare an `Exchanger<List<String>>` field named `exchanger`. This will be the exchanger object that will be used to synchronize the producer and consumer:

   ```
   private final Exchanger<List<String>> exchanger;
   ```

3. Implement the constructor of the class that will initialize the two attributes:

   ```
   public Producer (List<String> buffer, Exchanger<List<String>>
                    exchanger){
     this.buffer=buffer;
     this.exchanger=exchanger;
   }
   ```

4. Implement the `run()` method. Inside it, implement 10 cycles of interchange:

   ```
   @Override
   public void run() {
     for (int cycle = 1; cycle <= 10; cycle++){
       System.out.printf("Producer: Cycle %d\n",cycle);
   ```

5. In each cycle, add 10 strings to the buffer:

   ```
   for (int j=0; j<10; j++){
     String message="Event "+(((cycle-1)*10)+j);
     System.out.printf("Producer: %s\n",message);
     buffer.add(message);
   }
   ```

6. Call the `exchange()` method to interchange data with the consumer. As this method can throw an `InterruptedException` exception, you have to add some code to process it.

```
try {
  buffer=exchanger.exchange(buffer);
} catch (InterruptedException e) {
  e.printStackTrace();
}
  System.out.println("Producer: "+buffer.size());
}
```

7. Now, implement the consumer. Create a class named `Consumer` and specify that it implements the `Runnable` interface:

```
public class Consumer implements Runnable {
```

8. Declare a `List<String>` field named `buffer`. This will be the data structure that the producer will interchange with the consumer:

```
private List<String> buffer;
```

9. Declare an `Exchanger<List<String>>` field named `exchanger`. This will be the `exchanger` object that will be used to synchronize the producer and consumer:

```
private final Exchanger<List<String>> exchanger;
```

10. Implement the constructor of the class that will initialize the two attributes:

```
public Consumer(List<String> buffer, Exchanger<List<String>>
              exchanger){
  this.buffer=buffer;
  this.exchanger=exchanger;
}
```

11. Implement the `run()` method. Inside it, implement 10 cycles of interchange:

```
@Override
public void run() {
  for (int cycle=1; cycle <= 10; cycle++){
    System.out.printf("Consumer: Cycle %d\n",cycle);
```

12. In each cycle, begin with a call to the `exchange()` method to synchronize with the producer. The consumer needs data to consume. As this method can throw an `InterruptedException` exception, you have to add some code to process it:

```
try {
  buffer=exchanger.exchange(buffer);
} catch (InterruptedException e) {
  e.printStackTrace();
}
```

13. Write the 10 strings the producer sent in its buffer to the console and delete them from the buffer to leave it empty:

```
System.out.println("Consumer: "+buffer.size());
for (int j=0; j<10; j++){
  String message=buffer.get(0);
  System.out.println("Consumer: "+message);
  buffer.remove(0);
}
}
```

14. Now, implement the `main` class of the example by creating a class named `Main` and adding the `main()` method to it:

```
public class Main {
  public static void main(String[] args) {
```

15. Create two buffers that will be used by the producer and consumer:

```
List<String> buffer1=new ArrayList<>();
List<String> buffer2=new ArrayList<>();
```

16. Create the `Exchanger` object that will be used to synchronize the producer and consumer:

```
Exchanger<List<String>> exchanger=new Exchanger<>();
```

17. Create the `Producer` and `Consumer` objects:

```
Producer producer=new Producer(buffer1, exchanger);
Consumer consumer=new Consumer(buffer2, exchanger);
```

18. Create the threads to execute the producer and consumer and start the threads:

```
Thread threadProducer=new Thread(producer);
Thread threadConsumer=new Thread(consumer);

threadProducer.start();
threadConsumer.start();
```

How it works...

The consumer begins with an empty buffer and calls `Exchanger` to synchronize with the producer. It needs data to consume. The producer begins its execution with an empty buffer. It creates 10 strings, stores them in the buffer, and uses the `Exchanger` to synchronize with the consumer.

At this point, both the threads (producer and consumer) are in `Exchanger`, which changes the data structures. So when the consumer returns from the `exchange()` method, it will have a buffer with 10 strings. When the producer returns from the `exchange()` method, it will have an empty buffer to fill again. This operation will be repeated 10 times.

If you execute the example, you will see how producer and consumer do their jobs concurrently and how the two objects interchange their buffers in every step. As it occurs with other synchronization utilities, the first thread that calls the `exchange()` method is put to sleep until the other threads arrive.

There's more...

The `Exchanger` class has another version of the `exchange` method: `exchange(V data, long time, TimeUnit unit)`. where, `V` is the type used as a parameter in the declaration of `Phaser` (`List<String>` in our case). The thread will sleep until it's interrupted, another thread arrives, or the specified time passes. In this case, a `TimeoutException` is thrown. The `TimeUnit` class is an enumeration with the following constants: DAYS, HOURS, MICROSECONDS, MILLISECONDS, MINUTES, NANOSECONDS, and SECONDS.

Completing and linking tasks asynchronously

Java 8 Concurrency API includes a new synchronization mechanism with the CompletableFuture class. This class implements the Future object and the CompletionStage interface that gives it the following two characteristics:

- As the Future object, a CompletableFuture object will return a result sometime in future
- As the CompletionStage object, you can execute more asynchronous tasks after the completion of one or more CompletableFuture objects

You can work with a CompletableFuture class in different ways:

- You can create a CompletableFuture object explicitly and use it as a synchronization point between tasks. One task will establish the value returned by CompletableFuture, using the complete() method, and the other tasks will wait for this value, using the get() or join() methods.
- You can use a static method of the CompletableFuture class to execute Runnable or Supplier with the runAsync() and supplyAsync() methods. These methods will return a CompletableFuture object that will be completed when these tasks end their execution. In the second case, the value returned by Supplier will be the completion value of CompletableFuture.
- You can specify other tasks to be executed in an asynchronous way after the completion of one or more CompletableFuture objects. This task can implement the Runnable, Function, Consumer or BiConsumer interfaces.

These characteristics make the `CompletableFuture` class very flexible and powerful. In this chapter, you will learn how to use this class to organize different tasks. The main purpose of the example is that the tasks will be executed, as specified in the following diagram:

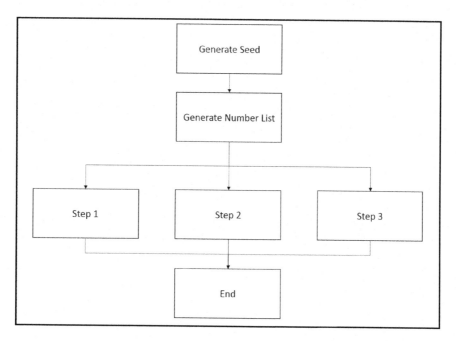

First, we're going to create a task that will generate a seed. Using this seed, the next task will generate a list of random numbers. Then, we will execute three parallel tasks:

1. Step 1 will calculate the nearest number to 1,000, in a list of random numbers.
2. Step 2 will calculate the biggest number in a list of random numbers.
3. Step 3 will calculate the average number between the largest and smallest numbers in a list of random numbers.

Getting ready

The example of this recipe has been implemented using the Eclipse IDE. If you use Eclipse or a different IDE, such as NetBeans, open it and create a new Java project.

How to do it...

Follow these steps to implement the example:

1. First, we're going to implement the auxiliary tasks we will use in the example. Create a class named `SeedGenerator` that implements the `Runnable` interface. It will have a `CompletableFuture` object as an attribute, and it will be initialized in the constructor of the class:

```
public class SeedGenerator implements Runnable {

    private CompletableFuture<Integer> resultCommunicator;

    public SeedGenerator (CompletableFuture<Integer> completable) {
        this.resultCommunicator=completable;
    }
```

2. Then, implement the `run()` method. It will sleep the current thread for 5 seconds (to simulate a long operation), calculate a random number between 1 and 10, and then use the `complete()` method of the `resultCommunicator` object to complete `CompletableFuture`:

```
@Override
public void run() {

    System.out.printf("SeedGenerator: Generating seed...\n");
    // Wait 5 seconds
    try {
        TimeUnit.SECONDS.sleep(5);
    } catch (InterruptedException e) {
        e.printStackTrace();
    }
        int seed=(int) Math.rint(Math.random() * 10);

    System.out.printf("SeedGenerator: Seed generated: %d\n",
                      seed);

    resultCommunicator.complete(seed);
}
```

3. Create a class named `NumberListGenerator` that implements the `Supplier` interface parameterized with the `List<Long>` data type. This means that the `get()` method provided by the `Supplier` interface will return a list of large numbers. This class will have an integer number as a private attribute, which will be initialized in the constructor of the class:

```
public class NumberListGenerator implements Supplier<List<Long>> {

  private final int size;

  public NumberListGenerator (int size) {
    this.size=size;
  }
```

4. Then, implement the `get()` method that will return a list with millions of numbers, as specified in the size parameter of larger random numbers:

```
@Override
public List<Long> get() {
  List<Long> ret = new ArrayList<>();
  System.out.printf("%s : NumberListGenerator : Start\n",
                  Thread.currentThread().getName());

  for (int i=0; i< size*1000000; i++) {
    long number=Math.round(Math.random()*Long.MAX_VALUE);
    ret.add(number);
  }
  System.out.printf("%s : NumberListGenerator : End\n",
                  Thread.currentThread().getName());

  return ret;
}
```

5. Finally, create a class named `NumberSelector` that implements the `Function` interface parameterized with the `List<Long>` and `Long` data types. This means that the `apply()` method provided by the `Function` interface will receive a list of large numbers and will return a `Long` number:

```
public class NumberSelector implements Function<List<Long>, Long> {

  @Override
  public Long apply(List<Long> list) {

    System.out.printf("%s: Step 3: Start\n",
                    Thread.currentThread().getName());
    long max=list.stream().max(Long::compare).get();
    long min=list.stream().min(Long::compare).get();
    long result=(max+min)/2;
    System.out.printf("%s: Step 3: Result - %d\n",
                    Thread.currentThread().getName(), result);
    return result;
  }
}
```

6. Now it's time to implement the `Main` class and the `main()` method:

```
public class Main {
   public static void main(String[] args) {
```

7. First, create a `CompletableFuture` object and a `SeedGenerator` task and execute it as a `Thread`:

```
System.out.printf("Main: Start\n");
CompletableFuture<Integer> seedFuture = new CompletableFuture<>();
Thread seedThread = new Thread(new SeedGenerator(seedFuture));
seedThread.start();
```

8. Then, wait for the seed generated by the `SeedGenerator` task, using the `get()` method of the `CompletableFuture` object:

```
System.out.printf("Main: Getting the seed\n");
int seed = 0;
try {
   seed = seedFuture.get();
} catch (InterruptedException | ExecutionException e) {
   e.printStackTrace();
}
System.out.printf("Main: The seed is: %d\n", seed);
```

9. Now create another `CompletableFuture` object to control the execution of a `NumberListGenerator` task, but in this case, use the static method `supplyAsync()`:

```
System.out.printf("Main: Launching the list of numbers
                 generator\n");
NumberListGenerator task = new NumberListGenerator(seed);
CompletableFuture<List<Long>> startFuture = CompletableFuture
                                       .supplyAsync(task);
```

10. Then, configure the three parallelized tasks that will make calculations based on the list of numbers generated in the previous task. These three steps can't start their execution until the `NumberListGenerator` task has finished its execution, so we use the `CompletableFuture` object generated in the previous step and the `thenApplyAsync()` method to configure these tasks. The first two steps are implemented in a functional way, and the third one is an object of the `NumberSelector` class:

```
System.out.printf("Main: Launching step 1\n");
CompletableFuture<Long> step1Future = startFuture
                                    .thenApplyAsync(list -> {
   System.out.printf("%s: Step 1: Start\n",
                  Thread.currentThread().getName());
   long selected = 0;
   long selectedDistance = Long.MAX_VALUE;
   long distance;
   for (Long number : list) {
     distance = Math.abs(number - 1000);
     if (distance < selectedDistance) {
       selected = number;
       selectedDistance = distance;
     }
   }
   System.out.printf("%s: Step 1: Result - %d\n",
                  Thread.currentThread().getName(), selected);
   return selected;
});

System.out.printf("Main: Launching step 2\n");
CompletableFuture<Long> step2Future = startFuture
.thenApplyAsync(list -> list.stream().max(Long::compare).get());

CompletableFuture<Void> write2Future = step2Future
                                    .thenAccept(selected -> {
   System.out.printf("%s: Step 2: Result - %d\n",
                  Thread.currentThread().getName(), selected);
});

System.out.printf("Main: Launching step 3\n");
NumberSelector numberSelector = new NumberSelector();
CompletableFuture<Long> step3Future = startFuture
                           .thenApplyAsync(numberSelector);
```

11. We wait for the finalization of the three parallel steps with the `allOf()` static method of the `CompletableFuture` class:

```
System.out.printf("Main: Waiting for the end of the three
                  steps\n");
CompletableFuture<Void> waitFuture = CompletableFuture
                           .allOf(step1Future, write2Future,
                                  step3Future);
```

12. Also, we execute a final step to write a message in the console:

```
CompletableFuture<Void> finalFuture = waitFuture
                                .thenAcceptAsync((param) -> {
    System.out.printf("Main: The CompletableFuture example has
                     been completed.");
});
finalFuture.join();
```

How it works...

We can use a `CompletableFuture` object with two main purposes:

- Wait for a value or an event that will be produced in future (creating an object and using the `complete()` and `get()` or `join()` methods).
- To organize a set of tasks to be executed in a determined order so one or more tasks won't start their execution until others have finished their execution.

In this example, we made both uses of the `CompletableFuture` class. First, we created an instance of this class and sent it as a parameter to a `SeedGenerator` task. This task uses the `complete()` method to send the calculated value, and the `main()` method uses the `get()` method to obtain the value. The `get()` method sleeps the current thread until `CompletableFuture` has been completed.

Then, we used the `supplyAsync()` method to generate a `CompletableFuture` object. This method receives an implementation of the `Supplier` interface as a parameter. This interface provides the `get()` method that must return a value. The `supplyAsync()` method returns `CompletableFuture`, which will be completed when the `get()` method finishes its execution; the value of completion is the value returned by that method. The `CompletableFuture` object returned will be executed by a task in the `ForkJoinPool` returns the static method `commonPool()`.

Then, we used the `thenApplyAsync()` method to link some tasks. You call this method in a `CompletableFuture` object, and you must pass an implementation of the `Function` interface as a parameter that can be expressed directly in the code using a functional style or an independent object. One powerful characteristic is that the value generated by `CompletableFuture` will be passed as a parameter to the `Function`. That is to say, in our case, all the three steps will receive a random list of numbers as parameters. The `CompletableFuture` class returned will be executed by a task in the `ForkJoinPool` returns the static method `commonPool()`.

Finally, we used the `allOf()` static method of the `CompletableFuture` class to wait for the finalization of various tasks. This method receives a variable list of `CompletableFuture` objects and returns a `CompletableFuture` class that will be completed when all the `CompletableFuture` class passed as parameters are completed. We also used the `thenAcceptAsync()` method as another way to synchronize tasks because this method receives `Consumer` as a parameter that is executed by the default executor when the `CompletableFuture` object used to call the method is completed. Finally, we used the `join()` method to wait for the finalization of the last `CompletableFuture` object.

The following screenshot shows the execution of the example. You can see how the tasks are executed in the order we organized:

```
Problems  @ Javadoc  Declaration  Search  Console  Error Log
<terminated> Main (16) [Java Application] C:\Program Files\Java\jdk-9\bin\javaw.exe (10 sept. 2016 1:25:34)
Main: Start
Main: Getting the seed
SeedGenerator: Generating seed...
SeedGenerator: Seed generated: 7
Main: The seed is: 7
Main: Launching the list of numbers generator
Main: Launching step 1
ForkJoinPool.commonPool-worker-1 : NumberListGenerator : Start
Main: Launching step 2
Main: Launching step 3
Main: Waiting for the end of the three steps
ForkJoinPool.commonPool-worker-1 : NumberListGenerator : End
ForkJoinPool.commonPool-worker-1: Step 1: Start
ForkJoinPool.commonPool-worker-2: Step 3: Start
ForkJoinPool.commonPool-worker-1: Step 1: Result - 3442504078336
ForkJoinPool.commonPool-worker-3: Step 2: Result - 9223370183966876672
ForkJoinPool.commonPool-worker-2: Step 3: Result - -4611685223619298304
Main: The CompletableFuture example has been completed.
```

There's more...

In the example of this recipe, we used the `complete()`, `get()`, `join()`, `supplyAsync()`, `thenApplyAsync()`, `thenAcceptAsync()`, and `allOf()` methods of the `CompletableFuture` class. However, this class has a lot of useful methods that help increase the power and flexibility of this class. These are the most interesting ones:

- Methods to complete a `CompletableFuture` object: In addition to the `complete()` method, the `CompletableFuture` class provides the following three methods:
    - `cancel()`: This completes `CompletableFuture` with a `CancellationException` exception.
    - `completeAsync()`: This completes `CompletableFuture` with the result of the `Supplier` object passed as a parameter. The `Supplier` object is executed in a different thread by the default executor.
    - `completeExceptionally()`: This method completes `CompletableFuture` with the exception passed as a parameter.

- Methods to execute a task: In addition to the `supplyAsync()` method, the `CompletableFuture` class provides the following method:
    - `runAsync()`: This is a static method of the `CompletableFuture` class that returns a `CompletableFuture` object. This object will be completed when the `Runnable` interface is passed as a parameter to finish its execution. It will be completed with a void result.

- Methods to synchronize the execution of different tasks: In addition to the `allOf()`, `thenAcceptAsync()`, and `thenApplyAsync()` methods, the `CompletableFuture` class provides the following methods to synchronize the execution of tasks:
    - `anyOf()`: This is a static method of the `CompletableFuture` class. It receives a list of `CompletableFuture` objects and returns a new `CompletableFuture` object. This object will be completed with the result of the first `CompletableFuture` parameter that is completed.

- `runAfterBothAsync()`: This method receives `CompletionStage` and `Runnable` objects as parameters and returns a new `CompletableFuture` object. When `CompletableFuture` (which does the calling) and `CompletionStage` (which is received as a parameter) are completed, the `Runnable` object is executed by the default executor and then the `CompletableFuture` object returned is completed.
- `runAfterEitherAsync()`: This method is similar to the previous one, but here, the `Runnable` interface is executed after one of the two (`CompletableFuture` or `CompletionStage`) are completed.
- `thenAcceptBothAsync()`: This method receives `CompletionStage` and `BiConsumer` objects as parameters and returns `CompetableFuture` as a parameter. When `CompletableFuture` (which does the calling) and `CompletionStage` (which is passed as a parameter), `BiConsumer` is executed by the default executor. It receives the results of the two `CompletionStage` objects as parameters but it won't return any result. When `BiConsumer` finishes its execution, the returned `CompletableFuture` class is completed without a result.
- `thenCombineAsync()`: This method receives a `CompletionStage` object and a `BiFunction` object as parameters and returns a new `CompletableFuture` object. When `CompletableFuture` (which does the calling) and `CompletionStage` (which is passed as a parameter) are completed, the `BiFunction` object is executed; it receives the completion values of both the objects and returns a new result that will be the completion value of the returned `CompletableFuture` class.
- `thenComposeAsync()`:This method is analogous to `thenApplyAsync()`, but it is useful when the supplied function returns `CompletableFuture` too.
- `thenRunAsync()`: This method is analogous to the `thenAcceptAsync()` method, but in this case, it receives a `Runnable` object as a parameter instead of a `Consumer` object.

- Methods to obtain the completion value: In addition to the `get()` and `join()` methods, the `CompletableFuture` object provides the following method to get the completion value:
  - `getNow()`: This receives a value of the same type of the completion value of `CompletableFuture`. If the object is completed, it returns the completion value. Else, it returns the value passed as the parameter.

See also...

- The *Creating a thread executor and controlling its rejected tasks* and *Executing tasks in an executor that returns a result* recipes in `Chapter 4`, *Thread Executors*

4
Thread Executors

In this chapter, we will cover the following topics:

- Creating a thread executor and controlling its rejected tasks
- Executing tasks in an executor that returns a result
- Running multiple tasks and processing the first result
- Running multiple tasks and processing all the results
- Running a task in an executor after a delay
- Running a task in an executor periodically
- Canceling a task in an executor
- Controlling a task finishing in an executor
- Separating the launching of tasks and the processing of their results in an executor

Introduction

Usually, when you develop a simple, concurrent programming application in Java, first you create some `Runnable` objects and then the corresponding `Thread` objects to execute them. If you have to develop a program that runs a lot of concurrent tasks, this approach will present the following disadvantages:

- You will have to implement all of the code-related information to manage `Thread` objects (creating, ending, and obtaining results).
- You will have to create a `Thread` object per task. Executing a huge number of tasks can affect the throughput of the application.
- You will have to control and manage the resources of the computer efficiently. If you create too many threads, you could saturate the system.

Since Java 5, the Java concurrency API provides a mechanism that aims to resolve these problems. This mechanism is called the **Executor framework** and is around the `Executor` interface, its subinterface `ExecutorService`, and the `ThreadPoolExecutor` class that implements both these interfaces.

This mechanism separates task creation and execution. With an executor, you only have to implement either `Runnable` or `Callable` objects and send them to the executor. It is responsible for their execution, running them with the necessary threads. But it goes beyond this; it improves performance using a pool of threads. When you send a task to the executor, it tries to use a pooled thread for the execution of the task. It does so to avoid the continuous spawning of threads. Another important advantage of the `Executor` framework is the `Callable` interface. It's similar to the `Runnable` interface but offers two improvements, which are as follows:

- The main method of this interface, named `call()`, may return a result.
- When you send a `Callable` object to an executor, you get an object that implements the `Future` interface. You can use this object to control the status and the result of the `Callable` object.

This chapter presents nine recipes that show you how to work with the `Executor` framework using the classes mentioned earlier and other variants provided by the Java Concurrency API.

Creating a thread executor and controlling its rejected tasks

The first step toward working with the `Executor` framework is to create an object of the `ThreadPoolExecutor` class. You can use the four constructors provided by this class or use a factory class named `Executors`, which creates `ThreadPoolExecutor`. Once you have an executor, you can send `Runnable` or `Callable` objects to be executed.

When you want to finish the execution of an executor, use the `shutdown()` method. The executor waits for the completion of tasks that are either running or waiting for their execution. Then, it finishes the execution.

If you send a task to an executor between the `shutdown()` method and the end of its execution, the task will be rejected. This is because the executor no longer accepts new tasks. The `ThreadPoolExecutor` class provides a mechanism, which is called when a task is rejected.

In this recipe, you will learn how to use the `Executors` class to create a new `ThreadPoolExecutor` object, how to send tasks to the `Executor`, and how to control the rejected tasks of the `Executor` class.

Getting ready

You should read the *Creating, running, and setting the characteristics of a thread* recipe in `Chapter 1`, *Thread Management*, to learn the basic mechanism of thread creation in Java. You can compare both the mechanisms and select one, depending on the problem.

The example of this recipe has been implemented using the Eclipse IDE. If you use Eclipse or a different IDE, such as NetBeans, open it and create a new Java project.

How to do it...

Follow these steps to implement the example:

1. First, implement the tasks that will be executed by the server. Create a class named `Task` that implements the `Runnable` interface:

   ```
   public class Task implements Runnable {
   ```

2. Declare a `Date` attribute named `initDate` to store the creation date of the task and a `String` attribute called `name` to store the name of the task:

   ```
   private final Date initDate;
   private final String name;
   ```

3. Implement the constructor of the class that initializes both the attributes:

   ```
   public Task(String name){
     initDate=new Date();
     this.name=name;
   }
   ```

4. Implement the `run()` method:

   ```
   @Override
   public void run() {
   ```

5. First, write the `initDate` attribute and the actual date, which is the starting date of the task:

```
System.out.printf("%s: Task %s: Created on: %s\n",
                  Thread.currentThread().getName(),
                  name,initDate);
System.out.printf("%s: Task %s: Started on: %s\n",
                  Thread.currentThread().getName(),
                  name,new Date());
```

6. Then, put the task to sleep for a random period of time:

```
try {
  Long duration=(long)(Math.random()*10);
  System.out.printf("%s: Task %s: Doing a task during %d
                    seconds\n", Thread.currentThread().getName(),
                    name,duration);
  TimeUnit.SECONDS.sleep(duration);
} catch (InterruptedException e) {
  e.printStackTrace();
}
```

7. Finally, write the completion date of the task in the console:

```
System.out.printf("%s: Task %s: Finished on: %s\n",
                  Thread.currentThread().getName(),
                  name,new Date());
```

8. Create a class named `RejectedTaskController` that implements the `RejectedExecutionHandler` interface. Implement the `rejectedExecution()` method of this interface. Then write the name of the task that has been rejected and the name and status of the executor:

```
public class RejectedTaskController implements
                                    RejectedExecutionHandler {
  @Override
  public void rejectedExecution(Runnable r,
                        ThreadPoolExecutor executor) {
    System.out.printf("RejectedTaskController: The task %s has been
                      rejected\n",r.toString());
    System.out.printf("RejectedTaskController: %s\n",
                      executor.toString());
    System.out.printf("RejectedTaskController: Terminating: %s\n",
                      executor.isTerminating());
    System.out.printf("RejectedTaksController: Terminated: %s\n",
                      executor.isTerminated());
  }
```

9. Now implement the `Server` class that will execute every task it receives using an executor. Create a class named `Server`:

```
public class Server {
```

10. Declare a `ThreadPoolExecutor` attribute named `executor`:

```
private final ThreadPoolExecutor executor;
```

11. Implement the constructor of the class that initializes the `ThreadPoolExecutor` object using the `Executors` class, and establish a handler for rejected tasks:

```
public Server(){
   executor =( ThreadPoolExecutor ) Executors.newFixedThreadPool(
                  Runtime.getRuntime().availableProcessors() );
   RejectedTaskController controller=new
                                  RejectedTaskController();
   executor.setRejectedExecutionHandler(controller);
}
```

12. Implement the `executeTask()` method. It receives a `Task` object as a parameter and sends it to the executor. First, write a message to the console indicating that a new task has arrived:

```
public void executeTask(Task task){
   System.out.printf("Server: A new task has arrived\n");
```

13. Then, call the `execute()` method of the executor and send it to the task:

```
executor.execute(task);
```

14. Finally, write some executor data to the console to see its status:

```
System.out.printf("Server: Pool Size: %d\n",
                  executor.getPoolSize());
System.out.printf("Server: Active Count: %d\n",
                  executor.getActiveCount());
System.out.printf("Server: Task Count: %d\n",
                  executor.getTaskCount());
System.out.printf("Server: Completed Tasks: %d\n",
                  executor.getCompletedTaskCount());
```

15. Next, implement the `endServer()` method. In this method, call the `shutdown()` method of the executor to finish its execution:

```
public void endServer() {
   executor.shutdown();
}
```

16. Implement the main class of the example by creating a class named `Main` and adding the `main()` method to it. First, create 100 tasks and send them to `Executor`:

```
public class Main {
   public static void main(String[] args) {
      Server server=new Server();

      System.out.printf("Main: Starting.\n");
         for (int i=0; i<100; i++){
            Task task=new Task("Task "+i);
            server.executeTask(task);
      }
```

17. Then call the `endServer()` method of `Server` to shut down the executor:

```
System.out.printf("Main: Shuting down the Executor.\n");
server.endServer();
```

18. Finally, send a new task. This task will be rejected, so we will see how this mechanism works:

```
System.out.printf("Main: Sending another Task.\n");
Task task=new Task("Rejected task");
server.executeTask(task);

System.out.printf("Main: End.\n");
```

How it works...

The key of this example is the `Server` class. This class creates and uses `ThreadPoolExecutor` to execute tasks.

The first important point is the creation of ThreadPoolExecutor in the constructor of the Server class. The ThreadPoolExecutor class has four different constructors, but due to their complexity, the Java concurrency API provides the Executors class to construct executors and other related objects. Although you can create ThreadPoolExecutor directly using one of its constructors, it's recommended that you use the Executors class.

In this case, you created a cached thread pool using the newFixedThreadPool() method of the Executors class in order to create the executor. This method creates an executor with the maximum number of threads. If the number of tasks you send is more than the number of threads, the remaining tasks will be blocked until there is a free thread available to process them. This method receives the maximum number of threads you want to have in your executor as parameters. In our case, we used the availableProcessors() method of the Runtime class that returns the number of processors available to JVM. Normally, this number matches the number of cores of the computer.

Reutilization of threads has the advantage that it reduces the time taken for thread creation. The cached thread pool, however, has the disadvantage of having constant lying threads for new tasks. Therefore, if you send too many tasks to this executor, you could overload the system.

Once you have created the executor, you can send tasks of the Runnable or Callable type for execution using the execute() method. In this case, you sent objects of the Task class that implements the Runnable interface.

You also printed some log messages with information about the executor. Specifically, you used the following methods:

- getPoolSize(): This method returned the actual number of threads in the pool of the executor.
- getActiveCount(): This method returned the number of threads that were executing tasks in the executor.
- getTaskCount(): This method returned the number of tasks that were scheduled for execution. The returned value is only an approximation because it changes dynamically.
- getCompletedTaskCount(): This method returned the number of tasks completed by the executor.

One critical aspect of the `ThreadPoolExecutor` class, and of executors in general, is that you have to end them explicitly. If you don't do this, the executor will continue its execution and the program won't end. If the executor doesn't have tasks to execute, it continues waiting for new tasks and doesn't end its execution. A Java application won't end until all its non-daemon threads finish their execution. So, if you don't terminate the executor, your application will never end.

To indicate to the executor that you want to finish it, use the `shutdown()` method of the `ThreadPoolExecutor` class. When the executor finishes the execution of all the pending tasks, it finishes its execution as well. After you call the `shutdown()` method, if you try to send another task to the executor, it will be rejected and the executor will throw a `RejectedExecutionException` exception, unless you have implemented a manager for rejected tasks, as in our case. To manage the rejected tasks of an executor, you need to create a class that implements the `RejectedExecutionHandler` interface. This interface has a method called `rejectedExecution()` with two parameters:

- A `Runnable` object that stores the task that has been rejected
- An `Executor` object that stores the executor that rejected the task

This method is called for every task that is rejected by the executor. You need to establish the handler of the rejected tasks using the `setRejectedExecutionHandler()` method of the `ThreadPoolExecutor` class.

The following screenshot shows part of an execution of this example:

```
Server: Task Count: 99
Server: Completed Tasks: 0
Server: A new task has arrived
Server: Pool Size: 4
Server: Active Count: 4
Server: Task Count: 100
Server: Completed Tasks: 0
Main: Shuting down the Executor.
Main: Sending another Task.
Server: A new task has arrived
RejectedTaskController: The task com.packtpub.java9.concurrency.cookbook.chapter04.recipe01.task.Task@42dafa95 has been rejected
RejectedTaskController: java.util.concurrent.ThreadPoolExecutor@6500df86[Shutting down, pool size = 4, active threads = 4, queued tasks = 96, completed tasks = 0]
RejectedTaskController: Terminating: true
RejectedTaksController: Terminated: false
```

See that when the last task arrives at the executor, both the number of threads in the pool and the number of threads that are being executed are represented by 4. This refers to the number of cores of the PC on which the example was executed, and it is the number returned by the `availableProcessors()` method. Once this is done, we shut down the executor and the next task is rejected. `RejectedTaskController` writes information about the task and the executor in the console.

There's more...

The Executors class provides other methods to create ThreadPoolExecutor:

- newCachedThreadPool(): This method returns an ExecutorService object, so it's been cast to ThreadPoolExecutor to have access to all its methods. The cached thread pool you created creates new threads, if needed, to execute new tasks. Plus, it reuses the existing ones if they have finished the execution of the tasks they were running.

- newSingleThreadExecutor(): This is an extreme case of a fixed-size thread executor. It creates an executor with only one thread so it can only execute one task at a time.

The ThreadPoolExecutor class provides a lot of methods to obtain information about its status. We used the getPoolSize(), getActiveCount(), and getCompletedTaskCount() methods in the example to obtain information about the size of the pool, the number of threads, and the number of completed tasks of the executor. You can also use the getLargestPoolSize() method; it returns the maximum number of threads that have been in the pool at a time.

The ThreadPoolExecutor class also provides other methods related to the finalization of the executor. These methods are:

- shutdownNow(): This shuts down the executor immediately. It doesn't execute pending tasks. It returns a list with all the pending tasks. Tasks that are running when you call this method continue with their execution, but the method doesn't wait for their finalization.

- isTerminated(): This method returns true if you call either the shutdown() or shutdownNow() method; the executor finishes the process of shutting it down accordingly.

- isShutdown(): This method returns true if you call the shutdown() method of the executor.

- awaitTermination(long timeout, TimeUnit unit): This method blocks the calling thread until the tasks of the executor end or a timeout occurs. The TimeUnit class is an enumeration with the following constants: DAYS, HOURS, MICROSECONDS, MILLISECONDS, MINUTES, NANOSECONDS, and SECONDS.

 If you want to wait for the completion of tasks, regardless of their duration, use a big timeout, for example, DAYS.

See also

- The *Monitoring an Executor framework* recipe in `Chapter 9`, *Testing Concurrent Applications*

Executing tasks in an executor that returns a result

One of the advantages of the `Executor` framework is that it allows you to run concurrent tasks that return a result. The Java Concurrency API achieves this with the following two interfaces:

- `Callable`: This interface has the `call()` method. In this method, you have to implement the logic of the task. The `Callable` interface is a parameterized interface, meaning you have to indicate the type of data the `call()` method will return.
- `Future`: This interface has some methods to obtain the result generated by a `Callable` object and manage its state.

In this recipe, you will learn how to implement tasks that return a result and run them on an executor.

Getting ready

The example of this recipe has been implemented using the Eclipse IDE. If you use Eclipse or a different IDE, such as NetBeans, open it and create a new Java project.

How to do it...

Follow these steps to implement the example:

1. Create a class named `FactorialCalculator`. Specify that it implements the `Callable` interface parameterized by the `Integer` type:

```
public class FactorialCalculator implements Callable<Integer> {
```

2. Declare a private `Integer` attribute called `number` to store the number that this task will use for its calculations:

```
private final Integer number;
```

3. Implement the constructor of the class that initializes the attribute of the class:

```
public FactorialCalculator(Integer number){
    this.number=number;
}
```

4. Implement the `call()` method. This method returns the factorial of the number attribute of `FactorialCalculator`:

```
@Override
public Integer call() throws Exception {
```

5. First, create and initialize the internal variables used in the method:

```
int result = 1;
```

6. If the number is 0 or 1, return 1. Otherwise, calculate the factorial of the number. Between two multiplications, for educational purposes, put this task to sleep for 20 milliseconds:

```
if ((number==0)||(number==1)) {
    result=1;
} else {
    for (int i=2; i<=number; i++) {
        result*=i;
        TimeUnit.MILLISECONDS.sleep(20);
    }
}
```

7. Write a message to the console with the result of the operation:

```
System.out.printf("%s: %d\n",Thread.currentThread().getName(),
                  result);
```

8. Return the result of the operation:

```
return result;
```

9. Implement the main class of the example by creating a class named `Main` and adding the `main()` method to it:

```
public class Main {
  public static void main(String[] args) {
```

10. Create `ThreadPoolExecutor` to run the tasks using the `newFixedThreadPool()` method of the `Executors` class. Pass 2 as the parameter, that is, as the number of threads in the executor:

```
ThreadPoolExecutor executor=(ThreadPoolExecutor)Executors
                            .newFixedThreadPool(2);
```

11. Create a list of `Future<Integer>` objects:

```
List<Future<Integer>> resultList=new ArrayList<>();
```

12. Create a random number generator with the `Random` class:

```
Random random=new Random();
```

13. Make a loop with ten steps. In every step, we generate a random number:

```
for (int i=0; i<10; i++){
  Integer number= random.nextInt(10);
```

14. Then, we create a `FactorialCalculator` object passing the generated random number as parameter:

```
FactorialCalculator calculator=new FactorialCalculator(number);
```

15. Call the `submit()` method of the executor to send the `FactorialCalculator` task to the executor. This method returns a `Future<Integer>` object to manage the task and eventually get its result:

```
Future<Integer> result=executor.submit(calculator);
```

16. Add the `Future` object to the list created before:

```
resultList.add(result);
}
```

17. Create a do loop to monitor the status of the executor:

```
do {
```

18. First, write a message to the console indicating the number of completed tasks, using the `getCompletedTaskNumber()` method of the executor:

```
System.out.printf("Main: Number of Completed Tasks: %d\n",
                  executor.getCompletedTaskCount());
```

19. Then, for the 10 `Future` objects in the list, write a message indicating whether the tasks that it manages have finished or not. Do this using the `isDone()` method:

```
for (int i=0; i<resultList.size(); i++) {
    Future<Integer> result=resultList.get(i);
    System.out.printf("Main: Task %d: %s\n",i,result.isDone());
}
```

20. Put the thread to sleep for 50 milliseconds:

```
try {
    TimeUnit.MILLISECONDS.sleep(50);
} catch (InterruptedException e) {
    e.printStackTrace();
}
```

21. Repeat this loop when the number of completed tasks of the executor is less than 10:

```
} while (executor.getCompletedTaskCount()<resultList.size());
```

22. In the console, write the results obtained by each task. For each `Future` object, get the `Integer` object returned by its task, using the `get()` method:

```
System.out.printf("Main: Results\n");
for (int i=0; i<resultList.size(); i++) {
    Future<Integer> result=resultList.get(i);
    Integer number=null;
    try {
        number=result.get();
    } catch (InterruptedException e) {
        e.printStackTrace();
    } catch (ExecutionException e) {
        e.printStackTrace();
    }
}
```

23. Then, print the number to the console:

```
    System.out.printf("Main: Task %d: %d\n",i,number);
}
```

24. Finally, call the `shutdown()` method of the executor to finalize its execution:

```
executor.shutdown();
```

How it works...

In this recipe, you learned how to use the `Callable` interface to launch concurrent tasks that return a result. You implemented the `FactorialCalculator` class that implements the `Callable` interface with `Integer` as the type of the result. Hence, the `call()` method returns an `Integer` value.

The other critical point of this example is the `Main` class. You sent a `Callable` object to be executed in an executor using the `submit()` method. This method receives a `Callable` object as a parameter and returns a `Future` object that you can use with two main objectives:

- You can control the status of the task you can cancel the task and check whether it has finished or not. For this purpose, you used the `isDone()` method.
- You can get the result returned by the `call()` method. For this purpose, you used the `get()` method. This method waits until the `Callable` object has finished the execution of the `call()` method and has returned its result. If the thread is interrupted while the `get()` method is waiting for the result, it throws an `InterruptedException` exception. If the `call()` method throws an exception, then the `get()` method throws an `ExecutionException` exception as well.

There's more...

When you call the `get()` method of a `Future` object and the task controlled by this object hasn't finished yet, the method is blocked until the task is finished. The `Future` interface provides another version of the `get()` method:

- `get(long timeout, TimeUnit unit)`: This version of the `get` method, if the result of the task isn't available, waits for the specified time. If the specified period of time passes and the result is still not available, it throws a `TimeoutException` exception. The `TimeUnit` class is an enumeration with the following constants: DAYS, HOURS, MICROSECONDS, MILLISECONDS, MINUTES, NANOSECONDS, and SECONDS.

See also

- The *Creating a thread executor and controlling its rejected tasks, Running multiple tasks and processing the first result,* and *Running multiple tasks and processing all the results recipes* in this chapter

Running multiple tasks and processing the first result

A common problem in concurrent programming arises when you have various concurrent tasks available to solve a problem, but you are only interested in the first result. For example, you want to sort an array. You have various sort algorithms. You can launch all of them and get the result of the first one that sorts the array, that is, the fastest sorting algorithm for a given array.

In this recipe, you will learn how to implement this scenario using the ThreadPoolExecutor class. You are going to use two mechanisms to try and validate a user. The user will be validated if one of these mechanisms is able to validate it.

Getting ready

The example of this recipe has been implemented using the Eclipse IDE. If you use Eclipse or a different IDE, such as NetBeans, open it and create a new Java project.

How to do it...

Follow these steps to implement the example:

1. Create a class named UserValidator that will implement the process of user validation:

   ```
   public class UserValidator {
   ```

2. Declare a private `String` attribute called `name` that will store the name of the user validation system:

```
private final String name;
```

3. Implement the constructor of the class that initializes its attributes:

```
public UserValidator(String name) {
   this.name=name;
}
```

4. Implement the `validate()` method. It receives two `String` parameters with the name and password of the user you want to validate:

```
public boolean validate(String name, String password) {
```

5. Create a `Random` object named `random`:

```
Random random=new Random();
```

6. Wait for a random period of time to simulate the process of user validation:

```
try {
   long duration=(long)(Math.random()*10);
   System.out.printf("Validator %s: Validating a user during %d
                     seconds\n", this.name,duration);
   TimeUnit.SECONDS.sleep(duration);
} catch (InterruptedException e) {
   return false;
}
```

7. Return a random Boolean value. The `validate()` method returns `true` when the user is validated, and `false` otherwise:

```
   return random.nextBoolean();
}
```

8. Implement `getName()`. This method returns the value of the name attribute:

```
public String getName(){
   return name;
}
```

9. Now, create a class named `ValidatorTask` that will execute a validation process with the `UserValidation` object as a concurrent task. Specify that it implements the `Callable` interface parameterized by the `String` class:

```
public class ValidatorTask implements Callable<String> {
```

10. Declare a private `UserValidator` attribute named `validator`:

```
private final UserValidator validator;
```

11. Declare two private `String` attributes, named `user` and `password`:

```
private final String user;
private final String password;
```

12. Implement the constructor of the class that will initialize all the attributes:

```
public ValidatorTask(UserValidator validator, String user,
                     String password){
    this.validator=validator;
    this.user=user;
    this.password=password;
}
```

13. Implement the `call()` method that will return a `String` object:

```
@Override
public String call() throws Exception {
```

14. If the user is not validated by the `UserValidator` object, write a message to the console indicating this and throw `Exception`:

```
if (!validator.validate(user, password)) {
    System.out.printf("%s: The user has not been found\n",
                      validator.getName());
    throw new Exception("Error validating user");
}
```

15. Otherwise, write a message to the console indicating that the user has been validated and return the name of the `UserValidator` object:

```
System.out.printf("%s: The user has been found\n",
                  validator.getName());
return validator.getName();
```

16. Now implement the main class of the example by creating a class named `Main` and adding the `main()` method to it:

```
public class Main {
    public static void main(String[] args) {
```

17. Create two `String` objects named `user` and `password` and initialize them with the test value:

```
String username="test";
String password="test";
```

18. Create two `UserValidator` objects, named `ldapValidator` and `dbValidator`:

```
UserValidator ldapValidator=new UserValidator("LDAP");
UserValidator dbValidator=new UserValidator("DataBase");
```

19. Create two `TaskValidator` objects, named `ldapTask` and `dbTask`. Initialize them with `ldapValidator` and `dbValidator`, respectively:

```
TaskValidator ldapTask=new TaskValidator(ldapValidator,
                                    username, password);
TaskValidator dbTask=new TaskValidator(dbValidator,
                                    username, password);
```

20. Create a list of `TaskValidator` objects and add to it the two objects that you have created:

```
List<TaskValidator> taskList=new ArrayList<>();
taskList.add(ldapTask);
taskList.add(dbTask);
```

21. Create a new `ThreadPoolExecutor` object using the `newCachedThreadPool()` method of the `Executors` class and a string variable named `result`:

```
ExecutorService executor=(ExecutorService)Executors
                            .newCachedThreadPool();
String result;
```

22. Call the `invokeAny()` method of the executor object. This method receives `taskList` as a parameter and returns `String`. Also, it writes the `String` object that is returned to the console:

```
try {
    result = executor.invokeAny(taskList);
    System.out.printf("Main: Result: %s\n",result);
```

```
      } catch (InterruptedException e) {
        e.printStackTrace();
      } catch (ExecutionException e) {
        e.printStackTrace();
      }
```

23. Terminate the executor using the `shutdown()` method and write a message to the console to indicate that the program has ended:

```
executor.shutdown();
System.out.printf("Main: End of the Execution\n");
```

How it works...

The key of the example is in the `Main` class. The `invokeAny()` method of the `ThreadPoolExecutor` class receives a list of tasks, then launches them, and returns the result of the first task that finishes without throwing an exception. This method returns the same data type that the `call()` method of the tasks returns. In this case, it returned a `String` value.

The following screenshot shows the output of an execution of the example when one of the tasks validates the user:

```
<terminated> Main (79) [Java Application] C:\Program Files\Java\jdk-9\bin\j
Validator LDAP: Validating a user during 3 seconds
Validator DataBase: Validating a user during 9 seconds
LDAP: The user has been found
Main: Result: LDAP
DataBase: The user has not been found
Main: End of the Execution
```

The example has two `UserValidator` objects that return a random Boolean value. Each `UserValidator` object is used by a `Callable` object, implemented by the `TaskValidator` class. If the `validate()` method of the `UserValidator` class returns a false value, the `TaskValidator` class throws `Exception`. Otherwise, it returns the `true` value.

So, we have two tasks that can return the `true` value or throw `Exception`. You can have the following four possibilities:

- Both tasks return the `true` value. Here, the result of the `invokeAny()` method is the name of the task that finishes in the first place.
- The first task returns the `true` value and the second one throws `Exception`. Here, the result of the `invokeAny()` method is the name of the first task.

- The first task throws Exception and the second one returns the true value. Here, the result of the invokeAny() method is the name of the second task.
- Both tasks throw Exception. In such a class, the invokeAny() method throws an ExecutionException exception.

If you run the examples several times, you will get each of the four possible solutions.

The following screenshot shows the output of the application when both the tasks throw an exception:

```
<terminated> Main (79) [Java Application] C:\Program Files\Java\jdk-9\bin\javaw.exe (28 mar. 2017 0:23:40)
Validator DataBase: Validating a user during 4 seconds
Validator LDAP: Validating a user during 2 seconds
LDAP: The user has not been found
DataBase: The user has not been found
java.util.concurrent.ExecutionException: java.lang.Exception: Error validating user
        at java.util.concurrent.FutureTask.report(java.base@9-ea/FutureTask.java:122)
        at java.util.concurrent.FutureTask.get(java.base@9-ea/FutureTask.java:191)
        at java.util.concurrent.AbstractExecutorService.doInvokeAny(java.base@9-ea/AbstractExecutorService.java:199)
        at java.util.concurrent.AbstractExecutorService.invokeAny(java.base@9-ea/AbstractExecutorService.java:220)
        at com.packtpub.java9.concurrency.cookbook.chapter04.recipe03.core.Main.main(Main.java:49)
Caused by: java.lang.Exception: Error validating user
```

There's more...

The ThreadPoolExecutor class provides another version of the invokeAny() method:

- invokeAny(Collection<? extends Callable<T>> tasks, long timeout, TimeUnit unit): This method executes all the tasks and returns the result of the first one that finishes without throwing an exception, if it does so before the given timeout is passed. The TimeUnit class is an enumeration with the following constants: DAYS, HOURS, MICROSECONDS, MILLISECONDS, MINUTES, NANOSECONDS, and SECONDS.

See also

- The *Running multiple tasks and processing all the results* recipe in this chapter

Running multiple tasks and processing all the results

The `Executor` framework allows you to execute concurrent tasks without worrying about thread creation and execution. It provides you with the `Future` class, which you can use to control the status and get the results of any task executed in an executor.

When you want to wait for the finalization of a task, you can use the following two methods:

- The `isDone()` method of the `Future` interface returns `true` if the task has finished its execution
- The `awaitTermination()` method of the `ThreadPoolExecutor` class puts the thread to sleep until all the tasks have finished their execution after a call to the `shutdown()` method

These two methods have some drawbacks. With the first one, you can only control the completion of a task. With the second one, you have to shut down the executor to wait for a thread; otherwise, the method's call is returned immediately.

The `ThreadPoolExecutor` class provides a method that allows you to send a list of tasks to the executor and wait for the finalization of all the tasks in the list. In this recipe, you will learn how to use this feature by implementing an example with 10 tasks executed and their results printed out when they have finished.

Getting ready

The example of this recipe has been implemented using the Eclipse IDE. If you use Eclipse or a different IDE, such as NetBeans, open it and create a new Java project.

How to do it...

Follow these steps to implement the example:

1. Create a class named `Result` to store the results generated in the concurrent tasks of this example:

   ```
   public class Result {
   ```

2. Declare two private attributes, namely a `String` attribute called `name` and an `int` attribute named `value`:

```
private String name;
private int value;
```

3. Implement the corresponding `get()` and `set()` methods to set and return the value of the name and value attributes:

```
public String getName() {
   return name;
}
public void setName(String name) {
   this.name = name;
}
public int getValue() {
   return value;
}
public void setValue(int value) {
   this.value = value;
}
```

4. Create a class named `Task` that implements the `Callable` interface parameterized by the `Result` class:

```
public class Task implements Callable<Result> {
```

5. Declare a private `String` attribute called `name`:

```
private final String name;
```

6. Implement the constructor of the class that initializes its attribute:

```
public Task(String name) {
   this.name=name;
}
```

7. Implement the `call()` method of the class. In this case, the method will return a `Result` object:

```
@Override
public Result call() throws Exception {
```

8. First, write a message to the console to indicate that the task is getting started:

```
System.out.printf("%s: Staring\n",this.name);
```

9. Then, wait for a random period of time:

```
try {
   long duration=(long)(Math.random()*10);
   System.out.printf("%s: Waiting %d seconds for results.\n",
                     this.name,duration);
   TimeUnit.SECONDS.sleep(duration);
} catch (InterruptedException e) {
   e.printStackTrace();
}
```

10. To generate an `int` value to be returned in the `Result` object, calculate the sum of five random numbers:

```
int value=0;
for (int i=0; i<5; i++){
   value+=(int)(Math.random()*100);
}
```

11. Create a `Result` object and initialize it with the name of this `Task` object and the result of the operation done earlier:

```
Result result=new Result();
result.setName(this.name);
result.setValue(value);
```

12. Write a message to the console to indicate that the task has finished:

```
System.out.println(this.name+": Ends");
```

13. Return the `Result` object:

```
   return result;
}
```

14. Finally, implement the main class of the example by creating a class named `Main` and adding the `main()` method to it:

```
public class Main {

   public static void main(String[] args) {
```

15. Create a `ThreadPoolExecutor` object using the `newCachedThreadPool()` method of the `Executors` class:

```
ExecutorService executor=(ExecutorService)Executors
                          .newCachedThreadPool();
```

16. Create a list of `Task` objects. Create 10 `Task` objects and save them on this list:

```
List<Task> taskList=new ArrayList<>();
for (int i=0; i<10; i++){
  Task task=new Task("Task-"+i);
  taskList.add(task);
}
```

17. Create a list of `Future` objects. These objects are parameterized by the `Result` class:

```
List<Future<Result>>resultList=null;
```

18. Call the `invokeAll()` method of the `ThreadPoolExecutor` class. This class will return the list of the `Future` objects created earlier:

```
try {
  resultList=executor.invokeAll(taskList);
} catch (InterruptedException e) {
  e.printStackTrace();
}
```

19. Finalize the executor using the `shutdown()` method:

```
executor.shutdown();
```

20. Write the results of the tasks processing the list of `Future` objects.

```
System.out.println("Main: Printing the results");
for (int i=0; i<resultList.size(); i++){
  Future<Result> future=resultList.get(i);
  try {
    Result result=future.get();
    System.out.println(result.getName()+": "+result.getValue());
  } catch (InterruptedException | ExecutionException e) {
    e.printStackTrace();
  }
}
```

How it works...

In this recipe, you learned how to send a list of tasks to an executor and wait for the finalization of all of them using the invokeAll() method. This method receives a list of Callable objects and returns a list of Future objects. This list will have a Future object per task. The first object in the list of Future objects will be the object that controls the first task in the list of Callable objects, the second object the second task, and so on.

The first point to take into consideration is that the type of data used for the parameterization of the Future interface in the declaration of the list that stores the result objects must be compatible with the one used to parameterize Callable objects. In this case, you used the same type of data: the Result class.

Another important point about the invokeAll() method is that you will use Future objects only to get the results of the tasks. As the method finishes when all the tasks finish, if you call the isDone() method of Future objects that are returned, all the calls will return the true value.

There's more...

The ExecutorService class provides another version of the invokeAll() method:

- invokeAll(Collection<? extends Callable<T>> tasks, long timeout, TimeUnit unit): This method executes all the tasks and returns the result of their execution when all of them are finished, that is, if they finish before the given timeout has passed. The TimeUnit class is an enumeration with the following constants: DAYS, HOURS, MICROSECONDS, MILLISECONDS, MINUTES, NANOSECONDS, and SECONDS.

See also

- The *Executing tasks in an executor that returns a result* and *Running multiple tasks and processing the first result* recipes in this chapter

Running a task in an executor after a delay

The `Executor` framework provides the `ThreadPoolExecutor` class to execute `Callable` and `Runnable` tasks with a pool of threads, which helps you avoid all thread creation operations. When you send a task to the executor, it's executed as soon as possible, according to the configuration of the executor. There are use cases when you are not interested in executing a task as soon as possible. You may want to execute a task after a period of time or do it periodically. For these purposes, the Executor framework provides the `ScheduledExecutorService` interface along with its implementation, namely the `ScheduledThreadPoolExecutor` class.

In this recipe, you will learn how to create `ScheduledThreadPoolExecutor` and use it to schedule the execution of a task after a given period of time.

Getting ready

The example of this recipe has been implemented using the Eclipse IDE. If you use Eclipse or a different IDE, such as NetBeans, open it and create a new Java project.

How to do it...

Follow these steps to implement the example:

1. Create a class named `Task` that implements the `Callable` interface parameterized by the `String` class:

   ```
   public class Task implements Callable<String> {
   ```

2. Declare a private `String` attribute called `name` that will store the name of the task:

   ```
   private final String name;
   ```

3. Implement the constructor of the class that initializes the name attribute:

   ```
   public Task(String name) {
     this.name=name;
   }
   ```

4. Implement the `call()` method. Write a message to the console with the actual date and return some text, for example, `Hello, world`:

```
public String call() throws Exception {
    System.out.printf("%s: Starting at : %s\n",name,new Date());
    return "Hello, world";
}
```

5. Implement the main class of the example by creating a class named `Main` and adding the `main()` method to it:

```
public class Main {
    public static void main(String[] args) {
```

6. Create an executor of the `ScheduledThreadPoolExecutor` class using the `newScheduledThreadPool()` method of the `Executors` class, passing 1 as a parameter:

```
ScheduledExecutorService executor=Executors
                            .newScheduledThreadPool(1);
```

7. Initialize and start a few tasks (five in our case) with the `schedule()` method of the `ScheduledThreadPoolExecutor` instance:

```
System.out.printf("Main: Starting at: %s\n",new Date());
for (int i=0; i<5; i++) {
  Task task=new Task("Task "+i);
  executor.schedule(task,i+1 , TimeUnit.SECONDS);
}
```

8. Request the finalization of the executor using the `shutdown()` method:

```
executor.shutdown();
```

9. Wait for the finalization of all the tasks using the `awaitTermination()` method of the executor:

```
try {
  executor.awaitTermination(1, TimeUnit.DAYS);
} catch (InterruptedException e) {
  e.printStackTrace();
}
```

10. Write a message to indicate the time when the program will finish:

```
System.out.printf("Main: Ends at: %s\n",new Date());
```

How it works...

The key point of this example is the `Main` class and the management of `ScheduledThreadPoolExecutor`. As with the `ThreadPoolExecutor` class, to create a scheduled executor, Java recommends that you utilize the `Executors` class. In this case, you used the `newScheduledThreadPool()` method. You passed the number 1 as a parameter to this method. This parameter refers to the number of threads you want to have in the pool.

To execute a task in this scheduled executor after a period of time, you have to use the `schedule()` method. This method receives the following three parameters:

- The task you want to execute
- The period of time you want the task to wait before its execution
- The unit of the period of time, specified as a constant of the `TimeUnit` class

In this case, each task will wait for a number of seconds (`TimeUnit.SECONDS`) equal to its position in the array of tasks plus one.

 If you want to execute a task at a given time, calculate the difference between that date and the current date and use the difference as the delay of the task.

The following screenshot shows the output of an execution of this example:

```
🔲 Problems  📖 Javadoc  🔍 Declaration  🔍 Search  🔲 Console ⊠  📋 Error Log
<terminated> Main (30) [Java Application] C:\Program Files\Java\jdk-9\bin\javaw.exe (
Main: Starting at: Tue Sep 13 23:13:42 GMT+01:00 2016
Task 0: Starting at : Tue Sep 13 23:13:43 GMT+01:00 2016
Task 1: Starting at : Tue Sep 13 23:13:44 GMT+01:00 2016
Task 2: Starting at : Tue Sep 13 23:13:45 GMT+01:00 2016
Task 3: Starting at : Tue Sep 13 23:13:46 GMT+01:00 2016
Task 4: Starting at : Tue Sep 13 23:13:47 GMT+01:00 2016
Core: Ends at: Tue Sep 13 23:13:47 GMT+01:00 2016
```

You can see how the tasks start their execution, one per second. All the tasks are sent to the executor at the same time but with a delay of 1 second later than the previous task.

There's more...

You can also use the `Runnable` interface to implement the tasks because the `schedule()` method of the `ScheduledThreadPoolExecutor` class accepts both types of tasks.

Although the `ScheduledThreadPoolExecutor` class is a child class of the `ThreadPoolExecutor` class (and therefore inherits all its features), Java recommends that you use `ScheduledThreadPoolExecutor` only for scheduled tasks.

Finally, you can configure the behavior of the `ScheduledThreadPoolExecutor` class when you call the `shutdown()` method, and there are pending tasks waiting for the end of their delay time. The default behavior is that these tasks will be executed despite the finalization of the executor. You can change this behavior using the `setExecuteExistingDelayedTasksAfterShutdownPolicy()` method of the `ScheduledThreadPoolExecutor` class. If you call the `setExecuteExistingDelayedTasksAfeterShutdownsPolicy()` passing the `false` value as parameter, pending tasks won't be executed after you call the `shutdown()` method.

See also

- The *Executing tasks in an executor that returns a result* recipe in this chapter

Running a task in an executor periodically

The Executor framework provides the `ThreadPoolExecutor` class to execute concurrent tasks using a pool of threads that helps you avoid all thread creation operations. When you send a task to the executor, it executes the task as soon as possible according to its configuration. When it ends, the task is deleted from the executor, and if you want to execute it again, you have to send it to the executor again.

However, the Executor framework provides the possibility of executing periodic tasks through the `ScheduledThreadPoolExecutor` class. In this recipe, you will learn how to use this functionality of the class to schedule a periodic task.

Getting ready

The example of this recipe has been implemented using the Eclipse IDE. If you use Eclipse or a different IDE, such as NetBeans, open it and create a new Java project.

How to do it...

Follow these steps to implement the example:

1. Create a class named `Task` and specify that it implements the `Runnable` interface:

```
public class Task implements Runnable {
```

2. Declare a private `String` attribute called `name` that will store the name of the task:

```
private final String name;
```

3. Implement the constructor of the class that initializes the attribute:

```
public Task(String name) {
    this.name=name;
}
```

4. Implement the `run()` method. Write a message to the console with the actual date to verify that the task is executed within the specified period:

```
@Override
public void run() {
    System.out.printf("%s: Executed at: %s\n",name,new Date());
}
```

5. Implement the main class of the example by creating a class named `Main` and adding the `main()` method to it:

```
public class Main {
    public static void main(String[] args) {
```

6. Create `ScheduledExecutorService` using the `newScheduledThreadPool()` method of the `Executors` class. Pass 1 to this method as a parameter:

```
ScheduledExecutorService executor=Executors
                            .newScheduledThreadPool(1);
```

7. Write a message to the console with the actual date:

```
System.out.printf("Main: Starting at: %s\n",new Date());
```

8. Create a new `Task` object:

```
Task task=new Task("Task");
```

9. Send this object to the executor using the `scheduledAtFixRate()` method. Use the tasks created earlier as parameters: the number one, the number two, and the constant `TimeUnit.SECONDS`. This method returns a `ScheduledFuture` object that you can use to control the status of the task:

```
ScheduledFuture<?> result=executor.scheduleAtFixedRate(task, 1,
                                          2, TimeUnit.SECONDS);
```

10. Create a loop with 10 steps to write the time remaining for the next execution of the task. In the loop, use the `getDelay()` method of the `ScheduledFuture` object to get the number of milliseconds until the next execution of the task:

```
for (int i=0; i<10; i++){
   System.out.printf("Main: Delay: %d\n",result
                              .getDelay(TimeUnit.MILLISECONDS));
```

11. Sleep the thread during 500 milliseconds.

```
   try {
      TimeUnit.MILLISECONDS.sleep(500);
   } catch (InterruptedException e) {
      e.printStackTrace();
   }
}
```

12. Finish the executor using the `shutdown()` method:

```
executor.shutdown();
```

13. Put the thread to sleep for 5 seconds to verify that the periodic tasks have finished:

```
try {
   TimeUnit.SECONDS.sleep(5);
} catch (InterruptedException e) {
   e.printStackTrace();
}
```

14. Write a message to indicate the end of the program:

```
System.out.printf("Main: Finished at: %s\n",new Date());
```

How it works...

When you want to execute a periodic task using the Executor framework, you need a `ScheduledExecutorService` object. To create it (as with every executor), Java recommends the use of the `Executors` class. This class works as a factory of executor objects. In this case, you used the `newScheduledThreadPool()` method to create a `ScheduledExecutorService` object. This method receives the number of threads of the pool as a parameter. Since you had only one task in this example, you passed 1 as a parameter.

Once you had the executor needed to execute a periodic task, you sent the task to the executor. You used the `scheduledAtFixedRate()` method. This method accepts four parameters: the task you want to execute periodically, the delay of time until the first execution of the task, the period between two executions, and the time unit of the second and third parameters. It's a constant of the `TimeUnit` class. The `TimeUnit` class is an enumeration with the following constants: DAYS, HOURS, MICROSECONDS, MILLISECONDS, MINUTES, NANOSECONDS, and SECONDS.

An important point to consider is that the period between two executions is the period of time between the start of those two executions. If you have a periodic task that takes 5 seconds to execute and you put in a period of 3 seconds, you will have two instances of the task executing at a time.

The `scheduleAtFixedRate()` method returns a `ScheduledFuture` object, which extends the `Future` interface, with methods to work with scheduled tasks. `ScheduledFuture` is a parameterized interface. In this example, as your task was a `Runnable` object that was not parameterized, you had to parameterize them with the `?` symbol as a parameter.

You used one method of the `ScheduledFuture` interface. The `getDelay()` method returns the time until the next execution of the task. This method receives a `TimeUnit` constant with the time unit in which you want to receive the results.

The following screenshot shows the output of an execution of the example:

```
Problems  Javadoc  Declaration  Search  Console ☒  Error Log
<terminated> Main (31) [Java Application] C:\Program Files\Java\jdk-9\bin\javaw.exe (13 sept. 2016 23:32:17)
Main: Starting at: Tue Sep 13 23:32:18 GMT+01:00 2016
Main: Delay: 999
Main: Delay: 492
Task: Executed at: Tue Sep 13 23:32:19 GMT+01:00 2016
Main: Delay: -7
Main: Delay: 1487
Main: Delay: 987
Main: Delay: 487
Task: Executed at: Tue Sep 13 23:32:21 GMT+01:00 2016
Main: Delay: 1987
Main: Delay: 1487
Main: Delay: 987
Main: Delay: 487
Task: Executed at: Tue Sep 13 23:32:23 GMT+01:00 2016
Main: No more tasks at: Tue Sep 13 23:32:23 GMT+01:00 2016
Main: Finished at: Tue Sep 13 23:32:28 GMT+01:00 2016
```

You can see the task being executed every 2 seconds (denoted by Task: prefix) and the delay written in the console every 500 milliseconds. That's how long the main thread has been put to sleep. When you shut down the executor, the scheduled task ends its execution and you don't see any more messages in the console.

There's more...

ScheduledThreadPoolExecutor provides other methods to schedule periodic tasks. It is the scheduleWithFixedRate() method. It has the same parameters as the scheduledAtFixedRate() method, but there is a difference worth noticing. In the scheduledAtFixedRate() method, the third parameter determines the period of time between the starting of two executions. In the scheduledWithFixedRate() method, the parameter determines the period of time between the end of an execution of the task and its beginning.

You can also configure the behavior of an instance of the ScheduledThreadPoolExecutor class with the shutdown() method. The default behavior is that the scheduled tasks finish when you call this method. You can change this behavior using the setContinueExistingPeriodicTasksAfterShutdownPolicy() method of the ScheduledThreadPoolExecutor class with a true value. Periodic tasks won't finish upon calling the shutdown() method.

See also

- The *Creating a thread executor and controlling its rejected tasks* and *Running a task in an executor after a delay* recipes in this chapter

Canceling a task in an executor

When you work with an executor, you don't have to manage threads. You only implement `Runnable` or `Callable` tasks and send them to the executor. It's the executor that's responsible for creating threads, managing them in a thread pool, and finishing them if they are not needed. Sometimes, you may want to cancel a task that you send to the executor. In that case, you can use the `cancel()` method of `Future`, which allows you to make the cancelation operation. In this recipe, you will learn how to use this method to cancel tasks that you have sent to an executor.

Getting ready

The example of this recipe has been implemented using the Eclipse IDE. If you use Eclipse or a different IDE, such as NetBeans, open it and create a new Java project.

How to do it...

Follow these steps to implement the example:

1. Create a class named `Task` and specify that it implements the `Callable` interface parameterized by the `String` class. Implement the `call()` method. Write a message to the console and put it to sleep for `100` milliseconds inside an infinite loop:

```
public class Task implements Callable<String> {
  @Override
  public String call() throws Exception {
    while (true){
      System.out.printf("Task: Test\n");
      Thread.sleep(100);
    }
  }
}
```

2. Implement the main class of the example by creating a class named `Main` and adding the `main()` method to it:

```
public class Main {
   public static void main(String[] args) {
```

3. Create a `ThreadPoolExecutor` object using the `newCachedThreadPool()` method of the `Executors` class:

```
ThreadPoolExecutor executor=(ThreadPoolExecutor)Executors
                            .newCachedThreadPool();
```

4. Create a new `Task` object:

```
Task task=new Task();
```

5. Send the task to the executor using the `submit()` method:

```
System.out.printf("Main: Executing the Task\n");
Future<String> result=executor.submit(task);
```

6. Put the main task to sleep for 2 seconds:

```
try {
   TimeUnit.SECONDS.sleep(2);
} catch (InterruptedException e) {
   e.printStackTrace();
}
```

7. Cancel the execution of the task using the `cancel()` method of the `Future` object, named `result`, returned by the `submit()` method. Pass the true value as a parameter of the `cancel()` method:

```
System.out.printf("Main: Canceling the Task\n");
result.cancel(true);
```

8. Write the result of a call to the `isCancelled()` and `isDone()` methods to the console. This is to verify that the task has been canceled, and hence, already done:

```
System.out.printf("Main: Canceled: %s\n",result.isCancelled());
System.out.printf("Main: Done: %s\n",result.isDone());
```

9. Finish the executor with the `shutdown()` method and write a message indicating the finalization of the program:

```
executor.shutdown();
System.out.printf("Main: The executor has finished\n");
```

How it works...

You use the `cancel()` method of the `Future` interface when you want to cancel a task that you have sent to an executor. Depending on the parameter of the `cancel()` method and the status of the task, the behavior of this method is different:

- If the task has finished or has been canceled earlier, or it can't be cancelled due to any other reason, the method will return the `false` value and the task won't be canceled.
- If the task is waiting in the executor to get a `Thread` object that will execute it, the task is canceled and will never begin its execution. If the task is already running, it depends on the parameter of the method. The `cancel()` method receives a Boolean value as a parameter. If the value of this parameter is `true` and the task is running, it will be canceled. If the value of the parameter is false and the task is running, it won't be canceled.

The following screenshot shows the output of an execution of this example:

```
<terminated> Main (32) [Java Application] C:\Program Files\Java\jdk-9\b
Task: Test
Task: Test
Task: Test
Task: Test
Task: Test
Task: Test
Task: Test
Main: Cancelling the Task
Main: Cancelled: true
Main: Done: true
Main: The executor has finished
```

There's more...

If you use the `get()` method of a `Future` object that controls a task that has been canceled, the `get()` method will throw a `CancellationException` exception.

See also

- The *Executing tasks in an executor that returns a result* recipe in this chapter

Controlling a task finishing in an executor

The Java API provides the FutureTask class as a cancelable asynchronous computation. It implements the Runnable and Future interfaces and provides the basic implementation of the Future interface. We can create a FutureTask class using a Callable or Runnable object (Runnable objects doesn't return a result, so we have to pass as parameter too in this case the result that the Future object will return). It provides methods to cancel the execution and obtain the result of the computation. It also provides a method called done() that allows you to execute some code after the finalization of a task executed in an executor. It can be used to make some postprocess operations, such as generating a report, sending results by e-mail, or releasing some resources. This method is called internally by the FutureTask class when the execution of the task that this FutureTask object is controlling finishes. The method is called after the result of the task is set and its status is changed to isDone, regardless of whether the task has been canceled or finished normally.

By default, this method is empty. You can override the FutureTask class and implement this method to change the behavior. In this recipe, you will learn how to override this method to execute code after the finalization of the tasks.

Getting ready

The example of this recipe has been implemented using the Eclipse IDE. If you use Eclipse or a different IDE, such as NetBeans, open it and create a new Java project.

How to do it...

Follow these steps to implement the example:

1. Create a class named ExecutableTask and specify that it implements the Callable interface parameterized by the String class:

```
public class ExecutableTask implements Callable<String> {
```

2. Declare a private `String` attribute called `name`. It will store the name of the task. Implement the `getName()` method to return the value of this attribute:

```
private final String name;
public String getName(){
  return name;
}
```

3. Implement the constructor of the class to initialize the name of the task:

```
public ExecutableTask(String name){
  this.name=name;
}
```

4. Implement the `call()` method. Put the task to sleep for a random period of time and return a message with the name of the task:

```
@Override
public String call() throws Exception {
  try {
    long duration=(long)(Math.random()*10);
    System.out.printf("%s: Waiting %d seconds for results.\n",
                    this.name,duration);
    TimeUnit.SECONDS.sleep(duration);
  } catch (InterruptedException e) {}
  return "Hello, world. I'm "+name;
}
```

5. Implement a class named `ResultTask` that extends the `FutureTask` class parameterized by the `String` class:

```
public class ResultTask extends FutureTask<String> {
```

6. Declare a private `String` attribute called `name`. It will store the name of the task:

```
private final String name;
```

7. Implement the constructor of the class. It has to receive a `Callable` object as a parameter. Call the constructor of the parent class and initialize the name attribute using the attribute of the task received:

```
public ResultTask(ExecutableTask callable) {
  super(callable);
  this.name= callable.getName();
}
```

8. Override the `done()` method. Check the value of the `isCancelled()` method and write a different message to the console, depending on the returned value:

```
@Override
protected void done() {
  if (isCancelled()) {
    System.out.printf("%s: Has been canceled\n",name);
  } else {
    System.out.printf("%s: Has finished\n",name);
  }
}
```

9. Implement the main class of the example by creating a class named `Main` and adding the `main()` method to it:

```
public class Main {
    public static void main(String[] args) {
```

10. Create `ExecutorService` using the `newCachedThreadPool()` method of the `Executors` class:

```
ExecutorService executor=Executors.newCachedThreadPool();
```

11. Create an array to store five `ResultTask` objects:

```
ResultTask resultTasks[]=new ResultTask[5];
```

12. Initialize the `ResultTask` objects. For each position in the array, first you have to create `ExecutorTask` and then `ResultTask` using the object. Then, send `ResultTask` to the executor using the `submit()` method:

```
for (int i=0; i<5; i++) {
    ExecutableTask executableTask=new ExecutableTask("Task "+i);
    resultTasks[i]=new ResultTask(executableTask);
    executor.submit(resultTasks[i]);
}
```

13. Put the main thread to sleep for 5 seconds:

```
try {
  TimeUnit.SECONDS.sleep(5);
} catch (InterruptedException e1) {
  e1.printStackTrace();
}
```

14. Cancel all the tasks you have sent to the executor:

```
for (int i=0; i<resultTasks.length; i++) {
  resultTasks[i].cancel(true);
}
```

15. Write the result of those tasks that haven't been canceled to the console, using the
`get()` method of the `ResultTask` objects:

```
for (int i=0; i<resultTasks.length; i++) {
  try {
    if (!resultTasks[i].isCancelled()){
      System.out.printf("%s\n",resultTasks[i].get());
    }
  } catch (InterruptedException | ExecutionException e) {
    e.printStackTrace();
  }
}
```

16. Finish the executor using the `shutdown()` method:

```
    executor.shutdown();
  }
}
```

How it works...

The `done()` method is called by the `FutureTask` class when the task that is being
controlled finishes its execution. In this example, you implemented a `Callable` object, the
`ExecutableTask` class, and then a subclass of the `FutureTask` class that controls the
execution of the `ExecutableTask` objects.

The `done()` method is called internally by the `FutureTask` class after establishing the
return value and changing the status of the task to `isDone`. You can't change the result
value of the task or change its status, but you can close resources used by the task, write log
messages, or send notifications. The `FutureTask` class might be used to ensure that a
specific task is run only once, as calling its `run()` method will execute its wrapped
`Runnable/Callable` interface only once (and the result can be fetched with `get` when it's
available).

See also

- The *Executing tasks in an executor that returns a result* recipe in this chapter

Separating the launching of tasks and the processing of their results in an executor

Normally, when you execute concurrent tasks using an executor, you will send `Runnable` or `Callable` tasks to the executor and get `Future` objects to control the method. You can find situations where you need to send the tasks to the executor in one object and process the results in another one. For such situations, the Java Concurrency API provides the `CompletionService` class.

The `CompletionService` class has a method to send tasks to an executor and a method to get the `Future` object for the next task that has finished its execution. Internally, it uses an `Executor` object to execute the tasks. This behavior has the advantage of sharing a `CompletionService` object and sending tasks to the executor so others can process the results. The limitation is that the second object can only get the `Future` objects for those tasks that have finished their execution, so these Future objects can only be used to get the results of the tasks.

In this recipe, you will learn how to use the `CompletionService` class to separate the process of launching tasks in an executor from the processing of their results.

Getting ready

The example of this recipe has been implemented using the Eclipse IDE. If you use Eclipse or a different IDE, such as NetBeans, open it and create a new Java project.

How to do it...

Follow these steps to implement the example:

1. Create a class named `ReportGenerator` and specify that it implements the `Callable` interface parameterized by the `String` class:

   ```
   public class ReportGenerator implements Callable<String> {
   ```

---

[193]

2. Declare two private `String` attributes named `sender` and `title`. These attributes will represent the data of the report:

```
private final String sender;
private final String title;
```

3. Implement the constructor of the class that initializes the two attributes:

```
public ReportGenerator(String sender, String title){
    this.sender=sender;
    this.title=title;
}
```

4. Implement the `call()` method. First, put the thread to sleep for a random period of time:

```
@Override
public String call() throws Exception {
    try {
        Long duration=(long)(Math.random()*10);
        System.out.printf("%s_%s: ReportGenerator: Generating a
                        report during %d seconds\n",this.sender,
                        this.title,duration);
        TimeUnit.SECONDS.sleep(duration);
    } catch (InterruptedException e) {
        e.printStackTrace();
    }
```

5. Then, generate the report as a string with the `sender` and `title` attributes and return that string:

```
    String ret=sender+": "+title;
    return ret;
}
```

6. Create a class named `ReportRequest` and specify that it implements the `Runnable` interface. Thiss class will simulate some report requests:

```
public class ReportRequest implements Runnable {
```

7. Declare a private `String` attribute called `name` to store the name of `ReportRequest`:

```
private final String name;
```

8. Declare a private `CompletionService` attribute named `service`. The `CompletionService` interface is a parameterized interface. Use the `String` class:

```
private final CompletionService<String> service;
```

9. Implement the constructor of the class that initializes the two attributes:

```
public ReportRequest(String name, CompletionService<String>
                     service){
   this.name=name;
   this.service=service;
}
```

10. Implement the `run()` method. Create three `ReportGenerator` objects and send them to the `CompletionService` object using the `submit()` method:

```
@Override
public void run() {
   ReportGenerator reportGenerator=new ReportGenerator(name,
                                                "Report");
   service.submit(reportGenerator);

}
```

11. Create a class named `ReportProcessor`. This class will get the results of the `ReportGenerator` tasks. Specify that it implements the `Runnable` interface:

```
public class ReportProcessor implements Runnable {
```

12. Declare a private `CompletionService` attribute named `service`. As the `CompletionService` interface is a parameterized interface, use the `String` class as a parameter of this `CompletionService` interface:

```
private final CompletionService<String> service;
```

13. Declare a private `Boolean` attribute named `end`. Add the `volatile` keyword to ensure that all the threads have access to the actual value of the attribute:

```
private volatile boolean end;
```

14. Implement the constructor of the class to initialize the two attributes:

```
public ReportProcessor (CompletionService<String> service){
    this.service=service;
    end=false;
}
```

15. Implement the `run()` method. While the `end` attribute is false, call the `poll()` method of the `CompletionService` interface to get the `Future` object of the next task executed by the completion service that has finished:

```
@Override
public void run() {
    while (!end){
        try {
            Future<String> result=service.poll(20, TimeUnit.SECONDS);
```

16. Then, get the results of the task using the `get()` method of the `Future` object and write the results to the console:

```
if (result!=null) {
    String report=result.get();
    System.out.printf("ReportReceiver: Report Received: %s\n",
                    report);
}
} catch (InterruptedException | ExecutionException e) {
    e.printStackTrace();
}
}
System.out.printf("ReportSender: End\n");
}
```

17. Implement the `stopProcessing()` method that modifies the value of the `end` attribute:

```
public void stopProcessing() {
    this.end = true;
}
```

18. Implement the main class of the example by creating a class named `Main` and adding the `main()` method to it:

```
public class Main {
    public static void main(String[] args) {
```

19. Create `ThreadPoolExecutor` using the `newCachedThreadPool()` method of the `Executors` class:

```
ExecutorService executor=Executors.newCachedThreadPool();
```

20. Create `CompletionService` using the executor created earlier as a parameter of the constructor:

```
CompletionService<String> service=new
                    ExecutorCompletionService<>(executor);
```

21. Create two `ReportRequest` objects and the threads to execute them:

```
ReportRequest faceRequest=new ReportRequest("Face", service);
ReportRequest onlineRequest=new ReportRequest("Online", service);
Thread faceThread=new Thread(faceRequest);
Thread onlineThread=new Thread(onlineRequest);
```

22. Create a `ReportProcessor` object and the thread to execute it:

```
ReportProcessor processor=new ReportProcessor(service);
Thread senderThread=new Thread(processor);
```

23. Start the three threads:

```
System.out.printf("Main: Starting the Threads\n");
faceThread.start();
onlineThread.start();
senderThread.start();
```

24. Wait for the finalization of the `ReportRequest` threads:

```
try {
  System.out.printf("Main: Waiting for the report generators.\n");
  faceThread.join();
  onlineThread.join();
} catch (InterruptedException e) {
  e.printStackTrace();
}
```

25. Finish the executor using the `shutdown()` method and wait for the finalization of the tasks with the `awaitTermination()` method:

```
System.out.printf("Main: Shutting down the executor.\n");
executor.shutdown();
try {
  executor.awaitTermination(1, TimeUnit.DAYS);
} catch (InterruptedException e) {
  e.printStackTrace();
}
```

26. Finish the execution of the `ReportSender` object setting the value of its end attribute to true:

```
processor.stopProcessing();
System.out.println("Main: Ends");
```

How it works...

In the main class of the example, you created `ThreadPoolExecutor` using the `newCachedThreadPool()` method of the `Executors` class. Then, you used that `Executor` object to initialize a `CompletionService` object because the completion service uses an executor to execute its tasks. To execute a task using the completion service, use the `submit()` method, as in the `ReportRequest` class.

When one of these tasks is executed when the completion service finishes its execution, the service stores the `Future` object used to control its execution in a queue. The `poll()` method accesses this queue to check whether there is any task that has finished its execution; if yes, it returns the first element of the queue, which is a `Future` object of a task that has finished its execution. When the `poll()` method returns a `Future` object, it deletes it from the queue. In this case, you passed two attributes to the method to indicate the time you want to wait for the finalization of a task, in case the queue with the results of the finished tasks is empty.

Once the `CompletionService` object is created, you create two `ReportRequest` objects that execute a `ReportGenerator` task, execute a `ReportGenerator` task using the `CompletionService` object create before and passed as parameter to the constructor of the `ReportRequest` objects

There's more...

The CompletionService class can execute Callable or Runnable tasks. In this example, you used Callable, but you could have also sent Runnable objects. Since Runnable objects don't produce a result, the philosophy of the CompletionService class doesn't apply in such cases.

This class also provides two other methods to obtain the Future objects of the finished tasks. These methods are as follows:

- poll(): The version of the poll() method without arguments checks whether there are any Future objects in the queue. If the queue is empty, it returns null immediately. Otherwise, it returns its first element and removes it from the queue.
- take(): This method, without arguments, checks whether there are any Future objects in the queue. If it is empty, it blocks the thread until the queue has an element. If the queue has elements, it returns and deletes its first element from the queue.

In our case, we used the poll() method with a timeout to control when we would like to end the execution of the ReportProcessor task.

See also

- The *Executing tasks in an executor that returns a result* recipe in this chapter

5

Fork/Join Framework

In this chapter, we will cover:

- Creating a fork/join pool
- Joining the results of the tasks
- Running tasks asynchronously
- Throwing exceptions in the tasks
- Canceling a task

Introduction

Normally, when you implement a simple, concurrent Java application, you implement some `Runnable` objects and then the corresponding `Thread` objects. You control the creation, execution, and status of those threads in your program. Java 5 introduced an improvement with the `Executor` and `ExecutorService` interfaces and the classes that implement them (for example, the `ThreadPoolExecutor` class).

The **Executor** framework separates the task creation and its execution. With it, you only have to implement the `Runnable` objects and use an `Executor` object. You send the `Runnable` tasks to the executor and it creates, manages, and finalizes the necessary threads to execute those tasks.

Java 7 goes a step further and includes an additional implementation of the `ExecutorService` interface oriented to a specific kind of problem. It's the **fork/join framework**.

This framework is designed to solve problems that can be broken into smaller tasks using the divide and conquer technique. Inside a task, you check the size of the problem you want to resolve, and if it's bigger than an established size, you divide it into smaller tasks that are executed using the framework. If the size of the problem is smaller than the established size, you solve the problem directly in the task, and then, optionally, it returns a result. The following diagram summarizes this concept:

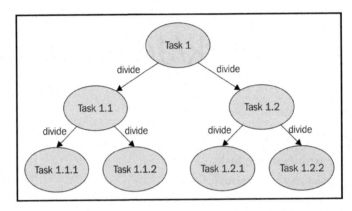

There is no formula to determine the reference size of a problem that determines if a task is to be subdivided or not, depending on its characteristics. You can use the number of elements to process in the task and an estimation of the execution time to determine the reference size. Test different reference sizes to choose the best one for your problem. You can consider ForkJoinPool as a special kind of Executor.

The framework is based on the following two operations:

- **Fork operation**: When you divide a task into smaller tasks and execute them using the framework.
- **Join operation**: When a task waits for the finalization of the tasks it has created. It's used to combine the results of those tasks.

The main difference between the fork/join and the Executor frameworks is the **work-stealing** algorithm. Unlike the Executor framework, when a task is waiting for the finalization of the subtasks it has created using the join operation, the thread that is executing that task (called **worker thread**) looks for other tasks that have not been executed yet and begins their execution. In this way, the threads take full advantage of their running time, thereby improving the performance of the application.

To achieve this goal, the tasks executed by the fork/join framework have the following limitations:

- Tasks can only use the `fork()` and `join()` operations as synchronization mechanisms. If they use other synchronization mechanisms, the worker threads can't execute other tasks when they are in the synchronization operation. For example, if you put a task to sleep in the fork/join framework, the worker thread that is executing that task won't execute another one during the sleeping time.
- Tasks should not perform I/O operations such as read or write data in a file.
- Tasks can't throw checked exceptions. They have to include the code necessary to process them.

The core of the fork/join framework is formed by the following two classes:

- `ForkJoinPool`: This class implements the `ExecutorService` interface and the work-stealing algorithm. It manages the worker threads and offers information about the status of the tasks and their execution.
- `ForkJoinTask`: This is the base class of the tasks that will execute in the `ForkJoinPool`. It provides the mechanisms to execute the `fork()` and `join()` operations inside a task and the methods to control the status of the tasks. Usually, to implement your fork/join tasks, you will implement a subclass of three subclasses of this class: `RecursiveAction` for tasks with no return result, `RecursiveTask` for tasks that return one result, and `CountedCompleter` for tasks that launch a completion action when all the subtasks have finished.

Most of the features provided by this framework were included in Java 7, but Java 8 included minor features in it. It included a default `ForkJoinPool` object. You can obtain it using the static method, `commonPool()`, of the `ForkJoinPool` class. This default fork/join executor will by default use the number of threads determined by the available processors of your computer. You can change this default behavior by changing the value of the system property, `java.util.concurrent.ForkJoinPool.common.parallelism`. This default pool is used internally by other classes of the Concurrency API. For example, **Parallel Streams** use it. Java 8 also included the `CountedCompleter` class mentioned earlier.

This chapter presents five recipes that show you how to work efficiently with the fork/join framework.

Creating a fork/join pool

In this recipe, you will learn how to use the basic elements of the fork/join framework. This includes the following:

- Creating a `ForkJoinPool` object to execute the tasks
- Creating a subclass of `ForkJoinTask` to be executed in the pool

The main characteristics of the fork/join framework you're going to use in this example are as follows:

- You will create `ForkJoinPool` using the default constructor.
- Inside the task, you will use the structure recommended by the Java API documentation:

```
if (problem size > default size){
  tasks=divide(task);
  execute(tasks);
} else {
  resolve problem using another algorithm;
}
```

- You will execute the tasks in a synchronized way. When a task executes two or more subtasks, it waits for their finalizations. In this way, the thread that was executing that task (called worker thread) will look for other tasks to execute, taking full advantage of their execution time.
- The tasks you're going to implement won't return any result, so you'll take the `RecursiveAction` class as the base class for their implementation.

Getting ready

The example in this recipe has been implemented using the Eclipse IDE. If you use Eclipse or other IDEs, such as NetBeans, open it and create a new Java project.

How to do it...

In this recipe, you are going to implement a task to update the price of a list of products. The initial task will be responsible for updating all the elements in a list. You will use a size 10 as the reference size, so if a task has to update more than 10 elements, it divides the part of the list assigned to it in two parts and creates two tasks to update the prices of the products in the respective parts.

Follow these steps to implement the example:

1. Create a class named `Product` that will store the name and price of a product:

   ```
   public class Product {
   ```

2. Declare a private `String` attribute named `name` and a `private` double attribute named `price`:

   ```
   private String name;
   private double price;
   ```

3. Implement getter and setter methods for those fields. They are very simple to implement, so its source code is not included.

4. Create a class named `ProductListGenerator` to generate a list of random products:

   ```
   public class ProductListGenerator {
   ```

4. Implement the `generate()` method. It receives an `int` parameter with the size of the list and returns a `List<Product>` object with the list of generated products:

   ```
   public List<Product> generate (int size) {
   ```

5. Create the object to return the list of products:

   ```
   List<Product> ret=new ArrayList<Product>();
   ```

6. Generate the list of products. Assign the same price to all of the products, for example, `10`, to check that the program works well:

   ```
   for (int i=0; i<size; i++){
     Product product=new Product();
     product.setName("Product "+i);
     product.setPrice(10);
     ret.add(product);
   ```

```
    }
    return ret;
}
```

7. Create a class named `Task`. Specify that it extends the `RecursiveAction` class:

```
public class Task extends RecursiveAction {
```

8. Declare a `private List<Product>` attribute named `products`:

```
private List<Product> products;
```

9. Declare two private `int` attributes named `first` and `last`. These attributes will determine the block of products this task has to process:

```
private int first;
private int last;
```

10. Declare a private `double` attribute named `increment` to store the increment of the price of the products:

```
private double increment;
```

11. Implement the constructor of the class that will initialize all the attributes of the class:

```
public Task (List<Product> products, int first, int last,
             double increment) {
    this.products=products;
    this.first=first;
    this.last=last;
    this.increment=increment;
}
```

12. Implement the `compute()` method, which will implement the logic of the task:

```
@Override
protected void compute() {
```

13. If the difference of the `last` and `first` attributes is less than `10` (the task has to update the price of less than `10` products), increment the price of that set of products using the `updatePrices()` method:

```
if (last - first<10) {
    updatePrices();
```

14. If the difference between the `last` and `first` attributes is greater than or equal to `10`, create two new `Task` objects, one to process the first half of the products and the other to process the second half, and execute them in `ForkJoinPool` using the `invokeAll()` method:

```
} else {
    int middle=(last+first)/2;
    System.out.printf("Task: Pending tasks:%s\n",
                    getQueuedTaskCount());
    Task t1=new Task(products, first,middle+1, increment);
    Task t2=new Task(products, middle+1,last, increment);
    invokeAll(t1, t2);
}
```

15. Implement the `updatePrices()` method. This method updates the products that occupy the positions between the values of the `first` and `last` attributes in the list of products:

```
private void updatePrices() {
    for (int i=first; i<last; i++){
        Product product=products.get(i);
        product.setPrice(product.getPrice()*(1+increment));
    }
}
```

16. Implement the main class of the example by creating a class named `Main` and add the `main()` method to it:

```
public class Main {
    public static void main(String[] args) {
```

17. Create a list of `10000` products using the `ProductListGenerator` class:

```
ProductListGenerator generator=new ProductListGenerator();
List<Product> products=generator.generate(10000);
```

18. Create a new `Task` object to update the `prices` of all the products in the list. The parameter `first` takes the value `0` and the `last` parameter takes the value `10000` (the size of the product list):

```
Task task=new Task(products, 0, products.size(), 0.20);
```

19. Create a `ForkJoinPool` object using the constructor without parameters:

```
ForkJoinPool pool=new ForkJoinPool();
```

20. Execute the task in the pool using the `execute()` method:

```
pool.execute(task);
```

21. Implement a block of code that shows information about the evolution of the pool every five milliseconds, writing to the console the value of some parameters of the pool until the task finishes its execution:

```
do {
  System.out.printf("Main: Thread Count:%d\n",
                    pool.getActiveThreadCount());
  System.out.printf("Main: Thread Steal:%d\n",
                    pool.getStealCount());
  System.out.printf("Main: Parallelism:%d\n",
                    pool.getParallelism());
  try {
    TimeUnit.MILLISECONDS.sleep(5);
  } catch (InterruptedException e) {
    e.printStackTrace();
  }
} while (!task.isDone());
```

22. Shut down the pool using the `shutdown()` method:

```
pool.shutdown();
```

23. Check if the task has finished without errors with the `isCompletedNormally()` method and in that case, write a message to the console:

```
if (task.isCompletedNormally()){
  System.out.printf("Main: The process has completed
                    normally.\n");
}
```

24. The expected price of all the products, after the increment, is 12. Write the name and price of all the products that have a price difference of 12 to check that all of them have increased their price correctly:

```
for (int i=0; i<products.size(); i++){
  Product product=products.get(i);
  if (product.getPrice()!=12) {
    System.out.printf("Product %s: %f\n",
                      product.getName(),product.getPrice());
  }
}
```

25. Write a message to indicate the finalization of the program:

```
System.out.println("Main: End of the program.\n");
```

How it works...

In this example, you created a `ForkJoinPool` object and a subclass of the `ForkJoinTask` class that you executed in the pool. To create the `ForkJoinPool` object, you used the constructor without arguments, so it will be executed with its default configuration. It creates a pool with a number of threads equal to the number of processors of the computer. When the `ForkJoinPool` object is created, those threads are created and they wait in the pool until some tasks arrive for their execution.

Since the `Task` class doesn't return a result, it extends the `RecursiveAction` class. In the recipe, you used the recommended structure for the implementation of the task. If the task has to update more than 10 products, it divides that set of elements into two blocks, creates two tasks, and assigns a block to each task. You used the `first` and `last` attributes in the `Task` class to know the range of positions that this task has to update in the list of products. You used the `first` and `last` attributes to use only one copy of the product list and not create different lists for each task.

To execute the subtasks that a task creates, it calls the `invokeAll()` method. This is a synchronous call, and the task waits for the finalization of the subtasks before continuing (potentially finishing) its execution. While the task is waiting for its subtasks, the worker thread that was executing it takes another task waiting for execution and executes it. With this behavior, the fork/join framework offers more efficient task management than the `Runnable` and `Callable` objects themselves.

The `invokeAll()` method of the `ForkJoinTask` class is one of the main differences between the Executor and the fork/join framework. In the Executor framework, all the tasks have to be sent to the executor while in this case, the tasks include methods to execute and control the tasks inside the pool. You used the `invokeAll()` method in the `Task` class, which extends the `RecursiveAction` class, which in turn extends the `ForkJoinTask` class.

You sent a unique task to the pool to update all the lists of products using the `execute()` method. In this case, it's an asynchronous call, and the main thread continues its execution.

You used some methods of the `ForkJoinPool` class to check the status and the evolution of the tasks that are running. The class includes more methods that can be useful for this purpose. See the *Monitoring a fork/join pool* recipe in `Chapter 9`, *Testing Concurrent Applications* for a complete list of those methods.

Finally, like with the Executor framework, you should finish `ForkJoinPool` using the `shutdown()` method.

The following screenshot shows part of an execution of this example:

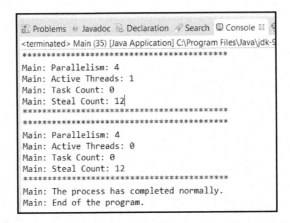

You can see the tasks finishing their work and the price of the products updated.

There's more...

The `ForkJoinPool` class provides other methods to execute a task. These methods are as follows:

- `execute (Runnable task)`: This is another version of the `execute()` method used in the example. In this case, you send a `Runnable` task to the `ForkJoinPool` class. Note that the `ForkJoinPool` class doesn't use the work-stealing algorithm with `Runnable` objects. It's only used with `ForkJoinTask` objects.
- `invoke(ForkJoinTask<T> task)`: While the `execute()` method makes an asynchronous call to the `ForkJoinPool` class, as you learned in the example, the `invoke()` method makes a synchronous call to the `ForkJoinPool` class. This call doesn't return until the task passed as a parameter finishes its execution.
- You can also use the `invokeAll()` and `invokeAny()` methods declared in the `ExecutorService` interface. These methods receive `Callable` objects as parameters. The `ForkJoinPool` class doesn't use the work-stealing algorithm with the `Callable` objects, so you'd be better off executing them using a `ThreadPoolExecutor`.

The `ForkJoinTask` class also includes other versions of the `invokeAll()` method used in the example. These versions are as follows:

- `invokeAll(ForkJoinTask<?>... tasks)`: This version of the method uses a variable list of arguments. You can pass to it as parameters as many `ForkJoinTask` objects as you want.
- `invokeAll(Collection<T> tasks)`: This version of the method accepts a collection (for example, an `ArrayList` object, a `LinkedList` object, or a `TreeSet` object) of objects of a generic type `T`. This generic type `T` must be the `ForkJoinTask` class or a subclass of it.

Although the `ForkJoinPool` class is designed to execute an object of `ForkJoinTask`, you can also execute the `Runnable` and `Callable` objects directly. You may also use the `adapt()` method of the `ForkJoinTask` class that accepts a `Callable` object or a `Runnable` object and returns a `ForkJoinTask` object to execute that task.

See also

- The *Monitoring a fork/join pool* recipe in `Chapter 9`, *Testing Concurrent Applications*

Joining the results of the tasks

The fork/join framework provides the ability to execute tasks that return a result. This kind of tasks is implemented by the `RecursiveTask` class. This class extends the `ForkJoinTask` class and implements the `Future` interface provided by the Executor framework.

Inside the task, you have to use the structure recommended by the Java API documentation:

```
if (problem size > size){
  tasks=Divide(task);
  execute(tasks);
  joinResults()
  return result;
} else {
  resolve problem;
  return result;
}
```

If the task has to resolve a problem bigger than a predefined size, you divide the problem into more subtasks and execute those subtasks using the fork/join framework. When they finish their execution, the initiating task obtains the results generated by all the subtasks, groups them, and returns the final result. Ultimately, when the initiating task executed in the pool finishes its execution, you obtain its result, which is effectively the final result of the entire problem.

In this recipe, you will learn how to use this kind of problem solving with fork/join framework by developing an application that looks for a word in a document. You will implement the following two kinds of tasks:

- A document task, which is going to search for a word in a set of lines of a document
- A line task, which is going to search a word in a part of the document

All the tasks will return the number of appearances of the word in the part of the document or line they process. In this recipe we will use the default fork/join pool provided by the Java Concurrency API.

How to do it...

Follow these steps to implement the example:

1. Create a class named `DocumentMock`. It will generate a string matrix that will simulate a document:

   ```
   public class DocumentMock {
   ```

2. Create an array of strings with some words. This array will be used in the generation of the strings matrix:

   ```
   private String words[]={"the","hello","goodbye","packt",
                           "java","thread","pool","random",
                           "class","main"};
   ```

3. Implement the `generateDocument()` method. It receives as parameters the number of lines, the number of words per line, and the word the example is going to look for. It returns a matrix of strings:

   ```
   public String[][] generateDocument(int numLines, int numWords,
                                      String word){
   ```

4. First, create the necessary objects to generate the document-the `String` matrix and a `Random` object to generate random numbers:

```
int counter=0;
String document[][]=new String[numLines][numWords];
Random random=new Random();
```

5. Fill the array with strings. Store in each position the string that is at a random position in the array of words and count the number of appearances of the word the program will look for in the generated array. You can use this value to check whether the program does its job properly:

```
for (int i=0; i<numLines; i++){
  for (int j=0; j<numWords; j++) {
    int index=random.nextInt(words.length);
    document[i][j]=words[index];
    if (document[i][j].equals(word)){
      counter++;
    }
  }
}
```

6. Write a message with the number of appearances of the word and return the matrix generated:

```
System.out.println("DocumentMock: The word appears "+ counter+"
                    times in the document");
return document;
```

7. Create a class named `DocumentTask` and specify that it extends the `RecursiveTask` class parameterized with the `Integer` class. This class will implement the task that will calculate the number of appearances of the word in a set of lines:

```
public class DocumentTask extends RecursiveTask<Integer> {
```

8. Declare a private `String` matrix named document and two private `int` attributes named `start` and `end`. Also, declare a private `String` attribute named `word`:

```
private String document[][];
private int start, end;
private String word;
```

9. Implement the constructor of the class to initialize all its attributes:

```
public DocumentTask (String document[][], int start, int end,
                     String word){
    this.document=document;
    this.start=start;
    this.end=end;
    this.word=word;
}
```

10. Implement the `compute()` method. If the difference between the `end` and `start` attributes is smaller than `10`, the task calculates the number of appearances of a word in the lines between those positions by calling the `processLines()` method:

```
@Override
protected Integer compute() {
    Integer result=null;
    if (end-start<10){
        result=processLines(document, start, end, word);
```

11. Otherwise, divide the group of lines into two objects, create two new `DocumentTask` objects to process those two groups, and execute them in the pool using the `invokeAll()` method:

```
} else {
    int mid=(start+end)/2;
    DocumentTask task1=new DocumentTask(document,start,mid,word);
    DocumentTask task2=new DocumentTask(document,mid,end,word);
    invokeAll(task1,task2);
```

12. Then, add the values returned by both the tasks using the `groupResults()` method. Finally, return the result calculated by the task:

```
    try {
        result=groupResults(task1.get(),task2.get());
    } catch (InterruptedException | ExecutionException e) {
        e.printStackTrace();
    }
}
return result;
```

13. Implement the `processLines()` method. It receives the string matrix, the `start` attribute, the `end` attribute, and the `word` attribute the task is searching for as parameters:

```
private Integer processLines(String[][] document, int start,
                             int end,String word) {
```

14. For every line the task has to process, create a `LineTask` object to process the complete line and store them in a list of tasks:

```
List<LineTask> tasks=new ArrayList<LineTask>();
for (int i=start; i<end; i++){
  LineTask task=new LineTask(document[i], 0,
                             document[i].length, word);
  tasks.add(task);
}
```

15. Execute all the tasks in that list using the `invokeAll()` method:

```
invokeAll(tasks);
```

16. Sum the value returned by all these tasks and return the result:

```
int result=0;
for (int i=0; i<tasks.size(); i++) {
  LineTask task=tasks.get(i);
  try {
    result=result+task.get();
  } catch (InterruptedException | ExecutionException e) {
    e.printStackTrace();
  }
}
return result;
```

17. Implement the `groupResults()` method. It adds two numbers and returns the result:

```
private Integer groupResults(Integer number1,Integer number2) {
  Integer result;
  result=number1+number2;
  return result;
}
```

18. Create a class named `LineTask` and specify that it extends the `RecursiveTask` class parameterized with the `Integer` class. This class will implement the task that will calculate the number of appearances of the word in a line:

```
public class LineTask extends RecursiveTask<Integer>{
```

19. Declare a private `String` array attribute named `line` and two private `int` attributes named `start` and `end`. Finally, declare a private `String` attribute named `word`:

```
private String line[];
private int start, end;
private String word;
```

20. Implement the constructor of the class to initialize all its attributes:

```
public LineTask(String line[],int start,int end,String word) {
    this.line=line;
    this.start=start;
    this.end=end;
    this.word=word;
}
```

21. Implement the `compute()` method of the class. If the difference between the `end` and `start` attributes is smaller than `100`, the task searches for the word in the fragment of the line determined by the `start` and `end` attributes using the `count()` method:

```
@Override
protected Integer compute() {
    Integer result=null;
    if (end-start<100) {
        result=count(line, start, end, word);
```

22. Otherwise, divide the group of words in the line in two, create two new `LineTask` objects to process those two groups, and execute them in the pool using the `invokeAll()` method:

```
} else {
    int mid=(start+end)/2;
    LineTask task1=new LineTask(line, start, mid, word);
    LineTask task2=new LineTask(line, mid, end, word);
    invokeAll(task1, task2);
```

23. Then, add the values returned by both the tasks using the `groupResults()` method. Finally, return the result calculated by the task:

```
try {
    result=groupResults(task1.get(),task2.get());
} catch (InterruptedException | ExecutionException e) {
    e.printStackTrace();
}
}
return result;
```

24. Implement the `count()` method. It receives the string array with the complete line, the `start` attribute, the `end` attribute, and the `word` attribute the task is searching for as parameters:

```
private Integer count(String[] line, int start, int end,
                      String word) {
```

25. Compare the words stored in the positions between the `start` and `end` attributes with the `word` attribute the task is searching for, and if they are equal, increment the `counter` variable:

```
int counter;
counter=0;
for (int i=start; i<end; i++){
    if (line[i].equals(word)){
        counter++;
    }
}
```

26. To slow the execution of the example, put the task to sleep for 10 milliseconds:

```
try {
    Thread.sleep(10);
} catch (InterruptedException e) {
    e.printStackTrace();
}
```

27. Return the value of the `counter` variable:

```
return counter;
```

28. Implement the `groupResults()` method. It sums two numbers and returns the result:

```
private Integer groupResults(Integer number1,Integer number2) {
    Integer result;
    result=number1+number2;
    return result;
}
```

29. Implement the main class of the example by creating a class named `Main` with a `main()` method:

```
public class Main{
    public static void main(String[] args) {
```

30. Create `Document` with `100` lines and `1000` words per line using the `DocumentMock` class:

```
DocumentMock mock=new DocumentMock();
String[][] document=mock.generateDocument(100, 1000, "the");
```

31. Create a new `DocumentTask` object to update the products of the entire document. The `start` parameter takes the value `0` and the `end` parameter takes the value `100`:

```
DocumentTask task=new DocumentTask(document, 0, 100, "the");
```

32. Get the default `ForkJoinPool` executor using the `commmonPool()` method and execute the task on it using the `execute()` method:

```
ForkJoinPool commonPool=ForkJoinPool.commonPool();
commonPool.execute(task);
```

33. Implement a block of code that shows information about the progress of the pool, writing every second to the console the value of some parameters of the pool until the task finishes its execution:

```
do {
    System.out.printf("**************************
                       ****************\n");
    System.out.printf("Main: Active Threads: %d\n",
                      commonPool.getActiveThreadCount());
    System.out.printf("Main: Task Count: %d\n",
                      commonPool.getQueuedTaskCount());
    System.out.printf("Main: Steal Count: %d\n",
                      commonPool.getStealCount());
```

```
System.out.printf("*********************************
******\n");
try {
  TimeUnit.SECONDS.sleep(1);
} catch (InterruptedException e) {
  e.printStackTrace();
}
} while (!task.isDone());
```

34. Shut down the pool using the shutdown() method:

```
pool.shutdown();
```

35. Wait for the finalization of the tasks using the awaitTermination() method:

```
try {
  pool.awaitTermination(1, TimeUnit.DAYS);
} catch (InterruptedException e) {
  e.printStackTrace();
}
```

36. Write the number of the appearances of the word in the document. Check that this number is the same as the number written by the DocumentMock class:

```
try {
  System.out.printf("Main: The word appears %d in the
                     document",task.get());
} catch (InterruptedException | ExecutionException e) {
  e.printStackTrace();
}
```

How it works...

In this example, you implemented two different tasks:

- DocumentTask: A task of this class has to process a set of lines of the document determined by the start and end attributes. If this set of lines has a size smaller than 10, it creates LineTask per line, and when they finish their execution, it sums the results of those tasks and returns the result of the sum. If the set of lines the task has to process has a size of 10 or bigger, it divides the set in two and creates two DocumentTask objects to process those new sets. When those tasks finish their execution, the tasks sum their results and return that sum as a result.

- `LineTask`: A task of this class has to process a set of words of a line of the document. If this set of words is smaller than `100`, the task searches the word directly in that set of words and returns the number of appearances of the word. Otherwise, it divides the set of words into two and creates two `LineTask` objects to process those sets. When those tasks finish their execution, the task sums the results of both the tasks and returns that sum as a `result`.

In the `Main` class, you used the default `ForkJoinPool` (obtained from the static method, `commonPool()`) and executed in it a `DocumentTask` class that has to process a document of `100` lines and `1000` words per line. This task will divide the problem using other `DocumentTask` objects and `LineTask` objects, and when all the tasks finish their execution, you can use the original task to get the total number of appearances of the word in the whole document. Since the tasks return a result, they extend the `RecursiveTask` class.

To obtain the result returned by `Task`, you used the `get()` method. This method is declared in the `Future` interface implemented by the `RecursiveTask` class.

When you execute the program, you can compare the first and the last lines written in the console. The first line is the number of appearances of the word calculated when the document is generated and the last is the same number calculated by the fork/join tasks.

There's more...

The `ForkJoinTask` class provides another method to finish the execution of a task and return a result, that is, the `complete()` method. This method accepts an object of the type used in the parameterization of the `RecursiveTask` class and returns that object as a result of the task when the `join()` method is called. It's use is recommended to provide results for asynchronous tasks.

Since the `RecursiveTask` class implements the `Future` interface, there's another version of the `get()` method:

- `get(long timeout, TimeUnit unit)`: This version of the `get()` method, if the result of the task isn't available, waits the specified time for it. If the specified period of time passes and the result isn't yet available, the method returns a `null` value. The `TimeUnit` class is an enumeration with these constants: DAYS, HOURS, MICROSECONDS, MILLISECONDS, MINUTES, NANOSECONDS, and SECONDS.

See also

- The *Creating a fork/join pool* recipe in this chapter
- The *Monitoring a fork/join pool* recipe in `Chapter 9`, *Testing Concurrent Applications*

Running tasks asynchronously

When you execute `ForkJoinTask` in `ForkJoinPool`, you can do it in a synchronous or an asynchronous way. When you do it in a synchronous way, the method that sends the task to the pool doesn't return until the task sent finishes its execution. When you do it in an asynchronous way, the method that sends the task to the executor returns immediately, so the task can continue with its execution.

You should be aware of a big difference between the two methods. When you use the synchronous methods, the task that calls one of these methods (for example, the `invokeAll()` method) is suspended until the tasks it sent to the pool finish their execution. This allows the `ForkJoinPool` class to use the work-stealing algorithm to assign a new task to the worker thread that executed the sleeping task. On the contrary, when you use the asynchronous methods (for example, the `fork()` method), the task continues with its execution, so the `ForkJoinPool` class can't use the work-stealing algorithm to increase the performance of the application. In this case, only when you call the `join()` or `get()` methods to wait for the finalization of a task, the `ForkJoinPool` class can use that algorithm.

In addition to the `RecursiveAction` and `RecursiveTask` classes, Java 8 introduced a new `ForkJoinTask` class with the `CountedCompleter` class. With this kind of tasks, you can include a completion action that will be executed when it is launched and there is no pending child task. This mechanism is based on a method included in the class (the `onCompletion()` method) and a counter of pending tasks.

This counter is initialized to zero by default and you can increment it when you need in an atomic way. Normally, you will increment this counter one by one as and when you launch a child task. Finally, when a task has finished its execution, you can try to complete the execution of the task and consequently execute the `onCompletion()` method. If the pending count is greater than zero, it is decremented by one. If it's zero, the `onCompletion()` method is executed and then the parent task is tried to be completed.

In this recipe, you will learn how to use the asynchronous methods provided by the
`ForkJoinPool` and `CountedCompleter` classes for the management of tasks. You are
going to implement a program that will search for files with a determined extension inside
a folder and its subfolders. The `CountedCompleter` class you're going to implement will
process the contents of a folder. For each subfolder inside that folder, it will send a new task
to the `ForkJoinPool` class in an asynchronous way. For each file inside that folder, the task
will check the extension of the file and add it to the result list if it proceeds. When a task is
completed, it will insert the result lists of all its child tasks in its result task.

How to do it...

Follow these steps to implement the example:

1. Create a class named `FolderProcessor` and specify that it extends the
    `CountedCompleter` class parameterized with the `List<String>` type:

    ```
    public class FolderProcessor extends
                              CountedCompleter<List<String>> {
    ```

2. Declare a private `String` attribute named `path`. This attribute will store the full
    path of the folder the task is going to process:

    ```
    private String path;
    ```

3. Declare a private `String` attribute named `extension`. This attribute will store
    the name of the extension of the files the task is going to look for:

    ```
    private String extension;
    ```

4. Declare two `List` private attributes named `tasks` and `resultList`. We will use
    the first one to store all the child tasks launched from this task and the other one
    to store the list of results of this task:

    ```
    private List<FolderProcessor> tasks;
    private List<String> resultList;
    ```

5. Implement one constructor for the class to initialize its attributes and its parent
    class. We declare this constructor as `protected` as it will only be used internally:

    ```
    protected FolderProcessor (CountedCompleter<?> completer,
                               String path, String extension) {
        super(completer);
        this.path=path;
    ```

```
    this.extension=extension;
  }
```

6. We implement the other public constructor to be used externally. As the task created by this constructor won't have a parent task, we don't include this object as a parameter:

```
public FolderProcessor (String path, String extension) {
  this.path=path;
  this.extension=extension;
}
```

7. Implement the `compute()` method. As the base class of our task is the `CountedCompleter` class, the return type of this method is `void`:

```
@Override
public void compute() {
```

8. First, initialize the two list attributes:

```
resultList=new ArrayList<>();
tasks=new ArrayList<>();
```

9. Get the contents of the folder:

```
File file=new File(path);
File content[] = file.listFiles();
```

10. For each element in the folder, if there is a subfolder, create a new `FolderProcessor` object and execute it asynchronously using the `fork()` method. We use the first constructor of the class and pass the current task as the completer task of the new one. We also increment the counter of pending tasks using the `addToPendingCount()` method:

```
if (content != null) {
  for (int i = 0; i < content.length; i++) {
    if (content[i].isDirectory()) {
      FolderProcessor task=new FolderProcessor(this,
                    content[i].getAbsolutePath(), extension);
      task.fork();
      addToPendingCount(1);
      tasks.add(task);
```

11. Otherwise, compare the extension of the file with the extension you are looking for, using the `checkFile()` method, and if they are equal, store the full path of the file in the list of strings declared earlier:

```
      } else {
        if (checkFile(content[i].getName())){
          resultList.add(content[i].getAbsolutePath());
        }
      }
    }
```

12. If the list of the `FolderProcessor` subtasks has more than 50 elements, write a message to the console to indicate this circumstance:

```
    if (tasks.size()>50) {
      System.out.printf("%s: %d tasks ran.\n",
                        file.getAbsolutePath(),tasks.size());
    }
  }
```

13. Finally, try to complete the current task using the `tryComplete()` method:

```
    tryComplete();
  }
```

14. Implement the `onCompletion()` method. This method will be executed when all the child tasks (all the tasks that have been forked from the current task) have finished their execution. We add the result list of all the child tasks to the result list of the current task:

```
  @Override
  public void onCompletion(CountedCompleter<?> completer) {
    for (FolderProcessor childTask : tasks) {
      resultList.addAll(childTask.getResultList());
    }
  }
```

15. Implement the `checkFile()` method. This method compares if the name of a file passed as a parameter ends with the `extension` you are looking for. If so, the method returns the `true` value, otherwise it returns the `false` value:

```
  private boolean checkFile(String name) {
    return name.endsWith(extension);
  }
```

16. Finally, implement the `getResultList()` method to return the result list of a task. The code of this method is very simple so it won't be included.

17. Implement the main class of the example by creating a class named `Main` with a `main()` method:

```
public class Main {
  public static void main(String[] args) {
```

18. Create `ForkJoinPool` using the default constructor:

```
ForkJoinPool pool=new ForkJoinPool();
```

19. Create three `FolderProcessor` tasks. Initialize each with a different folder path:

```
FolderProcessor system=new FolderProcessor("C:\\Windows",
                                           "log");
FolderProcessor apps=new FolderProcessor("C:\\Program Files",
                                           "log");
FolderProcessor documents=new FolderProcessor("C:\\Documents
                                And Settings","log");
```

20. Execute the three tasks in the pool using the `execute()` method:

```
pool.execute(system);
pool.execute(apps);
pool.execute(documents);
```

21. Write to the console information about the status of the pool every second until the three tasks have finished their execution:

```
do {
  System.out.printf("********************************
                    *******\n");
  System.out.printf("Main: Active Threads: %d\n",
                  pool.getActiveThreadCount());
  System.out.printf("Main: Task Count: %d\n",
                  pool.getQueuedTaskCount());
  System.out.printf("Main: Steal Count: %d\n",
                  pool.getStealCount());
  System.out.printf("********************************
                    *******\n");
  try {
    TimeUnit.SECONDS.sleep(1);
  } catch (InterruptedException e) {
    e.printStackTrace();
  }
```

```
    } while ((!system.isDone())||(!apps.isDone())||
            (!documents.isDone()));
```

22. Shut down `ForkJoinPool` using the `shutdown()` method:

```
pool.shutdown();
```

23. Write the number of results generated by each task to the console:

```
List<String> results;

results=system.join();
System.out.printf("System: %d files found.\n",results.size());

results=apps.join();
System.out.printf("Apps: %d files found.\n",results.size());

results=documents.join();
System.out.printf("Documents: %d files found.\n",
                  results.size());
```

How it works...

The following screenshot shows part of an execution of the preceding example:

The key to this example is in the `FolderProcessor` class. Each task processes the contents of a folder. As you know, this content has the following two kinds of elements:

- Files
- Other folders

If the task finds a folder, it creates another `FolderProcessor` object to process that folder and sends it to the pool using the `fork()` method. This method sends the task to the pool that will execute it if it has a free worker thread, or it can create a new one. The method returns immediately, so the task can continue processing the contents of the folder. For every file, a task compares its extension with the one it's looking for and, if they are equal, adds the name of the file to the list of `results`.

Once the task has processed all the contents of the assigned folder, we try to complete the current task. As we explained in the introduction of this recipe, when we try to complete a task, the code of the `CountedCompleter` looks for the value of the pending task counter. If this value is greater than 0, it decreases the value of that counter. On the contrary, if the value is 0, the task executes the `onCompletion()` method and then tries to complete its parent task. In our case, when a task is processing a folder and it finds a subfolder, it creates a new child task, launches that task using the `fork()` method, and increments the counter of the pending tasks. So, when a task has processed its entire content, the counter of pending tasks of the task will be equal to the number of child tasks we have launched. When we call the `tryComplete()` method, if the folder of the current task has subfolders, this call will decrease the number of pending tasks. Only when all its child tasks have been completed, its `onCompletion()` method is executed. If the folder of the current task hasn't got any subfolders, the counter of pending tasks will be zero; the `onComplete()` method will be called immediately, and then it will try to complete its parent task. In this way, we create a tree of tasks from top to bottom that are completed from bottom to top. In the `onComplete()` method, we process all the result lists of the child tasks and add their elements in the result list of the current task.

The `ForkJoinPool` class also allows the execution of tasks in an asynchronous way. You used the `execute()` method to send the three initial tasks to the pool. In the `Main` class, you also finished the pool using the `shutdown()` method and wrote information about the status and the evolution of the tasks that are running in it. The `ForkJoinPool` class includes more methods that can be useful for this purpose. See the *Monitoring a fork/join pool* recipe in `Chapter 9`, *Testing Concurrent Applications* to see a complete list of those methods.

There's more...

In this example we used the `addToPendingCount()` method to increment the counter of pending tasks, but we have other methods we can use to change the value of this counter:

- `setPendingCount()`: This method establishes the value of the counter of pending tasks.
- `compareAndSetPendingCount()`: This method receives two parameters. The first one is the expected value and the second one is the new value. If the value of the counter of pending tasks is equal to the expected value, establish its value to the new one.
- `decrementPendingCountUnlessZero()`: This method decrements the value of the counter of pending tasks unless it's equal to zero.

The `CountedCompleter` class also includes other methods to manage the completion of the tasks. The following are the most significant ones:

- `complete()`: This method executes the `onCompletion()` method independently of the value of the counter of pending tasks and tries to complete its completer (parent) task.
- `onExceptionalCompletion()`: This method is executed when the `completeExceptionally()` method has been called or the `compute()` method has thrown an `Exception`. Override this method to include your code to process such exceptions.

In this example, you used the `join()` method to wait for the finalization of tasks and get their results. You can also use one of the following two versions of the `get()` method with this purpose:

- `get(long timeout, TimeUnit unit)`: This version of the `get()` method, if the result of the task isn't available, waits the specified time for it. If the specified period of time passes and the result isn't yet available, the method returns a `null` value. The `TimeUnit` class is an enumeration with the following constants: DAYS, HOURS, MICROSECONDS, MILLISECONDS, MINUTES, NANOSECONDS, and SECONDS
- The `join()` method can't be interrupted. If you interrupt the thread that called the `join()` method, the method throws an `InterruptedException` exception.

See also

- The *Creating a fork/join pool* recipe in this chapter
- The *Monitoring a fork/join pool* recipe in `Chapter 9`, *Testing Concurrent Applications*

Throwing exceptions in the tasks

There are two kinds of exceptions in Java:

- **Checked exceptions**: These exceptions must be specified in the `throws` clause of a method or caught inside them. For example, `IOException` or `ClassNotFoundException`.
- **Unchecked exceptions**: These exceptions don't have to be specified or caught. For example, `NumberFormatException`.

You can't throw any checked exception in the `compute()` method of the `ForkJoinTask` class because this method doesn't include any `throws` declaration in its implementation. You have to include the necessary code to handle the checked exceptions. On the other hand, you can throw (or it can be thrown by any method or object used inside the method) an unchecked exception. The behavior of the `ForkJoinTask` and `ForkJoinPool` classes is different from what you may expect. The program doesn't finish execution and you won't see any information about the exception in the console. It's simply swallowed as if it weren't thrown. Only when you call the `get()` method of the initial task, the exception will be thrown. You can, however, use some methods of the `ForkJoinTask` class to know if a task has thrown an exception and if so, what kind of exception it was. In this recipe, you will learn how to get that information.

Getting ready

The example of this recipe has been implemented using the Eclipse IDE. If you use Eclipse or other IDE such as NetBeans, open it and create a new Java project.

How to do it...

Follow these steps to implement the example:

1. Create a class named `Task`. Specify that it implements the `RecursiveTask` class, parameterized with the `Integer` class:

```
public class Task extends RecursiveTask<Integer> {
```

2. Declare a private `int` array named `array`. It will simulate the array of data you are going to process in this example:

```
private int array[];
```

3. Declare two private `int` attributes named `start` and `end`. These attributes will determine the elements of the array this task has to process:

```
private int start, end;
```

4. Implement the constructor of the class that initializes its attributes:

```
public Task(int array[], int start, int end){
    this.array=array;
    this.start=start;
    this.end=end;
}
```

5. Implement the `compute()` method of the task. As you have parameterized the `RecursiveTask` class with the `Integer` class, this method has to return an `Integer` object. First, write a message to the console with the value of the `start` and `end` attributes:

```
@Override
protected Integer compute() {
    System.out.printf("Task: Start from %d to %d\n",start,end);
```

6. If the block of elements that this task has to process, determined by the `start` and `end` attributes, has a size smaller than `10`, check if the element in the fourth position in the array (index number three) is in that block. If that is the case, throw `RuntimeException`. Then, put the task to sleep for a second:

```
if (end-start<10) {
    if ((3>start)&&(3<end)){
        throw new RuntimeException("This task throws an"+
                    "Exception: Task from  "+start+" to "+end);
```

```
  }
  try {
    TimeUnit.SECONDS.sleep(1);
  } catch (InterruptedException e) {
    e.printStackTrace();
  }
```

7. Otherwise (the block of elements that this task has to process has a size of 10 or bigger), divide the block of elements in two, create two `Task` objects to process those blocks, and execute them in the pool using the `invokeAll()` method. Then, we write the results of these tasks to the console:

```
} else {
  int mid=(end+start)/2;
  Task task1=new Task(array,start,mid);
  Task task2=new Task(array,mid,end);
  invokeAll(task1, task2);
  System.out.printf("Task: Result form %d to %d: %d\n",
                    start,mid,task1.join());
  System.out.printf("Task: Result form %d to %d: %d\n",
                    mid,end,task2.join());
}
```

8. Write a message to the console indicating the end of the task, writing the value of the `start` and `end` attributes:

```
System.out.printf("Task: End form %d to %d\n",start,end);
```

9. Return the number 0 as the result of the task:

```
return 0;
```

10. Implement the main class of the example by creating a class named `Main` with a `main()` method:

```
public class Main {
  public static void main(String[] args) {
```

11. Create an array of 100 integer numbers:

```
int array[]=new int[100];
```

12. Create a `Task` object to process that `array`:

```
Task task=new Task(array,0,100);
```

13. Create a `ForkJoinPool` object using the default constructor:

```
ForkJoinPool pool=new ForkJoinPool();
```

14. Execute the task in the pool using the `execute()` method:

```
pool.execute(task);
```

15. Shut down the `ForkJoinPool` class using the `shutdown()` method:

```
pool.shutdown();
```

16. Wait for the finalization of the task using the `awaitTermination()` method. As you want to wait for the finalization of the task however long it takes to complete, pass the values 1 and `TimeUnit.DAYS` as parameters to this method:

```
try {
    pool.awaitTermination(1, TimeUnit.DAYS);
} catch (InterruptedException e) {
    e.printStackTrace();
}
```

17. Check if the task, or one of its subtasks, has thrown an exception using the `isCompletedAbnormally()` method. In such a case, write a message to the console with the exception that was thrown. Get that exception with the `getException()` method of the `ForkJoinTask` class:

```
if (task.isCompletedAbnormally()) {
    System.out.printf("Main: An exception has ocurred\n");
    System.out.printf("Main: %s\n",task.getException());
}
System.out.printf("Main: Result: %d",task.join());
```

How it works...

The `Task` class you implemented in this recipe processes an array of numbers. It checks if the block of numbers it has to process has 10 or more elements. In that case, it splits the block in two and creates two new `Task` objects to process those blocks. Otherwise, it looks for the element in the fourth position of the array (index number three). If that element is in the block the task has to process, it throws `RuntimeException`.

When you execute the program, the exception is thrown, but the program doesn't stop. In the `Main` class you have included a call to the `isCompletedAbnormally()` method of the `ForkJoinTask` class using the original task. This method returns `true` if that task, or one of its subtasks, has thrown an exception. You also used the `getException()` method of the same object to get the `Exception` object that it has thrown.

When you throw an unchecked exception in a task, it also affects its parent task (the task that sent it to the `ForkJoinPool` class) and the parent task of its parent task, and so on. If you revise the entire output of the program, you'll see that there aren't output messages for the finalization of some tasks. The starting messages of those tasks are as follows:

```
Task: Starting form 0 to 100
Task: Starting form 0 to 50
Task: Starting form 0 to 25
Task: Starting form 0 to 12
Task: Starting form 0 to 6
```

These tasks are the ones that threw the exception and its parent tasks. All of them have finished abnormally. Take this into account when you develop a program with the `ForkJoinPool` and `ForkJoinTask` objects that can throw exceptions if you don't want this behavior.

The following screenshot shows part of an execution of this example:

There's more...

In this example, you used the `join()` method to wait for the finalization of tasks and get their results. You can also use one of the following two versions of the `get()` method with this purpose:

- `get()`: This version of the `get()` method returns the value returned by the `compute()` method if `ForkJoinTask` has finished its execution, or it waits until its finalization.
- `get(long timeout, TimeUnit unit)`: This version of the `get()` method, if the result of the task isn't available, waits the specified time for it. If the specified period of time passes and the result isn't yet available, the method returns a `null` value. The `TimeUnit` class is an enumeration with the following constants: DAYS, HOURS, MICROSECONDS, MILLISECONDS, MINUTES, NANOSECONDS, and SECONDS.

There are two main differences between the `get()` and `join()` methods:

- The `join()` method can't be interrupted. If you interrupt the thread that called the `join()` method, the method throws `InterruptedException`.
- While the `get()` method will return `ExecutionException` if the tasks throw any unchecked exception, the `join()` method will return `RuntimeException`.

You can obtain the same result obtained in the example if, instead of throwing an exception, you use the `completeExceptionally()` method of the `ForkJoinTask` class. The code would be as follows:

```
Exception e=new Exception("This task throws an Exception: "+
                        "Task from  "+start+" to "+end);
completeExceptionally(e);
```

See also

- The *Creating a fork/join pool* recipe in this chapter

Canceling a task

When you execute the `ForkJoinTask` objects in a `ForkJoinPool` class, you can cancel them before they start their execution. The `ForkJoinTask` class provides the `cancel()` method for this purpose. There are some points you have to take into account when you want to cancel a task, which are as follows:

- The `ForkJoinPool` class doesn't provide any method to cancel all the tasks it has running or waiting in the pool
- When you cancel a task, you don't cancel the tasks this task has executed

In this recipe, you will implement an example of the cancellation of `ForkJoinTask` objects. You will look for the position of a number in an array. The first task that finds the number will cancel the remaining tasks. As that functionality is not provided by the fork/join framework, you will implement an auxiliary class to do this cancellation.

Getting ready...

The example of this recipe has been implemented using the Eclipse IDE. If you use Eclipse or other IDE such as NetBeans, open it and create a new Java project.

How to do it...

Follow these steps to implement the example:

1. Create a class named `ArrayGenerator`. This class will generate an array of random integer numbers with the specified size. Implement a method named `generateArray()`. It will generate the array of numbers. It receives the size of the array as a parameter:

```java
public class ArrayGenerator {
  public int[] generateArray(int size) {
    int array[]=new int[size];
    Random random=new Random();
    for (int i=0; i<size; i++){
      array[i]=random.nextInt(10);
    }
    return array;
  }
}
```

2. Create a class named `TaskManager`. We will use this class to store all the tasks executed in `ForkJoinPool` used in the example. Due to the limitations of the `ForkJoinPool` and `ForkJoinTask` classes, you will use this class to cancel all the tasks of the `ForkJoinPool` class:

```
public class TaskManager {
```

3. Declare a list of objects parameterized with the `ForkJoinTask` class, parameterized with the `Integer` class named `List`:

```
private final ConcurrentLinkedDeque<SearchNumberTask> tasks;
```

4. Implement the constructor of the class. It initializes the list of tasks:

```
public TaskManager(){
   tasks=new ConcurrentLinkedDeque<>();
}
```

5. Implement the `addTask()` method. It adds a `ForkJoinTask` object to the lists of tasks:

```
public void addTask(ForkJoinTask<Integer> task){
   tasks.add(task);
}
```

6. Implement the `cancelTasks()` method. It will cancel all the `ForkJoinTask` objects stored in the list using the `cancel()` method. It receives as a parameter the `ForkJoinTask` object that wants to cancel the rest of the tasks. The method cancels all the tasks:

```
public void cancelTasks(SearchNumberTask cancelTask){
   for (SearchNumberTask task   :tasks) {
     if (task!=cancelTask) {
       task.cancel(true);
       task.logCancelMessage();
     }
   }
}
```

7. Implement the `SearchNumberTask` class. Specify that it extends the `RecursiveTask` class parameterized with the `Integer` class. This class will look for a number in a block of elements of an integer array:

```
public class SearchNumberTask extends RecursiveTask<Integer> {
```

8. Declare a private array of `int` numbers named `numbers`:

```
private int numbers[];
```

9. Declare two private `int` attributes named `start` and `end`. These attributes will determine the elements of the array this task has to process:

```
private int start, end;
```

10. Declare a private `int` attribute named `number` to store the number you are going to look for:

```
private int number;
```

11. Declare a private `TaskManager` attribute named `manager`. You will use this object to cancel all the tasks:

```
private TaskManager manager;
```

12. Declare a private `int` constant and initialize it to −1. It will be the returned value by the task when it doesn't find the number:

```
private final static int NOT_FOUND=-1;
```

13. Implement the constructor of the class to initialize its attributes:

```
public SearchNumberTask(int numbers[], int start, int end,
                        int number, TaskManager manager){
  this.numbers=numbers;
  this.start=start;
  this.end=end;
  this.number=number;
  this.manager=manager;
}
```

14. Implement the `compute()` method. Start the method by writing a message to the console indicating the values of the `start` and `end` attributes:

```
@Override
protected Integer compute() {
  System.out.println("Task: "+start+":"+end);
```

15. If the difference between the `start` and `end` attributes is greater than `10` (the task has to process more than `10` elements of the array), call the `launchTasks()` method to divide the work of this task into two subtasks:

```
int ret;
if (end-start>10) {
   ret=launchTasks();
```

16. Otherwise, look for the number in the block of the array that the task calling the `lookForNumber()` method has to process:

```
} else {
   ret=lookForNumber();
}
```

17. Return the result of the task:

```
return ret;
```

18. Implement the `lookForNumber()` method:

```
private int lookForNumber() {
```

19. For all the elements in the block of elements this task has to process, compare the value stored in that element with the number you are looking for. If they are equal, write a message to the console indicating, in such a circumstance, to use the `cancelTasks()` method of the `TaskManager` object to cancel all the tasks, and return the position of the element where you found the number:

```
for (int i=start; i<end; i++){
   if (numbers[i]==number) {
      System.out.printf("Task: Number %d found in position %d\n",
                        number,i);
      manager.cancelTasks(this);
      return i;
   }
```

20. Inside the loop, put the task to sleep for one second:

```
try {
   TimeUnit.SECONDS.sleep(1);
} catch (InterruptedException e) {
   e.printStackTrace();
}
}
```

21. Finally, return the −1 value:

```
    return NOT_FOUND;
}
```

22. Implement the `launchTasks()` method. First, divide the block of numbers this task has to process into two, and then create two `Task` objects to process them:

```
private int launchTasks() {
    int mid=(start+end)/2;

    Task task1=new Task(numbers,start,mid,number,manager);
    Task task2=new Task(numbers,mid,end,number,manager);
```

23. Add the tasks to the `TaskManager` object:

```
manager.addTask(task1);
manager.addTask(task2);
```

24. Execute the two tasks asynchronously using the `fork()` method:

```
task1.fork();
task2.fork();
```

25. Wait for the finalization of the tasks, and return the result of the first task if it is not equal to −1 or the result of the second task, otherwise:

```
int returnValue;
returnValue=task1.join();
if (returnValue!=-1) {
    return returnValue;
}

returnValue=task2.join();
return returnValue;
```

26. Implement the `writeCancelMessage()` method to write a message when the task is canceled:

```
public void logCancelMessage(){
    System.out.printf("Task: Canceled task from %d to %d",
                        start,end);
}
```

27. Implement the main class of the example by creating a class named `Main` with a `main()` method:

```
public class Main {
    public static void main(String[] args) {
```

28. Create an array of `1000` numbers using the `ArrayGenerator` class:

```
ArrayGenerator generator=new ArrayGenerator();
int array[]=generator.generateArray(1000);
```

29. Create a `TaskManager` object:

```
TaskManager manager=new TaskManager();
```

30. Create a `ForkJoinPool` object using the default constructor:

```
ForkJoinPool pool=new ForkJoinPool();
```

31. Create a `Task` object to process the array generated before:

```
SearchNumberTask task=new SearchNumberTask (array,0,1000,
                                            5,manager);
```

32. Execute the task in the pool asynchronously using the `execute()` method:

```
pool.execute(task);
```

33. Shut down the pool using the `shutdown()` method:

```
pool.shutdown();
```

34. Wait for the finalization of the tasks using the `awaitTermination()` method of the `ForkJoinPool` class:

```
try {
    pool.awaitTermination(1, TimeUnit.DAYS);
} catch (InterruptedException e) {
    e.printStackTrace();
}
```

35. Write a message to the console indicating the end of the program:

```
System.out.printf("Main: The program has finished\n");
```

How it works...

The `ForkJoinTask` class provides the `cancel()` method that allows you to cancel a task if it hasn't been executed yet. This is a very important point. If the task has begun its execution, a call to the `cancel()` method has no effect. The method receives a parameter as a `Boolean` value called `mayInterruptIfRunning`. This name may make you think that, if you pass the true value to the method, the task will be canceled even if it is running. The Java API documentation specifies that, in the default implementation of the `ForkJoinTask` class, this attribute has no effect. The tasks are only canceled if they haven't started their execution. The cancellation of a task has no effect over the tasks that the cancelled task sent to the pool. They continue with their execution.

A limitation of the fork/join framework is that it doesn't allow the cancellation of all the tasks that are in `ForkJoinPool`. To overcome that limitation, you implemented the `TaskManager` class. It stores all the tasks that have been sent to the pool. It has a method that cancels all the tasks it has stored. If a task can't be canceled because it's running or has finished, the `cancel()` method returns the `false` value, so you can try to cancel all the tasks without being afraid of the possible collateral effects.

In the example, you have implemented a task that looks for a number in an array of numbers. You divided the problem into smaller subproblems as the fork/join framework recommends. You are only interested in one occurrence of the number, so when you find it, you cancel the other tasks.

The following screenshot shows part of an execution of this example:

```
Problems  Javadoc  Declaration  Search  Console    
<terminated> Main (37) [Java Application] C:\Program Files\Java\jdk-9\b
Task: 7:15
Task: 187:194
Task: 257:265
Task: Number 5 found in position 128
Task: Cancelled task from 0 to 500
Task: Cancelled task from 500 to 1000
Task: Cancelled task from 0 to 250
Task: Cancelled task from 250 to 500
Task: Cancelled task from 0 to 125
Task: Cancelled task from 125 to 250
Task: Cancelled task from 0 to 62
Task: Cancelled task from 62 to 125
Task: Cancelled task from 250 to 375
Task: Cancelled task from 375 to 500
Task: Cancelled task from 125 to 187
```

See also

- The *Creating a fork/join pool* recipe in this chapter

6
Parallel and Reactive Streams

In this chapter, we will cover the following recipes:

- Creating streams from different sources
- Reducing the elements of a stream
- Collecting the elements of a stream
- Applying an action to every element of a stream
- Filtering the elements of a stream
- Transforming the elements of a stream
- Sorting the elements of a stream
- Verifying conditions in the elements of a stream
- Reactive programming with reactive streams

Introduction

A **stream** in Java is a sequence of elements that can be processed (mapped, filtered, transformed, reduced, and collected) in a pipeline of declarative operations using **lambda expressions** in a sequential or parallel way. It was introduced in Java 8 and was one of the most significant new features of that version, together with lambda expressions. They have changed the way you can process big sets of elements in Java, optimizing the way the language processes those elements.

Streams have introduced the `Stream`, `DoubleStream`, `IntStream` and `LongStream` interfaces, some utility classes such as `Collectors` or `StreamSupport`, some functional-like interfaces such as `Collector`, and a lot of methods in different classes such as the `stream()` or `parallelStream()` methods in the `Collection` interface or the `lines()` method in the `Files` class.

Through the recipes of this chapter, you will learn how to effectively use streams in your application, but before that let's see the most important characteristics of streams:

- A stream is a sequence of data, not a data structure. Elements of data are processed by the stream but not stored in it.
- You can create streams from different sources, such as collections (lists, arrays and so on), files, and strings, or by creating a class that provides the elements of the stream.
- You can't access an individual element of the streams. You define the source of the stream and the operations you want to apply to its elements. Stream operations are defined in a functional way, and you can use lambda expressions in intermediate and terminal operations to define the actions you want to execute.
- You can't modify the source of the stream. If, for example, you filter some elements of the stream, you are skipping the elements on the stream and not in its source.
- Streams define two kinds of operations:

  - **Intermediate operations**: These operations always produce a new stream with their results. They can be used to transform, filter, and sort the elements of the stream.
  - **Terminal operations**: These operations process all the elements of the stream to generate a result or a side-effect. After their execution, the stream can't be used again.

- A stream pipeline is formed by zero or more intermediate operations and a final operation.
- Intermediate operations can be as follows:

  - **Stateless**: Processing an element of the stream is independent of the other elements. For example, filtering an element based on a condition.
  - **Stateful**: Processing an element of the stream depends on the other elements of the stream. For example, sorting the elements of the stream.

- **Laziness**: Intermediate operations are lazy. They're not executed until the terminal operation begins its execution. Java can avoid the execution of an intermediate operation over an element or a set of elements of the stream if it detects that it doesn't affect the final result of the operation.
- `Stream` can have an infinite number of elements. There are operations such as `limit()` or `findFirst()` that can be used to limit the elements used in the final computation. As the intermediate operations are lazy, an unbounded stream can finish its execution in a finite time.
- Streams can only be used once. As we mentioned before, when the terminal operation of a stream is executed, the stream is considered consumed, and it can't be used again. If you need to process the same data again to generate different results, you have to create a new `Stream` object from the same source. If you try to use a consumed stream, you will get an exception.
- You can process the elements of a stream sequentially or in a parallel way without any extra effort. You can specify the mode of execution of a stream more than once, but only the last time will be taken into account. You have to be careful with the selected mode. Stateful intermediate operations won't use all the possibilities of concurrency.

Java 9 has included a new kind of streams-the reactive streams-that allow you to communicate information to producers and consumers in an asynchronous way. This chapter presents nine recipes that will teach you how to create streams and use all their intermediate and terminal operations to process big collections of data in a parallel and functional way.

Creating streams from different sources

In this recipe, you will learn how to create streams from different sources. You have different options, as the following:

- The `parallelStream()` method of the `Collection` interface
- The `Supplier` interface
- A predefined set of elements
- `File` and a directory
- An array
- A random number generator
- The concatenation of two different streams

You can create a Stream object from other sources (that will be described in the *There's more* section), but we think that these are the more useful.

Getting ready

The example of this recipe has been implemented using the Eclipse IDE. If you use Eclipse or other IDE such as NetBeans, open it and create a new Java project.

How to do it...

In this recipe we'll implement an example where you will learn how to create streams from the sources described earlier. Follow these steps to implement the example:

1. First, we'll implement some auxiliary classes that we will use in the example. Create a class named Person with six attributes of different types: String, int, double and Date:

   ```java
   public class Person implements Comparable<Person> {

       private int id;
       private String firstName;
       private String lastName;
       private Date birthDate;
       private int salary;
       private double coeficient;
   ```

2. Create the methods to set and get the values of these attributes. Implement the comparteTo() method to compare two Person objects. Let's consider that two persons are the same it they have the same firstName and the same lastName

   ```java
   public int compareTo(Person otherPerson) {
      int compareLastNames = this.getLastName().compareTo
                               (otherPerson.getLastName());
      if (compareLastNames != 0) {
        return compareLastNames;
      } else {
      return this.getFirstName().compareTo
                               (otherPerson.getFirstName());

     }
   }
   ```

3. Then, create a class named `PersonGenerator` to create a random list of `Person` objects. Implement a static method named `generatePersonList()` in this class, which receives the number of persons you want to generate and returns a `List<Person>` object with the number of persons. Here, we include a version of this method, but feel free to change it:

```
public class PersonGenerator {

    public static List<Person> generatePersonList (int size) {
        List<Person> ret = new ArrayList<>();

        String firstNames[] = {"Mary","Patricia","Linda",
                               "Barbara","Elizabeth","James",
                               "John","Robert","Michael",
                               "William"};
        String lastNames[] = {"Smith","Jones","Taylor",
                              "Williams","Brown","Davies",
                              "Evans","Wilson","Thomas",
                              "Roberts"};

        Random randomGenerator=new Random();
        for (int i=0; i<size; i++) {
            Person person=new Person();
            person.setId(i);
            person.setFirstName(firstNames[randomGenerator
                                    .nextInt(10)]);
            person.setLastName(lastNames[randomGenerator
                                    .nextInt(10)]);
            person.setSalary(randomGenerator.nextInt(100000));
            person.setCoeficient(randomGenerator.nextDouble()*10);
            Calendar calendar=Calendar.getInstance();
            calendar.add(Calendar.YEAR, -randomGenerator
                                    .nextInt(30));
            Date birthDate=calendar.getTime();
            person.setBirthDate(birthDate);
            ret.add(person);
        }
        return ret;
    }
```

4. Now, create a class named `MySupplier` and specify that it implements the `Supplier` interface parameterized with the `String` class:

```
public class MySupplier implements Supplier<String> {
```

5. Declare a private `AtomicInteger` attribute named `counter` and initialize it in the constructor of the class:

```
private final AtomicInteger counter;
public MySupplier() {
  counter=new AtomicInteger(0);
}
```

6. Implement the `get()` method defined in the `Supplier` interface. This method will return the next element of the stream:

```
@Override
public String get() {
  int value=counter.getAndAdd(1);
  return "String "+value;
}
}
```

7. Now, create a class named `Main` and implement the `main()` method in it:

```
public class Main {
  public static void main(String[] args) {
```

8. First, we'll create a `Stream` object from a list of elements. Create the `PersonGenerator` class to create a list of 10,000 `Person` objects, and use the `parallelStream()` method of the `List` object to create the `Stream`. Then, use the `count()` method of the `Stream` object to get the number of elements of the `Stream`:

```
System.out.printf("From a Collection:\n");
List<Person> persons=PersonGenerator.generatePersonList(10000);
Stream<Person> personStream=persons.parallelStream();
System.out.printf("Number of persons: %d\n",
                personStream.count());
```

9. Then, we'll create a `Stream` from a generator. Create an object of the `MySupplier` class. Then, use the static method `generate()` of the `Stream` class, passing the created object as a parameter to create the stream. Finally, use the `parallel()` method to convert the stream created to a parallel stream, the `limit()` method to get the first ten elements of the stream, and the `forEach()` method to print the elements of the stream:

```
System.out.printf("From a Supplier:\n");
Supplier<String> supplier=new MySupplier();
Stream<String> generatorStream=Stream.generate(supplier);
generatorStream.parallel().limit(10).forEach(s->
                                   System.out.printf("%s\n",s));
```

10. Then, we'll create a stream from a predefined list of elements. Use the static `of()` method of the `Stream` class to create the `Stream`. This method receives a variable list of parameters. In this case, we'll pass three `String` objects. Then, use the `parallel()` method of the stream to convert it to a parallel one and the `forEach()` method to print the values in the console:

```
System.out.printf("From a predefined set of elements:\n");
Stream<String> elementsStream=Stream.of("Peter","John","Mary");
elementsStream.parallel().forEach(element ->
                          System.out.printf("%s\n", element));
```

11. Now, we'll create a stream to read the lines of a file. First, create a `BufferedReader` object to read the file you want to read. Then, use the `lines()` method of the `BufferedReader` class to get a stream of `String` objects. Each element of this stream will be a line from the file. Finally, use the `parallel()` method to get a parallel version of the stream and the `count()` method to get the number of elements of the `Stream`. We also have to close the `BufferedReader` object:

```
System.out.printf("From a File:\n");
try (BufferedReader br = new BufferedReader(new
                    FileReader("data\\nursery.data"));) {
  Stream<String> fileLines = br.lines();
  System.out.printf("Number of lines in the file: %d\n\n",
                 fileLines.parallel().count());
  System.out.printf("********************************
                    ***********************\n");
  System.out.printf("\n");
  br.close();
} catch (FileNotFoundException e) {
  e.printStackTrace();
} catch (IOException e) {
  e.printStackTrace();
}
```

12. Now, we'll create a `Stream` to process the contents of a folder. First, use the `list()` method of the `Files` class to get a stream of `Path` objects with the contents of the folder. Then, use the `parallel()` method of the `Stream` object to convert it to a parallel stream and the `count()` method to count its elements. Finally, in this case, we have to use the `close()` method to close the Stream:

```
System.out.printf("From a Directory:\n");
try {
  Stream<Path> directoryContent = Files.list(Paths.get
                              (System.getProperty("user.home")));
  System.out.printf("Number of elements (files and
                folders):%d\n\n",
                    directoryContent.parallel().count());
  directoryContent.close();
  System.out.printf("********************************
              ***********************\n");
  System.out.printf("\n");
} catch (IOException e) {
  e.printStackTrace();
}
```

13. The next source we'll use is an `Array`. First, create an `Array` of strings. Then, use the `stream()` method of the `Arrays` class to create a stream from the elements of the array. Finally, use the `parallel()` method to convert the stream into a parallel one and the `forEach()` method to print the elements of the stream to the console:

```
System.out.printf("From an Array:\n");
String array[]={"1","2","3","4","5"};
Stream<String> streamFromArray=Arrays.stream(array);
streamFromArray.parallel().forEach(s->System.out.printf("%s : ",
                                          s));
```

14. Now, we'll create a stream of random double numbers. First, create a `Random` object. Then, use the `doubles()` method to create a `DoubleStream` object. We'll pass the number `10` as a parameter to that method, so the stream we're going to create will have ten elements. Finally, use the `parallel()` method to convert the stream into a parallel one, the `peek()` method to write each element to the console, the `average()` method to calculate the average of the values of the stream, and the `getAsDouble()` method to get the value stored in the `Optional` object returned by the `average()` method:

```
Random random = new Random();
DoubleStream doubleStream = random.doubles(10);
double doubleStreamAverage = doubleStream.parallel().peek
                            (d -> System.out.printf("%f :",d))
                            .average().getAsDouble();
```

15. Finally, we'll create a stream concatenating two streams. First, we create two
    streams of `String` objects using the `of()` method of the `Stream` class. Then, we
    use the `concat()` method of the `Stream` class to concatenate those streams into a
    unique one. Finally, we use the `parallel()` method of the `Stream` class to
    convert the stream into a parallel one and the `forEach()` method to write all the
    elements to the console:

```
System.out.printf("Concatenating streams:\n");
Stream<String> stream1 = Stream.of("1", "2", "3", "4");
Stream<String> stream2 = Stream.of("5", "6", "7", "8");
Stream<String> finalStream = Stream.concat(stream1, stream2);
finalStream.parallel().forEach(s -> System.out.printf("%s : ",
                                                        s));
```

How it works...

Let's see in detail all the methods we used in this example to create streams:

- First, we used the `parallelStream()` method of the `List` class. In fact, this
  method is defined in the `Collection` interface, so all the classes that implement
  this interface, such as the `ArrayList`, `LinkedList`, or `TreeSet` classes
  implement that method. You can use the `stream()` method to create a sequential
  stream or the `parallelStream()` method to create a parallel one.

- Then, we used an implementation of the `Supplier` interface: the `MySupplier`
  class. The interface provides the `get()` method. This method is called each time
  the stream needs an element to process. You can create a stream with an infinite
  number of elements, so you should use a method that limits the number of
  elements of the stream, such as the `limit()` method.

- Then, we used the `of()` method of the `Stream` class. This is a static method that
  receives a variable number of parameters and returns a `Stream` with those
  parameters as elements.

- Then, we used the `lines()` method of the `BufferedStream` class. This method returns a stream where each element is a line read from the `BufferedStream`. We used this method to read all the lines of a file, but you can use it with other kinds of `BufferedReader`.

- Then, we used the `list()` method of the `Files` class. This method receives a `Path` object representing a folder of your system and returns a `Stream` of `Path` objects with the elements into that folder. You have to take into account that this method is not recursive, so if the folder has one or more subfolders, it doesn't process their content. As you will see later in the *There's more* section, the `Files` class has other methods to work with streams.

- Then, we used the `stream()` method of the `Arrays` class that receives an array and returns a `Stream` with the elements of the array. If the array is of the `double`, `int`, or `long` types, it returns a `DoubleStream`, `IntStream`, or `LongStream` object. These are special kinds of streams that allow you to work with such number types.

- Then, we generated a stream with random numbers. We used the `doubles()` method of the `Random` class. We passed to it the size of the `Stream` we wanted to obtain, but you can also pass to it the minimum and maximum numbers you want to obtain.

- Finally, we used the `concat()` method of the `Stream` class that takes two streams and returns one with the elements of both.

We also used some methods of the `Stream` class. Most of them will be described later in more detail, but here we provide a basic introduction to them:

- `count()`: This method returns the number of elements in the `Stream`. It's a terminal operation and returns a `long` number.

- `limit()`: This method receives a number as a parameter. If the stream has fewer elements than the number, it returns a stream with all the elements. Otherwise, it returns a stream with the number of elements specified in the parameter. It's an intermediate operation.

- `forEach()`: This method allows you to specify an action that will be applied to each of the elements of the `Stream`. We used this terminal operation to write some information to the console. We have used a lambda expression with this purpose.

- `peek()`: This method is an intermediate operation that allows you to perform an action over each of the elements of the stream and returns a stream with the same elements. This method is usually used as a debugging tool. Take into account that, like all intermediate operations, this is a lazy operation, so it will only be executed over those elements that are requested by the terminal operation.
- `average()`: This is a method that is declared in the `IntStream`, `DoubleStream`, and `LongStream` streams. It returns an `OptionalDouble` value. The `OptionalDouble` class represents a double number that can have a value or not. It won't generate a value for an empty `Stream`.
- `parallel()`: This method converts a sequential `Stream` into a parallel one. Most of the streams created in this example are sequential, but we can convert them into parallel ones using this method of the `Stream` class.

There's more...

The Java API includes other methods to create `Stream` objects. In this section, we enumerate some of them:

- The `Files` class provides more methods that create streams:
    - `find()`: This method returns the files contained in a folder, or in any of its subfolders, which meet the criteria specified in a lambda expression.
    - `walk()`: This method returns a stream of `Path` objects with the contents of a folder and all its subfolders.
- The `Stream` class also includes other static methods that allow you to create streams:
    - `iterate()`: This method produces a stream whose elements are generated by the application of a unary function to an initial element. The first element of the stream is the initial element, the second element, the result of applying the function to the initial element, the third, the result of applying the function to the second element, and so on.
- Finally, the `String` class has the `chars()` method. This method returns an `IntStream` with the values of the characters that forms the `String`.

See also

Now that you have created a stream, you have to process its elements. All the recipes in this chapter give you information about how to go about processing the elements of a stream.

Reducing the elements of a stream

MapReduce is a programming model used to process very large datasets in distributed environments using a lot of machines working in a cluster. This programming model has the following two operations:

- **Map**: This operation filters and transforms the original elements into a form more suitable to the reduction operation
- **Reduce**: This operation generates a summary result from all the elements, for example, the sum or the average of numeric values

This programming model has been commonly used in the functional programming world. In the Java ecosystem, the **Hadoop** project of the **Apache Software Foundation** provides an implementation of this model. The `Stream` class implements two different reduce operations:

- The pure reduce operation, implemented in the different versions of the `reduce()` method that process a stream of elements to obtain a value
- The mutable reduction implemented in the different versions of the `collect()` method that process a stream of elements to generate a mutable data structure, such as `Collection` or a `StringBuilder`.

In this recipe, you will learn how to use the different versions of the `reduce()` method to generate a result from a stream of values. As you may have already imagined, the `reduce()` method is a terminal operation in a `Stream`.

Getting ready

The example of this recipe has been implemented using the Eclipse IDE. If you use Eclipse or other IDE such as NetBeans, open it and create a new Java project.

How to do it...

Follow these steps to implement the example:

1. First, we'll create some auxiliary classes that we will use later in the example. Review the recipe, *Creating streams from different sources*, and include in this example the `Person` and `PersonGenerator` classes used in it.

2. Then, create a class named `DoubleGenerator`. Implement a method named `generateDoubleList()` to generate a list of double numbers. It receives two parameters with the size of the list we'll generate and the highest value in the list. It will generate a list of random double numbers:

```java
public class DoubleGenerator {

    public static List<Double> generateDoubleList(int size,
                                                  int max) {
        Random random=new Random();
        List<Double> numbers=new ArrayList<>();

        for (int i=0; i<size; i++) {
            double value=random.nextDouble()*max;
            numbers.add(value);
        }
        return numbers;
    }
}
```

3. Implement a method named `generateStreamFromList()`. This method receives a `List` of `double` numbers as a parameter and generates a `DoubleStream` stream with the elements of the list. For that purpose, we will use the `DoubleStream.Builder` class to construct the stream:

```java
public static DoubleStream generateStreamFromList(List<Double>
                                                  list) {
    DoubleStream.Builder builder=DoubleStream.builder();

    for (Double number : list) {
        builder.add(number);
    }
    return builder.build();
}
```

4. Create a class named `Point` with two double attributes, x and y, and the methods to get() and set() its value. The code of this class is very simple, so it won't be included.

5. Create a class named `PointGenerator` with a method named `generatePointList()`. This method receives the size of the list you want to generate and returns a list of random `Point` objects:

```
public class PointGenerator {
  public static List<Point> generatePointList (int size) {

    List<Point> ret = new ArrayList<>();
    Random randomGenerator=new Random();
    for (int i=0; i<size; i++) {
      Point point=new Point();
      point.setX(randomGenerator.nextDouble());
      point.setY(randomGenerator.nextDouble());
      ret.add(point);
    }
    return ret;
  }
}
```

6. Now create the `Main` class with the `main()` method. First, we'll generate a `List` of 10,000 double numbers using the `DoubleGenerator` class:

```
public class Main {
  public static void main (String args[]) {

    List<Double> numbers = DoubleGenerator.generateDoubleList
                                           (10000, 1000);
```

7. The `Stream` class and the specialized `DoubleStream`, `IntStream`, and `LongStream` classes implement some methods that are specialized reduce operations. In this case, we'll generate a `DoubleStream` using the `DoubleGenerator` class and use `count()`, `sum()`, `average()`, `max()` and `min()` to obtain the number of elements, the sum of all the elements, the average of all the elements, the maximum number in the stream, and the minimum number in the stream. As we can only process the elements of a stream once, we have to create a new stream per operation. Take into account that these methods are only present in the `DoubleStream`, `IntStream`, and `LongStream` classes. The `Stream` class only has the `count()` method. Some of these methods return an optional object. Take into account this object could not have any value, so you should check before obtaining the value:

```
DoubleStream doubleStream = DoubleGenerator
                                .generateStreamFromList(numbers);
long numberOfElements = doubleStream.parallel().count();
System.out.printf("The list of numbers has %d elements.\n",
                numberOfElements);

doubleStream = DoubleGenerator.generateStreamFromList(numbers);
double sum = doubleStream.parallel().sum();
System.out.printf("Its numbers sum %f.\n", sum);

doubleStream = DoubleGenerator.generateStreamFromList(numbers);
double average = doubleStream.parallel().average()
                                    .getAsDouble();
System.out.printf("Its numbers have an average value of %f.\n",
                average);

doubleStream = DoubleGenerator.generateStreamFromList(numbers);
double max = doubleStream.parallel().max().getAsDouble();
System.out.printf("The maximum value in the list is %f.\n",
                max);

doubleStream = DoubleGenerator.generateStreamFromList(numbers);
double min = doubleStream.parallel().min().getAsDouble();
System.out.printf("The minimum value in the list is %f.\n",
                min);
```

8. Then, we'll use the first version of the `reduce()` method. This method receives as parameter an associative `BinaryOperator` that receives two objects of the same type and returns an object of that type. When the operation has processed all the elements of the `Stream`, it returns an `Optional` object parameterized with the same type. For example, we'll use this version to calculate the sum of both the coordinates of a random list of `Point` objects:

```
List<Point> points=PointGenerator.generatePointList(10000);
Optional<Point> point=points.parallelStream().reduce((p1,p2) -> {
  Point p=new Point();
  p.setX(p1.getX()+p2.getX());
  p.setY(p1.getY()+p2.getY());
  return p;
});
System.out.println(point.get().getX()+":"+point.get().getY());
```

9. Then, we'll use the second version of the `reduce()` method. It's similar to the previous one, but in this case, in addition to the associative `BinaryOperator` object, it receives the identity value for that operator (for example `0` for a sum or `1` for a product) and returns an element of the type we're working with. If the stream has no values, the identity value will be returned. In this case, we use this version of the `reduce()` method to calculate the total amount of money we need to spend in salaries. We use the `map()` method to convert each `Person` object in an `int` value (its salary) so our `Stream` object will have `int` values when it executes the `reduce()` method. You will get more information about the `map()` method in the *Transforming the elements of a stream* recipe:

```
System.out.printf("Reduce, second version\n");
List<Person> persons = PersonGenerator.generatePersonList
                                                      (10000);
long totalSalary=persons.parallelStream().map
                 (p -> p.getSalary()).reduce(0, (s1,s2) -> s1+s2);
System.out.printf("Total salary: %d\n",totalSalary);
```

10. Finally, we'll use the third version of the `reduce()` method. This version is used when the type of result of the reduce operation is different from the type of stream elements. We have to provide the identity value of the return type, an accumulator that implements the `BiFunction` interfaces and will receive an object of the return type, an element of the stream to generate a value of the return type, and a combiner function that implements the `BinaryOperator` interface and receives two objects of the return type to generate an object of that type. In this case, we have used this version of the method to calculate the number of persons with a salary higher than 50,000 in a list of random persons:

```
Integer value=0;
value=persons.parallelStream().reduce(value, (n,p) -> {
    if (p.getSalary() > 50000) {
       return n+1;
    } else {
       return n;
    }
}, (n1,n2) -> n1+n2);
System.out.printf("The number of people with a salary bigger
                   that 50,000 is %d\n",value);
```

How it works...

In this example, you learned how to use the different reduce operations provided by Java streams. First, we used some specialized reduce operations provided by the DoubleStream, IntStream and LongStream classes. These operations allow you to count the number of elements of the stream, calculate the sum of all the elements of the stream, calculate the average value of the elements of the stream, and calculate the highest and lowest value of the elements of the stream. If you work with a generic Stream, you will only have the count() method to count the elements of the stream.

Then we used the three versions of the reduce() method provided by the Stream class. The first one receives only one parameter, a BinaryOperator. We specified that operator as a lambda expression and you will normally do that, but you can also use an object of a class that implements the BinaryOperator interface. That operator will receive two elements of the stream and will have to generate a new element of the same type. For example, we receive two Point objects and generate a new Point object. The operation implemented by that BinaryOperator has to be associative, that is to say, the following expression must be true:

(a op b) op c = a op (b op c)

Here op is our BinaryOperator.

This version of the reduce() method returns an Optional object; Optional because if the stream has no elements, there won't be a result value to return and the Optional object will be empty.

The second version of the reduce() method receives an *identity* value and a BinaryOperator. The BinaryOperator has to be associative as in the other version of the reduce() method. For the *identity* value, it has to be a true expression:

identity op a = a op identity = a

In this case, the reduce() method returns an element of the same type of elements of the stream. If the stream has no elements, the identity value will be returned.

The last version of the reduce() method is used when we want to return a value of a type different from the elements of the stream. In this case, the method has three parameters, an *identity* value, an *accumulator* operator, and a *combiner* operator. The *accumulator* operator receives a value of the return type and an element of the stream and generates a new object of the return type.

The *combiner* function receives two objects of the return type to calculate a new object of the return type. The *identity* value is the *identity* value of the return type, and it has to verify the following expression:

combiner (u, accumulator(identity, t)) == accumulator(u, t)

Here, *u* is an object of the return type and *t* an element of the stream.

The following screenshot shows the output of an execution of the example:

```
<terminated> Main (20) [Java Application] C:\Program Files\Java\jdk-9\bin\javaw.exe
**********************************************************
Main: Examples of reduce methods.
Main: Creating a list of double numbers.
**********************************************************

**********************************************************
The list of numbers has 10000 elements.
**********************************************************

**********************************************************
Its numbers sum 4959788,847481.
**********************************************************

**********************************************************
Its numbers have an average value of 495,978885.
**********************************************************

**********************************************************
The maximum value in the list is 999,803291.
**********************************************************

**********************************************************
The minimum value in the list is 0,000832.
**********************************************************

**********************************************************
Reduce - First Version
5012.111966489925:4965.503439268661
**********************************************************

**********************************************************
Reduce, second version
Total salary: 497495920
**********************************************************

**********************************************************
Reduce, third version
The number of people with a salary bigger that 50,000 is 4944
**********************************************************
```

There's more...

We have implemented all the parameters of the `reduce()` method as lambda expressions. The first two versions of the `reduce()` method receive a `BinaryOperator` and the third version receives a `BiFunction` and a `BinaryOperator`. If you want to reuse a complex operator, you can implement a class that implements the necessary interface and use an object of that class as the parameter to these and to the other methods of the `Stream` class.

See also

- The *Creating streams from different sources* recipe in this chapter

Collecting the elements of a stream

Java streams allow you to process a sequence of elements in a sequential or parallel way. You can create a stream from different data sources, as a `Collection`, a `File` or an `Array` and apply to its elements a sequence of operations normally defined with lambda expressions. Those operations can be divided into two different classes:

- **Intermediate operations**: These operations return other `Stream` as a result and allow you to filter, transform, or sort the elements of the stream
- **Terminal operations**: These operations return a result after processing the elements of the stream

A stream has a source, zero or more intermediate operations, and a terminal operation. The two most important terminal operations are:

- The reduce operation, which allows you to obtain a unique result after processing the elements of the stream. This result usually is a summary of the processed data. The *Reducing the elements of a stream* recipe explains you how to use reduce operations in Java.
- The collect operation that allows you to generate a data structure with the results of processing the elements of the stream. This is also called a mutable reduction operation as the result is a mutable data structure.

In this recipe, we will learn how to execute collect operations in Java streams with the different versions of the `collect()` method and the auxiliary `Collectors` class.

Getting ready

The example of this recipe has been implemented using the Eclipse IDE. If you use Eclipse or other IDE such as NetBeans, open it and create a new Java project.

How to do it...

Follow these steps to implement the example:

1. First, let's implement some auxiliary classes we will use in the example. Implement the `Person` class to store some basic data about a person and the `PersonGenerator` class to generate a random list of persons. You can check the *Creating streams from different sources* recipe to see the source code of both the classes.

2. In that class, override the `toString()` method with the following code, which returns the first name and the last name of the person:

```java
@Override
public String toString() {
    return firstName + " " + lastName;
}
```

3. Then, create a class named `Counter` with two attributes: a `String` attribute named `value` and an `int` attribute named `counter`. Generate the methods to `get()` and `set()` the values of both attributes. The source code of this class is very simple, so it won't be included.

4. Now, create the `Main` class with the `main()` method. Then, create a random `List` of `Person` objects using the `PersonGenerator` class:

```java
public class Main {

    public static void main(String args[]) {
        List<Person> persons = PersonGenerator.generatePersonList
                                                            (100);
```

5. The first collect operation we will implement will generate a `Map` where the keys will be first name of the person and the values will be a list with all the persons with that first name. To implement this, we use the `collect()` method of the `Stream` class and the `Collectors.groupingByConcurrent` collector. Then, we process all the keys (first names) of the map using the `forEach()` method and print in the console the number of persons with that key: As parameter of the `groupingByConcurrent()` method we pass a method reference. We can use this mechanism in a lambda expression if it only calls to an existing method as in this case.

```
Map<String, List<Person>> personsByName = persons
                .parallelStream().collect(Collectors
                .groupingByConcurrent(Person::getFirstName));
personsByName.keySet().forEach(key -> {
  List<Person> listOfPersons = personsByName.get(key);
  System.out.printf("%s: There are %d persons with that name\n",
                  key, listOfPersons.size());
```

6. The second collect operation we will implement will concatenate all the names of all the persons in the stream. To implement this operation, we use the `toString()` method of the `Person` object, the `collect()` method, of the `Stream` class, and the `joining()` method of the `Collectors` class that concatenates all the elements of the stream separated by the specified char sequence:

```
String message = persons.parallelStream().map
          (p -> p.toString()).collect(Collectors.joining(","));
System.out.printf("%s\n", message);
```

7. With the next collect operation we'll implement, we will separate the persons on the stream in two groups. The first one will have the persons with a salary greater than 50,000 and the second one will have the others. The result of the operation will be a `Map` object with a `Boolean` value as the key and a `List` of persons as the value. To implement this, we will use the `collect()` method of the `Stream` class and the `partitionBy()` method of the `Collectors` class that receives as a parameter a `Boolean` expression that allows you two divide the elements of the stream in `true` or `false`. Then we use the `forEach()` method to write the number of elements in the generated lists:

```
Map<Boolean, List<Person>> personsBySalary = persons
                .parallelStream().collect(Collectors
                .partitioningBy(p -> p.getSalary() > 50000));
```

```
personsBySalary.keySet().forEach(key -> {
    List<Person> listOfPersons = personsBySalary.get(key);
    System.out.printf("%s: %d \n", key, listOfPersons.size());
});
```

8. Then, we'll implement a collect operation that will generate another Map. In this case, the keys will be the first name of the persons and the value will be the last names of the people with the same first name concatenated in one String. To implement this behavior, we have use the collect() method of the Stream class and the toConcurrentMap() method of the Collectors class. We pass as parameters to that method a lambda expression to obtain the key, a lambda expression to obtain the value, and a lambda expression to resolve the situations where the key exists in the final Map. Then, we use the forEach() method to process all the keys and write its associated values:

```
ConcurrentMap<String, String> nameMap = persons
               .parallelStream().collect(Collectors
               .toConcurrentMap(p -> p.getFirstName(),
                             p -> p.getLastName(),
                             (s1, s2) -> s1 + ", " + s2));
nameMap.forEach((key, value) -> {
    System.out.printf("%s: %s \n", key, value);
});
```

9. Until now, in all the examples of the collect() method we have implemented, we used the version of that method that receives an implementation of the Collector interface. But there's another version of the collect() method. With this version of the collect() method, we will implement a collect operation that generates a List with the persons who have a salary greater than 50,000. We pass to the collect() method an expression to create the List (the List::new method), a lambda expression to process a list and an element of the stream, and an expression to process the two lists (the List::addAll method):

```
List<Person> highSalaryPeople = persons
               .parallelStream().collect(
    ArrayList::new, (list, person) -> {
        if (person.getSalary() > 50000) {
            list.add(person);
        }
    },
    ArrayList::addAll
);
System.out.printf("High Salary People: %d\n",
                highSalaryPeople.size());
```

10. Finally, we'll implement an example that generates a ConcurrentHashMap with the first names that appears in the list of People objects and the number of times that each name appears. We will use the first name of the persons as key and Counter objects as values. The first parameter of the collect method will create a new ConcurrentHashMap object. The second parameter is an implementation of the BiConsumer interface that receives as parameters a ConcurrentHashMap and a Person. First, we use the computeIfPresent() method of the hash to increment the Counter of the person if the person exists. Then, we use the computeIfAbsent() method of the hash to insert a new person name if it doesn't exists. The third argument of the collect() method is an implementation of the BiConsumer interface that receives two ConcurrentHashMap objects and we use the merge() method to process all the elements of the second hash and insert them in the first hash if they are not present or increment the counters if they are.

```
System.out.printf("Collect, second example\n");
ConcurrentHashMap<String, Counter> peopleNames = persons
                        .parallelStream().collect(
  ConcurrentHashMap::new, (hash, person) -> {
    hash.computeIfPresent(person.getFirstName(), (name,
                                            counter) -> {
      counter.increment();
      return counter;
    });
    hash.computeIfAbsent(person.getFirstName(), name -> {
      Counter c=new Counter();
      c.setValue(name);
      return c;
    });
  },
  (hash1, hash2) -> {
    hash2.forEach (10, (key, value) -> {
      hash1.merge(key, value, (v1,v2) -> {
        v1.setCounter(v1.getCounter()+v2.getCounter());
        return v1;
      });
    });
  });

  peopleNames.forEach((name, counter) -> {
    System.out.printf("%s: %d\n", name, counter.getCounter());
  });
```

How it works...

As we mentioned in the introduction of this recipe, the `collect()` method allows you to do a mutable reduction of the elements of a `Stream`. We call it a mutable reduction because the final result of the stream will be a mutable data structure, such as `Map` or `List`. The `Stream` class of the Java Concurrency API provides two versions of the `collect()` method.

The first one receives only one parameter that is an implementation of the `Collector` interface. This interface has seven methods, so you normally won't implement your own collectors. Instead of this, you will use the utility class `Collectors`, which has a lot of methods that return ready-to-use `Collector` objects for your reduce operations. In our example, we have used the following methods of the `Collectors` class:

- `groupingByConcurrent()`: This method returns a `Collector` object that implements a group by operating with the elements of `Stream` in a concurrent way, generating `Map` as the resultant data structure. It receives as parameter an expression to obtain the value of the key used in the map from the element of the stream. It generates `Map` where the keys will be of the type returned by the parameter expression and the value will be a `List` of elements of the stream.
- `joining()`: This method returns `Collector` that concatenates the elements of the stream into `String`. You can specify three `CharSequence` objects with a separator for the elements, a prefix of the final `String`, and a suffix of the final `String`.
- `partitioningBy()`: This method returns `Collector` similar to the first one. It receives as parameter a `Boolean` expression with the elements of `Stream` and organizes the elements of the stream in two groups: the ones that meet the expressions and the ones that don't. The final result will be `Map` with a `Boolean` key and `List` of the type of elements of the stream as value.
- `toConcurrentMap()`: This method returns `Collector` that generates `ConcurrentMap` in a concurrent way. It receives three parameters:
    - An expression to generate the key from an element of the stream
    - An expression to generate the value from an element of the stream
    - An expression to generate a value from two values when there are two or more elements with the same key

`Collector` has a set of `Characteristics` that define its behavior and can be defined or not for a specific collector. For us, the most important is the CONCURRENT one that indicates if the collector can work in a concurrent way or not. In this case, we can't take advantage of our multicore processor by creating only a parallel stream. If we use a collect operation with `Collector`, we have to also take into account the value of the CONCURRENT characteristic of that `Collector`. We will only have a concurrent reduction if the next three conditions are true:

- The `Stream` is parallel (we have used `parallelStream()` of the `parallel()` methods in the stream)
- The collector has the CONCURRENT characteristic
- Either the stream is unordered, or the collector has the UNORDERED characteristic

In our case, `groupingByConcurrent()` and `toConcurrentMap()` return collectors which have the CONCURRENT characteristic and the `joining()` and `partitionBy()` methods return collectors that don't have such characteristics.

However, there's another version of the `collect()` method that can be used with parallel streams. This version of the `collect()` method receives the following three parameters:

- A supplier function that generates a data structure of the type of the final result of the collect operation. With parallel streams, this function will be called as many times as there are threads executing the operation.
- An accumulator function that receives a data structure and an element of the stream and makes the process of the element.
- A combiner function that receives two data structures and generates a unique data structure of the same type.

You can use lambda expressions to implement these functions, but you can also implement the `Supplier` interface for the supplier function or the `BiConsumer` interface for the accumulator and combiner functions (always parameterized with the adequate data types). You can also use method references (`Class::Method`) if the input and output parameters are adequate. For example, we have used the `List::new` reference as the supplier function and the `List::addAll` method as the combiner function. We could use the `List::add` method as the accumulator function. There are more methods you can use as parameters to the `collect()` method.

The following screenshot shows the output of the `groupingByConcurrent()` operation:

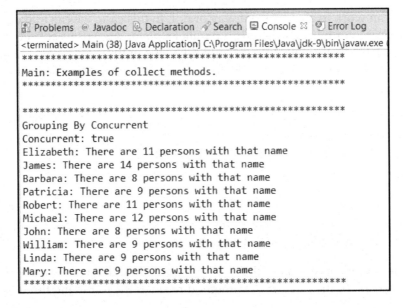

The following screenshot shows the output of the `toConcurrentMap()` operation:

```
**********************************************************
To Concurrent Map
Concurrent: true
Elizabeth: Wilson, Smith, Davies, Wilson, Roberts, Roberts, Wilson, Smith, Evans, Wilson, Williams
Barbara: Wilson, Taylor, Williams, Roberts, Evans, Thomas, Williams, Smith
James: Evans, Smith, Thomas, Roberts, Davies, Williams, Wilson, Jones, Davies, Davies, Jones, Wilson, Evans, Jones
Robert: Williams, Williams, Evans, Brown, Smith, Wilson, Thomas, Evans, Wilson, Williams, Evans
Patricia: Wilson, Brown, Williams, Davies, Evans, Williams, Williams, Davies, Taylor
Michael: Roberts, Williams, Davies, Evans, Jones, Smith, Davies, Brown, Thomas, Williams, Brown, Davies
John: Jones, Roberts, Taylor, Jones, Taylor, Williams, Jones, Roberts
William: Davies, Jones, Smith, Smith, Williams, Jones, Thomas, Thomas, Roberts
Linda: Roberts, Taylor, Davies, Wilson, Brown, Williams, Brown, Brown, Roberts
Mary: Taylor, Davies, Thomas, Brown, Thomas, Davies, Taylor, Wilson, Roberts
**********************************************************
```

There's more...

The `Collectors` class has many more methods that return `Collector` objects that can be used in the `collect()` method. The following are the most interesting:

- `toList()`: This method returns `Collector` that groups all the elements of `Stream` into `List`.
- `toCollection()`: This method returns `Collector` that groups all the elements of `Stream` into `Collection`. This method returns as parameter an expression that creates `Collection`, which will be used internally by `Collector` and returned at the end of its execution.
- `averagingInt()`, `averagingLong()`, and `averagingDouble()`: These methods return `Collector` that calculates the average of `int`, `long`, and `double` values, respectively. They receive as parameters an expression to convert an element of the stream into `int`, `long`, or `double`. The three methods return a double value.

See also

- The *Creating streams from different sources* and *Reducing the elements of a stream* recipes in this chapter

Applying an action to every element of a stream

In this recipe, you will learn how to apply an action to all the elements of the stream. We will use three methods: two terminal operations, the `forEach()` and `forEachOrdered()`, and an intermediate operation, the `peek()` method.

Getting ready

The example of this recipe has been implemented using the Eclipse IDE. If you use Eclipse or other IDE such as NetBeans, open it and create a new Java project.

How to do it...

Follow these steps to implement the example:

1. First, we will implement some auxiliary classes we will use in the example. Create a class named `Person` with the basic characteristics of a person. Check the *Creating streams from different sources* recipe to see the source code of this class.

2. As we'll work with methods that depend on the order of the elements of the stream, we have to override some methods in the `Person` class. First, we'll override the `compareTo()` method that compares two persons. We'll create a static `Comparator` object using the `Comparator` interface to compare two `Person` objects using their first name and last name. Then, we'll use that comparator in the `compareTo()` method:

```
private static Comparator<Person> comparator=Comparator
                    .comparing(Person::getLastName)
                    .thenComparing(Person::getFirstName);

@Override
public int compareTo(Person otherPerson) {
  return comparator.compare(this, otherPerson);
}
```

3. Then, we override the `equals()` method that determines if two `Person` objects are equal. As we made in the `compareTo()` method, we use the `Comparator` static object we have created before.

```
@Override
public boolean equals(Object object) {
  return this.compareTo((Person)object)==0;
}
```

4. Finally, we override the `hashCode()` method that calculates a hash value for a `Person` object. In Java, equal objects must produce the same hash code, so we have to override this method and generate the hash code of a `Person` object using the first name and last name attributes and the `hash()` method of the `Objects` class:

```
public int hashCode() {
  String sequence=this.getLastName()+this.getFirstName();
  return sequence.hashCode();
}
```

5. In this example, we will also use the `PersonGenerator` and `DoubleGenerator` classes used in the *Creating streams from different sources* recipe.

6. Now, create the `Main` class with the `main()` method. First, we create a `List` of ten random `Person` objects:

```
public class Main {

    public static void main(String[] args) {
        List<Person> persons=PersonGenerator.generatePersonList(10);
```

7. Then, we'll use the `forEach()` method to write the names of all the persons of the generated list. The `forEach()` method receives as parameter the expression we want to apply to each element. In our case, we use a lambda expression to write the information to the console:

```
persons.parallelStream().forEach(p -> {
    System.out.printf("%s, %s\n", p.getLastName(),
                        p.getFirstName());
});
```

8. Then, you'll learn how to apply an action to each element in an ordered way. First, we create a list of random `Double` numbers using the `DoubleGenerator` class. Then, we create a parallel stream, sort the elements of the stream using the `sorted()` method, and then use the `forEachOrdered()` method to write the numbers to the console in an ordered way:

```
List<Double> doubles= DoubleGenerator.generateDoubleList(10, 100);
System.out.printf("Parallel forEachOrdered() with numbers\n");
doubles.parallelStream().sorted().forEachOrdered(n -> {
    System.out.printf("%f\n",n);
});
```

9. Now, let's see what happens if you sort the elements of the stream but don't use the `forEachOrdered()` method. Repeat the same sentence as before but use the `forEach()` method instead:

```
System.out.printf("Parallel forEach() after sorted()
                    with numbers\n");
doubles.parallelStream().sorted().forEach(n -> {
    System.out.printf("%f\n",n);
});
```

10. Then, we'll test how the `forEachOrdered()` method works with a stream of `Person` objects:

```
persons.parallelStream().sorted().forEachOrdered( p -> {
    System.out.printf("%s, %s\n", p.getLastName(),
                      p.getFirstName());
});
```

11. Finally, let's test the `peek()` method. This method is similar to the `forEach()` method, but it's an intermediate operation. It's normally used for log purposes:

```
doubles
  .parallelStream()
  .peek(d -> System.out.printf("Step 1: Number: %f\n",d))
  .peek(d -> System.out.printf("Step 2: Number: %f\n",d))
  .forEach(d -> System.out.printf("Final Step: Number: %f\n",d));
```

How it works...

In this recipe you learnt how to use three methods to process all the elements of a stream and apply an action to them. These methods are:

- `forEach()`: This is a terminal operation that applies an action to all the elements of `Stream` and returns a `void` value. It receives as parameter the action to apply to the elements defined as a lambda expression or as an implementation of the `Consumer` interface. There's no guarantee about the order in which the action will be applied to the elements of a parallel stream.

- `forEachOrdered()`: This is a terminal operation that applies an action to all the elements of `Stream` in the order of the stream, if the stream is an ordered stream, and returns a void value. You can use this method after the `sorted()` method. You first sort the elements of the stream with the `sorted()` method and then apply the action in an ordered way using the `forEachOrdered()` method. This behavior is guaranteed with parallel streams too, but its performance will be worse than the `forEach()` method with unordered streams.

- `peek()`: This is an intermediate operation that returns `Stream` with the same elements of the stream that call the method and applies the action specified as a parameter to all the elements consumed from the stream. The action applied to the elements is specified as a lambda expression or as an implementation of the `Consumer` interface. Take into account that, as the intermediate operations are lazy, the operation will only be applied to the elements consumed by the stream when the terminal operation is executed.

There's more...

Take into account that if you use the sorted method, you have to provide `Comparator` that can be applied to the elements you want to sort or the elements of the stream must implement the `Comparable` interface. In our case, the `Person` class implements that interface and the `compareTo()` method to sort the elements of the stream according to their first and last names.

See also

- The *Creating streams from different sources, Reducing the elements of a stream* and *Sorting the elements of a stream* recipes in this chapter

Filtering the elements of a stream

One of the most commons actions you will apply to a stream will be the filtering operation that selects the elements that continue with the processing. In this recipe, you will learn the different methods provided by the `Stream` class to select the elements of a stream.

Getting ready

The example of this recipe has been implemented using the Eclipse IDE. If you use Eclipse or other IDE such as NetBeans, open it and create a new Java project.

How to do it...

Follow these steps to implement the example:

1. First, we'll implement some auxiliary classes we will use in the example. First, implement the `Person` class that stores the basic attributes of a person, and the `PersonGenerator` class that generates a `List` of random `Person` objects. Please, check the recipe *Apply an action to all the elements of a stream* to see the source code of both the classes.

2. Then, we'll implement the `Main` class with the `main()` method. First, create a `List` of random `Person` objects using the `PersonGenerator` class. Use the `forEach()` method to print the generated elements:

```
public class Main {
    public static void main(String[] args) {
        List<Person> persons=PersonGenerator
                                .generatePersonList(10);
        persons.parallelStream().forEach(p-> {
            System.out.printf("%s, %s\n", p.getLastName(),
                              p.getFirstName());
        });
```

3. Then, we'll eliminate the duplicate objects using the `distinct()` method. Use the `forEach()` method to write the elements that pass the filter:

```
persons.parallelStream().distinct().forEach(p-> {
    System.out.printf("%s, %s\n", p.getLastName(),
                      p.getFirstName());
});
```

4. Then, we'll test the `distinct()` method with an `Array` of numbers. Create an array of numbers repeating some of them. Convert them to a `List` using the `asList()` method of the `Arrays` class. Create a parallel stream with the `parallelStream()` method, convert the stream into an `IntStream` stream with the `mapToInt()` method, use the `distinct()` method to delete the repeated elements, and finally use the `forEach()` method to write the final elements to the console:

```
Integer[] numbers={1,3,2,1,2,2,1,3,3,1,1,3,2,1};
Arrays.asList(numbers).parallelStream().mapToInt(n -> n)
                    .distinct().forEach( n -> {
    System.out.printf("Number: %d\n", n);
});
```

5. Now, we'll get the persons of the random person list with a salary lower than 3,000 using the filter method and a predicate expressed as a lambda expression with that condition. As with the other examples, use the `forEach()` method to write the resultant elements:

```
persons.parallelStream().filter(p -> p.getSalary() < 30000)
                                        .forEach( p -> {
    System.out.printf("%s, %s\n", p.getLastName(),
                         p.getFirstName());
});
```

6. Then, we'll test the `filter()` method with an `IntStream` getting the numbers less than two:

```
Arrays.asList(numbers).parallelStream().mapToInt(n -> n)
                         .filter( n -> n<2).forEach(  n-> {
    System.out.printf("%d\n", n);
});
```

7. Now, we'll use the `limit()` method to limit the number of elements in the stream. For example, create a parallel stream from the random list of persons, convert them into a `DoubleStream` with the `mapToDouble()` method, and get the first five elements using the `limit()` method:

```
persons.parallelStream().mapToDouble(p -> p.getSalary())
                     .sorted().limit(5).forEach(s-> {
    System.out.printf("Limit: %f\n",s);
});
```

8. Finally, we'll use the `skip()` method to ignore a number of elements of the stream. Create a parallel stream from the random list of persons, convert them into a `DoubleStream` with the `mapToDouble()` method, and ignore the first five elements using the `skip()` method:

```
persons.parallelStream().mapToDouble(p -> p.getSalary())
                     .sorted().skip(5).forEach(s-> {
    System.out.printf("Skip: %f\n",s);
});
```

How it works...

In this recipe we have used four methods to filter the elements in a stream. These methods are:

- `distinct()`: This method returns a stream with the distinct elements of the current stream according to the `equals()` method of the elements of the `Stream` class. In our case, we have tested this method with `Person` objects and `int` numbers. We have implemented the `equals()` and `hashCode()` methods in the `Person` class. If we don't do this, the `equals()` method will only return `true` if the two compared objects hold the same reference. Take into account that this operation is a stateful operation, so it won't get a good performance with parallel streams (as the Java documentation reflects, '... under parallel computation, some pipelines containing stateful intermediate operations may require multiple passes on the data or may need to buffer significant data...').
- `filter()`: This method receives a `Predicate` as parameter. This predicate can be expressed as a lambda expression that returns a `boolean` value. The `filter()` method returns a stream with the elements that make the `Predicate` true.
- `limit()`: This method receives an `int` value as a parameter and returns a stream with no more than as many number of elements. The performance of this method can also be bad with ordered parallel streams, especially when the number of elements you want to get is big, because the method will return the first elements of the stream and that will imply additional computation. This circumstance doesn't occur with unordered streams because in that case, it doesn't matter what elements are returned.
- `skip()`: This method returns a stream with the elements of the original stream after discarding the first elements. The number of discarded elements is specified as the parameter of this method. This method has the same performance problems as with the `limit()` method.

There's more...

The stream class also has other two methods that can be used to filter the elements of a stream:

- dropWhile(): This method receives a Predicate expression as the parameter. It has a different behavior with ordered and unordered streams. With ordered streams, the method deletes the first elements that match the predicate from the stream. It deletes elements when the elements match the predicate. When it finds an element that doesn't match the predicate, it stops deleting the elements and returns the rest of the stream. With unordered streams, its behavior is not deterministic. It deletes a subset of elements that match the predicate but is not specified what subset of elements it will delete. As with the other methods, it may have a bad performance with parallel ordered streams.
- takeWhile(): This method is equivalent to the previous one, but it takes the elements instead of deleting them.

See also

- The *Creating streams from different sources, Reducing the elements of a stream* and *Collecting the elements of a stream* recipes in this chapter

Transforming the elements of a stream

Some of the most useful intermediate operations you can use with streams are those that allow you to transform the elements of the stream. These operations receive elements of a class and return the elements of a different class. You can even change the type of stream and generate an IntStream, LongStream, or DoubleStream from Stream.

In this recipe, you will learn how to use the transforming intermediate operations provided by the Stream class to convert its elements into a different class.

Getting ready

The example of this recipe has been implemented using the Eclipse IDE. If you use Eclipse or other IDE such as NetBeans, open it and create a new Java project.

How to do it...

Follow these steps to implement the example:

1. First, we'll implement some auxiliary classes we will use in the example. First, implement the `Person` class, which stores the basic attributes of a person, and the `PersonGenerator` class, which generates a `List` of random `Person` objects. Please, check the recipe *Apply an action to all the elements of a stream* to see the source code of both the classes.

2. Create a class named `BasicPerson`. This class will have a `String` attribute named `name` and a `long` attribute named `age`. Create the methods to get and set the value of both the attributes. As the source code of this class is very simple, it won't be included here.

3. Create another auxiliary class named `FileGenerator`. This class will have a method named `generateFile()` that receives the number of lines in the simulated file and returns its content as a `List` of `String`:

```java
public class FileGenerator {
  public static List<String> generateFile(int size) {
    List<String> file=new ArrayList<>();
    for (int i=0; i<size; i++) {
      file.add("Lorem ipsum dolor sit amet,
               consectetur adipiscing elit. Morbi lobortis
               cursus venenatis. Mauris tempus elit ut
               malesuada luctus. Interdum et malesuada fames
               ac ante ipsum primis in faucibus. Phasellus
               laoreet sapien eu pulvinar rhoncus. Integer vel
               ultricies leo. Donec vel sagittis nibh.
               Maecenas eu quam non est hendrerit pu");
    }
    return file;
  }
}
```

4. Then, create the `Main` class with the `main()` method. First, create a list of random `Person` objects using the `PersonGenerator` class:

```java
public class Main {

  public static void main(String[] args) {

    // Create list of persons
    List<Person> persons = PersonGenerator.generatePersonList(100);
```

5. Then, we'll use the `mapToDouble()` method to convert the stream of `Person` objects into `DoubleStream` of double values. Create a parallel stream using the `parallelStream()` method and then use the `mapToDouble()` method, passing as parameter a lambda expression that receives a `Person` object and returns its salary, which is a double number. Then use the `distinct()` method to get the unique values and the `forEach()` method to write them to the console. We also get the number of different elements written using the `count()` method:

```
DoubleStream ds = persons.parallelStream().mapToDouble
                                    (p -> p.getSalary());
ds.distinct().forEach(d -> {
  System.out.printf("Salary: %f\n", d);
});
ds = persons.parallelStream().mapToDouble(p -> p.getSalary());
long size = ds.distinct().count();
System.out.printf("Size: %d\n", size);
```

6. Now, we'll transform the `Person` objects of the stream into `BasicPerson` objects. Create the stream using the `parallelStream()` method and use the `map()` method to transform the objects. This method receives as parameter a lambda expression that receives a `Person` object, creates a new `BasicPerson` object, and establishes the value of its attributes. Then, we write the values of the attributes of the `BasicPerson` object using the `forEach()` method:

```
List<BasicPerson> basicPersons = persons.parallelStream().map
                                                   (p -> {
  BasicPerson bp = new BasicPerson();
  bp.setName(p.getFirstName() + " " + p.getLastName());
  bp.setAge(getAge(p.getBirthDate()));
  return bp;
}).collect(Collectors.toList());

basicPersons.forEach(bp -> {
  System.out.printf("%s: %d\n", bp.getName(), bp.getAge());
});
```

7. Finally, we'll learn how to manage the situations where an intermediate operation returns `Stream`. In this case, we'll work with a `Stream` of streams, but we can concatenate all these `Stream` objects into a unique `Stream` using the `flatMap()` method. Generate `List<String>` with 100 elements using the `FileGenerator` class. Then, create a parallel stream with the `parallelStream()` method. We'll split each line to get its words using the `split()` method, and with the `of()` method of the `Stream` class, we convert the resultant `Array` into `Stream`. If we use the `map()` method, we are generating a `Stream` of streams, but using the `flatMap()` method we'll get a unique `Stream` of `String` objects with all the words of the whole List. Then, we get the words with a length greater than zero with the `filter()` method, sort the stream with the `sorted()` method, and collect it to `Map` using the `groupingByConcurrent()` method where the keys are the words and the values are the number of times each word appears in the stream:

```
List<String> file = FileGenerator.generateFile(100);
Map<String, Long> wordCount = file.parallelStream()
  .flatMap(line -> Stream.of(line.split("[ ,.]")))
  .filter(w -> w.length() > 0).sorted()
  .collect(Collectors.groupingByConcurrent(e -> e, Collectors
    .counting()));

wordCount.forEach((k, v) -> {
  System.out.printf("%s: %d\n", k, v);
});
```

8. Finally, we have to implement the `getAge()` method used previously in the code. This method receives the date of birth of a `Person` object and returns its age:

```
private static long getAge(Date birthDate) {
  LocalDate start = birthDate.toInstant()
              .atZone(ZoneId.systemDefault()).toLocalDate();
  LocalDate now = LocalDate.now();
  long ret = ChronoUnit.YEARS.between(start, now);
  return ret;
}
```

How it works...

In this recipe you learnt how to convert the elements of the stream using an intermediate operation and an expression that makes the conversion between the source and the destination types. We used three different methods in our example:

- mapToDouble(): We used this method to convert Stream of objects into DoubleStream with double numbers as elements. This method receives as parameter a lambda expression or an implementation of the ToDoubleFunction interface. This expression receives an element of Stream and has to return a double value.
- map(): We can use this method when we have to convert the elements of Stream to a different class. For example, in our case, we convert the Person class to a BasicPerson class. This method receives as parameter a lambda expression or an implementation of the Function interface. This expression must create the new object and initialize its attributes.
- flatMap(): This method is useful in a more complex situation when you have to work with a Stream of Stream objects and you want to convert them to a unique Stream. This method receives as parameter a lambda expression or an implementation of the Function interface as the map() function, but in this case, this expression has to return a Stream object. The flatMap() method will automatically concatenate all those streams into a unique Stream.

There's more...

The Stream class provides other methods to transform the elements of a Stream:

- mapToInt(), mapToLong(): These methods are identical to the mapToDouble() method, but they generate IntStream and LongStream objects, respectively.
- flatMapToDouble(), flatMapToInt(), flatMapToLong(): These methods are identical to the flatMap() method, but they work with DoubleStream, IntStream, and LongStream, respectively.

See also

- The *Creating streams from different sources, Reducing the elements of a stream* and *Collecting the elements of a stream recipes* in this chapter

Sorting the elements of a stream

Another typical operation you will want to do with a Stream is sorting its elements. For example, you may want to sort the elements of the Stream by name, postal code, or any other numeric value.

With streams, we have other considerations with the so-called encounter order. Some streams may have a defined encounter order (it depends on the source of the Stream). Some operations work with the elements of the stream in its encountered ordered, such as limit(), skip(), and others. This makes that parallel computation for this methods doesn't give us good performance. In these cases, you can speed-up the execution of these methods by deleting the ordering constraint.

In this recipe, you will learn how to sort the elements of Stream and how to delete the ordering constraint in situations where we don't need the encounter order of Stream.

Getting ready

The example of this recipe has been implemented using the Eclipse IDE. If you use Eclipse or other IDE such as NetBeans, open it and create a new Java project.

How to do it...

Follow these steps to implement the example:

1. First, we'll implement some auxiliary classes we will use in the example. First, implement the Person class, which stores the basic attributes of a person, and the PersonGenerator class, which generates a List of random Person objects. Please, check the recipe *Apply an action to all the elements of a stream* to see the source code of both the classes.

2. Now, implement the Main class with the main() method. First, we'll create an Array of int numbers. Then, we'll create a parallel stream with the parallelStream() method from this array, use the sorted() method to sort the elements of the array, and use the forEachOrdered() method to write the elements in an ordered way. Take into account that this operation won't use all the power of our multi-core processor as it has to write the elements in the specified order:

```
public class Main {
  public static void main(String args[]) {
    int[] numbers={9,8,7,6,5,4,3,2,1,2,3,4,5,6,7,8,9};
    Arrays.stream(numbers).parallel().sorted().forEachOrdered
                                                        (n -> {
      System.out.printf("%d\n", n);
    });
```

3. Now, let's try the same principles with a Stream of Person objects. Create a list of 10 random Person objects using the PersonGenerator class and use the same methods, sorted() and forEachOrdered(), to see how the persons are written in an ordered way:

```
List<Person> persons=PersonGenerator.generatePersonList(10);
persons.parallelStream().sorted().forEachOrdered(p -> {
  System.out.printf("%s, %s\n",p.getLastName(),p.getFirstName());
});
```

4. Finally, we'll see how to eliminate the encounter order of a data structure using the unordered() method. First, we'll create TreeSet from our List of random Person objects. We use TreeSet because it orders the elements internally. Then, we make a loop to repeat the operations ten times and see how there's a difference between the ordered and the unordered operations:

```
TreeSet<Person> personSet=new TreeSet<>(persons);
for (int i=0; i<10; i++) {
```

5. Then, we create a stream from PersonSet using the stream() method, convert it to parallel with the parallel() method, get the first element with the limit() method, and return the Person object, collecting it to a list and getting the first element:

```
Person person= personSet.stream().parallel().limit(1)
                       .collect(Collectors.toList()).get(0);
System.out.printf("%s %s\n", person.getFirstName(),
                   person.getLastName());
```

6. Now, we perform the same operation but remove the ordered constraint with the unordered() method between the stream() and parallel() methods:

```
person=personSet.stream().unordered().parallel().limit(1)
                       .collect(Collectors.toList()).get(0);
System.out.printf("%s %s\n", person.getFirstName(),
                   person.getLastName());
```

How it works...

There are Stream objects that may have an encounter order depending on its source and the intermediate operations you have applied before. This encounter order imposes a restriction about the order in which the elements must be processed by certain methods. For example, if you use the limit() or skip() methods in Stream with an encounter order, they will get and ignore the first elements according to that encounter order. There are other operations, such as the forEach() method, that don't take into account the encounter order. If you apply the same operations to a stream with an encounter order, the result will always be the same. If the stream doesn't have an encounter order, the results may vary.

When you work with sequential streams, the encounter order doesn't have any impact on the performance of the application, but with parallel streams it can affect it greatly. Depending on the operations, it would be necessary to process more than once the elements of Stream or to store in a buffer a big amount of data. In this case, removing the encounter order using the unordered() method, as we did in this recipe, will significantly increase the performance of the application.

On the other hand, the sorted() method sorts the elements of the Stream. If you use this method, the elements of Stream must implement the Comparable interface. Otherwise, you can pass a Comparator as a parameter that will be used to sort the elements. If you use this method, you are creating an ordered stream, so all the things explained before to the streams with an encounter order are applicable to the resultant stream.

Finally, the forEach() method doesn't take into account the encounter order of the stream. If you want to take this encounter order into account, say, to write the elements of the stream order after sorting them, you can use the forEachOrdered() method.

The following screenshot shows part of the output of the example:

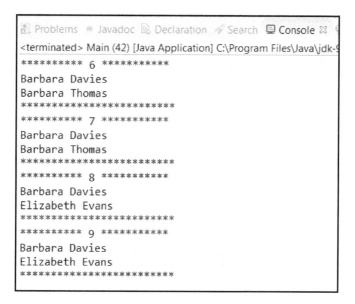

You can see that when you call the `limit(1)` method in the parallel stream generated from `TreeSet`, you always obtain the same result because the Stream API respects the encounter order of that structure. But when we include a call to the `unordered()` method, the encounter order is not taken into account and the result obtained should vary, as in this case.

There's more...

When you use the `unordered()` method, you're not executing any code that internally changes the order of the elements in the data structure. You're only deleting a condition that would be taken into account for some methods otherwise. It's possible that the results of a stream with the `unordered()` method and the results of the same stream without the method are equal. Its use may have consequences in possibly giving different processing results for parallel streams. For example, if you try our example using a `List` of `Person` objects instead of `personSet` a `TreeSet`, you will always obtain the same result in both the cases.

As we mentioned before, the main purpose of the `unordered()` method is to delete a constraint that limits the performance of parallel streams.

See also

- The *Creating streams from different sources, Reducing the elements of a stream* and *Collecting the elements of a stream* recipes in this chapter

Verifying conditions in the elements of a stream

One interesting option provided by the `Stream` class is the possibility to check if the elements of the stream verify a condition or not. This functionality is provided by the terminal operations that return a `Boolean` value.

In this recipe, you will learn which methods provide the `Stream` class to check conditions in the elements of a stream and how to use them.

Getting ready

The example of this recipe has been implemented using the Eclipse IDE. If you use Eclipse or other IDE such as NetBeans, open it and create a new Java project.

How to do it...

Follow these steps to implement the example:

1. First, we'll implement some auxiliary classes we will use in the example. First, implement the `Person` class, which stores the basic attributes of a person, and the `PersonGenerator` class, which generates a `List` of random `Person` objects. Please, check the recipe *Apply an action to all the elements of a stream* to see the source code of both classes.

2. Then, create the `Main` class with the `main()` method. First, we'll create a `List` of random `Person` objects using the `PersonGenerator` class:

```
public class Main {
  public static void main(String[] args) {
    List<Person> persons=PersonGenerator.generatePersonList(10);
```

3. Then, calculate the maximum and minimum values of the salary field to verify that all our calculations are correct. We use two streams for the calculation, the first one with the `map()` and `max()` methods and the second one with the `mapToInt()` and `min()` methods:

```
int maxSalary = persons.parallelStream().map(p -> p.getSalary())
                              .max(Integer::compare).get();
int minSalary = persons.parallelStream().mapToInt(p -> p
                    .getSalary()).min().getAsInt();
System.out.printf("Salaries are between %d and %d\n", minSalary,
                    maxSalary);
```

4. Now, we'll test some conditions. First, let's verify that all the `Person` objects generated have a salary greater than zero with the `allMatch()` method and the corresponding lambda expression:

```
boolean condition;
condition=persons.parallelStream().allMatch
                              (p -> p.getSalary() > 0);
System.out.printf("Salary > 0: %b\n", condition);
```

5. We repeat the condition to test if all the salaries are greater than 10,000 and 30,000.

```
condition=persons.parallelStream().allMatch
                              (p -> p.getSalary() > 10000);
System.out.printf("Salary > 10000: %b\n",condition);
condition=persons.parallelStream().allMatch
                              (p -> p.getSalary() > 30000);
System.out.printf("Salary > 30000: %b\n",condition);
```

6. Then, we'll use the `anyMatch()` method to test if there is someone with a salary greater than 50,000 and 100,000:

```
condition=persons.parallelStream().anyMatch
                              (p -> p.getSalary() > 50000);
System.out.printf("Any with salary > 50000: %b\n",condition);
condition=persons.parallelStream().anyMatch
                              (p -> p.getSalary() > 100000);
System.out.printf("Any with salary > 100000: %b\n",condition);
```

7. To finish this block of tests, we use the `noneMatch()` method to verify that there's none with a salary greater than 100,000

```
condition=persons.parallelStream().noneMatch
                              (p -> p.getSalary() > 100000);
System.out.printf("None with salary > 100000: %b\n",condition);
```

8. After that, we use the `findAny()` method to get a random element of the stream of `Person` objects:

```
Person person = persons.parallelStream().findAny().get();
System.out.printf("Any: %s %s: %d\n", person.getFirstName(),
                  person.getLastName(), person.getSalary());
```

9. Then, we use the `findFirst()` method to get the first element of the stream of Person objects:

```
person = persons.parallelStream().findFirst().get();
System.out.printf("First: %s %s: %d\n", person.getFirstName(),
                  person.getLastName(), person.getSalary());
```

10. Finally, we sort the stream by salary using the `sorted()` method, passing `Comparator` expressed as a lambda expression, and use the `findFirst()` method to obtain, in this case, the `Person` object with the lowest salary:

```
person = persons.parallelStream().sorted((p1,p2) -> {
    return p1.getSalary() - p2.getSalary();
}).findFirst().get();
System.out.printf("First Sorted: %s %s: %d\n",
                  person.getFirstName(), person.getLastName(),
                  person.getSalary());
```

How it works...

In this recipe, we used three different methods to verify conditions over the elements of a Stream:

- `allMatch()`: This method is a terminal operation that receives as parameter an implementation of the `Predicate` interface expressed as a lambda expression or as an object that implements it and returns a `Boolean` value. It returns `true` if the `Predicate` introduced is true for all the elements of the `Stream` and `false` otherwise.

- anyMatch(): This method is a terminal operation that receives as parameter an implementation of the Predicate interface expressed as a lambda expression or as an object that implements it and returns a Boolean value. It returns true if the Predicate introduced is true for at least one of the elements of the Stream and false otherwise.
- noneMatch(): This method is a terminal operation that receives as parameter a Predicate expressed as a lambda expression or as an implementation of interface and returns a Boolean value. It returns true if the Predicate introduced is false for all the elements of the Stream and false otherwise.

We also used two methods to obtain the elements of Stream:

- findAny(): This method is a terminal operation that doesn't receive parameters and returns an Optional object parameterized with the class of the elements of Stream with some element of Stream. There's no guarantee about the element returned by this method. If Stream has no elements, the Optional object returned will be empty.
- findFirst(): This method is a terminal operation that doesn't receive parameters and returns an Optional parameterized with the class of the elements of Stream. It returns the first element of Stream if the stream has a determined encounter order or any element if the stream has no encounter order. If Stream has no elements, the Optional returned will be empty.

There's more...

In this recipe we used an interface and a class provided by the Java API. The Predicate interface is a functional interface that is usually expressed as a lambda expression. This expression will receive an element of Stream and return a Boolean value. If you want to implement a class that implements this interface, you only have to implement the test() method that receives an object of the parameterized type and returns a Boolean value. The interface defines more methods, but they have a default implementation.

The Optional class is used when a terminal operation of Stream may or may not return a value. In this way, Java guarantees that the operation will always return a value, the Optional object, that may have a value we obtain using the get() method or may be an empty object, the condition we can check with the isPresent() method. If you use the get() method with an empty Optional object, a NoSuchElementException will be thrown.

See also

- The *Creating streams from different sources*, *Reducing the elements of a stream* and *Collecting the elements of a stream* recipes in this chapter

Reactive programming with reactive streams

Reactive streams (http://www.reactive-streams.org/) define a mechanism to provide asynchronous stream processing with non-blocking back pressure.

Reactive streams are based on the following three elements:

- A publisher of information
- One or more subscribers of that information
- A subscription between the publisher and a consumer

The reactive streams specification determines how these classes should interact among them, according to the following rules:

- The publisher will add the subscribers that want to be notified
- The subscriber receives a notification when they're added to a publisher
- The subscribers request one or more elements from the publisher in an asynchronous way, that is to say, the subscriber requests the element and continues with the execution
- When the publisher has an element to publish, it sends it to all its subscribers that have requested an element

As we mentioned before, all this communication is asynchronous, so we can take advantage of all the power of our multi-core processor.

Java 9 has included three interfaces, the `Flow.Publisher`, the `Flow.Subscriber`, and the `Flow.Subscription`, and a utility class, the `SubmissionPublisher` class, to allow us to implement reactive stream applications. In this recipe, you will learn how to use all these elements to implement a basic reactive stream application.

Getting ready

The example of this recipe has been implemented using the Eclipse IDE. If you use Eclipse or other IDE such as NetBeans, open it and create a new Java project.

How to do it...

Follow these steps to implement the example:

1. Create a class named Item that will represent the items of information sent from the publisher to the subscribers. This class has two String attributes, named title and content, and the methods to get() and set() their values. Its source code is very simple, so it won't be included here.

2. Then, create a class named Consumer1 and specify that it implements the Subscriber interface parameterized with the Item class. We have to implement four methods. First, we implement the onComplete() method. It simply writes a message to the console:

```java
public class Consumer1 implements Flow.Subscriber<Item> {

    @Override
    public void onComplete() {
        System.out.printf("%s: Consumer 1: Completed\n",
                          Thread.currentThread().getName());

    }
```

3. Then, we implement the onError() method. It simply writes information about the error to the console:

```java
    @Override
    public void onError(Throwable exception) {
        System.out.printf("%s: Consumer 1: Error\n",
                          Thread.currentThread().getName());
        exception.printStackTrace(System.err);
    }
```

4. Then, we implement the `onNext()` method. It simply writes information about the received item to the console:

```
@Override
public void onNext(Item item) {
    System.out.printf("%s: Consumer 1: Item received\n",
                    Thread.currentThread().getName());
    System.out.printf("%s: Consumer 1: %s\n",
                    Thread.currentThread().getName(),
                    item.getTitle());
    System.out.printf("%s: Consumer 1: %s\n",
                    Thread.currentThread().getName(),
                    item.getContent());
}
```

5. And finally, we implement the `onSubscribe()` method. It simply writes a message to the console and doesn't request any item using the `request()` method of the `Subscription` object:

```
@Override
public void onSubscribe(Flow.Subscription subscription) {
    System.out.printf("%s: Consumer 1: Subscription received\n",
                    Thread.currentThread().getName());
    System.out.printf("%s: Consumer 1: No Items requested\n",
                    Thread.currentThread().getName());
}
```

6. Now, it's time for the `Consumer2` class. Specify that it also implements the `Subscriber` interface parameterized with the `Item` class. In this case, we have a private `Subscription` attribute to store the subscription object. The `onComplete()` and `onError()` methods are equivalent to the ones of the `Consumer1` class:

```
public class Consumer2 implements Flow.Subscriber<Item> {

    private Subscription subscription;

    @Override
    public void onComplete() {
        System.out.printf("%s: Consumer 2: Completed\n",
                        Thread.currentThread().getName());
    }
```

```
@Override
public void onError(Throwable exception) {
  System.out.printf("%s: Consumer 2: Error\n",
                    Thread.currentThread().getName());
  exception.printStackTrace(System.err);
}
```

7. The onNext() method has an additional line to request another element:

```
@Override
public void onNext(Item item) {
  System.out.printf("%s: Consumer 2: Item received\n",
                    Thread.currentThread().getName());
  System.out.printf("%s: Consumer 2: %s\n",
                    Thread.currentThread().getName(),
                    item.getTitle());
  System.out.printf("%s: Consumer 2: %s\n",
                    Thread.currentThread().getName(),
                    item.getContent());
  subscription.request(1);
}
```

8. The onSubscribe() method also has an additional line to request the first element:

```
@Override
public void onSubscribe(Flow.Subscription subscription) {
  System.out.printf("%s: Consumer 2: Subscription received\n",
                    Thread.currentThread().getName());
  this.subscription=subscription;
  subscription.request(1);
}
```

9. Now, implement a class called Consumer3 and specify that it implements the Subscriber interface parameterized with the Item class. The onComplete() and onError() methods are equivalent to those of the previous classes:

```
public class Consumer3 implements Flow.Subscriber<Item> {

  @Override
  public void onComplete() {
    System.out.printf("%s: Consumer 3: Completed\n",
                      Thread.currentThread().getName());

  }
```

```
@Override
public void onError(Throwable exception) {
    System.out.printf("%s: Consumer 3: Error\n",
                      Thread.currentThread().getName());
    exception.printStackTrace(System.err);
}
```

10. The `onNext()` method, in this case, writes information about the item to the console but doesn't request any element:

```
@Override
public void onNext(Item item) {
    System.out.printf("%s: Consumer 3: Item received\n",
                      Thread.currentThread().getName());
    System.out.printf("%s: Consumer 3: %s\n",
                      Thread.currentThread().getName(),
                      item.getTitle());
    System.out.printf("%s: Consumer 3: %s\n",
                      Thread.currentThread().getName(),
                      item.getContent());
}
```

11. In the `onSubscribe()`, method we request three items:

```
@Override
public void onSubscribe(Flow.Subscription subscription) {
    System.out.printf("%s: Consumer 3: Subscription received\n",
                      Thread.currentThread().getName());
    System.out.printf("%s: Consumer 3: Requested three items\n",
                      Thread.currentThread().getName());
    subscription.request(3);
}
```

12. Finally, implement the `Main` class with the `main()` method. First, create three consumers, one of each class:

```
public class Main {
    public static void main(String[] args) {

        Consumer1 consumer1=new Consumer1();
        Consumer2 consumer2=new Consumer2();
        Consumer3 consumer3=new Consumer3();
```

13. Now, create a `SubmissionPublisher` object parameterized with the `Item` class and add the three consumers using the `subscribe()` method:

```
SubmissionPublisher<Item> publisher=new SubmissionPublisher<>();

publisher.subscribe(consumer1);
publisher.subscribe(consumer2);
publisher.subscribe(consumer3);
```

14. Now, create ten `Item` objects and publish them using the `submit()` method of the `SubmissionPublisher` object. Wait a second between each item:

```
for (int i=0; i<10; i++) {
  Item item =new Item();
  item.setTitle("Item "+i);
  item.setContent("This is the item "+i);
  publisher.submit(item);
  try {
    TimeUnit.SECONDS.sleep(1);
  } catch (InterruptedException e) {
    e.printStackTrace();
  }
}
```

15. Finally, close the publisher with the `close()` method:

```
    publisher.close();
  }
}
```

How it works...

The main goal of reactive streams is provide a mechanism to process asynchronous stream of data with non-blocking back pressure. We want that the receivers of information optimize their resources. As the mechanism is asynchronous, receivers don't need to use their resources to look for new elements. They will be called when a new element comes in. The non-blocking back pressure allows receivers to consume new elements only when the receivers are ready, so they can use a bounded queue to store the incoming elements and they won't be saturated by producers of new elements.

The reactive streams in Java are based on three interfaces:

- `Flow.Publisher`: This interface has only one method:
    - `subscribe()`: This method receives a `Subscriber` object as parameter. The publisher should take this subscriber into account when it publishes an Item.
- `Flow.Subscriber`: This interface has four methods:
    - `onComplete()`: This method will be called when the `Publisher` has finished its execution
    - `onError()`: This method will be called when there is an error that must be notified to the subscribers
    - `onNext()`: This method will be called when the `Publisher` has a new element
    - `onSubscribe()`: This method will be called when the publisher has added the subscriber with the `subscribe()` method
- `Flow.Subscription`: This interface has one methods:
    - `request()`: This method is used by the `Subscriber` to request an element from the publisher

Take into account that these are only interfaces and you can implement them and use them as you want. The supposed flow is as follows:

1. Someone calls the `subscribe()` method of a `Publisher`, sending it a `Subscriber`.
2. The `Publisher` creates a `Subscription` object and sends it to the `onSubscribe()` method of the `Subscriber`.
3. The `Subscriber` uses the `request()` method of the `Subscription` to request elements to the `Publisher`.
4. When the publisher has an element to publish, it sends them to all `Subscribers` that have requested elements, calling their `onNext()` method.
5. When the publisher ends its execution, it calls the `onComplete()` method of the subscribers.

Java API provides the `SubmissionPublisher` class that implements the Publisher interface and implements this behavior.

The following screenshot shows the output of the example and you can see how the behavior of the reactive streams is as expected:

```
Problems  @ Javadoc  Declaration  Search  Console   Error Log
<terminated> Main (44) [Java Application] C:\Program Files\Java\jdk-9\bin\javaw.exe (19 oct.
ForkJoinPool.commonPool-worker-1: Consumer 1: Subscription received
ForkJoinPool.commonPool-worker-2: Consumer 3: Subscription received
ForkJoinPool.commonPool-worker-2: Consumer 3: Requested three items
ForkJoinPool.commonPool-worker-3: Consumer 2: Subscription received
ForkJoinPool.commonPool-worker-2: Consumer 3: Item received
ForkJoinPool.commonPool-worker-2: Consumer 3: Item 0
ForkJoinPool.commonPool-worker-2: Consumer 3: This is the item 0
ForkJoinPool.commonPool-worker-1: Consumer 1: No Items requested
ForkJoinPool.commonPool-worker-3: Consumer 2: Item received
ForkJoinPool.commonPool-worker-3: Consumer 2: Item 0
ForkJoinPool.commonPool-worker-3: Consumer 2: This is the item 0
ForkJoinPool.commonPool-worker-1: Consumer 2: Item received
ForkJoinPool.commonPool-worker-1: Consumer 2: Item 1
ForkJoinPool.commonPool-worker-1: Consumer 2: This is the item 1
```

The three `Subscriber` objects receive their `Subscription`. As `Consumer1` doesn't request any `Item`, it won't receive them. `Consumer3` has requested three, so you will see in the output of the example that it will receive those three `Item` objects. Finally, the `Consumer2` object will receive the ten `Item` objects and the notification about the end of execution of the `Publisher`.

There's more...

There is an additional interface that should be used with reactive streams. It's the `Flow.Processor` interface and groups the `Flow.Publisher` and the `Flow.Subscriber` interfaces. Its main purpose is to be an element between a publisher and a subscriber to transform the elements produced by the first one into a format that can be processed by the second one. You can have more than one processors in a chain so the output of one of them could be processed by the next one.

Java also defines the `Flow` class that includes the four interfaces explained before.

7

Concurrent Collections

In this chapter, we will cover the following topics:

- Using non-blocking thread-safe deques
- Using blocking thread-safe deques
- Using blocking thread-safe queue ordered by priority
- Using thread-safe lists with delayed elements
- Using thread-safe navigable maps
- Using thread-safe HashMaps
- Using atomic variables
- Using atomic arrays
- Using the volatile keyword
- Using variable handles

Introduction

Data structure is a basic element of programming. Almost every program uses one or more types of data structure to store and manage data. The Java API provides the **Java Collections framework**. It contains interfaces, classes, and algorithms that implement a lot of different data structures that you can use in your programs.

When you need to work with data collections in a concurrent program, you must be very careful with the implementation you choose. Most collection classes do not work with concurrent applications because they can't control concurrent access to their data. If a concurrent task shares a data structure that is unable to work with another concurrent task, you might have data inconsistency errors that will affect the operation of the program. One example of this kind of data structure is the `ArrayList` class.

Java provides data collection processes that you can use in your concurrent programs without any problems or inconsistency. Basically, Java provides two kinds of collections to use in concurrent applications:

- **Blocking collections**: This kind of collection includes operations to add and remove data. If the operation can't be done immediately, because the collection is either full or empty, the thread that makes the call will be blocked until the operation could be carried out.
- **Non-blocking collections**: This kind of collection also includes operations to add and remove data. But in this case, if the operation can't be done immediately, it returns a `null` value or throws an exception; the thread that makes the call won't be blocked here.

Through the recipes in this chapter, you will learn how to use some Java collections in your concurrent applications. These include:

- Non-blocking deques, using the `ConcurrentLinkedDeque` class
- Blocking deques, using the `LinkedBlockingDeque` class
- Blocking queues to be used with producers and consumers of data, using the `LinkedTransferQueue` class
- Blocking queues that order elements by priority, using the `PriorityBlockingQueue` class
- Blocking queues with delayed elements, using the `DelayQueue` class
- Non-blocking navigable maps, using the `ConcurrentSkipListMap` class
- Non-blocking hash tables, using the `ConcurrentHashMap` class
- Atomic variables, using the `AtomicLong` and `AtomicIntegerArray` classes
- Variables stored in fields marked with the `volatile` keyword
- Atomic operations on the fields of individual classes, using variable handles.

Using non-blocking thread-safe deques

"List" is referred to as the most basic collection. It has an undetermined number of elements, and you can add, read, or remove an element from any position. Concurrent lists allow various threads to add or remove elements from the list at a time, without producing any data inconsistency errors. Similar to lists, we have deques. A deque is a data structure similar to a queue, but in a deque, you can add or remove elements from either the front (head) or back (tail).

In this recipe, you will learn how to use a non-blocking deque in a concurrent program. Non-blocking deques provide operations that, if not done immediately (for example, you want to get an element from a list but the list is empty), throw an exception or return a `null` value, depending on the operation. Java 7 introduced the `ConcurrentLinkedDeque` class that implements a non-blocking concurrent deque.

We are going to implement an example with the following two different tasks:

- One that adds thousands of elements to the deque
- One that removes data from the deque

Getting ready

The example of this recipe has been implemented using the Eclipse IDE. If you use Eclipse or a different IDE, such as NetBeans, open it and create a new Java project.

How to do it...

Follow these steps to implement the example:

1. Create a class named `AddTask` and specify that it implements the `Runnable` interface:

   ```
   public class AddTask implements Runnable {
   ```

2. Declare a private `ConcurrentLinkedDeque` attribute parameterized by the `String` class named `list`:

   ```
   private final ConcurrentLinkedDeque<String> list;
   ```

3. Implement the constructor of the class to initialize its attribute:

   ```
   public AddTask(ConcurrentLinkedDeque<String> list) {
     this.list=list;
   }
   ```

4. Implement the `run()` method of the class. This method will have a loop with 5000 cycles. In each cycle, we will take the first and last elements of the deque so we will take a total of 10,000 elements:

```
@Override
public void run() {
    String name=Thread.currentThread().getName();
    for (int i=0; i<10000; i++){
        list.add(name+": Element "+i);
    }
}
```

5. Create a class named `PollTask` and specify that it implements the `Runnable` interface:

```
public class PollTask implements Runnable {
```

6. Declare a private `ConcurrentLinkedDeque` attribute parameterized by the `String` class named `list`:

```
private final ConcurrentLinkedDeque<String> list;
```

7. Implement the constructor of the class to initialize its attribute:

```
public PollTask(ConcurrentLinkedDeque<String> list) {
    this.list=list;
}
```

8. Implement the `run()` method of the class. It takes out 10,000 elements of the deque in a loop with 5,000 steps, taking off two elements in each step:

```
@Override
public void run() {
    for (int i=0; i<5000; i++) {
        list.pollFirst();
        list.pollLast();
    }
}
```

9. Implement the main class of the example by creating a class named `Main` and adding the `main()` method to it:

```
public class Main {

    public static void main(String[] args) {
```

10. Create a `ConcurrentLinkedDeque` object parameterized by the `String` class named `list`:

```
ConcurrentLinkedDeque<String> list=new ConcurrentLinkedDeque<>();
```

11. Create an array of 100 `Thread` objects named `threads`:

```
Thread threads[]=new Thread[100];
```

12. Create 100 `AddTask` objects and threads to run each one of them. Store every thread in the array created earlier and start them:

```
for (int i=0; i<threads.length ; i++){
  AddTask task=new AddTask(list);
  threads[i]=new Thread(task);
  threads[i].start();
}
System.out.printf("Main: %d AddTask threads have been launched\n",
                  threads.length);
```

13. Wait for the completion of the threads using the `join()` method:

```
for (int i=0; i<threads.length; i++) {
  try {
    threads[i].join();
  } catch (InterruptedException e) {
    e.printStackTrace();
  }
}
```

14. Write the size of the list in the console:

```
System.out.printf("Main: Size of the List: %d\n",list.size());
```

15. Create 100 `PollTask` objects and threads to run each one of them. Store every thread in the array created earlier and start them:

```
for (int i=0; i< threads.length; i++){
  PollTask task=new PollTask(list);
  threads[i]=new Thread(task);
  threads[i].start();
}
System.out.printf("Main: %d PollTask threads have been launched\n",
                  threads.length);
```

16. Wait for the finalization of the threads using the `join()` method:

```
for (int i=0; i<threads.length; i++) {
  try {
    threads[i].join();
  } catch (InterruptedException e) {
    e.printStackTrace();
  }
}
```

17. Write the size of the list in the console:

```
System.out.printf("Main: Size of the List: %d\n",list.size());
```

How it works...

In this recipe, we used the `ConcurrentLinkedDeque` object parameterized by the `String` class to work with a non-blocking concurrent deque of data. The following screenshot shows the output of an execution of this example:

```
Problems  @ Javadoc  Declaration  Search  Console ⊠  Error Log
<terminated> Main (45) [Java Application] C:\Program Files\Java\jdk-9\bin\javaw.exe
Main: 100 AddTask threads have been launched
Main: Size of the List: 1000000
Main: 100 PollTask threads have been launched
Main: Size of the List: 0
```

First, you executed 100 `AddTask` tasks to add elements to the list. Each one of these tasks inserts 10,000 elements to the list using the `add()` method. This method adds new elements at the end of the deque. When all the tasks had finished, you wrote the number of elements of the deque in the console. At that moment, the deque had 1,000,000 elements.

Then, you executed 100 `PollTask` tasks to remove elements from the deque. Each one of these tasks removes 10,000 elements from the deque using the `pollFirst()` and `pollLast()` methods. The `pollFirst()` method returns and removes the first element of the deque, and the `pollLast()` method returns and removes the last element of the deque. If the deque is empty, they return a `null` value. When all the tasks had finished, you wrote the number of elements of the deque in the console. At that moment, the list had zero elements. Take into account that the `ConcurrentLinkedDeque` data structure doesn't allow you to add `null` values.

To write the number of elements in the deque, you used the `size()` method. You have to take into account that this method can return a value that is not real, especially if you use it when there are threads adding to or deleting data from the list. The method has to traverse the entire deque to count the elements, and the contents of the list can change with this operation. Only if you use them when there aren't any threads modifying the deque, you will have the guarantee that the returned result would be correct.

There's more...

The `ConcurrentLinkedDeque` class provides more methods to get elements from the deque:

- `getFirst()` and `getLast()`: These methods return the first and last element from the deque, respectively. They don't remove the returned element from the deque. If the deque is empty, they throw a `NoSuchElementExcpetion` exception.

- `peek()`, `peekFirst()`, and `peekLast()`: These methods return the first and the last element of the deque, respectively. They don't remove the returned element from the deque. If the deque is empty, they return a `null` value.

- `remove()`, `removeFirst()`, and `removeLast()`: These methods return the first and last element of the deque, respectively. They remove the returned element as well. If the deque is empty, they throw a `NoSuchElementException` exception.

Using blocking thread-safe deques

The most basic collection is referred to as a list. A list has an unlimited number of elements, and you can add, read, or remove an element from any position. A concurrent list allows various threads to add or remove elements from the list at a time without producing any data inconsistency. Similar to lists, we have deques. A deque is a data structure similar to a queue, but in a deque, you can add or remove elements from either the front (head) or back (tail).

In this recipe, you will learn how to use blocking deques in your concurrent programs. The main difference between blocking deques and non-blocking deques is that blocking deques have methods to insert and delete elements that, if not done immediately because the list is either full or empty, block the thread that make the call until the operation could be carried out. Java includes the `LinkedBlockingDeque` class that implements a blocking deque.

You are going to implement an example with the following two tasks:

- One that adds thousands of elements to the deque
- One that massively removes data from the same list

Getting ready

The example of this recipe has been implemented using the Eclipse IDE. If you use Eclipse or a different IDE, such as NetBeans, open it and create a new Java project.

How to do it...

Follow the steps described next to implement the example:

1. Create a class named `Client` and specify that it implements the `Runnable` interface:

   ```
   public class Client implements Runnable{
   ```

2. Declare a private `LinkedBlockingDeque` attribute parameterized by the `String` class named `requestList`:

   ```
   private final LinkedBlockingDeque<String> requestList;
   ```

3. Implement the constructor of the class to initialize its attributes:

```
public Client (LinkedBlockingDeque<String> requestList) {
    this.requestList=requestList;
}
```

4. Implement the `run()` method. Insert five `String` objects into the deque per second using the `put()` method of the `requestList` object. Repeat this cycle three times:

```
@Override
public void run() {
    for (int i=0; i<3; i++) {
        for (int j=0; j<5; j++) {
            StringBuilder request=new StringBuilder();
            request.append(i);
            request.append(":");
            request.append(j);
            try {
                requestList.put(request.toString());
            } catch (InterruptedException e) {
                e.printStackTrace();
            }
            System.out.printf("Client added: %s at %s.\n",request,
                                new Date());
        }
        try {
            TimeUnit.SECONDS.sleep(2);
        } catch (InterruptedException e) {
            e.printStackTrace();
        }
    }
    System.out.printf("Client: End.\n");
}
```

5. Create the main class of the example by creating a class named `Main` and adding the `main()` method to it:

```
public class Main {
    public static void main(String[] args) throws Exception {
```

6. Declare and create `LinkedBlockingDeque` parameterized by the `String` class named list specifying a fixed size of three:

```
LinkedBlockingDeque<String> list=new LinkedBlockingDeque<>(3);
```

7. Create and start a `Thread` object to execute a client task:

```
Client client=new Client(list);
Thread thread=new Thread(client);
thread.start();
```

8. Get three `String` objects from the list every 300 milliseconds using the `take()` method of the list object. Repeat this cycle five times. Write the strings in the console:

```
for (int i=0; i<5 ; i++) {
  for (int j=0; j<3; j++) {
    String request=list.take();
    System.out.printf("Main: Removed: %s at %s. Size: %d\n",
                   request,new Date(), list.size());
  }
  TimeUnit.MILLISECONDS.sleep(300);
}
```

9. Write a message to indicate the end of the program:

```
System.out.printf("Main: End of the program.\n");
```

How it works...

In this recipe, you used `LinkedBlockingDeque`, parameterized by the `String` class, to work with a non-blocking concurrent deque of data.

The `Client` class uses the `put()` method to insert strings into the deque. If the deque is full (because you have created it with fixed capacity), the method will block the execution of its thread until there is empty space in the list.

The `Main` class uses the `take()` method to get strings from the deque. If the deque is empty, the method blocks the execution of its thread until there are elements in the deque.

Both the methods of the `LinkedBlockingDeque` class used in this example can throw an `InterruptedException` exception if they are interrupted while they are being blocked. So, you have to include the necessary code to catch this exception.

There's more...

The `LinkedBlockingDeque` class also provides methods to insert and get elements from the deque that, instead of being blocked, throws an exception or returns the `null` value. These methods are as follows:

- `takeFirst()` and `takeLast()`: These return the first and last element of the deque, respectively. They remove the returned element from the deque. If the deque is empty, they block the thread until there are elements in the deque.
- `getFirst()` and `getLast()`: These return the first and last element of the deque, respectively. They don't remove the returned element from the deque. If the deque is empty, they throw a `NoSuchElementExcpetion` exception.
- `peek()`, `peekFirst()`, and `peekLast()`: The `peekFirst()` and `peekLast()` methods return the first and last element of the deque, respectively. They don't remove the returned element from the deque. If the deque is empty, they return a `null` value.
- `poll()`, `pollFirst()`, and `pollLast()`: The `pollFirst()` and `pollLast()` methods return the first and last element of the deque, respectively. They remove the returned element from the deque. If the list is empty, they return a `null` value.
- `add()`, `addFirst()`, and `addLast()`: The `addFirst()` and `addLast()` methods add an element to the first and last position, respectively. If the deque is full (created with fixed capacity), they throw an `IllegalStateException` exception.

See also

- The *Using non-blocking thread-safe deques* recipe in this chapter

Using blocking thread-safe queue ordered by priority

When you work with data structures, you may typically feel the need to have an ordered queue. Java provides `PriorityBlockingQueue` that has this functionality.

All the elements you want to add to `PriorityBlockingQueue` have to implement the `Comparable` interface; alternatively, you can include `Comparator` in the queue's constructor. This interface has a method called `compareTo()` that receives an object of the same type. So you have two objects to compare: the one that is executing the method and the one that is received as a parameter. The method must return a number less than zero if the local object is less than the parameter. It should return a number bigger than zero if the local object is greater than the parameter. The number must be zero if both the objects are equal.

`PriorityBlockingQueue` uses the `compareTo()` method when you insert an element in it to determine the position of the element inserted. Bigger elements will either be the tail or head of the queue, depending on the `compareTo()` method.

Another important characteristic of `PriorityBlockingQueue` is that it's a **blocking data structure**. It has methods that, if unable to perform the operation immediately, will block the thread until they are able to do it.

In this recipe, you will learn how to use the `PriorityBlockingQueue` class by implementing an example, where you are going to store a lot of events with different priorities in the same list, to check that the queue will be ordered as you want.

Getting ready

The example of this recipe has been implemented using the Eclipse IDE. If you use Eclipse or a different IDE, such as NetBeans, open it and create a new Java project.

How to do it...

Follow these steps to implement the example:

1. Create a class named `Event` and specify that it implements the `Comparable` interface parameterized by the `Event` class:

   ```
   public class Event implements Comparable<Event> {
   ```

2. Declare a private `int` attribute named `thread` to store the number of threads that have created the event:

   ```
   private final int thread;
   ```

3. Declare a private `int` attribute named `priority` to store the priority of the event:

```
private final int priority;
```

4. Implement the constructor of the class to initialize its attributes:

```
public Event(int thread, int priority){
  this.thread=thread;
  this.priority=priority;
}
```

5. Implement the `getThread()` method to return the value of the thread attribute:

```
public int getThread() {
  return thread;
}
```

6. Implement the `getPriority()` method to return the value of the priority attribute:

```
public int getPriority() {
  return priority;
}
```

7. Implement the `compareTo()` method. It receives `Event` as a parameter and compares the priority of the current event and the one received as a parameter. It returns −1 if the priority of the current event is bigger, 0 if both the priorities are equal, and 1 if the priority of the current event is smaller. Note that this is the opposite of most `Comparator.compareTo()` implementations:

```
@Override
public int compareTo(Event e) {
  if (this.priority>e.getPriority()) {
    return -1;
  } else if (this.priority<e.getPriority()) {
    return 1;
  } else {
    return 0;
  }
}
```

8. Create a class named `Task` and specify that it implements the `Runnable` interface:

```
public class Task implements Runnable {
```

9. Declare a private `int` attribute named `id` to store the number that identifies the task:

```
private final int id;
```

10. Declare a private `PriorityBlockingQueue` attribute parameterized by the `Event` class named `queue` to store the events generated by the task:

```
private final PriorityBlockingQueue<Event> queue;
```

11. Implement the constructor of the class to initialize its attributes:

```
public Task(int id, PriorityBlockingQueue<Event> queue) {
    this.id=id;
    this.queue=queue;
}
```

12. Implement the `run()` method. It stores 1,000 events in the queue, using its ID, to identify the task that creates the event and we assign to each event a different priority from 1 to 1000. Use the `add()` method to store the events in the queue:

```
@Override
public void run() {
    for (int i=0; i<1000; i++){
        Event event=new Event(id,i);
        queue.add(event);
    }
}
```

13. Implement the main class of the example by creating a class named `Main` and adding the `main()` method to it:

```
public class Main{
    public static void main(String[] args) {
```

14. Create a `PriorityBlockingQueue` object parameterized by the `Event` class named `queue`:

```
PriorityBlockingQueue<Event> queue=new PriorityBlockingQueue<>();
```

15. Create an array of five `Thread` objects to store the threads that will execute the five tasks:

```
Thread taskThreads[]=new Thread[5];
```

16. Create five `Task` objects. Store the threads in the array created earlier:

```
for (int i=0; i<taskThreads.length; i++){
  Task task=new Task(i,queue);
  taskThreads[i]=new Thread(task);
}
```

17. Start the five threads created earlier:

```
for (int i=0; i<taskThreads.length ; i++) {
  taskThreads[i].start();
}
```

18. Wait for the finalization of the five threads using the `join()` method:

```
for (int i=0; i<taskThreads.length ; i++) {
  try {
    taskThreads[i].join();
  } catch (InterruptedException e) {
    e.printStackTrace();
  }
}
```

19. Write the actual size of the queue in the console and the events stored in it. Use the `poll()` method to take off the events from the queue:

```
System.out.printf("Main: Queue Size: %d\n",queue.size());
for (int i=0; i<taskThreads.length*1000; i++){
  Event event=queue.poll();
  System.out.printf("Thread %s: Priority %d\n",
                event.getThread(),event.getPriority());
}
```

20. Write a message to the console with the final size of the queue:

```
System.out.printf("Main: Queue Size: %d\n",queue.size());
System.out.printf("Main: End of the program\n");
```

How it works...

In this example, you implemented a priority queue of `Event` objects using `PriorityBlockingQueue`. As mentioned in the introduction, all the elements stored in `PriorityBlockingQueue` have to implement the `Comparable` interface or provide a `Comparator` object to the constructor of the queue. In this case, you used the first approach, so you implemented the `compareTo()` method in the `Event` class.

All the events have a priority attribute. The elements that have a higher value of priority will be the first elements in the queue. When you implement the compareTo() method, if the event executing the method has a priority higher than the priority of the event passed as a parameter, it returns -1 as the result. In another case, if the event executing the method has a priority lower than the priority of the event passed as a parameter, it returns 1 as the result. If both objects have the same priority, the compareTo() method returns 0. In this case, the PriorityBlockingQueue class doesn't guarantee the order of the elements.

We implemented the Task class to add the Event objects to the priority queue. Each task object adds 1,000 events to the queue, with priorities between 0 and 999, using the add() method.

The main() method of the Main class creates five Task objects and executes them in the corresponding threads. When all the threads had finished their execution, you wrote all the elements to the console. To get the elements from the queue, we used the poll() method. This method returns and removes the first element from the queue.

The following screenshot shows part of the output of an execution of the program:

```
 Problems  @ Javadoc   Declaration   Search   Console ⊠   Error Log
<terminated> Main (47) [Java Application] C:\Program Files\Java\jdk-9\bin\javaw.exe
Main: Queue Size: 5000
Thread 1: Priority 999
Thread 3: Priority 999
Thread 2: Priority 999
Thread 0: Priority 999
Thread 4: Priority 999
Thread 2: Priority 998
Thread 0: Priority 998
Thread 3: Priority 998
Thread 1: Priority 998
Thread 4: Priority 998
Thread 2: Priority 997
Thread 0: Priority 997
Thread 3: Priority 997
Thread 1: Priority 997
Thread 4: Priority 997
Thread 2: Priority 996
```

You can see how the queue has a size of 5,000 elements and how the first elements have the biggest priority value.

There's more...

The `PriorityBlockingQueue` class has other interesting methods. The following is a description of some of them:

- `clear()`: This method removes all the elements of the queue.
- `take()`: This method returns and removes the first element of the queue. If the queue is empty, it blocks its thread until the queue has elements.
- `put(E e)`: This is the class used to parameterize the `PriorityBlockingQueue` class. It inserts the element that is passed as a parameter into the queue.
- `peek()`: This method returns the first element of the queue but doesn't remove it.

See also

- The *Using blocking thread-safe deques* recipe in this chapter

Using thread-safe lists with delayed elements

An interesting data structure provided by the Java API, which you can use in concurrent applications, is implemented in the `DelayQueue` class. In this class, you can store elements with an activation date. The methods that return or extract elements from the queue will ignore these elements whose data will appear in the future. They are invisible to these methods. To obtain this behavior, the elements you want to store in the `DelayQueue` class need to have the `Delayed` interface implemented. This interface allows you to work with delayed objects. This interface has the `getDelay()` method that returns the time until the activation of the element. This interface forces you to implement the following two methods:

- `compareTo(Delayed o)`: The `Delayed` interface extends the `Comparable` interface. This method will return a value less than zero if the object that is executing the method has a delay smaller than the object passed as a parameter. It will return a value greater than zero if the object that is executing the method has a delay bigger than the object passed as a parameter. It will return zero if both the objects have the same delay.

- `getDelay(TimeUnit unit)`: This method has to return the time remaining until the activation date in units, as specified by the unit parameter. The `TimeUnit` class is an enumeration with the following constants: DAYS, HOURS, MICROSECONDS, MILLISECONDS, MINUTES, NANOSECONDS, and SECONDS.

In this example, you will learn how to use the `DelaydQueue` class by storing in it some events with different activation dates.

Getting ready

The example of this recipe has been implemented using the Eclipse IDE. If you use Eclipse or a different IDE, such as NetBeans, open it and create a new Java project.

How to do it...

Follow these steps to implement the example:

1. Create a class named `Event` and specify that it implements the `Delayed` interface:

   ```
   public class Event implements Delayed {
   ```

2. Declare a private `Date` attribute named `startDate`:

   ```
   private final Date startDate;
   ```

3. Implement the constructor of the class to initialize its attribute:

   ```
   public Event (Date startDate) {
     this.startDate=startDate;
   }
   ```

4. Implement the `compareTo()` method. It receives a `Delayed` object as its parameter. Return the difference between the delay of the current object and the one passed as a parameter:

   ```
   @Override
   public int compareTo(Delayed o) {
     long result=this.getDelay(TimeUnit.NANOSECONDS)-o.getDelay
                                         (TimeUnit.NANOSECONDS);
     if (result<0) {
       return -1;
   ```

```
    } else if (result>0) {
      return 1;
    }
    return 0;
  }
```

5. Implement the `getDelay()` method. Return the difference between the start date of the object and the actual date in `TimeUnit`, which is received as a parameter:

```
public long getDelay(TimeUnit unit) {
  Date now=new Date();
  long diff=startDate.getTime()-now.getTime();
  return unit.convert(diff,TimeUnit.MILLISECONDS);
}
```

6. Create a class named `Task` and specify that it implements the `Runnable` interface:

```
public class Task implements Runnable {
```

7. Declare a private `int` attribute named `id` to store a number that identifies this task:

```
private final int id;
```

8. Declare a private `DelayQueue` attribute parameterized by the `Event` class named queue:

```
private final DelayQueue<Event> queue;
```

9. Implement the constructor of the class to initialize its attributes:

```
public Task(int id, DelayQueue<Event> queue) {
  this.id=id;
  this.queue=queue;
}
```

10. Implement the `run()` method. First, calculate the activation date of the events that this task is going to create. Then, add the number of seconds equal to the ID of the object to the actual date:

```
@Override
public void run() {
    Date now=new Date();
    Date delay=new Date();
    delay.setTime(now.getTime()+(id*1000));
    System.out.printf("Thread %s: %s\n",id,delay);
```

11. Store 100 events in the queue using the `add()` method:

```
for (int i=0; i<100; i++) {
    Event event=new Event(delay);
    queue.add(event);
}
}
```

12. Implement the main class of the example by creating a class named `Main` and adding the `main()` method to it:

```
public class Main {
    public static void main(String[] args) throws Exception {
```

13. Create a `DelayQueue` object parameterized by the `Event` class:

```
DelayQueue<Event> queue=new DelayQueue<>();
```

14. Create an array of five `Thread` objects to store the tasks you're going to execute:

```
Thread threads[]=new Thread[5];
```

15. Create five `Task` objects with different IDs:

```
for (int i=0; i<threads.length; i++){
    Task task=new Task(i+1, queue);
    threads[i]=new Thread(task);
}
```

16. Launch all the five tasks created earlier:

```
for (int i=0; i<threads.length; i++) {
    threads[i].start();
}
```

17. Wait for the finalization of the threads using the `join()` method:

```
for (int i=0; i<threads.length; i++) {
   threads[i].join();
}
```

18. Write to the console the events stored in the queue. When the size of the queue is bigger than zero, use the `poll()` method to obtain an `Event` class. If it returns `null`, put the main thread to sleep for 500 milliseconds for the activation of more events:

```
do {
   int counter=0;
   Event event;
   do {
      event=queue.poll();
      if (event!=null) counter++;
   } while (event!=null);
   System.out.printf("At %s you have read %d events\n",
                      new Date(), counter);
   TimeUnit.MILLISECONDS.sleep(500);
} while (queue.size()>0);
   }
}
```

How it works...

In this recipe, we implemented the `Event` class. This class has a unique attribute, the activation date of the events, and it implements the `Delayed` interface. You can store `Event` objects in the `DelayQueue` class.

The `getDelay()` method returns the number of nanoseconds between the activation date and the actual date. Both dates are objects of the `Date` class. You used the `getTime()` method that returns a date converted into milliseconds. Then, you converted this value into `TimeUnit`, which was received as a parameter. The `DelayQueue` class works in nanoseconds, but at this point, it's transparent to you.

The `compareTo()` method returns a value less than zero if the delay of the object executing the method is smaller than the delay of the object passed as a parameter. It returns a value greater than zero if the delay of the object executing the method is bigger than the delay of the object passed as a parameter. It returns 0 if both the delays are equal.

You also implemented the `Task` class. This class has an `integer` attribute named `id`. When a `Task` object is executed, it adds the number of seconds that is equal to the ID of the task to the actual date, and this refers to the activation date of the events stored by this task in the `DelayQueue` class. Each `Task` object stores 100 events in the queue using the `add()` method.

Finally, in the `main()` method of the `Main` class, you created five `Task` objects and executed them in their corresponding threads. When these threads finished their execution, you wrote all the events using the `poll()` method in the console. This method retrieves and removes the first element of the queue. If the queue does not have any active element, it returns the `null` value. You call the `poll()` method, and if it returns an `Event` class, you increment a counter. When it returns the `null` value, you write the value of the counter in the console and put the thread to sleep for half a second to wait for more active events. When you obtained the 500 events stored in the queue, the execution of the program finished.

The following screenshot shows part of the output of an execution of the program:

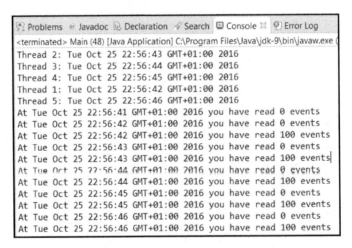

You can see how the program only gets 100 events when it is activated.

You must be very careful with the `size()` method. It returns the total number of elements in the list that includes both active and non-active elements.

There's more...

The `DelayQueue` class has other interesting methods, which are as follows:

- `clear()`: This method removes all the elements of the queue.
- `offer(E e)`: Here, `E` represents the class used to parameterize the `DelayQueue` class. This method inserts the element that is passed as a parameter into the queue.
- `peek()`: This method retrieves but doesn't remove the first element of the queue.
- `take()`: This method retrieves and removes the first element of the queue. If there aren't any active elements, the thread that is executing the method will be blocked until the thread gets some active elements.

See also

- The *Using blocking thread-safe deques* recipe in this chapter

Using thread-safe navigable maps

The `ConcurrentNavigableMap` is an interface that defines interesting data structures provided by the Java API that you can use in your concurrent programs. The classes that implement the `ConcurrentNavigableMap` interface stores elements in two parts:

- A **key** that uniquely identifies an element
- The rest of the data that defines the element, called **value**

The Java API also provides a class that implements `ConcurrentSkipListMap`, which is the interface that implements a non-blocking list with the behavior of the `ConcurrentNavigableMap` interface. Internally, it uses a **Skip List** to store data. A Skip List is a data structure based on parallel lists that allow us to get the kind of efficiency that is associated with a binary tree. You can get more information about Skip Lists at `https://en.wikipedia.org/wiki/Skip_list`. With it, you can get a sorted data structure, instead of a sorted list, with better access time to insert, search, or delete elements.

Skip List was introduced by William Pugh in 1990.

When you insert an element to a map, the map uses a key to order them; therefore, all the elements will be ordered. The keys have to implement the `Comparable` interface, or you have to supply a `Comparator` class to the constructor of the map. The class also provides methods to obtain a submap of the map, in addition to the ones that return a concrete element.

In this recipe, you will learn how to use the `ConcurrentSkipListMap` class to implement a map of contacts.

Getting ready

The example of this recipe has been implemented using the Eclipse IDE. If you use Eclipse or a different IDE, such as NetBeans, open it and create a new Java project.

How to do it...

Follow these steps to implement the example:

1. Create a class named `Contact`:

   ```
   public class Contact {
   ```

2. Declare two private `String` attributes named `name` and `phone`:

   ```
   private final String name;
   private final String phone;
   ```

3. Implement the constructor of the class to initialize its attributes:

   ```
   public Contact(String name, String phone) {
     this.name=name;
     this.phone=phone;
   }
   ```

4. Implement the methods to return the values of the `name` and `phone` attributes:

   ```
   public String getName() {
     return name;
   }

   public String getPhone() {
     return phone;
   }
   ```

5. Create a class named `Task` and specify that it implements the `Runnable` interface:

```
public class Task implements Runnable {
```

6. Declare a private `ConcurrentSkipListMap` attribute, parameterized by the `String` and `Contact` classes, named `map`:

```
private final ConcurrentSkipListMap<String, Contact> map;
```

7. Declare a private `String` attribute named `id` to store the ID of the current task:

```
private final String id;
```

8. Implement the constructor of the class to store its attributes:

```
public Task (ConcurrentSkipListMap<String, Contact> map,String id){
    this.id=id;
    this.map=map;
}
```

9. Implement the `run()` method. It stores 1,000 different contacts in the map using the ID of the task and an incremental number to create `Contact` objects. Use the `put()` method to store the contacts in the map:

```
@Override
public void run() {
    for (int i=0; i<1000; i++) {
        Contact contact=new Contact(id, String.valueOf(i+1000));
        map.put(id+contact.getPhone(), contact);
    }
}
```

10. Implement the main class of the example by creating a class named `Main` and adding the `main()` method to it:

```
public class Main {
    public static void main(String[] args) {
```

11. Create a `ConcurrentSkipListMap` object, parameterized by the `String` and `Conctact` classes, named `map`:

```
ConcurrentSkipListMap<String, Contact> map = new
                            ConcurrentSkipListMap<>();
```

12. Create an array for 26 `Thread` objects to store all the `Task` objects that you're going to execute:

```
Thread threads[]=new Thread[26];
int counter=0;
```

13. Create and launch 26 `task` objects and assign a capital letter to the ID of each task:

```
for (char i='A'; i<='Z'; i++) {
    Task task=new Task(map, String.valueOf(i));
    threads[counter]=new Thread(task);
    threads[counter].start();
    counter++;
}
```

14. Wait for the finalization of the threads using the `join()` method:

```
for (Thread thread : threads){
    try {
        threads[i].join();
    } catch (InterruptedException e) {
        e.printStackTrace();
    }
}
```

15. Get the first entry of the map using the `firstEntry()` method. Write its data to the console:

```
System.out.printf("Main: Size of the map: %d\n",map.size());

Map.Entry<String, Contact> element;
Contact contact;

element=map.firstEntry();
contact=element.getValue();
System.out.printf("Main: First Entry: %s: %s\n", contact.getName(),
                  contact.getPhone());
```

16. Get the last entry of the map using the `lastEntry()` method. Write its data to the console:

```
element=map.lastEntry();
contact=element.getValue();
System.out.printf("Main: Last Entry: %s: %s\n", contact.getName(),
                  contact.getPhone());
```

17. Obtain a submap of the map using the `subMap()` method. Write its data to the console:

```
System.out.printf("Main: Submap from A1996 to B1002: \n");
ConcurrentNavigableMap<String, Contact> submap=map
                                    .subMap("A1996","B1002");
do {
  element=submap.pollFirstEntry();
  if (element!=null) {
    contact=element.getValue();
    System.out.printf("%s: %s\n", contact.getName(),
                    contact.getPhone());
  }
} while (element!=null);
}
```

How it works...

In this recipe, we implemented a `Task` class to store `Contact` objects in a navigable map. Each contact has a name, which is the ID of the task that creates it, and a phone number, which is a number between 1,000 and 2,000. We concatenated these values as keys for the contacts. Each `Task` object creates 1,000 contacts; these contacts are stored in the navigable map using the `put()` method.

 If you insert an element with a key that exists in the map, the element associated with that key will be replaced by the new element.

The `main()` method of the `Main` class creates 26 `Task` objects, using the letters between A and Z as IDs. Then, you used some methods to obtain data from the map. The `firstEntry()` method returns a `Map.Entry` object with the first element of the map. This method doesn't remove the element from the map. The object contains the key and the element. To obtain the element, you called the `getValue()` method. You can use the `getKey()` method to obtain the key of that element.

The `lastEntry()` method returns a `Map.Entry` object with the last element of the map. The `subMap()` method returns the `ConcurrentNavigableMap` object with part of the elements of the map, in this case, the elements that had keys between `A1996` and `B1002`. You used the `pollFirst()` method to process the elements of the `subMap()` method. This method returns and removes the first `Map.Entry` object of the submap.

The following screenshot shows the output of an execution of the program:

```
Problems   @ Javadoc   Declaration   Search   Console ⅜   Error Log
<terminated> Main (49) [Java Application] C:\Program Files\Java\jdk-9\bin\javaw.exe (
Main: Size of the map: 25000
Main: First Entry: A: 1000
Main: Last Entry: Y: 1999
Main: Submap from A1996 to B1002:
A: 1996
A: 1997
A: 1998
A: 1999
B: 1000
B: 1001
```

There's more...

The `ConcurrentSkipListMap` class has other interesting methods. Some of them are as follows:

- `headMap(K toKey)`: Here, K is the class of the key values used in the parameterization of the `ConcurrentSkipListMap` object. This method returns a submap of the first elements of the map with the elements that have a key smaller than the one passed as a parameter.
- `tailMap(K fromKey)`: Here, K is the class of the key values used in the parameterization of the `ConcurrentSkipListMap` object. This method returns a submap of the last elements of the map with the elements that have a key greater than the one passed as a parameter.
- `putIfAbsent(K key, V Value)`: This method inserts the value specified as a parameter and also the key specified as a parameter if it doesn't exist in the map.
- `pollLastEntry()`: This method returns and removes a `Map.Entry` object with the last element of the map.
- `replace(K key, V Value)`: This method replaces the value associated with the key specified as a parameter if this key exists in the map.

See also

- The *Using non-blocking thread-safe deques* recipe in this chapter

Using thread-safe HashMaps

A hash table is a data structure that allows you to map a key to a value. Internally, it usually uses an array to store the elements and a hash function to calculate the position of the element in the array, using its key. The main advantage of this data structure is that the insert, delete, and search operations are very fast here, so it's very useful in situations when you have to carry out a lot of search operations.

The Java API provides different hash table implementations through the Map and ConcurrentMap interfaces. The ConcurrentMap interface provides thread-safety and atomic guarantees to all the operations, so you can use them in concurrent applications. The ConcurrentHashMap class implements the ConcurrentMap interface and adds some more methods to the ones defined in the interface. This class supports the following:

- Full concurrency of read operations
- High expected concurrency for insert and delete operations

Both the elements (class and interface) were introduced in Java version 5, but in version 8, a lot of new methods similar to the ones provided by the stream API were developed.

In this recipe, you will learn how to use the ConcurrentHashMap class in your application and the most important methods it provides.

Getting ready

The example of this recipe has been implemented using the Eclipse IDE. If you use Eclipse or a different IDE, such as NetBeans, open it and create a new Java project.

How to do it...

Follow these steps to implement the example:

1. Create a class named `Operation` with three attributes: a `String` attribute named `user`, a `String` attribute named `operation`, and a `Date` attribute named `time`. Add the methods to get and set the values of the attributes. The code of this class is very simple, so it won't be included here.

2. Create a class named `HashFiller`. Specify that it implements the `Runnable` interface:

   ```
   public class HashFiller implements Runnable {
   ```

3. Declare a private `ConcurrentHashMap` attribute named `userHash`. The key of the hash will be a `String` type and its value will be a `ConcurrentLinkedDeque` object of `Operation` objects. Implement the constructor of the class to initialize the attribute:

   ```
   private ConcurrentHashMap<String, ConcurrentLinkedDeque<Operation>>
           userHash;

   public HashFiller(ConcurrentHashMap<String, ConcurrentLinkedDeque
                     <Operation>> userHash) {
     this.userHash = userHash;
   }
   ```

4. Implement the `run()` method. We're going to fill `ConcurrentHashMap` with 100 random `Operation` objects. First, generate random data and then use the `addOperationToHash()` method to insert the object in the hash:

   ```
   @Override
   public void run() {

     Random randomGenerator = new Random();
     for (int i = 0; i < 100; i++) {
       Operation operation = new Operation();
       String user = "USER" + randomGenerator.nextInt(100);
       operation.setUser(user);
       String action = "OP" + randomGenerator.nextInt(10);
       operation.setOperation(action);
       operation.setTime(new Date());

       addOperationToHash(userHash, operation);
     }
   }
   ```

5. Implement the `addOperationToHash()` method. It receives the hash and the operation you want to add as parameters. The key in the map will be the user assigned to the operation. We use the `computeIfAbsent()` method to obtain the `ConcurrentLinkedDeque` object associated with the key. If the key exists, this method returns the value associated with it. If it doesn't, it executes the lambda expression passed as a parameter to this method to generate the value and associate it with the key. In this case, we generate a new `ConcurrentLinkedDeque` object. Finally, insert the operation to the deque:

```
private void addOperationToHash(ConcurrentHashMap<String,
                                ConcurrentLinkedDeque<Operation>>
                                userHash, Operation operation) {

    ConcurrentLinkedDeque<Operation> opList = userHash
                        .computeIfAbsent(operation.getUser(),
                        user -> new ConcurrentLinkedDeque<>());

    opList.add(operation);
}
```

6. Now implement the `Main` class and include the `main()` method. First, declare a `ConcurrentHashMap` object and a `HashFiller` task:

```
ConcurrentHashMap<String, ConcurrentLinkedDeque<Operation>>
    userHash = new ConcurrentHashMap<>();
HashFiller hashFiller = new HashFiller(userHash);
```

7. Execute 10 threads with the `HashFiller` class and wait for their finalization using the `join()` method:

```
Thread[] threads = new Thread[10];
for (int i = 0; i < 10; i++) {
  threads[i] = new Thread(hashFiller);
  threads[i].start();
}

for (int i = 0; i < 10; i++) {
  try {
    threads[i].join();
  } catch (InterruptedException e) {
    e.printStackTrace();
  }
}
```

8. Now, extract the information of `ConcurrentHashMap`. First, extract the number of elements stored in it with the `size()` method. Then, use the `forEach()` method to apply an action to all the elements stored in the hash. The first parameter is the parallelism threshold. This is the minimum number of elements required to make the operation execute in a concurrent way. We have specified the value 10 and the hash has 100 elements, so the operation will be executed in a parallel way. The lambda expression receives two parameters: key and value. Print the key and size of `ConcurrentLinkedDeque` stored as a value:

```
System.out.printf("Size: %d\n", userHash.size());

userHash.forEach(10, (user, list) -> {
    System.out.printf("%s: %s: %d\n", Thread.currentThread()
                        .getName(), user, list.size());
});
```

9. Then, use the `forEachEntry()` method. This is similar to the previous one, but the lambda expression receives an `Entry` object as a parameter instead of receiving two parameters. You can use this entry object to obtain the key and value:

```
userHash.forEachEntry(10, entry -> {
    System.out.printf("%s: %s: %d\n", Thread.currentThread()
                        .getName(), entry.getKey(),
    entry.getValue().size());
});
```

10. Then, use the `search()` method to find the first element that satisfies the search function specified. In our case, we search for an operation whose operation code ends in 1. As occurs with the `forEach()` method, we specify a parallelism threshold:

```
Operation op = userHash.search(10, (user, list) -> {
    for (Operation operation : list) {
        if (operation.getOperation().endsWith("1")) {
            return operation;
        }
    }
    return null;
});

System.out.printf("The operation we have found is: %s, %s, %s,\n",
                op.getUser(), op.getOperation(), op.getTime());
```

11. Use the `search()` method again, but this time, use it to find a user with more than 10 operations:

```
ConcurrentLinkedDeque<Operation> operations = userHash.search(10,
                                              (user, list) -> {
    if (list.size() > 10) {
      return list;
    }
    return null;
});

System.out.printf("The user we have found is: %s: %d operations\n",
                  operations.getFirst().getUser(),
                  operations.size());
```

12. Finally, use the `reduce()` method to calculate the total number of operations stored in the hash:

```
int totalSize = userHash.reduce(10, (user, list) -> {
    return list.size();
}, (n1, n2) -> {
    return n1 + n2;
});

System.out.printf("The total size is: %d\n", totalSize);
  }
}
```

How it works...

In this recipe, we implemented an application that uses `ConcurrentHashMap` to store information about operations made by users. Internally, the hash table uses the user attribute of the `Operation` class as a key and `ConcurrentLinkedDeque` (a non-blocking concurrent list) as its value to store all the operations associated with that user.

First, we filled the hash with some random data using 10 different threads. We implemented the `HashFiller` task for this purpose. The biggest problem with these tasks is what happens when you have to insert a key in the hash table. If two threads want to add the same key at the same time, you can lose the data inserted by one of the threads and have a data-race condition. To solve this problem, we used the `computeIfAbsent()` method.

This method receives a key and an implementation of the `Function` interface that can be expressed as a lambda expression; the key and implementation are received as parameters. If the key exists, the method returns the value associated with the key. If it doesn't, the method executes the `Function` object specified and adds the key and value returned by `Function` to the HashMap. In our case, the key didn't exist, so we created a new instance of the `ConcurrentLinkedDeque` class. The main advantage of this method is that it's executed atomically; so, if another thread tries to do the same operation, it will be blocked until this operation is finished.

Then, in the `main()` method, we used other methods of `ConcurrentHashMap` to process the information stored in the hash. We used the following methods:

- `forEach()`: This method receives an implementation of the `BiConsumer` interface that can be expressed as a lambda expression; it is received as a parameter. The other two parameters of this expression represent the key and value of the element we're processing. This method applies the expression to all the elements stored in `ConcurrentHashMap`.
- `forEachEntry()`: This method is equivalent to the previous one, but here the expression is an implementation of the `Consumer` interface. It receives an `Entry` object that stores the key and value of the entry we're processing as a parameter. This is another way to express the same functionality.
- `search()`: This method receives the implementation of the `BiFunction` interface that can be expressed as a lambda expression; it is received as a parameter. This function also receives the key and value of the entry of the `ConcurrentHashMap` object we're processing as parameters. It returns the first non-null value returned by `BiFunction`.
- `reduce()`: This method receives two `BiFunction` interfaces to reduce the elements of `ConcurrentHashMap` to a unique value. This allows you to implement a `MapReduce` operation with the elements of `ConcurrentHashMap`. The first `BiFunction` interface allows you to transform the key and value of the elements into a unique value, and the second `BiFunction` interface allows you to aggregate the values of two different elements.

All the methods described so far have a first parameter named `parallelismThreshold`. This parameter is described as ...*the (estimated) number of elements needed for this operation to be executed in parallel...*, that is to say, if `ConcurrentHashMap` has fewer elements than the value specified in the parameter, the method is executed in a sequential way. On the contrary (as in our case), the method is executed in a parallel way.

There's more...

`ConcurrentHashMap` has more methods than what's specified in the previous section. We enumerate some of them in the following list:

- `forEachKey()` and `forEachValue()`: These methods are similar to the `forEach()` methods, but in this case, the expression processes the keys and values stored in `ConcurrentHashMap`, respectively.

- `searchEntries()`, `searchKeys()`, and `searchValues()`: These methods are similar to the `search()` method explained before. However, in this case, the expression passed as a parameter receives an `Entry` object, a key, or a value of the elements stored in `ConcurrentHashMap`.

- `reduceEntries()`, `reduceKeys()`, and `reduceValues()`: These methods are similar to the `reduce()` method explained before. However, in this case, the expression passed as a parameter receives an `Entry` object, a key, or a value of the elements stored in `ConcurrentHashMap`.

- `reduceXXXToDouble()`, `reduceXXXToLong()`, and `reduceXXXToInt()`: These methods allow you to make a reduction of the elements of `ConcurrentHashMap` by generating a `double`, `long`, or `int` value, respectively.

- `computeIfPresent()`: This method complements the `computeIfAbsent()` method. In this case, it receives a key and an implementation of the `BiFunction` interface that can be expressed as a lambda expression. If the key exists in the `HashMap`, the method applies the expression to calculate the new value of the key. The `BiFunction` interface receives the key and the actual value of that key as parameters, and it returns the new value.

- `merge()`: This method receives a key, value, and implementation of the `BiFunction` interface that can be expressed as a lambda expression; they are received as parameters. If the key doesn't exist in `ConcurrentHashMap`, it inserts it there and associates the value parameter with it. If it exists, execute `BiFunction` to calculate the new value associated with the key. The `BiFunction` interface receives the key and its actual value as parameters and returns the new value associated with the key.

- `getOrDefault()`: This method receives a key and a default value as parameters. If the key exists in `ConcurrentHashMap`, it returns its associated value. Otherwise, it returns the default value.

See also

- The *Using thread-safe navigable maps* recipe in this chapter
- The *Reducing the elements of a stream* recipe in `Chapter 6`, *Parallel and Reactive Streams*

Using atomic variables

Atomic variables were introduced in Java version 5 to provide atomic operations on single variables. When you work with a normal variable, each operation that you implement in Java is transformed into several instructions of Java byte code that is understandable by the JVM when you compile the program. For example, when you assign a value to a variable, you only use one instruction in Java; however, when you compile this program, it is transformed into various instructions in the JVM language. This can lead to data inconsistency errors when you work with multiple threads that share a variable.

To avoid these problems, Java introduced atomic variables. When a thread is doing an operation with an atomic variable and if other threads want to do an operation with the same variable, the implementation of the class includes a mechanism to check that the operation is done atomically. Basically, the operation gets the value of the variable, changes the value to a local variable, and then tries to change the old value with the new one. If the old value is still the same, it is substituted; if not, the method begins the operation again. This operation is called **Compare and Set**. It implements the modification of the value of a variable in the following three steps:

1. You get the value of the variable, which is the old value of the variable
2. You change the value of the variable in a temporal variable, which is the new value of the variable.
3. You substitute the old value with the new value if the old value is equal to the actual value of the variable. The old value may be different from the actual value if another thread changes the value of the variable.

Some of these variables, for example, the `LongAccumulator` class, receive an operation as a parameter that could be executed inside some of its methods. These operations must be free from any side effects, as they might be executed multiple times in every value update.

Atomic variables don't use locks or other synchronization mechanisms to protect access to their values. All their operations are based on Compare and Set. It's guaranteed that several threads can work with an atomic variable at a time without generating data inconsistency errors; plus, they simplify the implementation.

Java 8 has added four new atomic classes. First we have the `LongAdder` and `DoubleAdder` classes; they store `long` and `double` values that are updated frequently by different threads. You can obtain the same functionality as that of the `LongAdder` class with the `AtomicLong` class, but the former provides better performance. The other two classes are `LongAccumulator` and `DoubleAccumulator`. These classes are similar to the previous one, but here, you have to specify two parameters in the constructor:

- The initial value of the counter.
- A `LongBinaryOperator` or `DoubleBinaryOperator` that can be indicated as a lambda expression. This expression receives the old value of the variable and the increment you want to apply and returns the new value of the variable.

In this recipe, you will learn how to use atomic variables implementing a bank account and two different tasks: one that adds money to the account and one that subtracts money from it. You will use the `AtomicLong` class in the implementation of the example.

Getting ready

The example of this recipe has been implemented using the Eclipse IDE. If you are using Eclipse or a different IDE, such as NetBeans, open it and create a new Java project.

How to do it...

Follow these steps to implement the example:

1. Create a class named `Account` to simulate a bank account:

```
public class Account {
```

2. Declare a private `AtomicLong` attribute named `balance` to store the balance of the account. In addition, declare a private `LongAdder` attribute named `operations` and a private `DoubleAccumulator` attribute named `commission`:

```
private final AtomicLong balance;
private final LongAdder operations;
private final DoubleAccumulator commission;
```

3. Implement the constructor of the class to initialize its attributes. For the `DoubleAccumulator` class, the identity value is `0` and we update the actual value with the result of multiply `0.2` to the increment passed as parameter:

```
public Account() {
    balance = new AtomicLong();
    operations = new LongAdder();
    commission = new DoubleAccumulator((x,y)-> x+y*0.2, 0);
}
```

4. Implement the method to get the value of the three attributes:

```
public long getBalance() {
    return balance.get();
}
public long getOperations() {
    return operations.longValue();
}
public double getCommission() {
    return commission.get();
}
```

5. Implement a method named `setBalance()` to establish the value of the balance attribute. We also have to initialize the operations and commission attributes using the `reset()` method:

```
public void setBalance(long balance) {
    this.balance.set(balance);
    operations.reset();
    commission.reset();
}
```

6. Implement a method named `addAmount()` to increment the value of the balance attribute. In addition, use the `increment()` method of the `LongAdder` class to increment the value of the `operations` attribute and the `accumulate()` method by one unit to add 20 percent of the amount value to the `commission` object:

```
public void addAmount(long amount) {
    this.balance.getAndAdd(amount);
    this.operations.increment();
    this.commission.accumulate(amount);
}
```

7. Implement a method named `substractAmount()` to decrement the value of the `balance` attribute. As it occurs with the `addAmount()` method, we modify the values of the `operations` and `commission` attributes:

```
public void subtractAmount(long amount) {
    this.balance.getAndAdd(-amount);
    this.operations.increment();
    this.commission.accumulate(amount);
}
```

8. Create a class named `Company` and specify that it implements the `Runnable` interface. This class will simulate the payments made by a company:

```
public class Company implements Runnable {
```

9. Declare a private `Account` attribute named `account`:

```
private final Account account;
```

10. Implement the constructor of the class to initialize its attribute:

```
public Company(Account account) {
    this.account=account;
}
```

11. Implement the `run()` method of the task. Use the `addAmount()` method of the account to make 10 increments of 1,000 each in its balance:

```
@Override
public void run() {
    for (int i=0; i<10; i++){
        account.addAmount(1000);
    }
}
```

12. Create a class named `Bank` and specify that it implements the `Runnable` interface. This class will simulate the withdrawal of money from the account:

```
public class Bank implements Runnable {
```

13. Declare a private `Account` attribute named `account`:

```
private final Account account;
```

14. Implement the constructor of the class to initialize its attribute:

```
public Bank(Account account) {
    this.account=account;
}
```

15. Implement the `run()` method of the task. Use the `subtractAmount()` method of the account to make 10 decrements of 1,000 each from its balance:

```
@Override
public void run() {
    for (int i=0; i<10; i++){
        account.subtractAmount(1000);
    }
}
```

16. Implement the main class of the example by creating a class named `Main` and adding the `main()` method to it:

```
public class Main {
    public static void main(String[] args) {
```

17. Create an `Account` object and set its balance to `1000`:

```
Account  account=new Account();
account.setBalance(1000);
```

18. Create a new `Company` task and a thread to execute it:

```
Company company=new Company(account);
Thread companyThread=new Thread(company);
```

19. Create a new `Bank` task and a thread to execute it:

```
Bank bank=new Bank(account);
Thread bankThread=new Thread(bank);
```

20. Write the initial balance of the account in the console:

```
System.out.printf("Account : Initial Balance: %d\n",
                    account.getBalance());
```

21. Start the threads:

```
companyThread.start();
bankThread.start();
```

22. Wait for the finalization of the threads using the `join()` method and write the final balance in the console, the number of operations, and the accumulated commission of the account:

```
try {
    companyThread.join();
    bankThread.join();
    System.out.printf("Account : Final Balance: %d\n",
                    account.getBalance());
    System.out.printf("Account : Number of Operations: %d\n",
                    account.getOperations().intValue());
    System.out.printf("Account : Accumulated commisions: %f\n",
                    account.getCommission().doubleValue());
} catch (InterruptedException e) {
    e.printStackTrace();
}
```

How it works...

The key to this example is in the `Account` class. In this class, we declared an `AtomicLong` variable named `balance` to store the balance of the account, a `LongAdder` variable named `operations` to store the number of operations we made with the account, and a `DoubleAccumulator` variable named `commission` to store the value of the commissions of the operations. In the constructor of the `commission` object, we specified that the value will be incremented with the expression `0.2*y`. With this, we wanted to specify that we will increment the actual value of the variable with the result of its multiplication by `0.2` and the value of the parameter we pass to the `accumulate()` method.

To implement the `getBalance()` method that returns the value of the `balance` attribute, we used the `get()` method of the `AtomicLong` class. To implement the `getOperations()` method that returns a `long` value with the number of operations, we used the `longValue()` method. To implement the `getCommission()` method, we used the `get()` method of the `DoubleAccumulator` class. To implement the `setBalance()` method that establishes the value of the balance attribute, we used the `set()` method of the `AtomicLong` class.

To implement the `addAmount()` method that adds an import to the balance of the account, we used the `getAndAdd()` method of the `AtomicLong` class that returns the value and increments it by the value specified as a parameter. We also used the `increment()` method of the `LongAdder` class that increments the value of the variable by one and the `accumulate()` method of the `DoubleAccumulator` class to increment the value of the `commission` attribute following the specified expression. Take into account that the `addAmount()` method is not atomic as a whole although it calls three atomic operations.

Finally, to implement the `subtractAmount()` method that decrements the value of the `balance` attribute, we used the `getAndAdd()` method. We also included calls to the `increment()` and `accumulate()` methods of the `LongAdder` and `DoubleAccumulator` classes.

Then, we implemented two different tasks:

- The `Company` class simulates a company that increments the balance of the account. Each task of this class makes 10 increments of 1,000 each.
- The `Bank` class simulates a bank where the proprietary of the bank account takes out its money. Each task of this class makes 10 decrements of 1,000 each.

In the `Main` class, you created an `Account` object with a balance of 1,000. Then, you executed a bank task and a company task so the final balance of the account is the same as the initial one.

When you execute the program, you will see how the final balance is the same as the initial one. The following screenshot shows the output of an execution of this example:

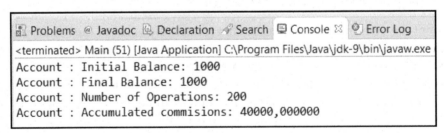

There's more...

As mentioned in the introduction, there are other atomic classes in Java. `AtomicBoolean`, `AtomicInteger`, and `AtomicReference` are other examples of atomic classes.

The `LongAdder` class provides other interesting methods as follows:

- `add()`: To increment the value of the internal counter by the value specified as a parameter
- `decrement()`: To decrement the internal counter by one
- `reset()`: To return the internal value to zero

You can also use the `DoubleAdder` class that is similar to `LongAdder`, but it doesn't have the `increment()` and `decrement()` methods and the internal counter is a `double` value.

You can also use the `LongAccumulator` class that is similar to `DoubleAccumulator` but with an internal `long` counter.

See also

- The *Synchronizing a method* recipe in `Chapter 2`, *Basic Thread Synchronization*

Using atomic arrays

Consider that you need to implement a concurrent application that has one or more objects shared by several threads. In such a scenario, you have to protect access to their attributes using a synchronization mechanism, such as locks or the `synchronized` keyword, to avoid data inconsistency errors.

These mechanisms have the following problems:

- Deadlock: This situation occurs when a thread is blocked waiting for a lock that is locked by other threads that will never free it. This situation blocks the program, so it will never finish.
- If only one thread is accessing the shared object, it has to execute the code necessary to get and release the lock.

To provide better performance in this situation, the **compare-and-swap operation** was developed. This operation implements the modification of the value of a variable in the following three steps:

1. You get the value of the variable, which is the old value of the variable.
2. You change the value of the variable in a temporal variable, which is the new value of the variable.
3. You substitute the old value with the new value if the old value is equal to the actual value of the variable. The old value may be different from the actual value if another thread has changed it.

With this mechanism, you don't need to use a synchronization mechanism, so you avoid deadlocks and you obtain better performance. This mechanism also has its drawbacks. Operations must be free from any side effects as they might be retried using livelocks with highly contended resources; they are also harder to monitor for performance when compared with standard locks.

Java implements this mechanism in **atomic variables**. These variables provide the `compareAndSet()` method, which is an implementation of the compare-and-swap operation and other methods based on it.

Java also introduced **atomic arrays** that provide atomic operations for arrays of `integer` or `long` numbers. In this recipe, you will learn how to use the `AtomicIntegerArray` class to work with atomic arrays. Take into account that if you use `AtomicInteger[]`, it's not a thread-safe object. The individual `AtomicInteger` objects are thread-safe, but the array as a data structure is not.

Getting ready

The example of this recipe has been implemented using the Eclipse IDE. If you use Eclipse or a different IDE, such as NetBeans, open it and create a new Java project.

How to do it...

Follow these steps to implement the example:

1. Create a class named `Incrementer` and specify that it implements the `Runnable` interface:

```
public class Incrementer implements Runnable {
```

2. Declare a private `AtomicIntegerArray` attribute named `vector` to store an array of `integer` numbers:

```
private final AtomicIntegerArray vector;
```

3. Implement the constructor of the class to initialize its attribute:

```
public Incrementer(AtomicIntegerArray vector) {
   this.vector=vector;
}
```

4. Implement the `run()` method. Increment all the elements of the array using the `getAndIncrement()` method:

```
@Override
public void run() {
   for (int i=0; i<vector.length(); i++){
     vector.getAndIncrement(i);
   }
}
```

5. Create a class named `Decrementer` and specify that it implements the `Runnable` interface:

```
public class Decrementer implements Runnable {
```

6. Declare a private `AtomicIntegerArray` attribute named `vector` to store an array of `integer` numbers:

```
private AtomicIntegerArray vector;
```

7. Implement the constructor of the class to initialize its attribute:

```
public Decrementer(AtomicIntegerArray vector) {
   this.vector=vector;
}
```

8. Implement the `run()` method. Decrement all the elements of the array using the `getAndDecrement()` method:

```
@Override
public void run() {
   for (int i=0; i<vector.length(); i++) {
     vector.getAndDecrement(i);
   }
}
```

9. Implement the main class of the example by creating a class named `Main` and adding the `main()` method to it:

```
public class Main {
    public static void main(String[] args) {
```

10. Declare a constant named `THREADS` and assign the value `100` to it. Create an `AtomicIntegerArray` object with 1,000 elements:

```
final int THREADS=100;
AtomicIntegerArray vector=new AtomicIntegerArray(1000);
```

11. Create an `Incrementer` task to work with the atomic array created earlier:

```
Incrementer incrementer=new Incrementer(vector);
```

12. Create a `Decrementer` task to work with the atomic array created earlier:

```
Decrementer decrementer=new Decrementer(vector);
```

13. Create two arrays to store 100 `Thread` objects:

```
Thread threadIncrementer[]=new Thread[THREADS];
Thread threadDecrementer[]=new Thread[THREADS];
```

14. Create and launch 100 threads to execute the `Incrementer` task and another 100 threads to execute the `Decrementer` task. Store the threads in the arrays created earlier:

```
for (int i=0; i<THREADS; i++) {
    threadIncrementer[i]=new Thread(incrementer);
    threadDecrementer[i]=new Thread(decrementer);

    threadIncrementer[i].start();
    threadDecrementer[i].start();
}
```

15. Wait for the finalization of the threads using the `join()` method:

```
for (int i=0; i<100; i++) {
    try {
        threadIncrementer[i].join();
        threadDecrementer[i].join();
```

```
    } catch (InterruptedException e) {
      e.printStackTrace();
    }
  }
```

16. In the console, write the elements of the atomic array distinct from zero. Use the `get()` method to obtain the elements of the atomic array:

```
int errors=0;
for (int i=0; i<vector.length(); i++) {
  if (vector.get(i)!=0) {
    System.out.println("Vector["+i+"] : "+vector.get(i));
    errors++;
  }
}
if (errors==0) {
  System.out.printf("No errors found\n");
}
```

17. Write a message in the console indicating the finalization of the example:

```
System.out.println("Main: End of the example");
```

How it works...

In this example, you implemented two different tasks to work with an `AtomicIntegerArray` object:

- `Incrementer`: This class increments all the elements of the array using the `getAndIncrement()` method
- `Decrementer`: This class decrements all the elements of the array using the `getAndDecrement()` method

In the `Main` class, you created `AtomicIntegerArray` with 1,000 elements, then you executed 100 incrementer and 100 decrementer tasks. At the end of these tasks, if there were no inconsistency errors, all the elements of the array must have the value `0`. If you execute the program, you will see how the program only writes the final message to the console because all the elements are zero.

There's more...

Nowadays, Java provides another atomic array class. It's called the `AtomicLongArray` class and it provides the same methods as the `IntegerAtomicArray` class.

Other interesting methods provided by these classes are:

- `get(int i)`: Returns the value of the array position specified by the parameter
- `set(int I, int newValue)`: Establishes the value of the array position specified by the parameter.

See also

- The *Using atomic variables* recipe in this chapter

Using the volatile keyword

Almost every application reads and writes data to the main memory of the computer. For performance reasons, these operations aren't performed directly in the memory. CPUs have a system of cache memory, so applications write data in the cache and then the data is moved from the cache to the main memory.

In multithread applications, concurrent threads run in different CPUs or cores inside a CPU. When a thread modifies a variable stored in the memory, the modification is made in the cache or the CPU or core where it's running. However, there's no guarantee about when that modification would reach the main memory. If another thread wants to read the value of the data, it's possible that it would not read the modified value because it's not in the main memory of the computer.

To solve this problem (there are other solutions, such as the `synchronized` keyword), the Java language includes the `volatile` keyword. It's a modifier that allows you to specify that a variable must always be read from and stored in the main memory, not the cache of your CPU. You should use the volatile keyword when it's important that other threads have visibility of the actual value of the variable; however, order of access to that variable is not important. In this scenario, the `volatile` keyword will give you better performance because it doesn't need to get any monitor or lock to access the variable. On the contrary, if the order of access to the variable is important, you must use another synchronization mechanism.

In this recipe, you will learn how to use the volatile keyword and the effects of its use.

Getting ready

The example of this recipe has been implemented using the Eclipse IDE. If you use Eclipse or a different IDE, such as NetBeans, open it and create a new Java project.

How to do it...

Follow these steps to implement the example:

1. Create a class named `Flag` with a public `Boolean` attribute named `flag` initialized to the `true` value:

```
public class Flag {
  public boolean flag=true;
}
```

2. Create a class named `VolatileFlag` with a public Boolean attribute named `flag` initialized to the `true` value. We add the `volatile` modifier to the declaration of this attribute:

```
public class VolatileFlag {
  public volatile boolean flag=true;
}
```

3. Create a class named `Task` and specify that it implements the `Runnable` interface. It has a private `Flag` attribute and a constructor to initialize it:

```
public class Task implements Runnable {
  private Flag flag;
  public Task(Flag flag) {
    this.flag = flag;
  }
```

4. Implement the `run()` method of this task. It will increment an `int` variable when the value of the `flag` attribute is `true`. Then, write the final value of the variable:

```
@Override
public void run() {
  int i = 0;
```

```
        while (flag.flag) {
          i++;
        }
        System.out.printf("VolatileTask: Stopped %d - %s\n", i,
                            new Date());
    }
```

5. Create a class named `VolatileTask` and specify that it implements the `Runnable` interface. It has a private `VolatileFlag` attribute and a constructor to initialize it:

```
public class VolatileTask implements Runnable {

    private VolatileFlag flag;
    public VolatileTask(VolatileFlag flag) {
        this.flag = flag;
    }
```

6. Implement the `run()` method of this task. It's equal to the one in the `Task` class, so it won't be included here:

7. Implement the `Main` class with the `main()` method. First, create four objects of the `VolatileFlag`, `Flag`, `VolatileTask`, and `Task` classes:

```
public class Main {

    public static void main(String[] args) {
        VolatileFlag volatileFlag=new VolatileFlag();
        Flag flag=new Flag();

        VolatileTask vt=new VolatileTask(volatileFlag);
        Task t=new Task(flag);
```

8. Then, create two threads to execute the tasks, start them, and sleep the main thread for a second:

```
Thread thread=new Thread(vt);
thread.start();
thread=new Thread(t);
thread.start();

try {
    TimeUnit.SECONDS.sleep(1);
} catch (InterruptedException e) {
    e.printStackTrace();
}
```

9. Then, change the value of the `volatileFlag` variable to stop the execution of `volatileTask` and sleep the main thread for a second:

```
System.out.printf("Main: Going to stop volatile task: %s\n",
                  new Date());
volatileFlag.flag=false;
System.out.printf("Main: Volatile task stoped: %s\n", new Date());

try {
  TimeUnit.SECONDS.sleep(1);
} catch (InterruptedException e) {
  e.printStackTrace();
}
```

10. Finally, change the value of the `task` object to stop the execution of the task and sleep the main thread for a second:

```
System.out.printf("Main: Going to stop task: %s\n", new Date());
flag.flag=false;
System.out.printf("Main: Volatile stop flag changed: %s\n",
                  new Date());

try {
  TimeUnit.SECONDS.sleep(1);
} catch (InterruptedException e) {
  e.printStackTrace();
}
```

How it works...

The following screenshot shows the output of the example:

```
 Problems  @ Javadoc  Declaration   Search  Console 
Main (52) [Java Application] C:\Program Files\Java\jdk-9\bin\javaw.exe (24 ene. 2017 0:36:5
Main: Going to stop volatile task: Tue Jan 24 00:36:56 CET 2017
Main: Volatile stop flag changed: Tue Jan 24 00:36:56 CET 2017
VolatileTask: Stoped 1646380285 - Tue Jan 24 00:36:56 CET 2017
Main: Going to stop task: Tue Jan 24 00:36:57 CET 2017
Main: Task stoped: Tue Jan 24 00:36:57 CET 2017
```

The application doesn't finish its execution because the `task` thread has not finished. When we change the value of `volatileFlag`-as its `flag` attribute is marked as `volatile`--the new value is written in the main memory and `VolatileTask` accesses the value immediately and finishes its execution. On the contrary, when you change the value of the `flag` object--as its `flag` attribute is not marked as volatile-the new value is stored in the cache of the main thread and the task object doesn't see the new value and never ends its execution. The `volatile` keyword is important not only because it requires that the writes are flushed, but also because it ensures that reads are not cached and they fetch the up-to-date value from the main memory. It's very important and very often neglected.

Take into account that the `volatile` keyword guarantees that modifications are written in the main memory, but its contrary is not always true. For example, if you work with a non-volatile integer value shared by more than one thread and make a lot of modifications, you may be able to see the modifications made by other threads because they were written in the main memory. However, there's no guarantee that these changes were passed from the cache to the main memory.

There's more...

The `volatile` keyword only works well when the value of the shared variable is only modified by one thread. If the variable is modified by multiple threads, the `volatile` keyword doesn't protect you from possible data-race conditions. It also doesn't make operations, such as + or –, atomic. For example, the ++ operator over a volatile variable is not thread-safe.

Since Java 5, **Java Memory Model** has a happens--before guarantee established with the `volatile` keyword. This fact has two implications:

- When you modify a volatile variable, its value is sent to the main memory. The value of all the variables modified previously by the same thread are sent too.
- Compilers can't reorder sentences that modify a volatile variable for an optimization purpose. It can reorder the previous operations and the later ones, but not the modifications of a volatile variable. The changes that happen before these modifications will be visible to those instructions.

See also

- The *Using atomic variables* and *Using atomic arrays* recipe in this chapter

Using variable handles

Variable handles are a new feature of Java 9 that allow you to get a typed reference to a variable (attribute, static field, or array element) in order to access it in different modes. You can, for example, protect access to this variable in a concurrent application by allowing atomic access to the variable. Until now, you could only obtain this behavior with atomic variables, but now, you can use variable handles to obtain the same functionality without using any synchronization mechanism. A variable handle also allows you to get additional access modes to a variable.

In this recipe, you will learn how to obtain and use a variable handle and the benefits you obtain using it.

Getting ready

The example of this recipe has been implemented using the Eclipse IDE. If you use Eclipse or a different IDE, such as NetBeans, open it and create a new Java project.

How to do it...

Follow these steps to implement the example:

1. Create a class named `Account` with two double public attributes named `amount` and `unsafeAmount`. Implement the constructor to initialize its values:

```java
public class Account {
  public double amount;
  public double unsafeAmount;

  public Account() {
    this.amount=0;
    this.unsafeAmount=0;
  }
}
```

2. Create a class named `Decrementer` and specify that it implements the `Runnable` interface. It has a private `Account` attribute initialized in the constructor of the class:

```java
public class Decrementer implements Runnable {

  private Account account;
```

```
      public Decrementer(Account account) {
         this.account = account;
      }
```

3. Implement the `run()` method. This method will make 10,000 decrement operations in the `amount` and `unsafeAmount` attributes. To modify the value of the amount attribute, use `VarHandle`. Obtain it using the `lookup()` method of the `MethodHandles` class, then use the `getAndAdd()` method to modify the value of the attribute. To modify the `unsafeAmount` attribute, use the `=` operator:

```
@Override
public void run() {
  VarHandle handler;
  try {
    handler = MethodHandles.lookup().in(Account.class)
                  .findVarHandle(Account.class, "amount",
                    double.class);
    for (int i = 0; i < 10000; i++) {
      handler.getAndAdd(account, -100);
      account.unsafeAmount -= 100;
    }
  } catch (NoSuchFieldException | IllegalAccessException e) {
    e.printStackTrace();
  }
}
```

4. Implement a class named `Incrementer`. This will be equivalent to the `Drementer` class, but it will increase the value of the account. The source code of this class won't be included here.

5. Finally, implement the `Main` class with the `main()` method. First, create an account object:

```
public class Main {
   public static void main(String[] args) {
      Account account = new Account();
```

6. Then, create a thread to execute an `Incrementer` task and a thread to execute a `Decrementer` task. Start them and wait for their finalization using the `join()` method:

```
Thread threadIncrementer = new Thread(new Incrementer(account));
Thread threadDecrementer = new Thread(new Decrementer(account));

threadIncrementer.start();
threadDecrementer.start();
```

```
try {
  threadIncrementer.join();
  threadDecrementer.join();
} catch (InterruptedException e) {
  e.printStackTrace();
}
```

7. Finally, write the value of the amount and `unsafeAmount` attributes in the console:

```
System.out.printf("Safe amount: %f\n", account.amount);
System.out.printf("Unsafe amount: %f\n", account.unsafeAmount);

  }
}
```

How it works...

The following screenshot shows the output of an execution of the application:

As you make the same number of increment and decrement operations, the expected result in both cases is 0. We obtain this result with the amount attribute because as we access it using the `VarHandle`, we guarantee atomic access to its modifications. On the other hand, the `unsafeAmount` doesn't have the expected value. Access to this value is not protected and we have a data-race condition.

To use a variable handle, first we have to obtain it using the `lookup()` method of the `MethodHandles` class, followed by the `in()` method and then the `findVarHandle()` method. The `lookup()` method returns a `Lookup` object, the `in()` method returns a `Lookup` object of the specified class—in our case, the `Account` class—and `findVarHandle()` generates `VarHandle` for the attribute we want to access.

Once we have the `VarHandle` object, we can use different methods to use different access modes. In this example, we used the `getAndAdd()` method. This method guarantees atomic access to increment the value of the attribute. We pass to them the object we want to access and the value of the increment.

The next section provides more information about the different access modes and the methods you can use in each case.

There's more...

You have four different access types to a variable with a variable handle:

- **Read mode**: This is used to get read mode access to a variable. You can use the following methods:
    - `get()`: Read the value of the variable as if it was declared non-volatile
    - `getVolatile()`: Read the value of the variable as if it was declared volatile
    - `getAcquire()`: Read the value of the variable and guarantee that the following instructions that modify or access this variable are not reordered before the instructions for optimization purposes
    - `getOpaque()`: Read the value of variable and guarantee that the instructions of the current thread are not reordered; no guarantee is provided for other threads

- **Write mode**: This is used to get write access mode to a variable. You can use the `set()`, `setVolatile()`, `setRelease()`, and `setOpaque()` methods. They are equivalent to the previous ones but with write access.
- **Atomic access mode**: This is used to get a functionality that is similar to the one provided by the atomic variables with operations to, for example, compare and get the value of the variable. You can use the following methods:
    - `compareAndSet()`: Change the value of the variable as it was declared as a volatile variable if the expected value passed as parameter is equal to the current value of the variable
    - `weakCompareAndSet()` and `weakCompareAndSetVolatile()`: Possibly atomically' changes the value of the variable as it was declared as non-volatile or volatile variables respectively if the expected value passed as parameter is equals to the current value of the variable

- **Numerical update access mode**: This is to modify numerical values in an atomic way.

See also

- The *Using atomic variables* and *Using atomic arrays* recipe in this chapter

8
Customizing Concurrency Classes

In this chapter, we will cover the following topics:

- Customizing the ThreadPoolExecutor class
- Implementing a priority-based Executor class
- Implementing the ThreadFactory interface to generate custom threads
- Using our ThreadFactory in an Executor object
- Customizing tasks running in a scheduled thread pool
- Implementing the ThreadFactory interface to generate custom threads for the fork/join framework
- Customizing tasks running in the fork/join framework
- Implementing a custom Lock class
- Implementing a transfer queue-based on priorities
- Implementing your own atomic object
- Implementing your own stream generator
- Implementing your own asynchronous stream

Introduction

The Java Concurrency API provides a lot of interfaces and classes to implement concurrent applications. They provide low-level mechanisms, such as the `Thread` class, the `Runnable` or `Callable` interfaces, or the `synchronized` keyword. They also provide high-level mechanisms, such as the `Executor` framework and the fork/join framework added in the Java 7 release, or the `Stream` framework added in Java 8, to process big sets of data. Despite this, you may find yourself developing a program where the default configuration and/or implementation of the Java API doesn't meet your needs.

In this case, you may need to implement your own custom concurrent utilities, based on the ones provided by Java. Basically, you can:

- Implement an interface to provide the functionality defined by that interface, for example, the `ThreadFactory` interface.
- Override some methods of a class to adapt its behavior to your needs. For example, overriding the `onAdvance()` method of the `Phaser` class that, by default, does nothing useful and is supposed to be overridden to offer some functionality.

Through the recipes of this chapter, you will learn how to change the behavior of some Java concurrency API classes without the need to design a concurrency framework from scratch. You can use these recipes as an initial point to implement your own customizations.

Customizing the ThreadPoolExecutor class

The `Executor` framework is a mechanism that allows you to separate thread creation from its execution. It's based on the `Executor` and `ExecutorService` interfaces with the `ThreadPoolExecutor` class that implements both the interfaces. It has an internal pool of threads and provides methods that allow you to send two kinds of tasks and execute them in the pooled threads. These tasks are:

- The `Runnable` interface to implement tasks that don't return a result
- The `Callable` interface to implement tasks that return a result

In both cases, you only send the task to the executor. The executor uses one of its pooled threads or creates a new one to execute those tasks. It also decides the moment in which the task is executed.

In this recipe, you will learn how to override some methods of the `ThreadPoolExecutor` class to calculate the execution time of the tasks that you will execute in the executor and write about the executor in console statistics when it completes its execution.

Getting ready

The example of this recipe has been implemented using the Eclipse IDE. If you use Eclipse or a different IDE, such as NetBeans, open it and create a new Java project.

How to do it...

Follow these steps to implement the example:

1. Create a class named `MyExecutor` that extends the `ThreadPoolExecutor` class:

   ```
   public class MyExecutor extends ThreadPoolExecutor {
   ```

2. Declare a private `ConcurrentHashMap` attribute parameterized by the `String` and `Date` classes, named `startTimes`:

   ```
   private final ConcurrentHashMap<Runnable, Date> startTimes;
   ```

3. Implement the constructor for the class. Call a constructor of the parent class using the `super` keyword and initialize the `startTime` attribute:

   ```
   public MyExecutor(int corePoolSize, int maximumPoolSize,
                   long keepAliveTime, TimeUnit unit,
                   BlockingQueue<Runnable> workQueue) {
      super(corePoolSize, maximumPoolSize, keepAliveTime, unit,
           workQueue);
      startTimes=new ConcurrentHashMap<>();
   }
   ```

4. Override the `shutdown()` method. Write in the console information about the executed, running, and pending tasks. Then, call the `shutdown()` method of the parent class using the `super` keyword:

   ```
   @Override
   public void shutdown() {
      System.out.printf("MyExecutor: Going to shutdown.\n");
      System.out.printf("MyExecutor: Executed tasks: %d\n",
                   getCompletedTaskCount());
   ```

```
        System.out.printf("MyExecutor: Running tasks: %d\n",
                        getActiveCount());
        System.out.printf("MyExecutor: Pending tasks: %d\n",
                        getQueue().size());
        super.shutdown();
    }
```

5. Override the `shutdownNow()` method. Write in the console information about the executed, running, and pending tasks. Then, call the `shutdownNow()` method of the parent class using the `super` keyword:

```
@Override
public List<Runnable> shutdownNow() {
    System.out.printf("MyExecutor: Going to immediately
                    shutdown.\n");
    System.out.printf("MyExecutor: Executed tasks: %d\n",
                    getCompletedTaskCount());
    System.out.printf("MyExecutor: Running tasks: %d\n",
                    getActiveCount());
    System.out.printf("MyExecutor: Pending tasks: %d\n",
                    getQueue().size());
    return super.shutdownNow();
}
```

6. Override the `beforeExecute()` method. Write a message in the console with the name of the thread that is going to execute the task and the hash code of the task. Store the start date in `HashMap` using the hash code of the task as the key:

```
@Override
protected void beforeExecute(Thread t, Runnable r) {
    System.out.printf("MyExecutor: A task is beginning: %s : %s\n",
                    t.getName(),r.hashCode());
    startTimes.put(r, new Date());
}
```

7. Override the `afterExecute()` method. Write a message in the console with the result of the task and calculate the running time of the task after subtracting the start date of the task stored in `HashMap` of the current date:

```
@Override
protected void afterExecute(Runnable r, Throwable t) {
    Future<?> result=(Future<?>)r;
    try {
        System.out.printf("**********************************\n");
        System.out.printf("MyExecutor: A task is finishing.\n");
```

```
            System.out.printf("MyExecutor: Result: %s\n",
                              result.get());
            Date startDate=startTimes.remove(r);
            Date finishDate=new Date();
            long diff=finishDate.getTime()-startDate.getTime();
            System.out.printf("MyExecutor: Duration: %d\n",diff);
            System.out.printf("********************************\n");
        } catch (InterruptedException | ExecutionException e) {
            e.printStackTrace();
        }
    }
  }
}
```

8. Create a class named `SleepTwoSecondsTask` that implements the `Callable` interface parameterized by the `String` class. Implement the `call()` method. Put the current thread to sleep for 2 seconds and return the current date converted into a `String` type:

```
public class SleepTwoSecondsTask implements Callable<String> {

  public String call() throws Exception {
    TimeUnit.SECONDS.sleep(2);
    return new Date().toString();
  }

}
```

9. Implement the main class of the example by creating a class named `Main` with a `main()` method:

```
public class Main {
  public static void main(String[] args) {
```

10. Create a `MyExecutor` object named `myExecutor`:

```
MyExecutor myExecutor=new MyExecutor(4, 8, 1000,
                      TimeUnit.MILLISECONDS,
                      new LinkedBlockingDeque<Runnable>());
```

11. Create a list of `Future` objects parameterized by the `String` class to store the resultant objects of the tasks you're going to send to the executor:

```
List<Future<String>> results=new ArrayList<>();
```

12. Submit 10 `Task` objects:

```
for (int i=0; i<10; i++) {
    SleepTwoSecondsTask task=new SleepTwoSecondsTask();
    Future<String> result=myExecutor.submit(task);
    results.add(result);
}
```

13. Get the result of the execution of the first five tasks using the `get()` method. Write them in the console:

```
for (int i=0; i<5; i++){
    try {
        String result=results.get(i).get();
        System.out.printf("Main: Result for Task %d : %s\n",
                            i,result);
    } catch (InterruptedException | ExecutionException e) {
        e.printStackTrace();
    }
}
```

14. Finish the execution of the executor using the `shutdown()` method:

```
myExecutor.shutdown();
```

15. Get the result of the execution of the last five tasks using the `get()` method. Write them in the console:

```
for (int i=5; i<10; i++){
    try {
        String result=results.get(i).get();
        System.out.printf("Main: Result for Task %d : %s\n",
                            i,result);
    } catch (InterruptedException | ExecutionException e) {
        e.printStackTrace();
    }
}
```

16. Wait for the completion of the executor using the `awaitTermination()` method:

```
try {
    myExecutor.awaitTermination(1, TimeUnit.DAYS);
} catch (InterruptedException e) {
    e.printStackTrace();
}
```

17. Write a message indicating the end of the execution of the program:

```
System.out.printf("Main: End of the program.\n");
```

How it works...

In this recipe, we implemented our custom executor by extending the
ThreadPoolExecutor class and overriding four of its methods. The beforeExecute()
and afterExecute() methods were used to calculate the execution time of a task. The
beforeExecute() method is executed before the execution of a task; in this case, we used
HashMap to store the start date of the task in it. The afterExecute() method is executed
after the execution of the task. You got startTime of the task that had finished from
HashMap and then calculate the difference between the actual date and and the startTime
to get the execution time of the task. You also overrode the shutdown() and
shutdownNow() methods to write statistics about the tasks executed in the executor to the
console. These tasks included:

- The executed tasks, using the getCompletedTaskCount() method
- The tasks that were running at the current time, using the getActiveCount()
  method
- The pending tasks, using the size() method of the blocking queue where the
  executor stores the pending tasks

The SleepTwoSecondsTask class that implements the Callable interface puts its
execution thread to sleep for 2 seconds and the Main class, where you send 10 tasks to your
executor, uses it and the other classes to demo their features.

Execute the program and you will see how the program shows the time span of each task
that is running and the statistics of the executor upon calling the shutdown() method.

See also

- The *Creating a thread executor and controlling its rejected tasks* recipe in Chapter 4,
  Thread Executors
- The *Using our ThreadFactory in an Executor object* recipe in this chapter

Implementing a priority-based Executor class

In the first version of the Java Concurrency API, you had to create and run all the threads of your application. In Java version 5, with the appearance of the Executor framework, a new mechanism was introduced for the execution of concurrency tasks.

With the Executor framework, you only have to implement your tasks and send them to the executor. The executor is responsible for the creation and execution of the threads that execute your tasks.

Internally, an executor uses a blocking queue to store pending tasks. These are stored in the order of their arrival at the executor. One possible alternative is to use a priority queue to store new tasks. This way, if a new task with high priority arrives to the executor, it will be executed before all the other threads that have already been waiting but have comparatively lower priority.

In this recipe, you will learn how to adapt an executor that will use a priority queue to store the tasks you send for execution.

Getting ready

The example of this recipe has been implemented using the Eclipse IDE. If you use Eclipse or a different IDE, such as NetBeans, open it and create a new Java project.

How to do it...

Follow these steps to implement the example:

1. Create a class named `MyPriorityTask` that implements the `Runnable` and `Comparable` interfaces parameterized by the `MyPriorityTask` class interface:

   ```
   public class MyPriorityTask implements Runnable,
                           Comparable<MyPriorityTask> {
   ```

2. Declare a private `int` attribute named `priority`:

   ```
   private int priority;
   ```

3. Declare a private String attribute called name:

```
private String name;
```

4. Implement the constructor of the class to initialize its attributes:

```
public MyPriorityTask(String name, int priority) {
  this.name=name;
  this.priority=priority;
}
```

5. Implement a method to return the value of the priority attribute:

```
public int getPriority(){
  return priority;
}
```

6. Implement the `compareTo()` method declared in the `Comparable` interface. It receives a `MyPriorityTask` object as a parameter and compares the priorities of the two objects: the current one and the parameter. You let tasks with higher priority be executed before tasks with lower priority:

```
@Override
public int compareTo(MyPriorityTask o) {
  return Integer.compare(o.getPriority(), this.getPriority());
}
```

7. Implement the `run()` method. Put the current thread to sleep for 2 seconds:

```
@Override
public void run() {
  System.out.printf("MyPriorityTask: %s Priority : %d\n",
                    name,priority);
  try {
    TimeUnit.SECONDS.sleep(2);
  } catch (InterruptedException e) {
    e.printStackTrace();
    Thread.currentThread().interrupt();
  }
}
```

8. Implement the main class of the example by creating a class named `Main` with a `main()` method:

```
public class Main {
  public static void main(String[] args) {
```

9. Create a `ThreadPoolExecutor` object named `executor`. Use `PriorityBlockingQueue`, parameterized by the `Runnable` interface, as the queue that this executor will use to store its pending tasks:

```
ThreadPoolExecutor executor=new ThreadPoolExecutor(4,4,1,
                            TimeUnit.SECONDS,
                            new PriorityBlockingQueue<Runnable>());
```

10. Send 10 tasks to the executor using the counter of the loop as the priority of the tasks. Use the `execute()` method to send the tasks to the executor:

```
for (int i=0; i<10; i++){
    MyPriorityTask task=new MyPriorityTask ("Task "+i,i);
    executor.execute(task);
}
```

11. Put the current thread to sleep for 1 second:

```
try {
    TimeUnit.SECONDS.sleep(1);
} catch (InterruptedException e) {
    e.printStackTrace();
}
```

12. Send 10 additional tasks to the executor using the counter of the loop as the priority of the tasks. Use the `execute()` method to send the tasks to the executor:

```
for (int i=10; i<20; i++) {
    MyPriorityTask task=new MyPriorityTask ("Task "+i,i);
    executor.execute(task);
}
```

13. Shut down the executor using the `shutdown()` method:

```
executor.shutdown();
```

14. Wait for the finalization of the executor using the `awaitTermination()` method:

```
try {
    executor.awaitTermination(1, TimeUnit.DAYS);
} catch (InterruptedException e) {
    e.printStackTrace();
}
```

15. Write a message in the console indicating the finalization of the program:

```
System.out.printf("Main: End of the program.\n");
```

How it works...

Converting a regular executor into a priority-based executor is simple. You only have to pass a `PriorityBlockingQueue` object, parameterized by the `Runnable` interface, as a parameter. But with the executor, you should know that all the objects stored in a priority queue have to implement the `Comparable` interface.

You implemented the `MyPriorityTask` class that implements the `Runnable` interface, which will act as a task, and the `Comparable` interface to be stored in the priority queue. This class has a `Priority` attribute that is used to store the priority of the tasks. If a task has a higher value for this attribute, it will be executed earlier. The `compareTo()` method determines the order of the tasks in the priority queue. In the `Main` class, you sent 20 tasks to the executor with different priorities. The first tasks you sent to the executor were the first tasks to be executed. As the executor was idle waiting for the tasks, it executed the first tasks immediately, as soon as they arrived. You created the executor with four execution threads, so the first four tasks will be the first ones that are executed. Then, the rest of the tasks will be executed based on their priority.

The following screenshot shows one execution of this example:

```
Problems   Javadoc   Declaration   Search   Console
<terminated> Main (56) [Java Application] C:\Program Files\Java\jdk
MyPriorityTask: Task 0 Priority : 0
MyPriorityTask: Task 3 Priority : 3
MyPriorityTask: Task 2 Priority : 2
MyPriorityTask: Task 1 Priority : 1
MyPriorityTask: Task 19 Priority : 19
MyPriorityTask: Task 18 Priority : 18
MyPriorityTask: Task 17 Priority : 17
MyPriorityTask: Task 16 Priority : 16
MyPriorityTask: Task 15 Priority : 15
MyPriorityTask: Task 14 Priority : 14
MyPriorityTask: Task 13 Priority : 13
MyPriorityTask: Task 12 Priority : 12
MyPriorityTask: Task 11 Priority : 11
MyPriorityTask: Task 10 Priority : 10
MyPriorityTask: Task 9 Priority : 9
MyPriorityTask: Task 8 Priority : 8
MyPriorityTask: Task 7 Priority : 7
MyPriorityTask: Task 6 Priority : 6
MyPriorityTask: Task 5 Priority : 5
MyPriorityTask: Task 4 Priority : 4
Main: End of the program.
```

There's more...

You can configure `Executor` to use any implementation of the `BlockingQueue` interface. One interesting implementation is `DelayQueue`. This class is used to store elements with delayed activation. It provides methods that only return active objects. You can use this class to implement your own version of the `ScheduledThreadPoolExecutor` class.

See also

- The *Creating a thread executor and controlling its rejected tasks* recipe in `Chapter 4, Thread Executors`
- The *Customizing the ThreadPoolExecutor class* recipe in this chapter
- The *Using blocking thread-safe queue ordered by priority* recipe in `Chapter 7, Concurrent Collections`

Implementing the ThreadFactory interface to generate custom threads

Factory pattern is a widely used design pattern in the object-oriented programming world. It is a creational pattern and its objective is to develop a class whose mission is to create objects of one or several classes. Then, when we want to create an object of one of those classes, we use the factory instead of using the new operator.

With this factory, we centralize the creation of objects, thereby gaining the advantage of easily changing the class of objects created or the way we create these objects, considering the limitations we have in creating objects with limited resources. For example, we can only have N objects of a type that has the ability to easily generate statistical data about the creation of objects.

Java provides the `ThreadFactory` interface to implement a `Thread` object factory. Some advanced utilities of the Java concurrency API, such as the `Executor` framework or the fork/join framework, use thread factories to create threads. Another example of the factory pattern in the Java Concurrency API is the `Executors` class. It provides a lot of methods to create different kinds of `Executor` objects. In this recipe, you will extend the `Thread` class by adding new functionalities, and you will implement a thread factory class to generate threads of this new class.

Getting ready

The example of this recipe has been implemented using the Eclipse IDE. If you use Eclipse or a different IDE, such as NetBeans, open it and create a new Java project.

How to do it...

Follow these steps to implement the example:

1. Create a class named `MyThread` that extends the `Thread` class:

   ```java
   public class MyThread extends Thread {
   ```

2. Declare three private `Date` attributes named `creationDate`, `startDate`, and `finishDate`:

   ```java
   private final Date creationDate;
   private Date startDate;
   private Date finishDate;
   ```

3. Implement a constructor of the class. It receives the name and the `Runnable` object to be executed as parameters. Initialize the creation date of the thread:

   ```java
   public MyThread(Runnable target, String name ){
     super(target,name);
     creationDate = new Date();
   }
   ```

4. Implement the `run()` method. Store the start date of the thread, call the `run()` method of the parent class, and store the finish date of the execution:

   ```java
   @Override
   public void run() {
     setStartDate();
     super.run();
     setFinishDate();
   }
   ```

5. Implement a method to establish the value of the `startDate` attribute:

   ```java
   public synchronized void setStartDate() {
     startDate=new Date();
   }
   ```

6. Implement a method to establish the value of the `finishDate` attribute:

```
public synchronized void setFinishDate() {
   finishDate=new Date();
}
```

7. Implement a method named `getExecutionTime()` that calculates the execution time of the thread as the difference between start and finish dates:

```
public synchronized long getExecutionTime() {
   return finishDate.getTime()-startDate.getTime();
}
```

8. Override the `toString()` method to return the creation date and execution time of the thread:

```
@Override
public synchronized String toString(){
   StringBuilder buffer=new StringBuilder();
   buffer.append(getName());
   buffer.append(": ");
   buffer.append(" Creation Date: ");
   buffer.append(creationDate);
   buffer.append(" : Running time: ");
   buffer.append(getExecutionTime());
   buffer.append(" Milliseconds.");
   return buffer.toString();
}
```

9. Create a class named `MyThreadFactory` that implements the `ThreadFactory` interface:

```
public class MyThreadFactory implements ThreadFactory {
```

10. Declare a private `AtomicInteger` attribute named `counter`:

```
private AtomicInteger counter;
```

11. Declare a private `String` attribute named `prefix`:

```
private String prefix;
```

12. Implement the constructor of the class to initialize its attributes:

```
public MyThreadFactory (String prefix) {
   this.prefix=prefix;
   counter=new AtomicInteger(1);
}
```

13. Implement the `newThread()` method. Create a `MyThread` object and increment the `counter` attribute:

```
@Override
public Thread newThread(Runnable r) {
   MyThread myThread=new MyThread(r,prefix+"-"+counter
                                     .getAndIncrement());
   return myThread;
}
```

14. Create a class named `MyTask` that implements the `Runnable` interface. Implement the `run()` method. Put the current thread to sleep for 2 seconds:

```
public class MyTask implements Runnable {
   @Override
   public void run() {
      try {
         TimeUnit.SECONDS.sleep(2);
      } catch (InterruptedException e) {
         e.printStackTrace();
      }
   }
}
```

15. Implement the main class of the example by creating a class named `Main` with a `main()` method:

```
public class Main {
   public static void main(String[] args) throws Exception {
```

16. Create a `MyThreadFactory` object:

```
MyThreadFactory myFactory=new MyThreadFactory
                                  ("MyThreadFactory");
```

17. Create a `Task` object:

```
MyTask task=new MyTask();
```

18. Create a `MyThread` object to execute the task using the `newThread()` method of the factory:

```
Thread thread=myFactory.newThread(task);
```

19. Start the thread and wait for its finalization:

```
thread.start();
thread.join();
```

20. Write information about the thread using the `toString()` method:

```
System.out.printf("Main: Thread information.\n");
System.out.printf("%s\n",thread);
System.out.printf("Main: End of the example.\n");
```

How it works...

In this recipe, you implemented a custom `MyThread` class extending the `Thread` class. This class has three attributes to store the creation date, the start date of its execution, and the end date of its execution. Using the start date and end date attributes, you implemented the `getExecutionTime()` method that returns the total time the thread spent in executing its task. Finally, you overrode the `toString()` method to generate information about a thread.

Once you had your own thread class, you implemented a factory to create objects of that class by implementing the `ThreadFactory` interface. It's not mandatory to make use of the interface if you're going to use your factory as an independent object, but if you want to use this factory with other classes of the Java Concurrency API, you must construct your factory by implementing this interface. The `ThreadFactory` interface has only one method: the `newThread()` method. This method receives a `Runnable` object as a parameter and returns a `Thread` object to execute the `Runnable` object. In your case, you returned a `MyThread` object.

To check these two classes, you implemented the `MyTask` class that implemented the `Runnable` object. This is the task to be executed in threads managed by the `MyThread` object. A `MyTask` instance puts its execution thread to sleep for 2 seconds.

In the main method of the example, you created a `MyThread` object using a `MyThreadFactory` factory to execute a `Task` object. If you execute the program, you will see a message with the start date and the execution time of the thread executed.

The following screenshot shows the output generated by this example:

```
Problems  Javadoc  Declaration  Search  Console ⊠  Error Log                                    ■ ✖ ✖ |
<terminated> Main (57) [Java Application] C:\Program Files\Java\jdk-9\bin\javaw.exe (6 nov. 2016 1:04:22)
Main: Thread information.
MyThreadFactory-1:  Creation Date: Sun Nov 06 01:04:22 GMT+01:00 2016 : Running time: 2001 Milliseconds.
Main: End of the example.
```

There's more...

The Java Concurrency API provides the `Executors` class to generate thread executors, usually objects of the `ThreadPoolExecutor` class. You can also use this class to obtain the most basic implementation of the `ThreadFactory` interface, using the `defaultThreadFactory()` method. The factory generated by this method generates basic `Thread` objects that belong to the same `ThreadGroup` object. You can use the `ThreadFactory` interface in your program for any purpose, not necessarily related only to the Executor framework.

Using our ThreadFactory in an Executor object

In the previous recipe, we introduced the factory pattern and provided an example of how to implement a factory of threads implementing the `ThreadFactory` interface.

The Executor framework is a mechanism that allows you to separate thread creation and its execution. It's based on the `Executor` and `ExecutorService` interfaces and the `ThreadPoolExecutor` class that implements both these interfaces. It has an internal pool of threads and provides methods that allow you to send two kinds of tasks to execute them in the pooled threads. These two kinds of tasks are as follows:

- Classes that implement the `Runnable` interface, to implement tasks that don't return a result
- Classes that implement the `Callable` interface, to implement tasks that return a result

Internally, the `Executor` framework uses a `ThreadFactory` interface to create threads that it uses to generate new threads. In this recipe, you will learn how to implement your own thread class, a thread factory to create threads of this class, and how to use this factory in an executor so the executor will execute your threads.

Getting ready

Read the previous recipe and implement its example.

The example of this recipe has been implemented using the Eclipse IDE. If you use Eclipse or another IDE, such as NetBeans, open it and create a new Java project.

How to do it...

Follow these steps to implement the example:

1. Copy the `MyThread`, `MyThreadFactory`, and `MyTask` classes into the project. They were implemented in the *Implementing the ThreadFactory interface to generate custom threads for the fork/join framework* recipe. You are going to use them in this example.

2. Implement the main class of the example by creating a class named `Main` with a `main()` method:

    ```
    public class Main {
        public static void main(String[] args) throws Exception {
    ```

3. Create a new `MyThreadFactory` object named `threadFactory`:

    ```
    MyThreadFactory threadFactory=new MyThreadFactory
                                    ("MyThreadFactory");
    ```

4. Create a new `Executor` object using the `newCachedThreadPool()` method of the `Executors` class. Pass the factory object created earlier as a parameter. The new `Executor` object will use this factory to create the necessary threads, so it will execute `MyThread` threads:

    ```
    ExecutorService executor=Executors.newCachedThreadPool
                                    (threadFactory);
    ```

5. Create a new `Task` object and send it to the executor using the `submit()` method:

```
MyTask task=new MyTask();
executor.submit(task);
```

6. Shut down the executor using the `shutdown()` method:

```
executor.shutdown();
```

7. Wait for the finalization of the executor using the `awaitTermination()` method:

```
executor.awaitTermination(1, TimeUnit.DAYS);
```

8. Write a message to indicate the end of the program:

```
System.out.printf("Main: End of the program.\n");
```

How it works...

In the *How it works...* section of the previous recipe, you have a detailed explanation of how the `MyThread`, `MyThreadFactory`, and `MyTask` classes work.

In the `main()` method of the example, you created an `Executor` object using the `newCachedThreadPool()` method of the `Executors` class. You passed the factory object created earlier as a parameter, so the `Executor` object created will use that factory to create the threads it needs and also execute threads of the `MyThread` class.

Execute the program and you will see a message with information about the thread's start date and its execution time. The following screenshot shows the output generated by this example:

```
Problems  Javadoc  Declaration  Search  Console  Error Log
<terminated> Main (58) [Java Application] C:\Program Files\Java\jdk-9\bin\javaw.exe (6 nov. 2016 1:25:16)
Main: End of the program.
Thread: MyThreadFactory-1:  Creation Date: Sun Nov 06 01:25:17 GMT+01:00 2016 : Running time: 2005 Milliseconds.
```

See also

- The *Implementing the ThreadFactory interface to generate custom threads for the fork/join framework* recipe in this chapter

Customizing tasks running in a scheduled thread pool

Scheduled thread pool is an extension of the basic thread pool of the `Executor` framework that allows you to schedule the execution of tasks to be executed after a period of time. It's implemented by the `ScheduledThreadPoolExecutor` class, and it permits the execution of the following two kinds of tasks:

- **Delayed tasks**: These kinds of tasks are executed only once after a period of time
- **Periodic tasks**: These kinds of tasks are executed after a delay and then periodically, every so often

Delayed tasks can execute both `Callable` and `Runnable` objects, but periodic tasks can only execute `Runnable` objects. All the tasks executed by a scheduled pool are an implementation of the `RunnableScheduledFuture` interface. In this recipe, you will learn how to implement your own implementation of the `RunnableScheduledFuture` interface to execute both delayed and periodic tasks.

Getting ready

The example of this recipe has been implemented using the Eclipse IDE. If you use Eclipse or a different IDE, such as NetBeans, open it and create a new Java project.

How to do it...

Follow these steps to implement the example:

1. Create a class named `MyScheduledTask` parameterized by a generic type named `V`. It extends the `FutureTask` class and implements the `RunnableScheduledFuture` interface:

   ```
   public class MyScheduledTask<V> extends FutureTask<V>
                       implements RunnableScheduledFuture<V> {
   ```

2. Declare a privateRunnableScheduledFuture attribute named `task`:

```
private RunnableScheduledFuture<V> task;
```

3. Declare a privateScheduledThreadPoolExecutor class named `executor`:

```
private ScheduledThreadPoolExecutor executor;
```

4. Declare a private `long` attribute named `period`:

```
private long period;
```

5. Declare a private `long` attribute named `startDate`:

```
private long startDate;
```

6. Implement a constructor of the class. It receives the `Runnable` object that is going to be executed by a task, the result that will be returned by this task, the `RunnableScheduledFuture` task that will be used to create the `MyScheduledTask` object, and the `ScheduledThreadPoolExecutor` object that is going to execute the task. Call the constructor of its parent class and store the task and `executor` attributes:

```
public MyScheduledTask(Runnable runnable, V result,
                       RunnableScheduledFuture<V> task,
                       ScheduledThreadPoolExecutor executor) {
  super(runnable, result);
  this.task=task;
  this.executor=executor;
}
```

7. Implement the `getDelay()` method. If the task is periodic and the `startDate` attribute has a value other than zero, calculate the returned value as the difference between the `startDate` attribute and the actual date. Otherwise, return the delay of the original task stored in the task attribute. Don't forget that you have to return the result in the time unit passed as a parameter:

```
@Override
public long getDelay(TimeUnit unit) {
  if (!isPeriodic()) {
    return task.getDelay(unit);
  } else {
    if (startDate==0){
      return task.getDelay(unit);
    } else {
```

```
    Date now=new Date();
    long delay=startDate-now.getTime();
    return unit.convert(delay, TimeUnit.MILLISECONDS);
  }
 }
}
```

8. Implement the `compareTo()` method. Call the `compareTo()` method of the original task:

```
@Override
public int compareTo(Delayed o) {
  return task.compareTo(o);
}
```

9. Implement the `isPeriodic()` method. Call the `isPeriodic()` method of the original task:

```
@Override
public boolean isPeriodic() {
  return task.isPeriodic();
}
```

10. Implement the `run()` method. If it's a periodic task, you have to update its `startDate` attribute with the start date of the next execution of the task. Calculate it as the sum of the actual date and period. Then, add the task again to the queue of the `ScheduledThreadPoolExecutor` object:

```
@Override
public void run() {
  if (isPeriodic() && (!executor.isShutdown())) {
    Date now=new Date();
    startDate=now.getTime()+period;
    executor.getQueue().add(this);
  }
}
```

11. Print a message to the console with the actual date. Execute the task calling the `runAndReset()` method and then print another message to the console with the actual date:

```
System.out.printf("Pre-MyScheduledTask: %s\n",new Date());
System.out.printf("MyScheduledTask: Is Periodic: %s\n",
              isPeriodic());
super.runAndReset();
System.out.printf("Post-MyScheduledTask: %s\n",new Date());
}
```

12. Implement the setPeriod() method to establish the period of this task:

```
public void setPeriod(long period) {
    this.period=period;
}
```

13. Create a class named MyScheduledThreadPoolExecutor to implement a ScheduledThreadPoolExecutor object that executes MyScheduledTask tasks. Specify that this class extends the ScheduledThreadPoolExecutor class:

```
public class MyScheduledThreadPoolExecutor extends
                                ScheduledThreadPoolExecutor {
```

14. Implement a constructor of the class that merely calls the constructor of its parent class:

```
public MyScheduledThreadPoolExecutor(int corePoolSize) {
    super(corePoolSize);
}
```

15. Implement the decorateTask() method. It receives the Runnable object that is going to be executed as a parameter and the RunnableScheduledFuture task that will execute this Runnable object. Create and return a MyScheduledTask task using these objects to construct them:

```
@Override
protected <V> RunnableScheduledFuture<V> decorateTask(
                        Runnable runnable,
                        RunnableScheduledFuture<V> task) {
    MyScheduledTask<V> myTask=new MyScheduledTask<V>(runnable,
                                        null, task,this);
    return myTask;
}
```

16. Override the scheduledAtFixedRate() method. Call the method of its parent class, convert the returned object into a MyScheduledTask object, and establish the period of that task using the setPeriod() method:

```
@Override
public ScheduledFuture<?> scheduleAtFixedRate(Runnable command,
            long initialDelay, long period, TimeUnit unit) {
    ScheduledFuture<?> task= super.scheduleAtFixedRate(command,
                            initialDelay, period, unit);
    MyScheduledTask<?> myTask=(MyScheduledTask<?>)task;
    myTask.setPeriod(TimeUnit.MILLISECONDS.convert(period,unit));
```

```
        return task;
    }
```

17. Create a class named `Task` that implements the `Runnable` interface:

```
public class Task implements Runnable {
```

18. Implement the `run()` method. Print a message at the start of the task, put the current thread to sleep for 2 seconds, and print another message at the end of the task:

```
@Override
public void run() {
    System.out.printf("Task: Begin.\n");
    try {
        TimeUnit.SECONDS.sleep(2);
    } catch (InterruptedException e) {
        e.printStackTrace();
    }
    System.out.printf("Task: End.\n");
}
```

19. Implement the main class of the example by creating a class named `Main` with a `main()` method:

```
public class Main {

    public static void main(String[] args) throws Exception{
```

20. Create a `MyScheduledThreadPoolExecutor` object named executor. Use `4` as a parameter to have two threads in the pool:

```
MyScheduledThreadPoolExecutor executor=new
                    MyScheduledThreadPoolExecutor(4);
```

21. Create a `Task` object named `task`. Write the actual date in the console:

```
Task task=new Task();
System.out.printf("Main: %s\n",new Date());
```

22. Send a delayed task to the executor using the `schedule()` method. The task will be executed after a 1-second delay:

```
executor.schedule(task, 1, TimeUnit.SECONDS);
```

23. Put the main thread to sleep for 3 seconds:

```
TimeUnit.SECONDS.sleep(3);
```

24. Create another `Task` object. Print the actual date in the console again:

```
task=new Task();
System.out.printf("Main: %s\n",new Date());
```

25. Send a periodic task to the executor using the `scheduleAtFixedRate()` method. The task will be executed after a 1-second delay and then it will be executed every 3 seconds:

```
executor.scheduleAtFixedRate(task, 1, 3, TimeUnit.SECONDS);
```

26. Put the main thread to sleep for 10 seconds:

```
TimeUnit.SECONDS.sleep(10);
```

27. Shut down the executor using the `shutdown()` method. Wait for the finalization of the executor using the `awaitTermination()` method:

```
executor.shutdown();
executor.awaitTermination(1, TimeUnit.DAYS);
```

28. Write a message in the console indicating the end of the program:

```
System.out.printf("Main: End of the program.\n");
```

How it works...

In this recipe, you implemented the `MyScheduledTask` class to implement a custom task that can be executed on a `ScheduledThreadPoolExecutor` executor. This class extends the `FutureTask` class and implements the `RunnableScheduledFuture` interface. It implements the `RunnableScheduledFuture` interface because all the tasks executed in a scheduled executor must implement this interface and extend the `FutureTask` class. This is because this class provides valid implementations of the methods declared in the `RunnableScheduledFuture` interface. All the interfaces and classes mentioned earlier are parameterized classes and they possess the type of data that will be returned by the tasks.

To use a MyScheduledTask task in a scheduled executor, you override the decorateTask() method in the MyScheduledThreadPoolExecutor class. This class extends the ScheduledThreadPoolExecutor executor, and the method provides a mechanism to convert the default scheduled tasks implemented by the ScheduledThreadPoolExecutor executor into MyScheduledTask tasks. So, when you implement your own version of scheduled tasks, you have to implement your own version of a scheduled executor.

The decorateTask() method simply creates a new MyScheduledTask object with four parameters. The first one is a Runnable object that is going to be executed in the task. The second one is the object that is going to be returned by the task. In this case, the task won't return a result, so you used the null value. The third one is the task that the new object is going to replace in the pool and the latest is the executor that will execute the task. In this case, you use the this keyword to reference the executor that is creating the task.

The MyScheduledTask class can execute delayed and periodic tasks. You implemented two methods with all of the necessary logic to execute both kinds of tasks. They are the getDelay() and run() methods.

The getDelay() method is called by the scheduled executor to know whether it has to execute a task. The behavior of this method changes in delayed and periodic tasks. As mentioned earlier, the constructor of the MyScheduledClass class receives the original ScheduledRunnableFuture object that was going to execute the Runnable object and stores it as an attribute of the class to have access to its methods and data. When we execute a delayed task, the getDelay() method returns the delay of the original task; however, in the case of a periodic task, the getDelay() method returns the difference between the startDate attribute and the actual date.

The run() method is the one that executes the task. One particularity of periodic tasks is that you have to put the next execution of the task in the queue of the executor as a new task if you want the task to be executed again. So, if you're executing a periodic task, you establish the startDate attribute value and add it to the actual date and period of the execution of the task and store the task again in the queue of the executor. The startDate attribute stores the date when the next execution of the task will begin. Then, you execute the task using the runAndReset() method provided by the FutureTask class. In the case of delayed tasks, you don't have to put them in the queue of the executor because they can only be executed once.

You also have to take into account whether the executor has been shut down. If yes, you don't have to store the periodic tasks in the queue of the executor again.

Finally, you overrode the `scheduleAtFixedRate()` method in the `MyScheduledThreadPoolExecutor` class. We mentioned earlier that for periodic tasks, you establish the value of the `startDate` attribute using the period of the task, but you haven't initialized that period yet. You have to override this method that receives this period as a parameter; do this to pass it to the `MyScheduledTask` class so it can use it.

The example is complete with the `Task` class that implements the `Runnable` interface, and it is the task executed in the scheduled executor. The main class of the example creates a `MyScheduledThreadPoolExecutor` executor and sends the following two tasks to them:

- A delayed task, which is to be executed 1 second after the actual date
- A periodic task, which is to be executed for the first time a second after the actual date and then every 3 seconds

The following screenshot shows part of the execution of this example. You can check whether the two kinds of tasks are executed properly:

```
📊 Problems  @ Javadoc  🔍 Declaration  🔍 Search  💻 Console ⊠  💡 Error Log
<terminated> Main (59) [Java Application] C:\Program Files\Java\jdk-9\bin\javaw.e
Main: Sun Nov 06 01:38:41 GMT+01:00 2016
Pre-MyScheduledTask: Sun Nov 06 01:38:42 GMT+01:00 2016
MyScheduledTask: Is Periodic: false
Task: Begin.
Main: Sun Nov 06 01:38:44 GMT+01:00 2016
Task: End.
Post-MyScheduledTask: Sun Nov 06 01:38:44 GMT+01:00 2016
Pre-MyScheduledTask: Sun Nov 06 01:38:45 GMT+01:00 2016
MyScheduledTask: Is Periodic: true
Task: Begin.
Task: End.
Post-MyScheduledTask: Sun Nov 06 01:38:47 GMT+01:00 2016
Pre-MyScheduledTask: Sun Nov 06 01:38:48 GMT+01:00 2016
MyScheduledTask: Is Periodic: true
Task: Begin.
Task: End.
Post-MyScheduledTask: Sun Nov 06 01:38:50 GMT+01:00 2016
Pre-MyScheduledTask: Sun Nov 06 01:38:51 GMT+01:00 2016
MyScheduledTask: Is Periodic: true
Task: Begin.
Task: End.
Post-MyScheduledTask: Sun Nov 06 01:38:53 GMT+01:00 2016
Main: End of the program.
```

There's more...

The `ScheduledThreadPoolExecutor` class provides another version of the `decorateTask()` method that receives a `Callable` object as a parameter, instead of a `Runnable` object.

See also

- The *Running a task in an executor after a delay* and *Running a task in an executor periodically* recipes in `Chapter 4`, *Thread Executors*

Implementing the ThreadFactory interface to generate custom threads for the fork/join framework

One of the most interesting features of Java 9 is the fork/join framework. It's an implementation of the `Executor` and `ExecutorService` interfaces that allows you to execute the `Callable` and `Runnable` tasks without managing the threads that execute them.

This executor is oriented to execute tasks that can be divided into smaller parts. Its main components are as follows:

- It's a special kind of task, which is implemented by the `ForkJoinTask` class.
- It provides two operations for dividing a task into subtasks (the fork operation) and to wait for the finalization of these subtasks (the join operation).
- It's an algorithm, denominating the work-stealing algorithm, that optimizes the use of the threads of the pool. When a task waits for its subtasks, the thread that was executing it is used to execute another thread.

The main class of the fork/join framework is the `ForkJoinPool` class. Internally, it has the following two elements:

- A queue of tasks that are waiting to be executed
- A pool of threads that execute the tasks

The `ForkJoinWorkerThread` adds new methods to the `Thread` class, such as the `onStart()` method that's executed when the thread is created and the `onTermination()` method that's called to clean up the resources used by the thread. The `ForkJoinPool` class uses an implementation of the `ForkJoinWorkerThreadFactory` interface to create the worker threads it uses.

In this recipe, you will learn how to implement a customized worker thread to be used in a `ForkJoinPool` class and how to use it with a factory extending the `ForkJoinPool` class and implementing the `ForkJoinWorkerThreadFactory` interface.

Getting ready

The example of this recipe has been implemented using the Eclipse IDE. If you use Eclipse or a different IDE, such as NetBeans, open it and create a new Java project.

How to do it...

Follow these steps to implement the example:

1. Create a class named `MyWorkerThread` that extends the `ForkJoinWorkerThread` class:

   ```
   public class MyWorkerThread extends ForkJoinWorkerThread {
   ```

2. Declare and create a private `ThreadLocal` attribute parameterized by the `Integer` class named `taskCounter`:

   ```
   private final static ThreadLocal<Integer> taskCounter=
                              new ThreadLocal<Integer>();
   ```

3. Implement a constructor of the class:

   ```
   protected MyWorkerThread(ForkJoinPool pool) {
     super(pool);
   }
   ```

4. Override the `onStart()` method. Call the method on its parent class, print a message to the console, and set the value of the `taskCounter` attribute of this thread to zero:

```
@Override
protected void onStart() {
  super.onStart();
  System.out.printf("MyWorkerThread %d: Initializing task
                    counter.\n", getId());
  taskCounter.set(0);
}
```

5. Override the `onTermination()` method. Write the value of the `taskCounter` attribute of this thread in the console:

```
@Override
protected void onTermination(Throwable exception) {
  System.out.printf("MyWorkerThread %d: %d\n",
                    getId(),taskCounter.get());
  super.onTermination(exception);
}
```

6. Implement the `addTask()` method. Increment the value of the `taskCounter` attribute:

```
public void addTask(){
  taskCounter.set(taskCounter.get() + 1);;
}
```

7. Create a class named `MyWorkerThreadFactory` that implements the `ForkJoinWorkerThreadFactory` interface. Implement the `newThread()` method. Create and return a `MyWorkerThread` object:

```
public class MyWorkerThreadFactory implements
               ForkJoinWorkerThreadFactory {
  @Override
  public ForkJoinWorkerThread newThread(ForkJoinPool pool) {
    return new MyWorkerThread(pool);
  }

}
```

8. Create a class named `MyRecursiveTask` that extends the `RecursiveTask` class parameterized by the `Integer` class:

```
public class MyRecursiveTask extends RecursiveTask<Integer> {
```

9. Declare a private `int` array named `array`:

```
private int array[];
```

10. Declare two private `int` attributes named `start` and `end`:

```
private int start, end;
```

11. Implement the constructor of the class that initializes its attributes:

```
public Task(int array[],int start, int end) {
  this.array=array;
  this.start=start;
  this.end=end;
}
```

12. Implement the `compute()` method to sum all the elements of the array between the start and end positions. First, convert the thread that is executing the task into a `MyWorkerThread` object and use the `addTask()` method to increment the counter of tasks for that thread:

```
@Override
protected Integer compute() {
  Integer ret;
  MyWorkerThread thread=(MyWorkerThread)Thread.currentThread();
  thread.addTask();
```

13. If the difference between the start and end positions in the array is higher than 100 elements, we calculate the position in the middle and create two new `MyRecursiveTask` tasks to process the first and second halves, respectively. If the difference is equal to or lower than 100, we calculate the sum of all the elements between the start and end positions:

```
if (end-start>100) {
  int mid=(start+end)/2;
  MyRecursiveTask task1=new MyRecursiveTask(array,start,mid);
  MyRecursiveTask task2=new MyRecursiveTask(array,mid,end);
  invokeAll(task1,task2);
  ret=addResults(task1,task2);
} else {
  int add=0;
  for (int i=start; i<end; i++) {
    add+=array[i];
  }
  ret=add;
}
```

14. Put the thread to sleep for 10 milliseconds and return the result of the task:

```
try {
   TimeUnit.MILLISECONDS.sleep(10);
} catch (InterruptedException e) {
   e.printStackTrace();
}
return ret;
}
```

15. Implement the `addResults()` method. Calculate and return the sum of the results of the two tasks received as parameters:

```
private Integer addResults(Task task1, Task task2) {
   int value;
   try {
      value = task1.get().intValue()+task2.get().intValue();
   } catch (InterruptedException e) {
      e.printStackTrace();
      value=0;
   } catch (ExecutionException e) {
      e.printStackTrace();
      value=0;
   }
}
```

16. Implement the main class of the example by creating a class named `Main` with a `main()` method:

```
public class Main {

   public static void main(String[] args) throws Exception {
```

17. Create a `MyWorkerThreadFactory` object named `factory`:

```
MyWorkerThreadFactory factory=new MyWorkerThreadFactory();
```

18. Create a `ForkJoinPool` object named `pool`. Pass the `factory` object, created earlier, to the constructor:

```
ForkJoinPool pool=new ForkJoinPool(4, factory, null, false);
```

19. Create an array of 100,000 integers. Initialize all the elements to 1:

```
int array[]=new int[100000];
for (int i=0; i<array.length; i++){
   array[i]=1;
}
```

20. Create a new `task` object to sum all the elements of the array:

```
MyRecursiveTask task=new MyRecursiveTask(array,0,array.length);
```

21. Send the task to the pool using the `execute()` method:

```
pool.execute(task);
```

22. Wait for the end of the task using the `join()` method:

```
task.join();
```

23. Shut down the pool using the `shutdown()` method:

```
pool.shutdown();
```

24. Wait for the finalization of the executor using the `awaitTermination()` method:

```
pool.awaitTermination(1, TimeUnit.DAYS);
```

25. Write the result of the task in the console, using the `get()` method:

```
System.out.printf("Main: Result: %d\n",task.get());
```

26. Write a message in the console indicating the end of the example:

```
System.out.printf("Main: End of the program\n");
```

How it works...

Threads used by the fork/join framework are called worker threads. Java includes the `ForkJoinWorkerThread` class that extends the `Thread` class and implements the worker threads used by the fork/join framework.

In this recipe, you implemented the `MyWorkerThread` class that extends the `ForkJoinWorkerThread` class and overrides two methods of the `ForkJoinWorkerThread` class. Your objective is to implement a counter of tasks in each worker thread so that you can know how many tasks a worker thread has executed. You implemented the counter with a `ThreadLocal` attribute. This way, each thread will have its own counter in a transparent way for you, the programmer.

You overrode the `onStart()` method of the `ForkJoinWorkerThread` class to initialize the task counter. This method is called when the worker thread begins its execution. You also overrode the `onTermination()` method to print the value of the task counter to the console. This method is called when the worker thread finishes its execution. In addition, you implemented a method in the `MyWorkerThread` class. The `addTask()` method increments the task counter of each thread.

The `ForkJoinPool` class, like with all the executors in the Java Concurrency API, creates its threads using a factory. So, if you want to use the `MyWorkerThread` thread in a `ForkJoinPool` class, you have to implement your thread factory. For the fork/join framework, this factory has to implement the `ForkJoinPool.ForkJoinWorkerThreadFactory` class. You implemented the `MyWorkerThreadFactory` class for this purpose. This class only has one method that creates a new `MyWorkerThread` object.

Finally, you only have to initialize a `ForkJoinPool` class with the factory you have created. You did this in the `Main` class, using the constructor of the `ForkJoinPool` class.

The following screenshot shows part of the output of the program:

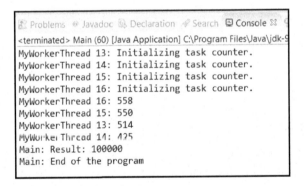

You can see how the `ForkJoinPool` object has executed four worker threads and how many tasks have executed each one of them.

There's more...

Take into account that the `onTermination()` method provided by the `ForkJoinWorkerThread` class is called when a thread finishes normally or throws an exception. The method receives a `Throwable` object as a parameter. If the parameter takes the null value, the worker thread finishes normally; however, if the parameter takes a value, the thread throws an exception. You have to include the necessary code to process this situation.

See also

- The *Creating a fork/join pool* recipe in `Chapter 5`, *Fork/Join Framework*
- The *Creating threads through a factory* recipe in `Chapter 1`, *Thread Management*

Customizing tasks running in the fork/join framework

The `Executor` framework separates task creation and its execution. With it, you only have to implement the `Runnable` objects and use an `Executor` object. You just need to send the `Runnable` tasks to the executor and it creates, manages, and finalizes the necessary threads to execute these tasks.

Java 9 provides a special kind of executor in the fork/join framework (introduced in Java 7). This framework is designed to solve problems that can be broken down into smaller tasks using the divide and conquer technique. Inside a task, you have to check the size of the problem you want to resolve; if it's bigger than the established size, you divide the problem into two or more tasks and execute them using the framework. If the size of the problem is smaller than the established size, you resolve the problem directly in the task; optionally, it returns a result. The fork/join framework implements the work-stealing algorithm that improves the overall performance of these kinds of problems.

The `main` class of the fork/join framework is the `ForkJoinPool` class. Internally, it has the following two elements:

- A queue of tasks that are waiting to be executed
- A pool of threads that execute the tasks

By default, the tasks executed by a `ForkJoinPool` class are objects of the `ForkJoinTask` class. You can also send the `Runnable` and `Callable` objects to a `ForkJoinPool` class, but they can't take advantage of all the benefits of the fork/join framework. Normally, you will send one of two subclasses of the `ForkJoinTask` class to the `ForkJoinPool` object:

- `RecursiveAction`: If your tasks don't return a result
- `RecursiveTask`: If your tasks return a result

In this recipe, you will learn how to implement your own tasks for the fork/join framework by implementing a task that extends the `ForkJoinTask` class. The task you're going to implement measures and writes its execution time in the console so you can control its evolution. You can also implement your own fork/join task to write log information, to get resources used in the tasks, or to postprocess the results of the tasks.

How to do it...

Follow these steps to implement the example:

1. Create a class named `MyWorkerTask` and specify that it extends the `ForkJoinTask` class parameterized by the `Void` type:

   ```
   public abstract class MyWorkerTask extends ForkJoinTask<Void> {
   ```

2. Declare a private `String` attribute called `name` to store the name of the task:

   ```
   private String name;
   ```

3. Implement the constructor of the class to initialize its attribute:

   ```
   public MyWorkerTask(String name) {
     this.name=name;
   }
   ```

4. Implement the `getRawResult()` method. This is one of the abstract methods of the `ForkJoinTask` class. As the `MyWorkerTask` tasks won't return any results, this method must return null:

   ```
   @Override
   public Void getRawResult() {
     return null;
   }
   ```

5. Implement the `setRawResult()` method. This is another abstract method of the `ForkJoinTask` class. As the `MyWorkerTask` tasks won't return any results, leave the body of this method empty:

```
@Override
protected void setRawResult(Void value) {

}
```

6. Implement the `exec()` method. This is the `main` method of the task. In this case, delegate the logic of the task to the `compute()` method. Calculate the execution time of this method and write it in the console:

```
@Override
protected boolean exec() {
    Date startDate=new Date();
    compute();
    Date finishDate=new Date();
    long diff=finishDate.getTime()-startDate.getTime();
    System.out.printf("MyWorkerTask: %s : %d Milliseconds to
                      complete.\n",name,diff);
    return true;
}
```

7. Implement the `getName()` method to return the name of the task:

```
public String getName(){
    return name;
}
```

8. Declare the abstract method `compute()`. As mentioned earlier, this method will implement the logic of the tasks, and it must be implemented by the child classes of the `MyWorkerTask` class:

```
protected abstract void compute();
```

9. Create a class named `Task` that extends the `MyWorkerTask` class:

```
public class Task extends MyWorkerTask {
```

10. Declare a private array of `int` values named `array`:

```
private int array[];
```

11. Implement a constructor of the class that initializes its attributes:

```
public Task(String name, int array[], int start, int end){
    super(name);
    this.array=array;
    this.start=start;
    this.end=end;
}
```

12. Implement the `compute()` method. This method increments the block of elements of the array determined by the start and end attributes. If this block of elements has more than 100 elements, divide the block into two parts and create two `Task` objects to process each part. Send these tasks to the pool using the `invokeAll()` method:

```
protected void compute() {
    if (end-start>100){
        int mid=(end+start)/2;
        Task task1=new Task(this.getName()+"1",array,start,mid);
        Task task2=new Task(this.getName()+"2",array,mid,end);
        invokeAll(task1,task2);
```

13. If the block of elements has less than 100 elements, increment all the elements using a `for` loop:

```
} else {
for (int i=start; i<end; i++) {
    array[i]++;
}
```

14. Finally, put the thread that is executing the task to sleep for 50 milliseconds:

```
    try {
        Thread.sleep(50);
    } catch (InterruptedException e) {
        e.printStackTrace();
    }
    }
}
```

15. Next, implement the main class of the example by creating a class named `Main` with a `main()` method:

```
public class Main {
    public static void main(String[] args) throws Exception {
```

16. Create an `int` array of 10,000 elements:

```
int array[]=new int[10000];
```

17. Create a `ForkJoinPool` object named `pool`:

```
ForkJoinPool pool=new ForkJoinPool();
```

18. Create a `Task` object to increment all the elements of the array. The parameter of the constructor is given `Task` as the name of the task, the array object, and the values 0 and 10000 to indicate to this task that it has to process the entire array:

```
Task task=new Task("Task",array,0,array.length);
```

19. Send the task to the pool using the `execute()` method:

```
pool.invoke(task);
```

20. Shut down the `pool` using the `shutdown()` method:

```
pool.shutdown();
```

21. Write a message in the console indicating the end of the program:

```
System.out.printf("Main: End of the program.\n");
```

How it works...

In this recipe, you implemented the `MyWorkerTask` class that extends the `ForkJoinTask` class. It's your own base class to implement tasks that can be executed in a `ForkJoinPool` executor and that can take advantage of all the benefits of the executor, as it's a work-stealing algorithm. This class is equivalent to the `RecursiveAction` and `RecursiveTask` classes.

When you extend the `ForkJoinTask` class, you have to implement the following three methods:

- `setRawResult()`: This method is used to establish the result of the task. As your tasks don't return any results, leave this method empty.
- `getRawResult()`: This method is used to return the result of the task. As your tasks don't return any results, this method returns null.

- `exec()`: This method implements the logic of the task. In this case, you delegated the logic to the abstract `compute()` method (as the `RecursiveAction` and `RecursiveTask` classes). However, in the `exec()` method, you measure the execution time of the method, writing it in the console.

Finally, in the main class of the example, you created an array of 10,000 elements, a `ForkJoinPool` executor, and a `Task` object to process the whole array. Execute the program and you'll see how the different tasks that are executed write their execution time in the console.

See also

- The *Creating a fork/join pool* recipe in `Chapter 5`, *Fork/Join Framework*
- The *Implementing the ThreadFactory interface to generate custom threads for the fork/join framework* recipe in this chapter

Implementing a custom Lock class

Locks are one of the basic synchronization mechanisms provided by the Java Concurrency API. They allow programmers to protect a critical section of code so only one thread can execute that block of code at a time. It provides the following two operations:

- `lock()`: You call this operation when you want to access a critical section. If there is another thread running this critical section, other threads are blocked until they're woken up by the lock to get access to the critical section.
- `unlock()`: You call this operation at the end of a critical section to allow other threads to access it.

In the Java Concurrency API, locks are declared in the `Lock` interface and implemented in some classes, for example, the `ReentrantLock` class.

In this recipe, you will learn how to implement your own `Lock` object by implementing a class that implements the `Lock` interface, which can be used to protect a critical section.

Getting ready

The example of this recipe has been implemented using the Eclipse IDE. If you use Eclipse or a different IDE, such as NetBeans, open it and create a new Java project.

How to do it...

Follow these steps to implement the example:

1. Create a class named `MyAbstractQueuedSynchronizer` that extends the `AbstractQueuedSynchronizer` class:

   ```
   public class MyAbstractQueuedSynchronizer extends
                               AbstractQueuedSynchronizer {
   ```

2. Declare a private `AtomicInteger` attribute named `state`:

   ```
   private final AtomicInteger state;
   ```

3. Implement the constructor of the class to initialize its attribute:

   ```
   public MyAbstractQueuedSynchronizer() {
     state=new AtomicInteger(0);
   }
   ```

4. Implement the `tryAcquire()` method. This method tries to change the value of the state variable from zero to one. If it can, it returns the `true` value; else, it returns `false`:

   ```
   @Override
   protected boolean tryAcquire(int arg) {
     return state.compareAndSet(0, 1);
   }
   ```

5. Implement the `tryRelease()` method. This method tries to change the value of the state variable from one to zero. If it can, it returns `true`; else, it returns `false`:

   ```
   @Override
   protected boolean tryRelease(int arg) {
     return state.compareAndSet(1, 0);
   }
   ```

6. Create a class named `MyLock` and specify that it implements the `Lock` interface:

```
public class MyLock implements Lock{
```

7. Declare a private `AbstractQueuedSynchronizer` attribute named `sync`:

```
private final AbstractQueuedSynchronizer sync;
```

8. Implement the constructor of the class to initialize the `sync` attribute with a new `MyAbstractQueueSynchronizer` object:

```
public MyLock() {
    sync=new MyAbstractQueuedSynchronizer();
}
```

9. Implement the `lock()` method. Call the `acquire()` method of the `sync` object:

```
@Override
public void lock() {
    sync.acquire(1);
}
```

10. Implement the `lockInterruptibly()` method. Call the `acquireInterruptibly()` method of the sync object:

```
@Override
public void lockInterruptibly() throws InterruptedException {
    sync.acquireInterruptibly(1);
}
```

11. Implement the `tryLock()` method. Call the `tryAcquireNanos()` method of the sync object:

```
@Override
public boolean tryLock() {
    try {
        return sync.tryAcquireNanos(1, 1000);
    } catch (InterruptedException e) {
        e.printStackTrace();
        Thread.currentThread().interrupt();
        return false;
    }
}
```

12. Implement another version of the `tryLock()` method with two parameters: a long parameter named time and a `TimeUnit` parameter named unit. Call the `tryAcquireNanos()` method of the sync object:

```
@Override
public boolean tryLock(long time, TimeUnit unit) throws
                                InterruptedException {
    return sync.tryAcquireNanos(1, TimeUnit.NANOSECONDS
                                .convert(time, unit));
}
```

13. Implement the `unlock()` method. Call the `release()` method of the `sync` object:

```
@Override
public void unlock() {
    sync.release(1);
}
```

14. Implement the `newCondition()` method. Create a new object of the internal class of the `sync` object, namely `ConditionObject`:

```
@Override
public Condition newCondition() {
    return sync.new ConditionObject();
}
```

15. Create a class named `Task` and specify that it implements the `Runnable` interface:

```
public class Task implements Runnable {
```

16. Declare a private `MyLock` attribute named `lock`:

```
private final MyLock lock;
```

17. Declare a private `String` attribute called `name`:

```
private final String name;
```

18. Implement the constructor of the class to initialize its attributes:

```
public Task(String name, MyLock lock){
    this.lock=lock;
    this.name=name;
}
```

19. Implement the `run()` method of the class. Acquire the `lock`, put the thread to sleep for 2 seconds, and then release the lock object:

```
@Override
public void run() {
  lock.lock();
  System.out.printf("Task: %s: Take the lock\n",name);
  try {
    TimeUnit.SECONDS.sleep(2);
    System.out.printf("Task: %s: Free the lock\n",name);
  } catch (InterruptedException e) {
    e.printStackTrace();
  } finally {
    lock.unlock();
  }
}
```

20. Implement the main class of the example by creating a class named `Main` with a `main()` method:

```
public class Main {
  public static void main(String[] args) {
```

21. Create a `MyLock` object named `lock`:

```
MyLock lock=new MyLock();
```

22. Create and execute 10 `Task` tasks:

```
for (int i=0; i<10; i++){
  Task task=new Task("Task-"+i,lock);
  Thread thread=new Thread(task);
  thread.start();
}
```

23. Try to get the lock using the `tryLock()` method. Wait for a second, and if you don't get the lock, write a message and try again:

```
boolean value;
do {
  try {
    value=lock.tryLock(1,TimeUnit.SECONDS);
    if (!value) {
      System.out.printf("Main: Trying to get the Lock\n");
    }
  } catch (InterruptedException e) {
    e.printStackTrace();
```

```
            value=false;
        }
    } while (!value);
```

24. Write a message indicating that you got the lock and release it:

    ```
    System.out.printf("Main: Got the lock\n");
    lock.unlock();
    ```

25. Write a message indicating the end of the program:

    ```
    System.out.printf("Main: End of the program\n");
    ```

How it works...

The Java Concurrency API provides a class that can be used to implement synchronization mechanisms with features of locks or semaphores. It's called `AbstractQueuedSynchronizer`, and as the name suggests, it's an abstract class. It provides operations to control access to a critical section and manage a queue of threads that are blocked and are awaiting access to the section. The operations are based on two abstract methods:

- `tryAcquire()`: This method is called to try and get access to a critical section. If the thread that calls it can access the critical section, the method returns the `true` value. Otherwise, it returns the `false` value.
- `tryRelease()`: This method is called to try and release access to a critical section. If the thread that calls it can release access, the method returns the `true` value. Else, it returns the `false` value.

In these methods, you have to implement the mechanism you use to control access to a critical section. In this case, you implemented the `MyAbstractQueuedSynchonizer` class that extends the `AbstractQueuedSyncrhonizer` class and implements the abstract methods using an `AtomicInteger` variable to control access to the critical section. This variable will store the value `0` if the lock is free, so a thread can have access to the critical section, and the value `1` if the lock is blocked, so a thread 'doesn't have access to the critical section.

You used the `compareAndSet()` method provided by the `AtomicInteger` class that tries to change the value you specify as the first parameter with the value you specify as the second parameter. To implement the `tryAcquire()` method, you try to change the value of the atomic variable from zero to one. Similarly, to implement the `tryRelease()` method, you try to change the value of the atomic variable from one to zero.

You have to implement `AtomicInteger` class because other implementations of the `AbstractQueuedSynchronizer` class (for example, the one used by `ReentrantLock`) are implemented as private classes internally. This is carried out in the class that uses it, so you don't have access to it.

Then, you implemented the `MyLock` class. This class implements the `Lock` interface and has a `MyQueuedSynchronizer` object as an attribute. To implement all the methods of the `Lock` interface, you used methods of the `MyQueuedSynchronizer` object.

Finally, you implemented the `Task` class that implements the `Runnable` interface and uses a `MyLock` object to get access to the critical section. This critical section puts the thread to sleep for 2 seconds. The `main` class creates a `MyLock` object and runs 10 `Task` objects that share the lock. The `main` class also tries to get access to the lock using the `tryLock()` method.

When you execute the example, you can see how only one thread has access to the critical section, and when that thread finishes, another one gets access to it.

You can use your own `Lock` interface to write log messages about its utilization, control the time that it's locked, or implement advanced synchronization mechanisms to control, for example, access to a resource so that it's only available at certain times.

There's more...

The `AbstractQueuedSynchronizer` class provides two methods that can be used to manage the state of the lock. They are the `getState()` and `setState()` methods. These methods receive and return an integer value with the state of the lock. You could have used them instead of the `AtomicInteger` attribute to store the state of the lock.

The Java Concurrency API provides another class to implement synchronization mechanisms. It's the `AbstractQueuedLongSynchronizer` class, which is equivalent to `AbstractQueuedSynchronizer` but uses a long attribute to store the state of the threads.

See also

- The *Synchronizing a block of code with locks* recipe in `Chapter 2`, *Basic Thread Synchronization*

Implementing a transfer queue-based on priorities

The Java 9 API provides several data structures to work with concurrent applications. From these, we want to highlight the following two data structures:

- `LinkedTransferQueue`: This data structure is supposed to be used in programs that have a producer/consumer structure. In such applications, you have one or more producers of data and one or more consumers of data, and a data structure is shared by all of them. Producers put data in the data structure and consumers take it from there. If the data structure is empty, consumers are blocked until they have data to consume. If it is full, producers are blocked until they have space to put data.

- `PriorityBlockingQueue`: In this data structure, elements are stored in an ordered way. They have to implement the `Comparable` interface with the `compareTo()` method. When you insert an element in the structure, it's compared to the elements of the structure until it finds its position.

Elements of `LinkedTransferQueue` are stored in the same order as they arrive, so the ones that arrived earlier are consumed first. It may be the case when you want to develop a producer/consumer program, where data is consumed according to some priority instead of arrival time. In this recipe, you will learn how to implement a data structure to be used in the producer/consumer problem whose elements will be ordered by priority; elements with higher priority will be consumed first.

Getting ready

The example of this recipe has been implemented using the Eclipse IDE. If you use Eclipse or a different IDE, such as NetBeans, open it and create a new Java project.

How to do it...

Follow these steps to implement the example:

1. Create a class named `MyPriorityTransferQueue` that extends the `PriorityBlockingQueue` class and implements the `TransferQueue` interface:

```
public class MyPriorityTransferQueue<E> extends
        PriorityBlockingQueue<E> implements TransferQueue<E> {
```

2. Declare a private `AtomicInteger` attribute named `counter` to store the number of consumers that are waiting to consume elements:

```
private final AtomicInteger counter;
```

3. Declare a private `LinkedBlockingQueue` attribute named `transferred`:

```
private final LinkedBlockingQueue<E> transfered;
```

4. Declare a private `ReentrantLock` attribute named `lock`:

```
private final ReentrantLock lock;
```

5. Implement the constructor of the class to initialize its attributes:

```
public MyPriorityTransferQueue() {
   counter=new AtomicInteger(0);
   lock=new ReentrantLock();
   transfered=new LinkedBlockingQueue<E>();
}
```

6. Implement the `tryTransfer()` method. This method tries to send the element to a waiting consumer immediately, if possible. If there isn't any consumer waiting, the method returns `false`:

```
@Override
public boolean tryTransfer(E e) {
   boolean value=false;
   try {
     lock.lock();
     if (counter.get() == 0) {
       value = false;
     } else {
       put(e);
       value = true;
     }
   } finally {
     lock.unlock();
   }
   return value;
}
```

7. Implement the `transfer()` method. This method tries to send the element to a waiting consumer immediately, if possible. If there is no consumer waiting, the method stores the element in a special queue to be sent to the first consumer that tries to get an element and blocks the thread until the element is consumed:

```
@Override
public void transfer(E e) throws InterruptedException {
    lock.lock();
    if (counter.get()!=0) {
        try {
            put(e);
        } finally {
            lock.unlock();
        }
    } else {
        try {
            transfered.add(e);
        } finally {
            lock.unlock();
        }
        synchronized (e) {
        e.wait();
        }
    }
}
```

8. Implement the `tryTransfer()` method that receives three parameters: the element, the time to wait for a consumer if there is none, and the unit of time used to specify the wait. If there is a consumer waiting, it sends the element immediately. Otherwise, it converts the time specified into milliseconds and uses the `wait()` method to put the thread to sleep. When the consumer takes the element, if the thread is sleeping in the `wait()` method, you need to wake it up using the `notify()` method, as you'll see in a moment:

```
@Override
public boolean tryTransfer(E e, long timeout, TimeUnit unit)
                            throws InterruptedException {
    lock.lock();
    if (counter.get() != 0) {
        try {
            put(e);
        } finally {
            lock.unlock();
        }
        return true;
    } else {
```

```
        long newTimeout=0;
        try {
           transfered.add(e);
           newTimeout = TimeUnit.MILLISECONDS.convert(timeout, unit);
        } finally {
           lock.unlock();
        }
        e.wait(newTimeout);
        lock.lock();
        boolean value;
        try {
           if (transfered.contains(e)) {
              transfered.remove(e);
              value = false;
           } else {
              value = true;
           }
        } finally {
           lock.unlock();
        }
        return value;
     }
   }
```

9. Implement the `hasWaitingConsumer()` method. Use the value of the counter attribute to calculate the return value of this method. If the counter has a value that is bigger than zero, it returns `true`; else, it returns `false`:

```
@Override
public boolean hasWaitingConsumer() {
   return (counter.get()!=0);
}
```

10. Implement the `getWaitingConsumerCount()` method. Return the value of the `counter` attribute:

```
@Override
public int getWaitingConsumerCount() {
   return counter.get();
}
```

11. Implement the `take()` method. This method is called by the consumers when they want to consume an element. First, get the lock defined earlier and increment the number of waiting consumers:

```
@Override
public E take() throws InterruptedException {
```

```
lock.lock();
try {
    counter.incrementAndGet();
```

12. If there aren't any elements in the transferred queue, free the lock and try to get an element from the queue using the `take()` element and get the lock again. If there aren't any elements in the queue, this method will put the thread to sleep until there are elements to consume:

```
E value=transfered.poll();
if (value==null) {
    lock.unlock();
    value=super.take();
    lock.lock();
```

13. Otherwise, take the element from the transferred queue and wake up the thread that is waiting to consume that element, if there is one. Take into account that you are synchronizing an object coming to this class from the outside. You have to guarantee that the object wouldn't be used for locking in other parts of the application:

```
} else {
    synchronized (value) {
        value.notify();
    }
}
```

14. Finally, decrement the counter of waiting consumers and free the lock:

```
    counter.decrementAndGet();
} finally {
    lock.unlock();
}
return value;
}
```

15. Next, implement a class named `Event` that extends the `Comparable` interface parameterized by the `Event` class:

```
public class Event implements Comparable<Event> {
```

16. Declare a private `String` attribute named `thread` to store the name of the thread that creates the event:

```
private final String thread;
```

17. Declare a private `int` attribute named `priority` to store the priority of the event:

```
private final int priority;
```

18. Implement the constructor of the class to initialize its attributes:

```
public Event(String thread, int priority){
    this.thread=thread;
    this.priority=priority;
}
```

19. Implement a method to return the value of the `thread` attribute:

```
public String getThread() {
    return thread;
}
```

20. Implement a method to return the value of the `priority` attribute:

```
public int getPriority() {
    return priority;
}
```

21. Implement the `compareTo()` method. This method compares the actual event with the event received as a parameter. Return –1 if the actual event has a higher priority than the parameter, 1 if the actual event has a lower priority than the parameter, and 0 if both the events have the same priority. You will get the list ordered by priority in descending order. Events with a higher priority will be stored first in the queue:

```
public int compareTo(Event e) {
    return Integer.compare(e.priority, this.getPriority());
}
```

22. Implement a class named `Producer` that implements the `Runnable` interface:

```
public class Producer implements Runnable {
```

23. Declare a private `MyPriorityTransferQueue` attribute parameterized by the `Event` class named `buffer` to store the events generated by this producer:

```
private final MyPriorityTransferQueue<Event> buffer;
```

24. Implement the constructor of the class to initialize its attributes:

```
public Producer(MyPriorityTransferQueue<Event> buffer) {
   this.buffer=buffer;
}
```

25. Implement the `run()` method of the class. Create 100 `Event` objects using its order of creation as priority (the latest event will have the highest priority) and insert them into the queue using the `put()` method:

```
@Override
public void run() {
   for (int i=0; i<100; i++) {
      Event event=new Event(Thread.currentThread().getName(),i);
      buffer.put(event);
   }
}
```

26. Implement a class named `Consumer` that implements the `Runnable` interface:

```
public class Consumer implements Runnable {
```

27. Declare a private `MyPriorityTransferQueue` attribute parameterized by the `Event` class named `buffer` to get the events consumed by this class:

```
private final MyPriorityTransferQueue<Event> buffer;
```

28. Implement the constructor of the class to initialize its attribute:

```
public Consumer(MyPriorityTransferQueue<Event> buffer) {
   this.buffer=buffer;
}
```

29. Implement the `run()` method. It consumes 1,002 events (all the events generated in the example) using the `take()` method and writes the number of threads that generated the event and their priority in the console:

```
@Override
public void run() {
   for (int i=0; i<1002; i++) {
      try {
         Event value=buffer.take();
         System.out.printf("Consumer: %s: %d\n",value.getThread(),
                           value.getPriority());
      } catch (InterruptedException e) {
         e.printStackTrace();
```

```
        }
      }
    }
```

30. Implement the main class of the example by creating a class named `Main` with a `main()` method:

```
public class Main {

    public static void main(String[] args) throws Exception {
```

31. Create a `MyPriorityTransferQueue` object named `buffer`:

```
MyPriorityTransferQueue<Event> buffer=new
                    MyPriorityTransferQueue<Event>();
```

32. Create a `Producer` task and launch 10 threads to execute this task:

```
Producer producer=new Producer(buffer);
Thread producerThreads[]=new Thread[10];
for (int i=0; i<producerThreads.length; i++) {
    producerThreads[i]=new Thread(producer);
    producerThreads[i].start();
}
```

33. Create and launch a `Consumer` task:

```
Consumer consumer=new Consumer(buffer);
Thread consumerThread=new Thread(consumer);
consumerThread.start();
```

34. Write the actual consumer count in the console:

```
System.out.printf("Main: Buffer: Consumer count: %d\n",
                buffer.getWaitingConsumerCount());
```

35. Transfer an event to the consumer using the `transfer()` method:

```
Event myEvent=new Event("Core Event",0);
buffer.transfer(myEvent);
System.out.printf("Main: My Event has ben transfered.\n");
```

36. Wait for the finalization of the producers using the `join()` method:

```
for (int i=0; i<producerThreads.length; i++) {
    try {
        producerThreads[i].join();
```

```
    } catch (InterruptedException e) {
      e.printStackTrace();
    }
  }
```

37. Put the thread to sleep for 1 second:

```
TimeUnit.SECONDS.sleep(1);
```

38. Write the actual consumer count:

```
System.out.printf("Main: Buffer: Consumer count: %d\n",
               buffer.getWaitingConsumerCount());
```

39. Transfer another event using the `transfer()` method:

```
myEvent=new Event("Core Event 2",0);
buffer.transfer(myEvent);
```

40. Wait for the finalization of the consumer using the `join()` method:

```
consumerThread.join();
```

41. Write a message indicating the end of the program:

```
System.out.printf("Main: End of the program\n");
```

How it works...

In this recipe, you implemented the `MyPriorityTransferQueue` data structure. It's a data structure to be used in the producer/consumer problem, but its elements are ordered by priority, not by their order of arrival. As Java doesn't allow multiple inheritances, the first decision you took was in relation to the base class of the `MyPriorityTransferQueue` class. You extend the class to use the operations implemented in the `PriorityBlockingQueue`, not to implement them. You also implemented the `TransferQueue` interface to add the methods related to the producer/consumer. We made this choice because we think it is easier to implement the methods of the `TransferQueue` interface than the methods implemented in the `PriorityBlockingQueue` class. However, you can implement the class that extends from the `LinkedTransferQueue` class and implements the necessary methods to get your own version of the `PriorityBlockingQueue` class.

The `MyPriortyTransferQueue` class has the following three attributes:

- An `AtomicInteger` attribute named `counter`: This attribute stores the number of consumers that are waiting to take an element from the data structure. When a consumer calls the `take()` operation to take an element from the data structure, the counter is incremented. When the consumer finishes the execution of the `take()` operation, the counter is decremented again. This counter is used in the implementation of the `hasWaitingConsumer()` and `getWaitingConsumerCount()` methods.
- A `ReentrantLock` attribute named `lock`: This attribute is used to control access to implemented operations. Only one thread is allowed to work with the data structure, as per this attribute.
- Finally, it has a `LinkedBlockingQueue` list to store transferred elements.

You implemented some methods in `MyPriorityTransferQueue`. All the methods are declared in the `TransferQueue` interface, and the `take()` method is implemented in the `PriorityBlockingQueue` interface. Both of these were described earlier. Here is a description of the rest:

- `tryTransfer(E e)`: This method tries to send an element directly to a consumer. If there is a consumer waiting, it stores the element in the priority queue to be consumed immediately by the consumer and then returns the `true` value. If no one's waiting, it returns the `false` value.
- `transfer(E e)`: This method transfers an element directly to a consumer. If there is a consumer waiting, it stores the element in the priority queue to be consumed immediately by the consumer. Otherwise, the element is stored in the list of transferred elements, and the thread is blocked until the element is consumed. While the thread is put to sleep, you have to free the lock because, if you don't do this, you will block the queue.
- `tryTransfer(E e, long timeout, TimeUnit unit)`: This method is similar to the `transfer()` method, but here, the thread blocks the period of time determined by its parameters. While the thread is put to sleep, you have to free the lock because, if you don't, you will block the queue.
- `take()`: This method returns the next element to be consumed. If there are elements in the list of transferred elements, the element is taken from the list. Otherwise, it is taken from the priority queue.

Once you implemented the data structure, you implemented the `Event` class. It is the class of the elements you have stored in the data structure. The `Event` class has two attributes to store the ID of the producer and the priority of the event, and it implements the `Comparable` interface because it is a requirement of your data structure.

Then, you implemented the `Producer` and `Consumer` classes. In the example, you had 10 producers and a consumer and they shared the same buffer. Each producer generated 100 events with incremental priority, so the events with a higher priority were the last generated ones.

The main class of the example created a `MyPriorityTransferQueue` object, 10 producers, and a consumer, and used the `transfer()` method of the `MyPriorityTransferQueue` buffer to transfer two events to the buffer.

The following screenshot shows part of the output of an execution of the program:

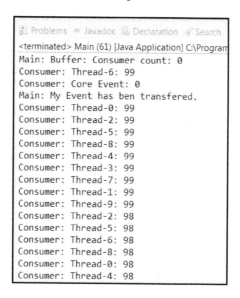

You can see how events with a higher priority are consumed first and that a consumer consumes the transferred event.

See also

- The *Using blocking thread-safe queue ordered by priority* and *Using blocking thread-safe deques* recipes in `Chapter 7`, *Concurrent Collections*

Implementing your own atomic object

Atomic variables were introduced in Java version 5; they provide atomic operations on single variables. When a thread does an operation with an atomic variable, the implementation of the class includes a mechanism to check that the operation is done atomically.

In this recipe, you will learn how to extend an atomic object and implement two operations that follow the mechanisms of the atomic objects to guarantee that all the operations are done in one step.

Getting ready

The example of this recipe has been implemented using the Eclipse IDE. If you use Eclipse or a different IDE, such as NetBeans, open it and create a new Java project.

How to do it...

Follow these steps to implement the example:

1. Create a class named `ParkingCounter` and specify that it extends the `AtomicInteger` class:

   ```
   public class ParkingCounter extends AtomicInteger {
   ```

2. Declare a private `int` attribute named `maxNumber` to store the maximum number of cars admitted into the parking lot:

   ```
   private final int maxNumber;
   ```

3. Implement the constructor of the class to initialize its attributes:

   ```
   public ParkingCounter(int maxNumber){
     set(0);
   ```

```
            this.maxNumber=maxNumber;
        }
```

4. Implement the `carIn()` method. This method increments the counter of cars if it has a value smaller than the established maximum value. Construct an infinite loop and get the value of the internal counter using the `get()` method:

```
public boolean carIn() {
    for (;;) {
        int value=get();
```

5. If the value is equal to the `maxNumber` attribute, the counter can't be incremented (the parking lot is full and the car can't enter). In this case, the method returns the `false` value:

```
if (value==maxNumber) {
    System.out.printf("ParkingCounter: The parking lot is full.\n");
    return false;
```

6. Otherwise, increment the value and use the `compareAndSet()` method to change the old value with the new one. This method returns the `false` value; the counter was not incremented, so you have to begin the loop again. If it returns `true`, it means the change was made and then you return the `true` value:

```
    } else {
        int newValue=value+1;
        boolean changed=compareAndSet(value,newValue);
        if (changed) {
            System.out.printf("ParkingCounter: A car has entered.\n");
            return true;
        }
    }
}
}
```

7. Implement the `carOut()` method. This method decrements the counter of cars if it has a value bigger than 0. Construct an infinite loop and get the value of the internal counter using the `get()` method:

```
public boolean carOut() {
    for (;;) {
        int value=get();
        if (value==0) {
            System.out.printf("ParkingCounter: The parking lot is
                                empty.\n");
            return false;
```

```
    } else {
      int newValue=value-1;
      boolean changed=compareAndSet(value,newValue);
      if (changed) {
        System.out.printf("ParkingCounter: A car has gone out.\n");
        return true;
      }
    }
  }
}
```

8. Create a class named `Sensor1` that implements the `Runnable` interface:

```
public class Sensor1 implements Runnable {
```

9. Declare a private `ParkingCounter` attribute named `counter`:

```
private final ParkingCounter counter;
```

10. Implement the constructor of the class to initialize its attribute:

```
public Sensor1(ParkingCounter counter) {
  this.counter=counter;
}
```

11. Implement the `run()` method. Call the `carIn()` and `carOut()` operations several times:

```
@Override
public void run() {
  counter.carIn();
  counter.carIn(),
  counter.carIn();
  counter.carIn();
  counter.carOut();
  counter.carOut();
  counter.carOut();
  counter.carIn();
  counter.carIn();
  counter.carIn();
}
```

12. Create a class named `Sensor2` that implements the `Runnable` interface:

```
public class Sensor2 implements Runnable {
```

13. Declare a private `ParkingCounter` attribute named `counter`:

```
private ParkingCounter counter;
```

14. Implement the constructor of the class to initialize its attribute:

```
public Sensor2(ParkingCounter counter) {
    this.counter=counter;
}
```

15. Implement the `run()` method. Call the `carIn()` and `carOut()` operations several times:

```
@Override
public void run() {
    counter.carIn();
    counter.carOut();
    counter.carOut();
    counter.carIn();
    counter.carIn();
    counter.carIn();
    counter.carIn();
    counter.carIn();
    counter.carIn();
}
```

16. Implement the main class of the example by creating a class named `Main` with a `main()` method:

```
public class Main {

    public static void main(String[] args) throws Exception {
```

17. Create a `ParkingCounter` object named `counter`:

```
ParkingCounter counter=new ParkingCounter(5);
```

18. Create and launch a `Sensor1` and `Sensor2` task:

```
Sensor1 sensor1=new Sensor1(counter);
Sensor2 sensor2=new Sensor2(counter);

Thread thread1=new Thread(sensor1);
Thread thread2=new Thread(sensor2);

thread1.start();
thread2.start();
```

19. Wait for the finalization of both the tasks:

```
thread1.join();
thread2.join();
```

20. Write the actual value of the counter in the console:

```
System.out.printf("Main: Number of cars: %d\n",counter.get());
```

21. Write a message indicating the end of the program in the console:

```
System.out.printf("Main: End of the program.\n");
```

How it works...

The `ParkingCounter` class extends the `AtomicInteger` class with two atomic operations: `carIn()` and `carOut()`. The example simulates a system that controls the number of cars inside a parking lot. The parking lot can admit a number of cars, represented by the `maxNumber` attribute.

The `carIn()` operation compares the actual number of cars in the parking lot with the maximum value. If they are equal, the car can't enter the parking lot and the method returns the `false` value. Otherwise, it uses the following structure of the atomic operations:

- Get the value of the atomic object in a local variable.
- Store the new value in a different variable.
- Use the `compareAndSet()` method to try and replace the old value with the new one. If this method returns `true`, it means the old value you sent as a parameter was the value of the variable; therefore, it changes the values. The operation was made in an atomic way as the `carIn()` method returns `true`. If the `compareAndSet()` method returns `false`, it means the old value you sent as a parameter is not the value of the variable (the other thread modified it); therefore, the operation can't be done in an atomic way. The operation begins again until it can be done in an atomic way.

The `carOut()` method is analogous to the `carIn()` method. You also implemented two `Runnable` objects that use the `carIn()` and `carOut()` methods to simulate the activity of parking. When you execute the program, you can see that the parking lot never exceeds the maximum value of cars.

See also

- The *Using atomic variables* recipe in `Chapter 7`, *Concurrent Collections*

Implementing your own stream generator

A stream is a sequence of data that allows you to apply a sequence of operations (usually represented with lambda expressions) to it in a sequential or parallel way in order to filter, transform, sort, reduce, or construct a new data structure. It was introduced in Java 8 and was one of the most important features introduced in that version.

Streams are based on the `Stream` interface and some related classes and interfaces included in the `java.util.stream` package. They have also provoked the introduction of new methods in a lot of classes to generate streams from different data structures. You can create a `Stream` interface from every data structure that implements the `Collection` interface: from `File`, `Directory`, `Array`, and a lot of other sources.

Java also included different mechanisms to create streams from your own sources. The most important ones are:

- The `Supplier` interface: This interface defines the `get()` method. It will be called by `Stream` when it needs to process another object. You can create `Stream` from a `Supplier` interface using the `generate()` static method of the `Stream` class. Take into account that this source is potentially infinite, so you must use a method such as `limit()` or similar to limit the number of elements in `Stream`.
- The `Stream.Builder` interface: This interface provides the `accept()` and `add()` elements to add elements to `Stream` and the `build()` method, which returns the `Stream` interface created with the elements added before.
- The `Spliterator` interface: This interface defines the necessary methods to traverse and split the elements of a source. You can use the `stream()` method of the `StreamSupport` class to generate the `Stream` interface to process the elements of `Spliterator`.

In this chapter, you will learn how to implement your own `Spliterator` interface and how to create a `Stream` interface to process its data. We will work with a matrix of elements. A normal `Stream` interface should process one element at a time, but we will use the `Spliterator` class to implement one row at a time.

Getting ready

The example of this recipe has been implemented using the Eclipse IDE. If you use Eclipse or another IDE, such as NetBeans, open it and create a new Java project.

How to do it...

Follow these steps to implement the example:

1. Create a class named `Item` to store the information of each element of the matrix. It will have three private attributes: a `String` attribute named `name` and two integer attributes named `row` and `column`. Create the methods to get and set the values of these attributes. The code of this class is very simple, so it won't be included here.

2. Create a class named `MySpliterator`. Specify that it implements the `Spliterator` interface parameterized by the `Item` class. This class has four attributes: a matrix of `Item` objects named `items` and three integer attributes named `start`, `end`, and `current` to store the first and last elements that will be processed by this `Spliterator` interface and the current element that is being processed. Implement the constructor of the class to initialize all these attributes:

   ```java
   public class MySpliterator implements Spliterator<Item> {

       private Item[][] items;
       private int start, end, current;

       public MySpliterator(Item[][] items, int start, int end) {
           this.items=items;
           this.start=start;
           this.end=end;
           this.current=start;
       }
   ```

3. Implement `characteristics()`. This method will return an `int` value that describes the behavior of `Spliterator`. The meaning of this value will be explained later in the *How it Works...* section:

   ```java
   @Override
   public int characteristics() {
     return ORDERED | SIZED | SUBSIZED;
   }
   ```

4. Implement `estimatedSize()`. This method will return the number of elements to be processed by this `Spliterator`. We will calculate it as the difference between the end and current attributes:

```
@Override
public long estimateSize() {
   return end - current;
}
```

5. Now implement `tryAdvance()`. This method will be called to try and process an element of the `Spliterator`. The input parameter of the `tryAdvance()` method is and object that implements the `Consumer` interface. It will be called by the Stream API, so we only have to worry about its implementation. In our case, as mentioned in the introduction to this chapter, we have a matrix of `Item` objects and we're going to process a row each time. The `Consumer` function received will process an `Item` object. Therefore, if the `Spliterator` interface still has elements to process, we will process all the items of the current row using the `accept()` method of the `Consumer` function:

```
@Override
public boolean tryAdvance(Consumer<? super Item> consumer) {
   System.out.printf("MySpliterator.tryAdvance.start: %d, %d, %d\n",
                  start,end,current);
     if (current < end) {
        for (int i=0; i<items[current].length; i++) {
          consumer.accept(items[current][i]);
        }
        current++;
        System.out.printf("MySpliterator.tryAdvance.end:true\n");
        return true;
     }
     System.out.printf("MySpliterator.tryAdvance.end:false\n");
     return false;
}
```

6. Now implement `forEachRemaining()`. This method will receive an implementation of the `Consumer` interface and will apply this function to the remaining elements of `Spliterator`. In our case, we will call the `tryAdvance()` method for all the remaining elements:

```
@Override
public void forEachRemaining(Consumer<? super Item> consumer) {
   System.out.printf("MySpliterator.forEachRemaining.start\n");
   boolean ret;
   do {
```

```
        ret=tryAdvance(consumer);
    } while (ret);
    System.out.printf("MySpliterator.forEachRemaining.end\n");
}
```

7. Finally, implement `trySplit()`. This method will be called by parallel streams to split `Spliterator` into two subsets. It will return a new `Spliterator` object with the elements that will be processed by another thread. The current thread will process the rest of the elements. If the `spliterator` object can't be split, you have to return a null value. In our case, we will calculate the element in the middle of the elements we have to process. The first half will be processed by the current thread, and the second half will be processed by another thread:

```
@Override
public Spliterator<Item> trySplit() {
    System.out.printf("MySpliterator.trySplit.start\n");

    if (end-start<=2) {
        System.out.printf("MySpliterator.trySplit.end\n");
        return null;
    }
    int mid=start+((end-start)/2);
    int newStart=mid;
    int newEnd=end;
    end=mid;
    System.out.printf("MySpliterator.trySplit.end: %d, %d, %d,
                       %d, %d, %d\n",start, mid, end, newStart,
                       newEnd, current);

    return new MySpliterator(items, newStart, newEnd);
}
```

8. Now implement the `Main` class of the project with the `main()` method. First, declare and initialize a matrix with 10 rows and 10 columns of `Item` objects:

```
public class Main {

    public static void main(String[] args) {
        Item[][] items;
        items= new Item[10][10];

        for (int i=0; i<10; i++) {
            for (int j=0; j<10; j++) {
                items[i][j]=new Item();
                items[i][j].setRow(i);
                items[i][j].setColumn(j);
```

```
                items[i][j].setName("Item "+i+" "+j);
            }
        }
    }
```

9. Then, create a `MySpliterator` object to process all the elements of the matrix:

```
MySpliterator mySpliterator=new MySpliterator(items, 0,
                                        items.length);
```

10. Finally, use the `stream()` method of the `StreamSupport` class to create a stream from `Spliterator`. Pass the `true` value as the second parameter to indicate that our stream will be in parallel. Then, use the `forEach()` method of the `Stream` class to write information about each element:

```
StreamSupport.stream(mySpliterator, true).forEach( item -> {
    System.out.printf("%s: %s\n",Thread.currentThread()
                        .getName(),item.getName());
    });
}
```

How it works...

The main element of this example is `Spliterator`. This interface defines methods that can be used to process and partition a source of elements to be used, for example, the source of a `Stream` object. You will rarely need to use a `Spliterator` object directly. Only if you want a different behavior--that is, if you want to implement your own data structure and create `Stream` from it--use a `Spliterator` object.

`Spliterator` has a set of characteristics that defines its behavior. They are as follows:

- CONCURRENT: The data source can be safely modified concurrently
- DISTINCT: All the elements of the data source are distinct
- IMMUTABLE: Elements can be added, deleted, or replaced in the data source
- NONNULL: There's no null element in the data source
- ORDERED: There's an encounter ordered in the elements of the data source
- SIZED: The value returned by the `estimateSize()` method is the exact size of the `Spliterator`
- SORTED: The elements of `Spliterator` are sorted
- SUBSIZED: After you call the `trySplit()` method, you can obtain the exact size of both the parts of `Spliterator`

In our case, we defined `Spliterator` with the `DISTINCT`, `IMMUTABLE`, `NONNULL`, `ORDERED`, `SIZED`, and `SUBSIZED` characteristics.

Then, we implemented all the methods defined by the `Spliterator` interface that don't have a default implementation:

- `characteristics()`: This method returns the characteristics of the `Spliterator` object. Specifically, it returns an integer value you calculate using the bitwise `or` operator (`|`) between the individual characteristics of your `Spliterator` object. Take into account that the value returned should be consistent with the real characteristics of your `Spliterator` object.
- `estimatedSize()`: This method returns the number of elements that would be processed by the `forEachRemaining()` method if it were called at the current moment. In our case, we returned the exact value as we know it, but the definition of the method talks about the estimated size.
- `tryAdvance()`: This method applies the function specified as a parameter to the next element to be processed, if there's one, and returns true. If there's no element to process, it will return false. In our case, this method received a `Consumer` that processed an Item object, but we processed a row of Item objects at a time. So we traversed all the items of the row and called the `accept()` method of `Consumer`.
- `trySplit()`: This method is used to divide the current `Spliterator` into two different parts so each one can be processed by different threads. In an ideal case, you should divide the data source into two halves with the same number of elements. But, in our case, we calculated the element in the middle between the start and end index and generated two blocks of elements. The start to the mid element part was processed by the current `Spliterator`, and the mid to the end element part was processed by the new `Spliterator` object. If you can't split the data source, this method returns a null value. In our case, the `Spliterator` had only two elements, so it won't be split.

The other methods of the `Spliterator` interface have a default implementation, but we overrode the `forEachRemaining()` method. This method applies the function received as a parameter (an implementation of the `Consumer` interface) to the elements of the `Spliterator` that haven't been processed yet. We implemented our own version to write a message in the console. We used the `tryAdvance()` method to process each individual item.

The following screenshot shows part of the output of this example:

```
Problems  Javadoc  Declaration  Search  Console
<terminated> Main (54) [Java Application] C:\Program Files\Java\jdk-
MySpliterator.trySplit.start
MySpliterator.trySplit.end: 0, 5, 5, 5, 10, 0
MySpliterator.trySplit.start
MySpliterator.trySplit.end: 0, 2, 2, 2, 5, 0
MySpliterator.trySplit.start
MySpliterator.trySplit.end: 5, 7, 7, 7, 10, 5
MySpliterator.trySplit.start
MySpliterator.trySplit.end
MySpliterator.trySplit.start
MySpliterator.trySplit.end: 2, 3, 3, 3, 5, 2
MySpliterator.trySplit.start
MySpliterator.trySplit.start
MySpliterator.trySplit.end
MySpliterator.forEachRemaining.start
MySpliterator.forEachRemaining.start
MySpliterator.tryAdvance.start: 5, 7, 5
ForkJoinPool.commonPool-worker-1: Item 5 0
ForkJoinPool.commonPool-worker-1: Item 5 1
```

First, the `trySplit()` method is called to divide the data source, then the
`forEachRemaining()` method is called to process all the elements of each `Spliterator`
generated by the `trySplit()` method.

There's more...

You can obtain an implementation of the `Spliterator` interface from different data
sources. The `BaseStream` class provides the `spliterator()` method that returns a
`Spliterator` from the elements of the `Stream`. Other data structures, such as
`ConcurrentLinkedDeque`, `ConcurrentLinkedQueue`, or `Collection`, also provide the
`spliterator()` method to get an implementation of that interface to process the elements
of those data structures.

See also

- The *Creating streams from different sources* recipe in `Chapter 6`, *Parallel and Reactive
  Streams*

Implementing your own asynchronous stream

Reactive streams (http://www.reactive-streams.org/) defines a mechanism to provide asynchronous stream processing with non-blocking back pressure.

Reactive streams are based on three elements:

- It is a publisher of information
- It has one or more subscribers of this information
- It provides subscription between the publisher and a consumer

Java 9 has included three interfaces--`Flow.Publisher`, `Flow.Subscriber`, and `Flow.Subscription`--and a utility class, `SubmissionPublisher`, to allow us to implement reactive stream applications.

In this recipe, you will learn how to implement your own reactive application using only three interfaces. Take into account that we will implement the expected behavior between the three elements. The publisher will only send elements to those subscribers who have requested them, and it will do this in a concurrent way. But you can modify this behavior easily by modifying the implementation of the methods.

Getting ready

The example of this recipe has been implemented using the Eclipse IDE. If you use Eclipse or another IDE, such as NetBeans, open it and create a new Java project.

How to do it...

Follow these steps to implement the example:

1. Implement a class named `News`. This class implements the elements sent from the publisher to the subscriber. It will have two private `String` attributes, named `title` and `content`, and a `Date` attribute named `date`. It will also have the methods to get and set the values of these attributes. The source code of this class is very simple, so it won't be included here.

2. Create a class named `Consumer` and specify that it implements the `Subscriber` interface parameterized by the `News` class. It will have two private attributes: a `Subscription` object named subscription and a `String` attribute called name. Implement the constructor of the class to initialize the name attribute:

```
public class Consumer implements Subscriber<News> {

    private Subscription subscription;
    private String name;

    public Consumer(String name) {
        this.name=name;
    }
```

3. Implement the `onComplete()` method. This method should be called by the publisher when it doesn't send any additional elements. In our case, we only write a message in the console:

```
@Override
public void onComplete() {
    System.out.printf("%s - %s: Consumer - Completed\n", name,
                    Thread.currentThread().getName());
}
```

4. Implement the `onError()` method. This method should be called by the publisher when an error has occurred. In our case, we only write a message in the console:

```
@Override
public void onError(Throwable exception) {
    System.out.printf("%s - %s: Consumer - Error: %s\n", name,
                    Thread.currentThread().getName(),
                    exception.getMessage());
}
```

5. Then, implement `onNext()`. This method receives a `News` object as a parameter, and it should be called by the publisher when he or she sends an item to the subscriber. In our case, we write the value of the attributes of the `News` object in the console, and we use the `request()` method of the `Subscription` object to request an additional item:

```
@Override
public void onNext(News item) {
    System.out.printf("%s - %s: Consumer - News\n", name,
                    Thread.currentThread().getName());
```

```
System.out.printf("%s - %s: Title: %s\n", name,
                Thread.currentThread().getName(),
                item.getTitle());
System.out.printf("%s - %s: Content: %s\n", name,
                Thread.currentThread().getName(),
                item.getContent());
System.out.printf("%s - %s: Date: %s\n", name,
                Thread.currentThread().getName(),
                item.getDate());
subscription.request(1);
}
```

6. Finally, implement `onSubscription()`. This method will be called by the publisher, and it will be the first method of `Subscriber` invoked by it. It receives the `Subscription` between the publisher and the subscriber. In our case, we store the `Subscription` object and request the first item to be processed by the subscriber using the `request()` method:

```
@Override
public void onSubscribe(Subscription subscription) {
    this.subscription = subscription;
    subscription.request(1);
    System.out.printf("%s: Consumer - Subscription\n",
                    Thread.currentThread().getName());
}
```

7. Implement a class named `MySubscription` and specify that it implements the `Subscription` interface. It will have a private `Boolean` attribute named canceled and a private integer attribute named requested:

```
public class MySubscription implements Subscription {

    private boolean canceled=false;
    private long requested=0;
```

8. Implement the `cancel()` method provided by the `Subscription` interface to cancel the communication between the publisher and the subscriber. In our case, we set to `true` the canceled attribute:

```
@Override
public void cancel() {
    canceled=true;
}
```

9. Implement the `request()` method provided by the `Subscription` interface. This method is used by the subscriber to request elements from the publisher. It receives as parameter the number of elements requested by the subscriber. In our case, we increment the value of the requested attribute:

```
@Override
public void request(long value) {
   requested+=value;
}
```

10. Implement the `isCanceled()` method to obtain the value of the canceled attribute, the `getRequested()` method to obtain the value of the requested attribute and the `decreaseRequested()` to decrease the value of the requested attribute:

```
public boolean isCanceled() {
   return canceled;
}

public long getRequested() {
   return requested;
}

public void decreaseRequested() {
   requested--;
}
```

11. Implement a class named `ConsumerData`. This class will be used by the publisher to store the information of every subscriber. It will have a private `Consumer` attribute named consumer and a private `MySubscription` attribute named subscription. It will also have the methods to `get()` and `set()` the value of those attributes. The source code of this class is very simple, so it won't be included here.

12. Implement a class named `PublisherTask` and specify that it implements the `Runnable` interface. It will have a private `ConsumerData` attribute named consumerData and a private `News` attribute named news. Implement a constructor to initialize both the attributes:

```
public class PublisherTask implements Runnable {

private ConsumerData consumerData;
private News news;

public PublisherTask(ConsumerData consumerData, News news) {
```

```
    this.consumerData = consumerData;
    this.news = news;
}
```

13. Implement the `run()` method. It will get the `MySubscription` object of the
    `ConsumerData` attribute. If the subscription is not canceled and it has requested
    elements (the value of the attribute is bigger than 0), we send the `News` object to
    the subscriber using its `onNext()` method and then decrement the value of the
    requested attribute:

```
@Override
public void run() {
    MySubscription subscription = consumerData.getSubscription();
    if (!(subscription.isCanceled() && (subscription.getRequested()
                                                          > 0))) {

        consumerData.getConsumer().onNext(news);
        subscription.decreaseRequested();
    }
}
```

14. Then, implement a class named `MyPublisher` and specify that it implements the
    `Publisher` interface parameterized by the `News` class. It will store a private
    `ConcurrentLinkedDeque` of `ConsumerData` objects and a
    `ThreadPoolExecutor` object named `executor`. Implement the constructor of
    the class to initialize both the attributes:

```
public class MyPublisher implements Publisher<News> {

    private ConcurrentLinkedDeque<ConsumerData> consumers;
    private ThreadPoolExecutor executor;

    public MyPublisher() {
        consumers=new ConcurrentLinkedDeque<>();
        executor = (ThreadPoolExecutor)Executors.newFixedThreadPool
                    (Runtime.getRuntime().availableProcessors());
    }
```

15. Now, implement `subscribe()`. This method will receive a `Subscriber` object
    that wants to receive the items of this publisher in the form of a parameter. We
    create `MySubscription` and `ConsumerData` objects, store `ConsumerData` in
    `ConcurrentLinkedDeque`, and call the `onSubscribe()` method of the
    subscriber to send the subscription object to the `Subscriber` object:

```
@Override
public void subscribe(Subscriber<? super News> subscriber) {

    ConsumerData consumerData=new ConsumerData();
    consumerData.setConsumer((Consumer)subscriber);

    MySubscription subscription=new MySubscription();
    consumerData.setSubscription(subscription);

    subscriber.onSubscribe(subscription);

    consumers.add(consumerData);
}
```

16. Now implement the `publish()` method. This method receives a `News` parameter and sends it to the subscribers that meet the conditions explained before. To do this, we create a `PublisherTask` method per `Subscriber` and send these tasks to the executor:

```
public void publish(News news) {
  consumers.forEach( consumerData -> {
    try {
      executor.execute(new PublisherTask(consumerData, news));
    } catch (Exception e) {
      consumerData.getConsumer().onError(e);
    }
  });
}
```

17. Finally, implement the `Main` class of the example with its `main()` method. We create a publisher and two subscribers and subscribe them to the publisher:

```
public class Main {

  public static void main(String[] args) {

    MyPublisher publisher=new MyPublisher();

    Subscriber<News> consumer1, consumer2;
    consumer1=new Consumer("Consumer 1");
    consumer2=new Consumer("Consumer 2");

    publisher.subscribe(consumer1);
    publisher.subscribe(consumer2);
```

18. Then, create a `News` object, send it to the publisher, sleep the main thread for a second, create another `News` object, and send it to the publisher again:

```
System.out.printf("Main: Start\n");

News news=new News();
news.setTitle("My first news");
news.setContent("This is the content");
news.setDate(new Date());

publisher.publish(news);

try {
   TimeUnit.SECONDS.sleep(1);
} catch (InterruptedException e) {
   e.printStackTrace();
}

news=new News();
news.setTitle("My second news");
news.setContent("This is the content of the second news");
news.setDate(new Date());
publisher.publish(news);

System.out.printf("Main: End\n");

}
```

How it works...

In this example, we implemented a reactive streams communication between a publisher and a subscriber using the interfaces provided by the Java 9 API and just followed the expected behavior defined in the reactive streams' specification.

We had a publisher implemented by the `MyPublisher` class and subscribers implemented by the `Consumer` class. There are subscriptions between the publishers, and each subscriber is implemented by the `MySubscription` object.

The cycle of the communication starts when a subscriber calls the `subscribe()` method of a publisher. The publisher has to create the subscription between them and send that subscription to the subscriber using the `onSubscribe()` method. The subscriber must use the `request()` method of the subscription to indicate that it's ready to process more elements from the publisher. When the publisher publishes an item, it will send it to all its subscribers who have requested elements from the publisher using the subscription between them.

We added all the necessary elements to guarantee this behavior in a concurrent way.

The following screenshot shows the output of an execution of this example:

```
Problems  @ Javadoc  Declaration  Search  Console  Error Log
Main (55) [Java Application] C:\Program Files\Java\jdk-9\bin\javaw.exe (7 nov. 2016 1:28:40)
Main: Start
Consumer 1 - pool-1-thread-1: Consumer - News
Consumer 2 - pool-1-thread-2: Consumer - News
Consumer 2 - pool-1-thread-2: Title: My first news
Consumer 2 - pool-1-thread-2: Content: This is the content
Consumer 2 - pool-1-thread-2: Date: Mon Nov 07 01:28:40 GMT+01:00 2016
Consumer 1 - pool-1-thread-1: Title: My first news
Consumer 1 - pool-1-thread-1: Content: This is the content
Consumer 1 - pool-1-thread-1: Date: Mon Nov 07 01:28:40 GMT+01:00 2016
Main: End
Consumer 1 - pool-1-thread-3: Consumer - News
Consumer 1 - pool-1-thread-3: Title: My second news
Consumer 1 - pool-1-thread-3: Content: This is the content of the second news
Consumer 1 - pool-1-thread-3: Date: Mon Nov 07 01:28:41 GMT+01:00 2016
Consumer 2 - pool-1-thread-4: Consumer - News
Consumer 2 - pool-1-thread-4: Title: My second news
Consumer 2 - pool-1-thread-4: Content: This is the content of the second news
Consumer 2 - pool-1-thread-4: Date: Mon Nov 07 01:28:41 GMT+01:00 2016
```

There's more...

The easiest way to create an application that uses reactive streams is to use the `SubmissionPublisher` class. This class implements the `Publisher` interface and provides the necessary methods to use it as the publisher part of the application.

See also

- The *Reactive programming with reactive streams* recipe in Chapter 6, *Parallel and Reactive Streams*

Testing Concurrent Applications

9

In this chapter, we will cover the following topics:

- Monitoring a Lock interface
- Monitoring a Phaser class
- Monitoring an Executor framework
- Monitoring a fork/join pool
- Monitoring a stream
- Writing effective log messages
- Analyzing concurrent code with FindBugs
- Configuring Eclipse for debugging concurrency code
- Configuring NetBeans for debugging concurrency code
- Testing concurrency code with MultithreadedTC
- Monitoring with JConsole

Introduction

Testing an application is a critical task. Before you make an application ready for end users, you have to demonstrate its correctness. You use a test process to prove that correctness is achieved and errors are fixed. Testing is a common task in any software development and quality assurance process. You can find a lot of literature about testing processes and the different approaches you can apply to your developments. There are a lot of libraries as well, such as JUnit, and applications, such as Apache JMeter, that you can use to test your Java applications in an automated way. Testing is even more critical in concurrent application development.

The fact that concurrent applications have two or more threads that share data structures and interact with each other adds more difficulty to the testing phase. The biggest problem you will face when you test concurrent applications is that the execution of threads is non-deterministic. You can't guarantee the order of the execution of threads, so it's difficult to reproduce errors.

Monitoring a Lock interface

A `Lock` interface is one of the basic mechanisms provided by the Java concurrency API to synchronize a block of code. It allows you to define a **critical section**. A critical section is a block of code that accesses a shared resource and can't be executed by more than one thread at the same time. This mechanism is implemented by the `Lock` interface and the `ReentrantLock` class.

In this recipe, you will learn what information you can obtain about a `Lock` object and how to obtain that information.

Getting ready

The example of this recipe has been implemented using the Eclipse IDE. If you use Eclipse or a different IDE, such as NetBeans, open it and create a new Java project.

How to do it...

Follow these steps to implement the example:

1. Create a class named `MyLock` that extends the `ReentrantLock` class:

    ```
    public class MyLock extends ReentrantLock {
    ```

2. Implement `getOwnerName()`. This method returns the name of the thread that has control of a lock (if any), using the protected method of the `Lock` class called `getOwner()`:

```
public String getOwnerName() {
  if (this.getOwner()==null) {
    return "None";
  }
  return this.getOwner().getName();
}
```

3. Implement `getThreads()`. This method returns a list of threads queued in a lock, using the protected method of the `Lock` class called `getQueuedThreads()`:

```
public Collection<Thread> getThreads() {
  return this.getQueuedThreads();
}
```

4. Create a class named `Task` that implements the `Runnable` interface:

```
public class Task implements Runnable {
```

5. Declare a private `Lock` attribute named `lock`:

```
private final Lock lock;
```

6. Implement a constructor of the class to initialize its attribute:

```
public Task (Lock lock) {
  this.lock=lock;
}
```

7. Implement the `run()` method. Create a loop with five steps:

```
@Override
public void run() {
  for (int i=0; i<5; i++) {
```

8. Acquire the lock using the `lock()` method and print a message:

```
lock.lock();
System.out.printf("%s: Get the Lock.\n",
                  Thread.currentThread().getName());
```

9. Put the thread to sleep for 500 milliseconds. Free the lock using the `unlock()` method and print a message:

```
try {
    TimeUnit.MILLISECONDS.sleep(500);
    System.out.printf("%s: Free the Lock.\n",
                    Thread.currentThread().getName());
} catch (InterruptedException e) {
    e.printStackTrace();
} finally {
    lock.unlock();
}
        }
    }
}
```

10. Create the main class of the example by creating a class named `Main` with a `main()` method:

```
public class Main {
    public static void main(String[] args) throws Exception {
```

11. Create a `MyLock` object named `lock`:

```
MyLock lock=new MyLock();
```

12. Create an array of five `Thread` objects:

```
Thread threads[]=new Thread[5];
```

13. Create and start five threads to execute five `Task` objects:

```
for (int i=0; i<5; i++) {
    Task task=new Task(lock);
    threads[i]=new Thread(task);
    threads[i].start();
}
```

14. Create a loop with 15 steps:

```
for (int i=0; i<15; i++) {
```

15. Write the name of the owner of the lock in the console:

```
System.out.printf("Main: Logging the Lock\n");
System.out.printf("************************\n");
System.out.printf("Lock: Owner : %s\n",lock.getOwnerName());
```

16. Display the number and name of the threads queued for the lock:

```
System.out.printf("Lock: Queued Threads: %s\n",
                  lock.hasQueuedThreads());
if (lock.hasQueuedThreads()){
  System.out.printf("Lock: Queue Length: %d\n",
                    lock.getQueueLength());
  System.out.printf("Lock: Queued Threads: ");
  Collection<Thread> lockedThreads=lock.getThreads();
  for (Thread lockedThread : lockedThreads) {
    System.out.printf("%s ",lockedThread.getName());
  }
  System.out.printf("\n");
}
```

17. Display information about the fairness and status of the Lock object:

```
System.out.printf("Lock: Fairness: %s\n",lock.isFair());
System.out.printf("Lock: Locked: %s\n",lock.isLocked());
System.out.printf("***********************\n");
```

18. Put the thread to sleep for 1 second and close the loop and the class:

```
      TimeUnit.SECONDS.sleep(1);
    }
  }
}
```

How it works...

In this recipe, you implemented the MyLock class that extends the ReentrantLock class to return information that wouldn't have been available otherwise-it's protected data of the ReentrantLock class. The methods implemented by the MyLock class are as follows:

- getOwnerName(): Only one thread can execute a critical section protected by a Lock object. The lock stores the thread that is executing the critical section. This thread is returned by the protected getOwner() method of the ReentrantLock class.

- `getThreads()`: When a thread is executing a critical section, other threads that try to enter it are put to sleep before they continue executing that critical section. The protected method `getQueuedThreads()` of the `ReentrantLock` class returns the list of threads that are waiting to execute the critical section.

We also used other methods that are implemented in the `ReentrantLock` class:

- `hasQueuedThreads()`: This method returns a `Boolean` value indicating whether there are threads waiting to acquire the calling `ReentrantLock`
- `getQueueLength()`: This method returns the number of threads that are waiting to acquire the calling `ReentrantLock`
- `isLocked()`: This method returns a `Boolean` value indicating whether the calling `ReentrantLock` is owned by a thread
- `isFair()`: This method returns a `Boolean` value indicating whether the calling `ReentrantLock` has fair mode activated

There's more...

There are other methods in the `ReentrantLock` class that can be used to obtain information about a `Lock` object:

- `getHoldCount()`: This returns the number of times the current thread has acquired the lock
- `isHeldByCurrentThread()`: This returns a `Boolean` value indicating whether the lock is owned by the current thread

See also

- The *Synchronizing a block of code with a lock* recipe in Chapter 2, *Basic Thread Synchronization*
- The *Implementing a custom Lock class* recipe in Chapter 8, *Customizing Concurrency Classes*

Monitoring a Phaser class

One of the most complex and powerful functionalities offered by the Java Concurrency API is the ability to execute concurrent-phased tasks using the `Phaser` class. This mechanism is useful when we have some concurrent tasks divided into steps. The `Phaser` class provides the mechanism to synchronize threads at the end of each step so no thread starts its second step until all the threads have finished the first one.

In this recipe, you will learn what information you can obtain about the status of a `Phaser` class and how to obtain that information.

Getting ready

The example of this recipe has been implemented using the Eclipse IDE. If you use Eclipse or a different IDE, such as NetBeans, open it and create a new Java project.

How to do it...

Follow these steps to implement the example:

1. Create a class named `Task` that implements the `Runnable` interface:

   ```
   public class Task implements Runnable {
   ```

2. Declare a private `int` attribute named `time`:

   ```
   private final int time;
   ```

3. Declare a private `Phaser` attribute named `phaser`:

   ```
   private final Phaser phaser;
   ```

4. Implement the constructor of the class to initialize its attributes:

   ```
   public Task(int time, Phaser phaser) {
     this.time=time;
     this.phaser=phaser;
   }
   ```

5. Implement the `run()` method. First, instruct the `phaser` attribute that the task starts its execution with the `arrive()` method:

```
@Override
public void run() {

    phaser.arrive();
```

6. Write a message in the console indicating the start of phase one. Put the thread to sleep for the number of seconds specified by the `time` attribute. Write a message in the console indicating the end of phase one. And, synchronize with the rest of the tasks using the `arriveAndAwaitAdvance()` method of the `phaser` attribute:

```
System.out.printf("%s: Entering phase 1.\n",
                  Thread.currentThread().getName());
try {
    TimeUnit.SECONDS.sleep(time);
} catch (InterruptedException e) {
    e.printStackTrace();
}
System.out.printf("%s: Finishing phase 1.\n",
                  Thread.currentThread().getName());
phaser.arriveAndAwaitAdvance();
```

7. Repeat this behavior in both second and third phases. At the end of the third phase, use the `arriveAndDeregister()` method instead of `arriveAndAwaitAdvance()`:

```
System.out.printf("%s: Entering phase 2.\n",
                  Thread.currentThread().getName());
try {
    TimeUnit.SECONDS.sleep(time);
} catch (InterruptedException e) {
    e.printStackTrace();
}
System.out.printf("%s: Finishing phase 2.\n",
                  Thread.currentThread().getName());
phaser.arriveAndAwaitAdvance();

System.out.printf("%s: Entering phase 3.\n",
                  Thread.currentThread().getName());
try {
    TimeUnit.SECONDS.sleep(time);
} catch (InterruptedException e) {
    e.printStackTrace();
}
```

```
System.out.printf("%s: Finishing phase 3.\n",
                  Thread.currentThread().getName());

phaser.arriveAndDeregister();
```

8. Implement the main class of the example by creating a class named `Main` with a `main()` method:

```
public class Main {

    public static void main(String[] args) throws Exception {
```

9. Create a new `Phaser` object named `phaser` with three participants:

```
Phaser phaser=new Phaser(3);
```

10. Create and launch three threads to execute three task objects:

```
for (int i=0; i<3; i++) {
  Task task=new Task(i+1, phaser);
  Thread thread=new Thread(task);
  thread.start();
}
```

11. Create a loop with 10 steps to write information about the `phaser` object:

```
for (int i=0; i<10; i++) {
```

12. Write information about the registered parties, the phase of the `phaser`, the arrived parties, and the unarrived parties:

```
System.out.printf("********************\n");
System.out.printf("Main: Phaser Log\n");
System.out.printf("Main: Phaser: Phase: %d\n",
                  phaser.getPhase());
System.out.printf("Main: Phaser: Registered Parties: %d\n",
                  phaser.getRegisteredParties());
System.out.printf("Main: Phaser: Arrived Parties: %d\n",
                  phaser.getArrivedParties());
System.out.printf("Main: Phaser: Unarrived Parties: %d\n",
                  phaser.getUnarrivedParties());
System.out.printf("********************\n");
```

13. Put the thread to sleep for 1 second and close the loop and the class:

```
TimeUnit.SECONDS.sleep(1);
        }
    }
}
```

How it works...

In this recipe, we implemented a phased task in the `Task` class. This phased task has three phases and uses a `Phaser` interface to synchronize with other `Task` objects. The main class launches three tasks, and when these tasks execute their respective phases, it prints information about the status of the `phaser` object to the console. We used the following methods to get the status of the `phaser` object:

- `getPhase()`: This method returns the actual phase of a `phaser` object
- `getRegisteredParties()`: This method returns the number of tasks that use a `phaser` object as a mechanism of synchronization
- `getArrivedParties()`: This method returns the number of tasks that have arrived at the end of the actual phase
- `getUnarrivedParties()`: This method returns the number of tasks that haven't yet arrived at the end of the actual phase

The following screenshot shows part of the output of the program:

```
 Problems  Javadoc  Declaration  Search
<terminated> Main (63) [Java Application] C:\Program
********************
Main: Phaser Log
Main: Phaser: Phase: 2
Main: Phaser: Registered Parties: 3
Main: Phaser: Arrived Parties: 2
Main: Phaser: Unarrived Parties: 1
********************
Thread-2: Finishing phase 2.
Thread-2: Entering phase 3.
Thread-1: Entering phase 3.
Thread-0: Entering phase 3.
********************
Main: Phaser Log
Main: Phaser: Phase: 3
Main: Phaser: Registered Parties: 3
Main: Phaser: Arrived Parties: 0
Main: Phaser: Unarrived Parties: 3
********************
```

See also

- The *Running concurrent-phased tasks* recipe in `Chapter 3`, *Thread Synchronization Utilities*

Monitoring an Executor framework

The `Executor` framework provides a mechanism that separates the implementation of tasks from thread creation and management to execute the tasks. If you use an executor, you only have to implement `Runnable` objects and send them to the executor. It is the responsibility of an executor to manage threads. When you send a task to an executor, it tries to use a pooled thread for executing the task in order to avoid the creation of new threads. This mechanism is offered by the `Executor` interface and its implementing classes as the `ThreadPoolExecutor` class.

In this recipe, you will learn what information you can obtain about the status of a `ThreadPoolExecutor` executor and how to obtain it.

Getting ready

The example of this recipe has been implemented using the Eclipse IDE. If you use Eclipse or a different IDE, such as NetBeans, open it and create a new Java project.

How to do it...

Follow these steps to implement the example:

1. Create a class named `Task` that implements the `Runnable` interface:

   ```
   public class Task implements Runnable {
   ```

2. Declare a private `long` attribute named `milliseconds`:

   ```
   private final long milliseconds;
   ```

3. Implement the constructor of the class to initialize its attribute:

```
public Task (long milliseconds) {
   this.milliseconds=milliseconds;
}
```

4. Implement the `run()` method. Put the thread to sleep for the number of milliseconds specified by the `milliseconds` attribute:

```
@Override
public void run() {

   System.out.printf("%s: Begin\n",
                     Thread.currentThread().getName());
   try {
      TimeUnit.MILLISECONDS.sleep(milliseconds);
   } catch (InterruptedException e) {
      e.printStackTrace();
   }
   System.out.printf("%s: End\n",
                     Thread.currentThread().getName());

}
```

5. Implement the main class of the example by creating a class named `Main` with a `main()` method:

```
public class Main {

   public static void main(String[] args) throws Exception {
```

6. Create a new `Executor` object using the `newCachedThreadPool()` method of the `Executors` class:

```
ThreadPoolExecutor executor = (ThreadPoolExecutor)
                     Executors.newCachedThreadPool();
```

7. Create and submit 10 `Task` objects to the executor. Initialize the objects with a random number:

```
Random random=new Random();
for (int i=0; i<10; i++) {
   Task task=new Task(random.nextInt(10000));
   executor.submit(task);
}
```

8. Create a loop with five steps. In each step, write information about the executor by calling the `showLog()` method and putting the thread to sleep for a second:

```
for (int i=0; i<5; i++){
    showLog(executor);
    TimeUnit.SECONDS.sleep(1);
}
```

9. Shut down the executor using the `shutdown()` method:

```
executor.shutdown();
```

10. Create another loop with five steps. In each step, write information about the executor by calling the `showLog()` method and putting the thread to sleep for a second:

```
for (int i=0; i<5; i++){
    showLog(executor);
    TimeUnit.SECONDS.sleep(1);
}
```

11. Wait for the finalization of the executor using the `awaitTermination()` method:

```
executor.awaitTermination(1, TimeUnit.DAYS);
```

12. Display a message indicating the end of the program:

```
    System.out.printf("Main: End of the program.\n");
}
```

13. Implement the `showLog()` method that receives `Executor` as a parameter. Write information about the size of the pool, the number of tasks, and the status of the executor:

```
private static void showLog(ThreadPoolExecutor executor) {
    System.out.printf("*********************");
    System.out.printf("Main: Executor Log");
    System.out.printf("Main: Executor: Core Pool Size: %d\n",
                    executor.getCorePoolSize());
    System.out.printf("Main: Executor: Pool Size: %d\n",
                    executor.getPoolSize());
    System.out.printf("Main: Executor: Active Count: %d\n",
                    executor.getActiveCount());
    System.out.printf("Main: Executor: Task Count: %d\n",
                    executor.getTaskCount());
```

```
System.out.printf("Main: Executor: Completed Task Count: %d\n",
            executor.getCompletedTaskCount());
System.out.printf("Main: Executor: Shutdown: %s\n",
            executor.isShutdown());
System.out.printf("Main: Executor: Terminating: %s\n",
            executor.isTerminating());
System.out.printf("Main: Executor: Terminated: %s\n",
            executor.isTerminated());
System.out.printf("*********************\n");
    }
```

How it works...

In this recipe, you implemented a task that blocks its execution thread for a random number of milliseconds. Then, you sent 10 tasks to an executor, and while you were waiting for their finalization, you wrote information about the status of the executor to the console. You used the following methods to get the status of the Executor object:

- getCorePoolSize(): This method returns an int number, which refers to the core number of threads. It's the minimum number of threads that will be in the internal thread pool when the executor is not executing any task.

- getPoolSize(): This method returns an int value, which refers to the actual size of the internal thread pool.

- getActiveCount(): This method returns an int number, which refers to the number of threads that are currently executing tasks.

- getTaskCount(): This method returns a long number, which refers to the number of tasks that have been scheduled for execution.

- getCompletedTaskCount(): This method returns a long number, which refers to the number of tasks that have been executed by this executor and have finished their execution.

- isShutdown(): This method returns a Boolean value when the shutdown() method of an executor is called to finish its execution.

- isTerminating(): This method returns a Boolean value when the executor performs the shutdown() operation but hasn't finished it yet.

- isTerminated(): This method returns a Boolean value when the executor finishes its execution.

See also

- The *Creating a thread executor and controlling its rejected tasks* recipe in `Chapter 4`, *Thread Executors*
- The *Customizing the ThreadPoolExecutor class* and *Implementing a priority-based Executor class* recipes in `Chapter 8`, *Customizing Concurrency Classes*

Monitoring a fork/join pool

The Executor framework provides a mechanism that allows you to separate task implementation from the creation and management of threads that execute the tasks. Java 9 includes an extension of the Executor framework for a specific kind of problem that will improve the performance of other solutions (using `Thread` objects directly or the Executor framework). It's the fork/join framework.

This framework is designed to solve problems that can be broken down into smaller tasks using the `fork()` and `join()` operations. The main class that implements this behavior is `ForkJoinPool`.

In this recipe, you will learn what information you can obtain about a `ForkJoinPool` class and how to obtain it.

Getting ready

The example of this recipe has been implemented using the Eclipse IDE. If you use Eclipse or a different IDE, such as NetBeans, open it and create a new Java project.

How to do it...

Follow these steps to implement the example:

1. Create a class named `Task` that extends the `RecursiveAction` class:

   ```
   public class Task extends RecursiveAction{
   ```

2. Declare a private `int` array attribute named `array` to store the array of elements you want to increment:

```
private final int array[];
```

3. Declare two private `int` attributes named `start` and `end` to store the start and end positions of the block of elements this task has to process:

```
private final int start;
private final int end;
```

4. Implement the constructor of the class to initialize its attributes:

```
public Task (int array[], int start, int end) {
    this.array=array;
    this.start=start;
    this.end=end;
}
```

5. Implement the `compute()` method with the main logic of the task. If the task has to process more than 100 elements, first divide the elements into two parts, create two tasks to execute these parts, start its execution with the `fork()` method, and finally, wait for its finalization with the `join()` method:

```
protected void compute() {
    if (end-start>100) {
        int mid=(start+end)/2;
        Task task1=new Task(array,start,mid);
        Task task2=new Task(array,mid,end);

        task1.fork();
        task2.fork();

        task1.join();
        task2.join();
```

6. If the task has to process 100 elements or less, increment the elements by putting the thread to sleep for 5 milliseconds after each operation:

```
    } else {
        for (int i=start; i<end; i++) {
            array[i]++;

            try {
                Thread.sleep(5);
            } catch (InterruptedException e) {
```

```
                 e.printStackTrace();
            }
        }
      }
    }
  }
```

7. Implement the main class of the example by creating a class named `Main` with a `main()` method:

```
public class Main {

    public static void main(String[] args) throws Exception {
```

8. Create a `ForkJoinPool` object named `pool`:

```
ForkJoinPool pool=new ForkJoinPool();
```

9. Create an array of integer numbers, named `array`, with 10,000 elements:

```
int array[]=new int[10000];
```

10. Create a new `Task` object to process the whole array:

```
Task task1=new Task(array,0,array.length);
```

11. Send the task for execution to the pool using the `execute()` method:

```
pool.execute(task1);
```

12. If the task doesn't finish its execution, call the `showLog()` method to write information about the status of the `ForkJoinPool` class and put the thread to sleep for a second:

```
while (!task1.isDone()) {
    showLog(pool);
    TimeUnit.SECONDS.sleep(1);
}
```

13. Shut down the pool using the `shutdown()` method:

```
pool.shutdown();
```

14. Wait for the finalization of the pool using the `awaitTermination()` method:

```
pool.awaitTermination(1, TimeUnit.DAYS);
```

15. Call the `showLog()` method to write information about the status of the
`ForkJoinPool` class and write a message in the console indicating the end of the
program:

```
showLog(pool);
System.out.printf("Main: End of the program.\n");
```

16. Implement the `showLog()` method. It receives a `ForkJoinPool` object as a
parameter and writes information about its status and the threads and tasks that
are being executed:

```
private static void showLog(ForkJoinPool pool) {
    System.out.printf("**********************\n");
    System.out.printf("Main: Fork/Join Pool log\n");
    System.out.printf("Main: Fork/Join Pool: Parallelism: %d\n",
                    pool.getParallelism());
    System.out.printf("Main: Fork/Join Pool: Pool Size: %d\n",
                    pool.getPoolSize());
    System.out.printf("Main: Fork/Join Pool: Active Thread Count:
                    %d\n", pool.getActiveThreadCount());
    System.out.printf("Main: Fork/Join Pool: Running Thread Count:
                    %d\n", pool.getRunningThreadCount());
    System.out.printf("Main: Fork/Join Pool: Queued Submission:
                    %d\n", pool.getQueuedSubmissionCount());
    System.out.printf("Main: Fork/Join Pool: Queued Tasks: %d\n",
                    pool.getQueuedTaskCount());
    System.out.printf("Main: Fork/Join Pool: Queued Submissions:
                    %s\n", pool.hasQueuedSubmissions());
    System.out.printf("Main: Fork/Join Pool: Steal Count: %d\n",
                    pool.getStealCount());
    System.out.printf("Main: Fork/Join Pool: Terminated : %s\n",
                    pool.isTerminated());
    System.out.printf("**********************\n");
}
```

How it works...

In this recipe, you implemented a task that increments the elements of an array, using a `ForkJoinPool` class, and a `Task` class that extends the `RecursiveAction` class. This is one of the tasks you can execute in a `ForkJoinPool` class. When the tasks were processing the array, you printed information about the status of the `ForkJoinPool` class to the console. You used the following methods to get the status of the `ForkJoinPool` class:

- `getPoolSize()`: This method returns an `int` value, which is the number of worker threads of the internal pool of a `ForkJoinPool` class
- `getParallelism()`: This method returns the desired level of parallelism established for a pool
- `getActiveThreadCount()`: This method returns the number of threads that are currently executing tasks
- `getRunningThreadCount()`: This method returns the number of working threads that are not blocked in any synchronization mechanism
- `getQueuedSubmissionCount()`: This method returns the number of tasks that have been submitted to a pool and haven't started their execution yet
- `getQueuedTaskCount()`: This method returns the number of tasks that have been submitted to a pool and have started their execution
- `hasQueuedSubmissions()`: This method returns a `Boolean` value indicating whether the pool has queued tasks that haven't started their execution yet
- `getStealCount()`: This method returns a `long` value specifying the number of times a worker thread has stolen a task from another thread
- `isTerminated()`: This method returns a `Boolean` value indicating whether the fork/join pool has finished its execution

See also

- The *Creating a fork/join pool* recipe in `Chapter 5`, *Fork/Join Framework*
- The *Implementing the ThreadFactory interface to generate custom threads for the fork/join framework* and *Customizing tasks running in the fork/join framework* recipes in `Chapter 8`, *Customizing Concurrency Classes*

Monitoring a stream

A stream in Java is a sequence of elements that could be processed (mapped, filtered, transformed, reduced, and collected) either parallelly or sequentially in a pipeline of declarative operations using `lambda` expressions. It was introduced in Java 8 to change the way one can process enormous sets of data in a functional way, with lambda expressions instead of the traditional imperative way.

The `Stream` interface doesn't provide a lot of methods as other concurrency classes to monitor its status. Only the `peek()` method allows you to write log information about the elements that are being processed. In this recipe, you will learn how to use this method to write information about a stream.

Getting ready

The example of this recipe has been implemented using the Eclipse IDE. If you use Eclipse or a different IDE, such as NetBeans, open it and create a new Java project.

How to do it...

Follow these steps to implement the example:

1. Create a class named `Main` with a `main()` method. Declare two private variables, namely an `AtomicInteger` variable called `counter` and a `Random` object called `random`:

   ```
   public class Main {
       public static void main(String[] args) {

           AtomicLong counter = new AtomicLong(0);
           Random random-new Random();
   ```

2. Create a stream of 1,000 random `double` numbers. The stream created is a sequential stream. You have to make it parallel using the `parallel()` method, and use the `peek()` method to increment the value of the `counter` variable and write a message in the console. Post this, use the `count()` method to count the number of elements in the array and store that number in an integer variable. Write the value stored in the `counter` variable and the value returned by the `count()` method in the console:

```
long streamCounter = random.doubles(1000).parallel()
                        .peek( number -> {
    long actual=counter.incrementAndGet();
    System.out.printf("%d - %f\n", actual, number);
}).count();

System.out.printf("Counter: %d\n", counter.get());
System.out.printf("Stream Counter: %d\n", streamCounter);
```

3. Now, set the value of the `counter` variable to 0. Create another stream of 1,000 random `double` numbers. Then, convert it into a parallel stream using the `parallel()` method, and use the `peek()` method to increment the value of the `counter` variable and write a message in the console. Finally, use the `forEach()` method to write all the numbers and the value of the counter variable in the console:

```
counter.set(0);
random.doubles(1000).parallel().peek(number -> {
    long actual=counter.incrementAndGet();
    System.out.printf("Peek: %d - %f\n", actual,number);
}).forEach( number -> {
    System.out.printf("For Each: %f\n", number);
});

System.out.printf("Counter: %d\n", counter.get());
    }
}
```

How it works...

In this example, we used the `peek()` method in two different situations to count the number of elements that pass by this step of the stream and write a message in the console.

As described in `Chapter 6`, *Parallel and Reactive Streams*, `Stream` has a source, zero or more intermediate operations, and a final operation. In the first case, our final operation is the `count()` method. This method doesn't need to process the elements to calculate the returned value, so the `peek()` method will never be executed. You won't see any of the messages of the peek method in the console, and the value of the counter variable will be 0.

The second case is different. The final operation is the `forEach()` method, and in this case, all the elements of the stream will be processed. In the console, you will see messages of both `peek()` and `forEach()` methods. The final value of the `counter` variable will be 1,000.

The peek() method is an intermediate operation of a stream. Like with all intermediate operations, they are executed lazily, and they only process the necessary elements. This is the reason why it's never executed in the first case.

See also

- The *Creating streams from different sources, Reducing the elements of a stream* and *Collecting the elements of a stream* recipes in Chapter 6, *Parallel and Reactive Streams*

Writing effective log messages

A **log** system is a mechanism that allows you to write information to one or more destinations. A **Logger** has the following components:

- **One or more handlers**: A handler will determine the destination and format of the log messages. You can write log messages in the console, a file, or a database.
- **A name**: Usually, the name of a Logger used in a class is based on the class name and its package name.

- **A level**: Log messages have different levels that indicate their importance. A Logger also has a level to decide what messages it is going to write. It only writes messages that are as important as, or more important, than its level.

You should use the log system because of the following two main reasons:

- Write as much information as you can when an exception is caught. This will help you localize the error and resolve it.
- Write information about the classes and methods that the program is executing.

In this recipe, you will learn how to use the classes provided by the java.util.logging package to add a log system to your concurrent application.

Getting ready

The example of this recipe has been implemented using the Eclipse IDE. If you use Eclipse or a different IDE, such as NetBeans, open it and create a new Java project.

How to do it...

Follow these steps to implement the example:

1. Create a class named `MyFormatter` that extends the `java.util.logging.Formatter` class. Implement the abstract `format()` method. It receives a `LogRecord` object as a parameter and returns a `String` object with a log message:

```
public class MyFormatter extends Formatter {
  @Override
  public String format(LogRecord record) {

    StringBuilder sb=new StringBuilder();
    sb.append("["+record.getLevel()+"] - ");
    sb.append(new Date(record.getMillis())+" : ");
    sb.append(record.getSourceClassName()+ "."
          +record.getSourceMethodName()+" : ");
    sb.append(record.getMessage()+"\n");.
    return sb.toString();
  }
```

2. Create a class named `MyLoggerFactory`:

```
public class MyLoggerFactory {
```

3. Declare a private static `Handler` attribute named `handler`:

```
private static Handler handler;
```

4. Implement the public static method `getLogger()` to create the `Logger` object that you're going to use to write log messages. It receives a `String` parameter called `name`. We synchronize this method with the `synchronized` keyword:

```
public synchronized static Logger getLogger(String name){
```

5. Get `java.util.logging.Logger` associated with the name received as a parameter using the `getLogger()` method of the `Logger` class:

```
Logger logger=Logger.getLogger(name);
```

6. Establish the log level to write all the log messages using the `setLevel()` method:

```
logger.setLevel(Level.ALL);
```

7. If the handler attribute has the null value, create a new `FileHandler` object to write log messages in the `recipe8.log` file. Assign a `MyFormatter` object to this handler; assign it as a formatter using the `setFormatter()` object:

```
try {
    if (handler==null) {
        handler=new FileHandler("recipe6.log");
        Formatter format=new MyFormatter();
        handler.setFormatter(format);
    }
```

8. If the `Logger` object does not have a handler associated with it, assign the handler using the `addHandler()` method:

```
        if (logger.getHandlers().length==0) {
            logger.addHandler(handler);
        }
    } catch (SecurityException e | IOException e) {
    e.printStackTrace();
}
```

9. Return the `Logger` object created:

```
    return logger;
}
```

10. Create a class named `Task` that implements the `Runnable` interface. It will be the task used to test your `Logger` object:

```
public class Task implements Runnable {
```

11. Implement the `run()` method:

```
@Override
public void run() {
```

12. First, declare a `Logger` object named `logger`. Initialize it using the `getLogger()` method of the `MyLogger` class by passing the name of this class as a parameter:

```
Logger logger= MyLogger.getLogger(this.getClass().getName());
```

13. Write a log message indicating the beginning of the execution of the method, using the `entering()` method:

```
logger.entering(Thread.currentThread().getName(), "run()");
```

14. Sleep the thread for two seconds:

```
try {
  TimeUnit.SECONDS.sleep(2);
} catch (InterruptedException e) {
  e.printStackTrace();
}
```

15. Write a log message indicating the end of the execution of the method, using the `exiting()` method:

```
logger.exiting(Thread.currentThread().getName(), "run()",
          Thread.currentThread());
}
```

16. Implement the main class of the example by creating a class named `Main` with a `main()` method:

```
public class Main {
  public static void main(String[] args) {
```

17. Declare a `Logger` object named `logger`. Initialize it using the `getLogger()` method of the `MyLogger` class by passing the `Core` string as a parameter:

```
Logger logger=MyLogger.getLogger(Main.class.getName());
```

18. Write a log message indicating the start of the execution of the main program, using the `entering()` method:

```
logger.entering(Main.class.getName(), "main()",args);
```

19. Create a `Thread` array to store five threads:

```
Thread threads[]=new Thread[5];
```

20. Create five `Task` objects and five threads to execute them. Write log messages to indicate that you're going to launch a new thread and that you have created the thread:

```
for (int i=0; i<threads.length; i++) {
  logger.log(Level.INFO,"Launching thread: "+i);
  Task task=new Task();
  threads[i]=new Thread(task);
  logger.log(Level.INFO,"Thread created: "+
            threads[i].getName());
  threads[i].start();
}
```

21. Write a log message to indicate that you have created the threads:

```
logger.log(Level.INFO,"Ten Threads created."+
          "Waiting for its finalization");
```

22. Wait for the finalization of the five threads using the `join()` method. After the finalization of each thread, write a log message indicating that the thread has finished:

```
for (int i=0; i<threads.length; i++) {
  try {
    threads[i].join();
    logger.log(Level.INFO,"Thread has finished its execution",
              threads[i]);
  } catch (InterruptedException e) {
    logger.log(Level.SEVERE, "Exception", e);
  }
}
```

23. Write a log message to indicate the end of the execution of the main program, using the `exiting()` method:

```
  logger.exiting(Main.class.getName(), "main()");
}
```

How it works...

In this recipe, you used the `Logger` class provided by the Java logging API to write log messages in a concurrent application. First of all, you implemented the `MyFormatter` class to assign a format to the log messages. This class extends the `Formatter` class that declares the abstract `format()` method. This method receives a `LogRecord` object with all of the information of the log message and returns a formatted log message. In your class, you used the following methods of the `LogRecord` class to obtain information about the log message:

- `getLevel()`: Returns the level of a message
- `getMillis()`: Returns the date when a message was sent to a `Logger` object
- `getSourceClassName()`: Returns the name of a class that had sent the message to the Logger
- `getSourceMessageName()`: Returns the name of the method that had sent the message to the Logger
- `getMessage()`: Returns the log message

The `MyLogger` class implements the static method `getLogger()`. This method creates a `Logger` object and assigns a `Handler` object to write log messages of the application to the `recipe6.log` file, using the `MyFormatter` formatter. You create the `Logger` object with the static method `getLogger()` of the `Logger` class. This method returns a different object per name that is passed as a parameter. You only created one `Handler` object, so all the `Logger` objects will write their log messages in the same file. You also configured the logger to write all the log messages, regardless of their level.

Finally, you implemented a `Task` object and a main program that writes different log messages in the log file. You used the following methods:

- `entering()`: To write a message with the `FINER` level indicating that a method has started its execution
- `exiting()`: To write a message with the `FINER` level indicating that a method has ended its execution
- `log()`: To write a message with the specified level

There's more...

When you work with a log system, you have to take into consideration two important points:

- **Write the necessary information**: If you write too little information, the logger won't be useful because it won't fulfil its purpose. If you write a lot of information, you will generate large unmanageable log files; this will make it difficult to get the necessary information.
- **Use the adequate level for the messages**: If you write high level information messages or low level error messages, you will confuse the user who will look at the log files. This will make it more difficult to know what happened in an error situation; alternatively, you will have too much of information making it difficult to know the main cause of the error.

There are other libraries that provide a log system that is more complete than the `java.util.logging` package, such as the `Log4j` or `slf4j` libraries. But the `java.util.logging` package is part of the Java API, and all its methods are multithread safe; therefore, we can use it in concurrent applications without problems.

See also

- The *Using non-blocking thread-safe deques, Using blocking thread-safe deques, Using blocking thread-safe queues ordered by priority, Using thread-safe lists with delayed elements* and *Using thread-safe navigable maps* recipes in `Chapter 7`, *Concurrent Collections*

Analyzing concurrent code with FindBugs

Static code analysis tools are a set of tools that analyze the source code of an application while looking for potential errors. These tools, such as Checkstyle, PMD, or FindBugs, have a set of predefined rules of good practices and parse the source code looking for violations of these rules. The objective is to find errors or places that cause poor performance at an early stage, before they are executed in production. Programming languages usually offer such tools, and Java is not an exception. One of the tools that helps analyze Java code is FindBugs. It's an open source tool that includes a series of rules to analyze Java-concurrent code.

In this recipe, you will learn how to use this tool to analyze your Java-concurrent application.

Getting ready

Before you start this recipe, download FindBugs from the project's web page (`http://findbugs.sourceforge.net/`). You can download a standalone application or an Eclipse plugin. In this recipe, I used the standalone version.

 At the time of this writing, the actual version of FindBugs (3.0.1) doesn't include support for Java 9. You can download a preview of the 3.1.0 version with support for Java 9 from `https://github.com/findbugsproject/findbugs/releases/tag/3.1.0_p review1`.

How to do it...

Follow these steps to implement the example:

1. Create a class named `Task` that extends the `Runnable` interface:

   ```
   public class Task implements Runnable {
   ```

2. Declare a private `ReentrantLock` attribute named `lock`:

   ```
   private ReentrantLock lock;
   ```

3. Implement a constructor of the class:

   ```
   public Task(ReentrantLock lock) {
     this.lock=lock;
   }
   ```

4. Implement the `run()` method. Get control of the lock, put the thread to sleep for 2 seconds, and free the lock:

```
@Override
public void run() {
    lock.lock();
    try {
        TimeUnit.SECONDS.sleep(1);
        lock.unlock();
    } catch (InterruptedException e) {
        e.printStackTrace();
    }
}
```

5. Create the main class of the example by creating a class named `Main` with a `main()` method:

```
public class Main {
    public static void main(String[] args) {
```

6. Declare and create a `ReentrantLock` object named `lock`:

```
ReentrantLock lock=new ReentrantLock();
```

7. Create 10 `Task` objects and 10 threads to execute the tasks. Start the threads by calling the `run()` method:

```
for (int i=0; i<10; i++) {
    Task task=new Task(lock);
    Thread thread=new Thread(task);
    thread.run();
}
}
```

8. Export the project as a `.jar` file. Call it `recipe7.jar`. Use the menu option of your IDE or the `javac` and `.jar` commands to compile and compress your application.

9. Start the FindBugs standalone application by running the `findbugs.bat` command in Windows or the `findbugs.sh` command in Linux.

10. Create a new project by clicking on the **New Project** option under the **File** menu in the menu bar:

11. The *FindBugs* application shows a window to configure the project. In the **Project name** field, type `Recipe07`. In the **Classpath for analysis field (jar, ear, war, zip, or directory)**, add the `.jar` file with the project. In the **Source directories field (optional; classes used when browsing found bugs)**, add the directory with the source code of the example. Refer to the following screenshot:

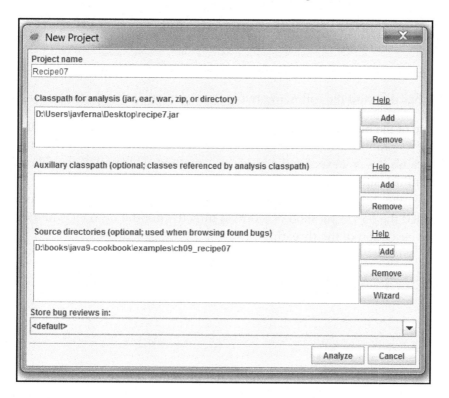

12. Click on the **Analyze** button to create the new project and analyze its code.

13. The *FindBugs* application shows the result of the analysis of the code. In this case, it has found two bugs.

14. Click on one of the bugs and you'll see the source code of the bug on the right-hand side panel and the description of the bug in the panel at the bottom of the screen.

How it works...

The following screenshot shows the result of the analysis by FindBugs:

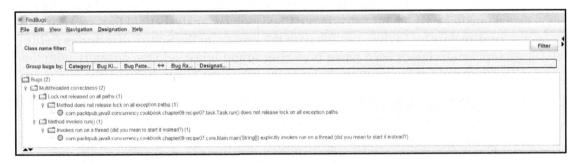

The analysis has detected the following two potential bugs in the application:

- One of the bugs is detected in the run() method of the Task class. If an InterruptedExeption exception is thrown, the task doesn't free the lock because it won't execute the unlock() method. This will probably cause a deadlock situation in the application.

- The other bug is detected in the main() method of the Main class because you called the run() method of a thread directly, not the start() method to begin the execution of the thread.

If you double-click on one of the two bugs, you will see detailed information about it. As you have included the source code reference in the configuration of the project, you will also see the source code where the bug was detected. The following screenshot shows you an example of this:

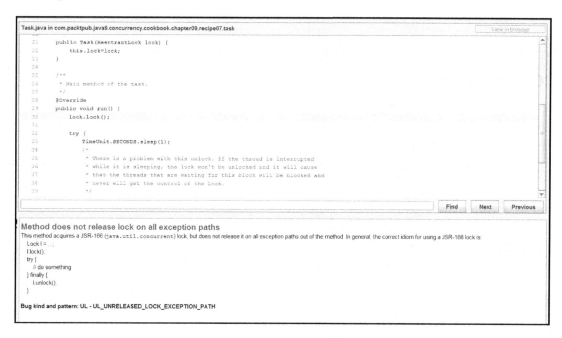

There's more...

Be aware that FindBugs can only detect some problematic situations (related or not to concurrency code). For example, if you delete the `unlock()` call in the `run()` method of the `Task` class and repeat the analysis, FindBugs won't alert you that you will get the lock in the task but you will never be able to free it.

Use the tools of the static code analysis as a form of assistance to improve the quality of your code, but do not expect it to detect all the bugs.

See also

- The *Configuring NetBeans for debugging concurrency code* recipe in this chapter

Configuring Eclipse for debugging concurrency code

Nowadays, almost every programmer, regardless of the programming language in use, create their applications with an IDE. They provide lots of interesting functionalities integrated in the same application, such as:

- Project management
- Automatic code generation
- Automatic documentation generation
- Integration with control version systems
- A debugger to test applications
- Different wizards to create projects and elements of the applications

One of the most helpful features of an IDE is a debugger. Using it, you can execute your application step by step and analyze the values of all the objects and variables of your program.

If you work with Java, Eclipse is one of the most popular IDEs. It has an integrated debugger that allows you to test your applications. By default, when you debug a concurrent application and the debugger finds a breakpoint, it only stops the thread that has the breakpoint while it allows the rest of the threads to continue with their execution. In this recipe, you will learn how to change this configuration to help you test concurrent applications.

Getting ready

You must have installed the Eclipse IDE. Open it and select a project with a concurrent application implemented, for example, one of the recipes implemented in the book.

How to do it...

Follow these steps to implement the example:

1. Navigate to **Window | Preferences**.
2. Expand the **Java** option in the left-hand side menu.
3. Then, select the **Debug** option. The following screenshot illustrates the window:

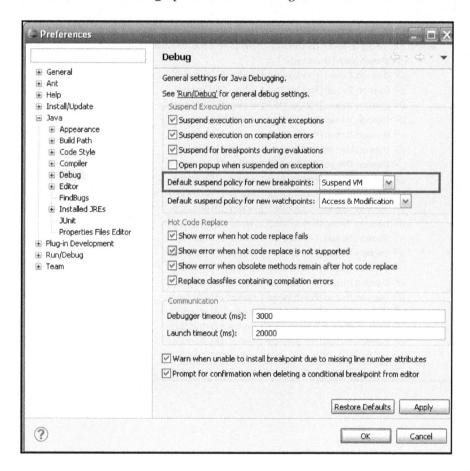

4. Change the value of **Default suspend policy for new breakpoints** from **Suspend Thread** to **Suspend VM** (marked in red in the screenshot).
5. Click on the **OK** button to confirm the change.

How it works...

As mentioned in the introduction of this recipe, by default, when you debug a concurrent Java application in Eclipse and the debug process finds a breakpoint, it only suspends the thread that hits the breakpoint first, but it allows other threads to continue with their execution. The following screenshot shows an example of this:

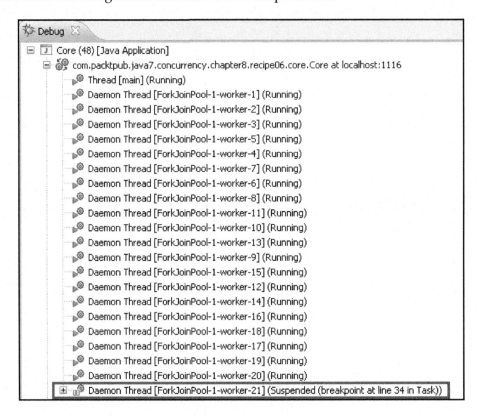

You can see that only **worker-21** is suspended (marked in red in the screenshot), while the rest of the threads are running. However, while debugging a concurrent application, if you change **Default suspend policy for new breakpoints** to **Suspend VM**, all the threads will suspend their execution and the debug process will hit a breakpoint.. The following screenshot shows an example of this situation:

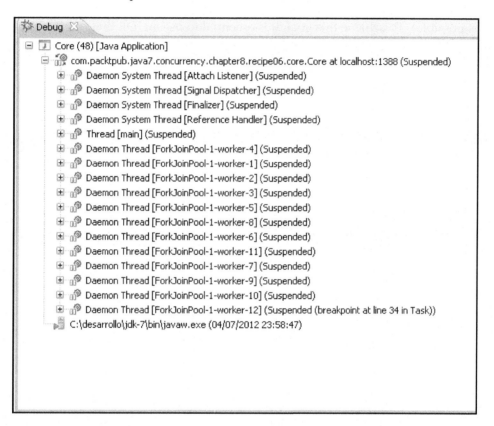

With the change, you can see that all the threads are suspended. You can continue debugging any thread you want. Choose the suspend policy that best suits your needs.

Configuring NetBeans for debugging concurrency code

Software is necessary to develop applications that work properly, meet the quality standards of the company, and could be easily modified in future (in limited time and cost as low as possible). To achieve this goal, it is essential to use an IDE that can integrate several tools (compilers and debuggers) that facilitate the development of applications under one common interface.

If you work with Java, NetBeans is one of the most popular IDEs. It has an integrated debugger that allows you to test your application.

In this recipe, you will learn how to change the configuration of the Netbeans debugger to help you test concurrent applications.

Getting ready

You should have the NetBeans IDE installed. Open it and create a new Java project.

How to do it...

Follow these steps to implement the example:

1. Create a class named Task1 and specify that it implements the Runnable interface:

    ```
    public class Task1 implements Runnable {
    ```

2. Declare two private Lock attributes, named lock1 and lock2:

    ```
    private Lock lock1, lock2;
    ```

3. Implement the constructor of the class to initialize its attributes:

    ```
    public Task1 (Lock lock1, Lock lock2) {
      this.lock1=lock1;
      this.lock2=lock2;
    }
    ```

4. Implement the `run()` method. First, get control of the `lock1` object using the `lock()` method and write aa message in the console indicating that you have got it:

```
@Override
public void run() {
    lock1.lock();
    System.out.printf("Task 1: Lock 1 locked\n");
```

5. Then, get control of `lock2` using the `lock()` method and write a message in the console indicating that you have got it:

```
lock2.lock();
System.out.printf("Task 1: Lock 2 locked\n");
```

6. Finally, release the two lock objects-first the `lock2` object and then the `lock1` object:

```
        lock2.unlock();
        lock1.unlock();
    }
```

7. Create a class named `Task2` and specify that it implements the `Runnable` interface:

```
public class Task2 implements Runnable{
```

8. Declare two private `Lock` attributes, named `lock1` and `lock2`:

```
private Lock lock1, lock2;
```

9. Implement the constructor of the class to initialize its attributes:

```
public Task2(Lock lock1, Lock lock2) {
    this.lock1=lock1;
    this.lock2=lock2;
}
```

10. Implement the `run()` method. First, get control of the `lock2` object using the `lock()` method and write a message in the console indicating that you have got it:

```
@Override
public void run() {
    lock2.lock();
    System.out.printf("Task 2: Lock 2 locked\n");
```

11. Then, get control of `lock1` using the `lock()` method and write a message in the console indicating that you have got it:

```
lock1.lock();
System.out.printf("Task 2: Lock 1 locked\n");
```

12. Finally, release the two lock objects-first `lock1` and then `lock2`:

```
        lock1.unlock();
        lock2.unlock();
    }
```

13. Implement the main class of the example by creating a class named `Main` and adding the `main()` method to it:

```
public class Main {
```

14. Create two lock objects named `lock1` and `lock2`:

```
Lock lock1, lock2;
lock1=new ReentrantLock();
lock2=new ReentrantLock();
```

15. Create a `Task1` object named `task1`:

```
Task1 task1=new Task1(lock1, lock2);
```

16. Create a `Task2` object named `task2`:

```
Task2 task2=new Task2(lock1, lock2);
```

17. Execute both the tasks using two threads:

```
    Thread thread1=new Thread(task1);
    Thread thread2=new Thread(task2);

    thread1.start();
    thread2.start();
```

18. When the two tasks finish their execution, write a message in the console every 500 milliseconds. Use the `isAlive()` method to check whether a thread has finished its execution:

```
while ((thread1.isAlive()) && (thread2.isAlive())) {
    System.out.println("Main: The example is"+ "running");
    try {
```

```
        TimeUnit.MILLISECONDS.sleep(500);
    } catch (InterruptedException ex) {
        ex.printStackTrace();
    }
}
```

19. Add a breakpoint in the first call to the `printf()` method of the `run()` method of the `Task1` class.

20. Debug the program. You will see the **Debugging** window in the top left-hand side corner of the main NetBeans window. The next screenshot illustrates the window with the thread that executes the `Task1` object. The thread is waiting in the breakpoint. The other threads of the application are running:

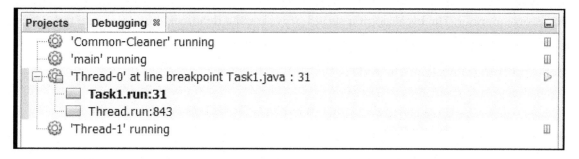

21. Pause the execution of the main thread. Select the thread, right-click on it, and select the **Suspend** option. The following screenshot shows the new appearance of the **Debugging** window. Refer to the following screenshot:

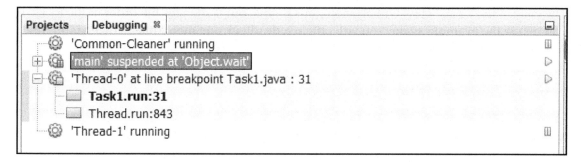

22. Resume the two paused threads. Select each thread, right-click on them, and select the **Resume** option.

How it works...

While debugging a concurrent application using NetBeans, when the debugger hits a breakpoint, it suspends the thread that hit the breakpoint and shows the **Debugging** window in the top left-hand side corner with the threads that are currently running. You can use the window to pause or resume the threads that are currently running, using the **Pause** or **Resume** options. You can also see the values of the variables or attributes of the threads using the **Variables** tab.

NetBeans also includes a deadlock detector. When you select the **Check for Deadlock** option in the **Debug** menu, NetBeans performs an analysis of the application that you're debugging to determine whether there's a deadlock situation. This example presents a clear deadlock. The first thread gets `lock1` first and then `lock2`. The second thread gets the locks in reverse manner. The breakpoint inserted provokes the deadlock, but if you use the NetBeans deadlock detector, you'll not find anything. Therefore, this option should be used with caution. Change the locks used in both the tasks by the `synchronized` keyword and debug the program again. The code of `Task1` is as follows:

```
@Override
public void run() {
  synchronized(lock1) {
    System.out.printf("Task 1: Lock 1 locked\n");
    synchronized(lock2) {
      System.out.printf("Task 1: Lock 2 locked\n");
    }
  }
}
```

The code of the `Task2` class will be analogous to this, but it changes the order of the locks. If you debug the example again, you will obtain a deadlock one more time. However, in this case, it's detected by the deadlock detector, as you can see in the following screenshot:

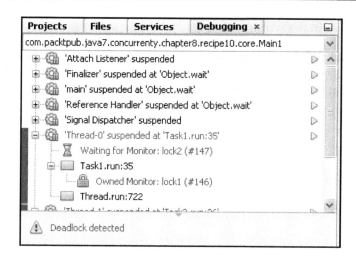

There's more...

There are options to control the debugger. Select **Options** from the **Tools** menu. Then, select the **Miscellaneous** option and the **Java Debugger** tab. The following screenshot illustrates this window:

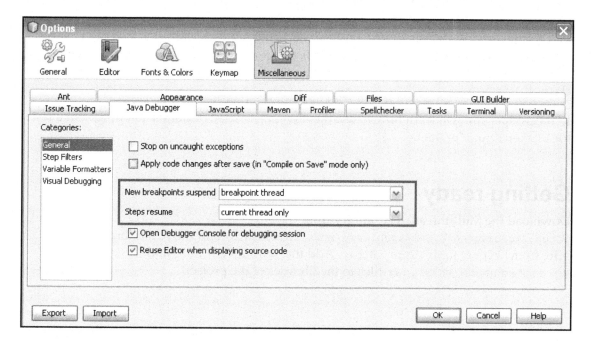

There are two options in the window that control the behavior described earlier:

- **New breakpoints suspend**: With this option, you can configure the behavior of NetBeans, which finds a breakpoint in a thread. You can suspend only that thread that has a breakpoint or all the threads of the application.
- **Steps resume**: With this option, you can configure the behavior of NetBeans when you resume a thread. You can resume only the current thread or all the threads.

Both the options have been marked in the screenshot presented earlier.

See also

- The *Configuring Eclipse for debugging concurrency code* recipe in this chapter

Testing concurrency code with MultithreadedTC

`MultithreadedTC` is a Java library for testing concurrent applications. Its main objective is to solve the problem of concurrent applications being non-deterministic. You can't control the order of execution of the different threads that form the application. For this purpose, it includes an internal **metronome**. These testing threads are implemented as methods of a class.

In this recipe, you will learn how to use the `MultithreadedTC` library to implement a test for `LinkedTransferQueue`.

Getting ready

Download the MultithreadedTC library from `https://code.google.com/archive/p/multithreadedtc/` and the JUnit library, version 4.10, from `http://junit.org/junit4/`. Add the `junit-4.10.jar` and `MultithreadedTC-1.01.jar` files to the libraries of the project.

How to do it...

Follow these steps to implement the example:

1. Create a class named `ProducerConsumerTest` that extends the `MultithreadedTestCase` class:

   ```
   public class ProducerConsumerTest extends MultithreadedTestCase {
   ```

2. Declare a private `LinkedTransferQueue` attribute parameterized by the `String` class named `queue`:

   ```
   private LinkedTransferQueue<String> queue;
   ```

3. Implement the `initialize()` method. This method won't receive any parameters and will return no value. It will call the `initialize()` method of its parent class and then initialize the queue attribute:

   ```
   @Override
   public void initialize() {
     super.initialize();
     queue=new LinkedTransferQueue<String>();
     System.out.printf("Test: The test has been initialized\n");
   }
   ```

4. Implement the `thread1()` method. It will implement the logic of the first consumer. Call the `take()` method of the queue and then write the returned value in the console:

   ```
   public void thread1() throws InterruptedException {
     String ret=queue.take();
     System.out.printf("Thread 1: %s\n",ret);
   }
   ```

5. Implement the `thread2()` method. It will implement the logic of the second consumer. First wait until the first thread has slept in the `take()` method. To put the thread to sleep, use the `waitForTick()` method. Then, call the `take()` method of the queue and write the returned value in the console:

   ```
   public void thread2() throws InterruptedException {
     waitForTick(1);
     String ret=queue.take();
     System.out.printf("Thread 2: %s\n",ret);
   }
   ```

6. Implement the `thread3()` method. It will implement the logic of a producer. First wait until the two consumers are blocked in the `take()` method; block this method using the `waitForTick()` method twice. Then, call the `put()` method of the queue to insert two strings in the queue:

```
public void thread3() {
  waitForTick(1);
  waitForTick(2);
  queue.put("Event 1");
  queue.put("Event 2");
  System.out.printf("Thread 3: Inserted two elements\n");
}
```

7. Finally, implement the `finish()` method. Write a message in the console to indicate that the test has finished its execution. Check that the two events have been consumed (so the size of the queue is 0) using the `assertEquals()` method:

```
public void finish() {
  super.finish();
  System.out.printf("Test: End\n");
  assertEquals(true, queue.size()==0);
  System.out.printf("Test: Result: The queue is empty\n");
}
```

8. Next, implement the main class of the example by creating a class named `Main` with a `main()` method:

```
public class Main {
  public static void main(String[] args) throws Throwable {
```

9. Create a `ProducerConsumerTest` object named `test`:

```
ProducerConsumerTest test=new ProducerConsumerTest();
```

10. Execute the test using the `runOnce()` method of the `TestFramework` class:

```
System.out.printf("Main: Starting the test\n");
TestFramework.runOnce(test);
System.out.printf("Main: The test has finished\n");
```

How it works...

In this recipe, you implemented a test for the LinkedTransferQueue class using the MultithreadedTC library. You can implement a test in any concurrent application or class using this library and its metronome. In the example, you implemented the classical producer/consumer problem with two consumers and a producer. You wanted to test that the first String object introduced in the buffer is consumed by the first consumer that arrives at the buffer, and the second String object introduced in the buffer is consumed by the second consumer that arrives at the buffer.

The MultithreadedTC library is based on the JUnit library, which is the most often used library to implement unit tests in Java. To implement a basic test using the MultithreadedTC library, you have to extend the MultithreadedTestCase class. This class extends the junit.framework.AssertJUnit class that includes all the methods to check the results of the test. It doesn't extend the junit.framework.TestCase class, so you can't integrate MultithreadedTC tests with other JUnit tests.

Then, you can implement the following methods:

- initialize(): The implementation of this method is optional. It's executed when you start the test, so you can use it to initialize objects that are using the test.
- finish(): The implementation of this method is optional. It's executed when the test has finished. You can use it to close or release resources used during the test or to check the results of the test.
- Methods that implement the test: These methods have the main logic of the test you implement. They have to start with the thread keyword, followed by a string, for example, thread1().

To control the order of execution of threads, you used the waitForTick() method. This method receives an integer value as a parameter and puts the thread that is executing the method to sleep until all the threads that are running in the test are blocked. When they are blocked, the MultithreadedTC library resumes the threads that are blocked by a call to the waitForTick() method.

The integer you pass as a parameter of the waitForTick() method is used to control the order of execution. The metronome of the MultithreadedTC library has an internal counter. When all the threads are blocked, the library increments this counter to the next number specified in the waitForTick() calls that are blocked.

Internally, when the `MultithreadedTC` library has to execute a test, first it executes the `initialize()` method. Then it creates a thread per method that starts with the `thread` keyword (in your example, the methods `thread1()`, `thread2()`, and `thread3()`). When all the threads have finished their execution, it executes the `finish()` method. To execute the test, you used the `runOnce()` method of the `TestFramework` class.

There's more...

If the `MultithreadedTC` library detects that all the threads of the test are blocked except in the `waitForTick()` method, the test is declared to be in a deadlock state and a `java.lang.IllegalStateException` exception is thrown.

See also

- The *Analyzing concurrent code with FindBugs* recipe in this chapter

Monitoring with JConsole

JConsole is a monitoring tool that follows the JMX specification that allows you to get information about the execution of an application as the number of threads, memory use, or class loading. It is included with the JDK and it can be used to monitor local or remote applications. In this recipe, you will learn how to use this tool to monitor a simple concurrent application.

Getting ready

The example of this recipe has been implemented using the Eclipse IDE. If you use Eclipse or a different IDE, such as NetBeans, open it and create a new Java project.

How to do it...

Follow these steps to implement the example:

1. Create a class named `Task` and specify the `Runnable` interface. Implement the `run()` method to write the message in the console during 100 seconds:

```
public class Task implements Runnable {

  @Override
  public void run() {

    Date start, end;
    start = new Date();
    do {
      System.out.printf("%s: tick\n",
                        Thread.currentThread().getName());
      end = new Date();
    } while (end.getTime() - start.getTime() < 100000);
  }
}
```

2. Implement the `Main` class with the `main()` method. Create 10 `Task` objects to create 10 threads. Start them and wait for their finalization using the `join()` method:

```
public class Main {
  public static void main(String[] args) {

    Thread[] threads = new Thread[10];

    for (int i=0; i<10; i++) {
      Task task=new Task();
      threads[i]=new Thread(task);
      threads[i].start();
    }

    for (int i=0; i<10; i++) {
      try {
        threads[i].join();
      } catch (InterruptedException e) {
        e.printStackTrace();
      }
    }
  }
}
```

3. Open a console window and execute the `JConsole` application. It's included in the bin directory of the JDK-9 installation:

How it works...

In this recipe, we implemented a very simple example: running 10 threads for 100 seconds. These are threads that write messages in the console.

When you execute JConsole, you will see a window that shows all the Java applications that are running in your system. You can choose the one you want to monitor. The window will be similar to the following one:

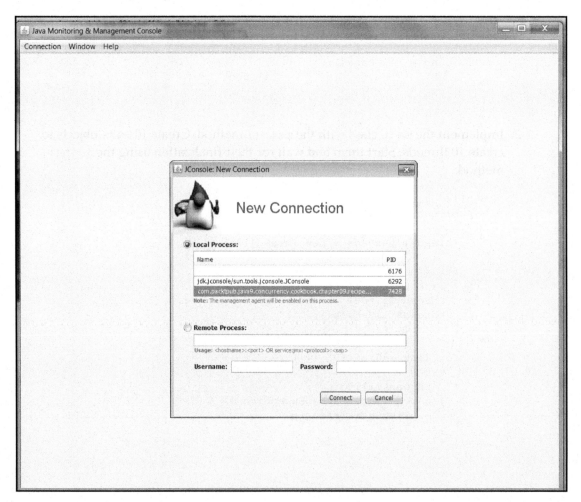

In this case, we select our sample app and click on the **Connect** button. Then, you will be asked to establish an insecure connection with the application, with a dialog similar to the following one:

Click on the **Insecure connection** button. JConsole will show you information about your application using six tabs:

- The **Overview** tab provides an overview of memory use, the number of threads running in the application, the number of objects created, and CPU usage of the application.
- The **Memory** tab shows the amount of memory used by the application. It has a combo where you can select the type of memory you want to monitor (heap, non-heap, or pools).
- The **Threads** tab shows you information about the number of threads in the application and detailed information about each thread.
- The **Classes** tab shows you information about the number of objects loaded in the application.
- The **VW Summary** tab provides a summary of the JVM running the application.
- The **MBeans** tab shows you information about the managed beans of the application.

The threads tab is similar to the following one:

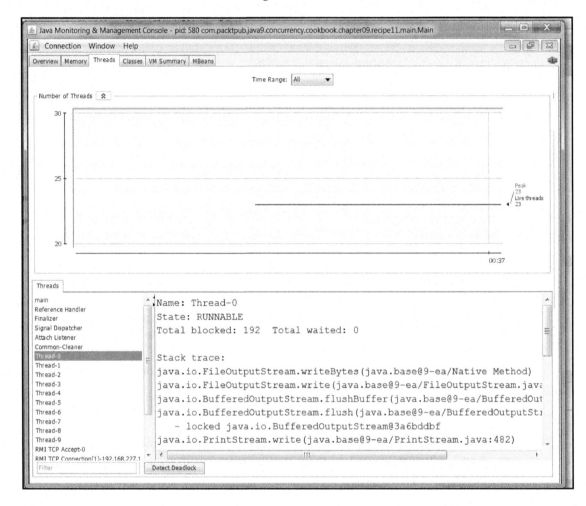

It has two different parts. In the upper part, you have real-time information about the **Peak** number of threads (with a red line) and the number of **Live Threads** (with a blue line). In the lower part, we have a list of active threads. When you select one of these threads, you will see detailed information about that thread, including its status and the actual stack trace.

There's more...

You can use other applications to monitor applications that run Java. For example, you can use VisualVM included with the JDK. You can obtain necessary information about visualvm at `https://visualvm.github.io`.

See also

- The *Testing concurrency code with MultithreadedTC* recipe in this chapter

10
Additional Information

In this chapter, we will cover the following topics:

- Processing results for Runnable objects in the Executor framework
- Processing uncontrolled exceptions in a ForkJoinPool class
- Using a blocking thread-safe queue to communicate with producers and consumers
- Monitoring a Thread class
- Monitoring a Semaphore class
- Generating concurrent random numbers

Introduction

This chapter include recipes about the `Executor` framework and the fork/join framework, concurrent data structures, monitoring concurrent objects, and generating concurrent random numbers.

Processing results for Runnable objects in the Executor framework

The `Executor` framework allows the execution of concurrent tasks that returns a result using the `Callable` and `Future` interfaces. The traditional concurrent programming in Java is based on `Runnable` objects, but this kind of object doesn't return a result.

In this recipe, you will learn how to adapt a `Runnable` object to simulate a `Callable` one, allowing a concurrent task to return a result.

Getting ready

The example of this recipe has been implemented using the Eclipse IDE. If you use Eclipse, or another IDE such as NetBeans, open it and create a new Java project.

How to do it...

Perform the following steps to implement the example:

1. Create a class named `FileSearch` and specify that it implements the `Runnable` interface. This class implements the file search operation:

   ```
   public class FileSearch implements Runnable {
   ```

2. Declare two private `String` attributes: one named `initPath`, which will store the initial folder for the search operation, and the other named end, which will store the extension of the files this task is going to look for:

   ```
   private String initPath;
   private String end;
   ```

3. Declare a private `List<String>` attribute named `results` that will store the full paths of the files that this task has found:

   ```
   private List<String> results;
   ```

4. Implement the constructor of the class that will initialize its attributes:

   ```
   public FileSearch(String initPath, String end) {
      this.initPath = initPath;
      this.end = end;
      results=new ArrayList<>();
   }
   ```

5. Implement the method `getResults()`. This method returns the list with the full paths of the files that this task has found:

```
public List<String> getResults() {
    return results;
}
```

6. Implement the `run()` method. First of all, write a log message to the console indicating that the task is starting its job:

```
@Override
public void run() {
    System.out.printf("%s: Starting\n",
                    Thread.currentThread().getName());
```

7. Then, if the `initPath` attribute stores the name of an existing folder, call the auxiliary method, `directoryProcess()`, to process its files and folders:

```
File file = new File(initPath);
    if (file.isDirectory()) {
        directoryProcess(file);
    }
```

8. Implement the auxiliary `diretoryProcess()` method, which receives a `File` object as a parameter. First of all, get the contents of the folder pointed to by the parameter:

```
private void directoryProcess(File file) {
    File list[] = file.listFiles();
```

9. With all the elements of the folder, if they are folders, make a recursive call to the `directoryProcess()` method. If they are files, call the `fileProcess()` auxiliary method:

```
if (list != null) {
    for (int i = 0; i < list.length; i++) {
        if (list[i].isDirectory()) {
            directoryProcess(list[i]);
        } else {
            fileProcess(list[i]);
        }
    }
}
```

10. Implement the auxiliary method `fileProcess()` that receives a `File` object with the full path of a file. This method checks if the file extension is equal to the one stored in the end attribute. If they are equal, add the full path of the file to the list of results:

```
private void fileProcess(File file) {
    if (file.getName().endsWith(end)) {
        results.add(file.getAbsolutePath());
    }
}
```

11. Implement a class named `Task` that extends the `FutureTask` class. You'll use `List<String>` as the parameterized type, as this will be the type of the data this task will return:

```
public class Task extends FutureTask<List<String>> {
```

12. Declare a private `FileSearch` attribute named `fileSearch`:

```
private FileSearch fileSearch;
```

13. Implement the constructor of this class. This constructor has two parameters: a `Runnable` object named `runnable` and a `List<String>` object named result. In the constructor, you have to call the constructor of the parent class, passing to it the same parameters. Then, store the `runnable` parameter, casting it to a `FileSearch` object:

```
public Task(Runnable runnable, List<String> result) {
    super(runnable, result);
    this.fileSearch=(FileSearch)runnable;
}
```

14. Override the `set()` method of the `FutureTask` class:

```
@Override
protected void set(List<String> v) {
```

15. If the parameter that it receives is null, store in it the result of calling the `getResults()` method of the `FileSearch` class:

```
v=fileSearch.getResults();
```

16. Then, call the parent's method passing the received parameter as a parameter:

```
super.set(v);
```

17. Finally, implement the main class of the example. Create a class named `Main` and implement the `main()` method:

```
public class Main {
  public static void main(String[] args) {
```

18. Create a `ThreadPoolExecutor` object named executor calling the `newCachedThreadPool()` method of the `Executors` class:

```
ExecutorService executor = Executors.newCachedThreadPool();
```

19. Create three `FileSearch` objects with a different initial folder for each one. You are going to look for files with the `log` extension:

```
FileSearch system=new FileSearch("C:\\Windows", "log");
FileSearch apps=new FileSearch("C:\\Program Files","log");
FileSearch documents=new FileSearch("C:\\Documents And
                                     Settings","log");
```

20. Create three `Task` objects to execute the search operations in the executor:

```
Task systemTask=new Task(system,null);
Task appsTask=new Task(apps,null);
Task documentsTask=new Task(documents,null);
```

21. Send these objects to the executor object using the `submit()` method. This version of the `submit()` method returns a `Future<?>` object, but you're going to ignore it. You have a class that extends the `FutureTask` class to control the execution of this task:

```
executor.submit(systemTask);
executor.submit(appsTask);
executor.submit(documentsTask);
```

22. Call the `shutdown()` method of the executor object to indicate that it should finish its execution when these three tasks have finished:

```
executor.shutdown();
```

23. Call the `awaitTermination()` method of the executor object, indicating a long waiting period to guarantee that this method won't return until the three tasks have finished:

```
try {
    executor.awaitTermination(1, TimeUnit.DAYS);
} catch (InterruptedException e) {
    e.printStackTrace();
}
```

24. For each task, write a message with the size of the result list using the `get()` method of the `Task` object:

```
try {
    System.out.printf("Main: System Task: Number of Results: %d\n",
                      systemTask.get().size());
    System.out.printf("Main: App Task: Number of Results: %d\n",
                      appsTask.get().size());
    System.out.printf("Main: Documents Task: Number of
                      Results: %d\n",documentsTask.get().size());
} catch (InterruptedException e) {
    e.printStackTrace();
} catch (ExecutionException e) {
    e.printStackTrace();
}
```

How it works...

The first point to take into consideration to understand this example is the difference between the `submit()` method of the `ThreadPoolExecutor` class when you pass a `Callable` object as the parameter and the `submit()` method when you pass a `Runnable` object as the parameter. In the first case, you can use the `Future` object that this method returns to control the status of the task and to get its result. But in the second case, when you pass a `Runnable` object, you can only use the `Future` object that this method returns to control the status of the task. If you call the `get()` method of that `Future` object, you will get a null value.

To override this behavior, you have implemented the `Task` class. This class extends the `FutureTask` class that is a class that implements the `Future` interface and the `Runnable` interface. When you call a method that returns a `Future` object (for example, the `submit()` method), you will normally get a `FutureTask` object. So you can use this class with two objectives:

1. First, execute the `Runnable` object (in this case, a `FileSearch` object).

2. Second, return the results that this task generates. To achieve this, you have overridden the `set()` method of the `Task` class. Internally, the `FutureTask` class controls when the task it has to execute has finished. At that moment, it makes a call to the `set()` method to establish the return value of the task. When you are executing a `Callable` object, this call is made with the value returned by the `call()` method, but when you are executing a `Runnable` object, this call is made with the null value. You have changed this null value with the list of results generated by the `FileSearch` object. The `set()` method will only have effect the first time it is called. When it's called for the first time, it marks the task as finished and the rest of the calls will not modify the return value of the task.

In the `Main` class, instead of sending the `FutureTasks` objects to the `Callable` or `Runnable` objects, you can send it to the executor object. The main difference is that you use the `FutureTasks` objects to get the results of the task instead of the `Future` object returned by the `submit()` method.

In this case, you can still use the `Future` object returned by the `submit()` method to control the status of the task but remember that, as this task executes a `Runnable` object (you have initialized the `FutureTasks` objects with the `FileSearch` objects that implement the `Runnable` interface), if you call the `get()` method in the `Future` objects, you will get the null value.

There's more...

The `FutureTask` class provides a method not included in the `Future` interface. It's the `setException()` method. This method receives a `Throwable` object as the parameter and when the `get()` method is called, an `ExecutionException` exception will be thrown. This call has an effect only if the `set()` method of the `FutureTask` object hasn't been called yet.

See also

-   The *Executing tasks in an executor that returns a result* recipe in `Chapter 4`, *Thread Executors*
-   The *Creating, running, and setting the characteristics of a thread* recipe in `Chapter 1`, *Thread Management*

Processing uncontrolled exceptions in a ForkJoinPool class

The fork/join framework gives you the possibility to set a handler for the exceptions thrown by the worker threads of a `ForkJoinPool` class. When you work with a `ForkJoinPool` class, you should understand the difference between tasks and worker threads.

To work with the fork/join framework, you implement a task extending the `ForkJoinTask` class or, usually, the `RecursiveAction` or `RecursiveTask` classes. The task implements the actions you want to execute concurrently with the framework. They are executed in the `ForkJoinPool` class by the worker threads. A worker thread will execute various tasks. In the work-stealing algorithm implemented by the `ForkJoinPool` class, a worker thread looks for a new task when the task it was executing finishes its execution or it is waiting for the completion of another task.

In this recipe, you will learn how to process the exceptions thrown by a worker thread. You'll have to implement two additional elements for it to work as described in the following items:

- The first element is an extended class of the `ForkJoinWorkerThread` class. This class implements the worker thread of a `ForkJoinPool` class. You will implement a basic child class that will throw an exception.
- The second element is a factory to create worker threads of your own custom type. The `ForkJoinPool` class uses a factory to create its worker threads. You have to implement a class that implements the `ForkJoinWorkerThreadFactory` interface and uses an object of that class in the constructor of the `ForkJoinPool` class. The `ForkJoinPool` object created will use that factory to create worker threads.

How to do it...

Perform the following steps to implement the example:

1. First, implement your own worker thread class. Create a class named `AlwaysThrowsExceptionWorkerThread` that extends the `ForkJoinWorkerThread` class:

```
public class AlwaysThrowsExceptionWorkerThread extends
                ForkJoinWorkerThread {
```

2. Implement the constructor of the class. It receives a `ForkJoinPool` class as a parameter and calls the constructor of its parent class:

```
protected AlwaysThrowsExceptionWorkerThread(ForkJoinPool pool) {
   super(pool);
}
```

3. Implement the `onStart()` method. This is a method of the `ForkJoinWorkerThread` class and is executed when the worker thread begins its execution. The implementation will throw a `RuntimeException` exception upon being called:

```
protected void onStart() {
   super.onStart();
   throw new RuntimeException("Exception from worker thread");
}
```

4. Now, implement the factory needed to create your worker threads. Create a class named `AlwaysThrowsExceptionWorkerThreadFactory` that implements the `ForkJoinWorkerThreadFactory` interface:

```
public class AlwaysThrowsExceptionWorkerThreadFactory implements
                     ForkJoinWorkerThreadFactory {
```

5. Implement the `newThread()` method. It receives a `ForkJoinPool` object as the parameter and returns a `ForkJoinWorkerThread` object. Create an `AlwaysThrowsExceptionWorkerThread` object and return it:

```
@Override
public ForkJoinWorkerThread newThread(ForkJoinPool pool) {
   return new AlwaysThrowsExceptionWorkerThread(pool);
}
```

6. Implement a class that will manage the exceptions thrown by worker threads. Implement a class named `Handler` that implements the `UncaughtExceptionHandler` interface:

```
public class Handler implements UncaughtExceptionHandler {
```

7. Implement the `uncaughtException()` method. It receives as parameters a Thread object and a `Throwable` object and is called by the `ForkJoinPool` class each time a worker thread throws an exception. Write a message to the console and exit the program:

```
@Override
public void uncaughtException(Thread t, Throwable e) {
    System.out.printf("Handler: Thread %s has thrown an
                        Exception.\n",t.getName());
    System.out.printf("%s\n",e);
    System.exit(-1);
}
```

8. Now, implement a task to be executed in the `ForkJoinPool` executor. Create a class named `OneSecondLongTask` that extends the `RecursiveAction` class:

```
public class OneSecondLongTask extends RecursiveAction{
```

9. Implement the `compute()` method. It simply puts the thread to sleep after one second:

```
@Override
protected void compute() {
    System.out.printf("Task: Starting.\n");
    try {
        TimeUnit.SECONDS.sleep(1);
    } catch (InterruptedException e) {
        e.printStackTrace();
    }
    System.out.printf("Task: Finish.\n");
}
```

10. Now, implement the main class of the example. Create a class named Main with a `main()` method:

```
public class Main {
    public static void main(String[] args) {
```

11. Create a new `OneSecondLongTask` object:

```
OneSecondLongTask task=new OneSecondLongTask();
```

12. Create a new Handler object:

```
Handler handler = new Handler();
```

13. Create a new `AlwaysThrowsExceptionWorkerThreadFactory` object:

```
AlwaysThrowsExceptionWorkerThreadFactory factory=new
                    AlwaysThrowsExceptionWorkerThreadFactory();
```

14. Create a new `ForkJoinPool` object. Pass as parameters the value `2`, the factory object, the handler object, and the value `false`:

```
ForkJoinPool pool=new ForkJoinPool(2,factory,handler,false);
```

15. Execute the task in the pool using the `execute()` method:

```
pool.execute(task);
```

16. Shut down the pool with the `shutdown()` method.

```
pool.shutdown();
```

17. Wait for the finalization of the tasks using the `awaitTermination()` method:

```
try {
  pool.awaitTermination(1, TimeUnit.DAYS);
} catch (InterruptedException e) {
  e.printStackTrace();
}
```

18. Write a message indicating the end of the program:

```
System.out.printf("Task: Finish.\n");
```

How it works...

In this recipe, you have implemented the following elements:

- **Your own worker thread class**: You have implemented the `AlwaysThrowsExceptionWorkerThread` class, which extends the `ForkJoinWorkerThread` class, which implements the worker threads of a fork/join pool. You have overridden the `onStart()` method. This method is executed when a worker thread starts its execution. It simply throws an exception `RuntimeException` upon being called.

- **Your own thread factory**: A `ForkJoinPool` class creates its worker threads using a factory. As you want to create a `ForkJoinPool` object that uses the `AlwaysThrowsExceptionWorkerThreadFactory` worker threads, you have implemented a factory that creates them. To implement a worker thread factory, you need to implement the `ForkJoinWorkerThreadFactory` interface. This interface only has a method named `newThread()`, which creates the worker thread and returns it to the `ForkJoinPool` class.
- **A task class**: The worker threads execute the tasks you send to the `ForkJoinPool` executor. As you want to start the execution of a worker thread, you need to send a task to the `ForkJoinPool` executor. The task sleeps for one second, but, as the `AlwaysThrowsExceptionWorkerThread` thread throws an exception, it will never be executed.
- **A handler class for uncaught exceptions**: When a worker thread throws an exception, the `ForkJoinPool` class checks whether an exception handler has been registered. You have implemented the `Handler` class for this purpose. This handler implements the `UncaughtExceptionHandler` interface, which only has one method, that is, the `uncaughtException()` method. This method receives as a parameter the thread that throws the exception and the exception it throws.

In the Main class, you have put together all these elements. You have passed to the constructor of the `ForkJoinPool` class four parameters: the parallelism level, the number of active worker threads you want to have, the worker thread factory you want to use in the `ForkJoinPool` object, the handler you want to use for the uncaught exceptions of the worker threads, and the async mode.

The following screenshot shows the result of an execution of this example:

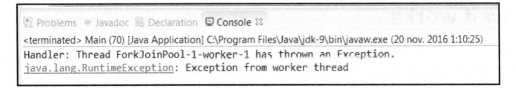

When you execute the program, a worker thread throws a `RuntimeException` exception. The `ForkJoinPool` class hands it over to your handler, which in turn writes the message to the console and exits the program. The task doesn't start its execution.

There's more...

You can test two interesting variants of this example:

- If you comment the following line in the Handler class and execute the program, you will see a lot of messages written in the console. The `ForkJoinPool` class tries to start a worker thread to execute the task and, as it can't because they always throw an exception, it tries it over and over again:

```
System.exit(-1);
```

- Something like that occurs if you change the third parameter (the exception handler) of the `ForkJoinPool` class constructor for the null value. In this case, you will see how the JVM writes the exceptions in the console.

- Take this into account when you implement your own worker threads that could throw exceptions.

See also

- The *Creating a fork/join pool* recipe in `Chapter 5`, *Fork/Join Framework*
- The *Customizing tasks running in the fork/join framework* and *Implementing the ThreadFactory interface to generate custom threads for the fork/join framework* recipes in `Chapter 8`, *Customizing Concurrency Classes*

Using a blocking thread-safe queue for communicating with producers and consumers

The producer/consumer problem is a classical problem in concurrent programming. You have one or more producers of data that store this data in a buffer. You also have one or more consumers of data that take the data from the same buffer. Both producers and consumers share the same buffer, so you have to control access to it to avoid data inconsistency problems. When the buffer is empty, the consumers wait until the buffer has elements. If the buffer is full, the producers wait until the buffer has empty space.

This problem has been implemented using almost all the techniques and synchronization mechanisms developed in Java and in other languages (refer to the *See Also* section to get more information). One advantage of this problem is that it can be extrapolated to a lot of real-world situations.

The Java 7 Concurrency API introduced a data structure oriented to be used in these kinds of problem. It's the `LinkedTransferQueue` class, and its main characteristics are as follows:

- It's a blocking data structure. The thread is blocked until the operation can be made, provided that the operations are performed immediately.
- Its size has no limit. You can insert as many elements as you want.
- It's a parameterized class. You have to indicate the class of the elements you're going to store in the list.

In this recipe, you will learn how to use the `LinkedTransferQueue` class running a lot of producer and consumer tasks that share a buffer of strings.

Getting ready

The example of this recipe has been implemented using the Eclipse IDE. If you use Eclipse or any other IDE such as NetBeans, open it and create a new Java project.

How to do it...

Perform the following steps to implement the example:

1. Create a class named `Producer` and specify that it implements the `Runnable` interface:

   ```
   public class Producer implements Runnable {
   ```

2. Declare a private `LinkedTransferQueue` attribute parameterized with the `String` class named buffer:

   ```
   private LinkedTransferQueue<String> buffer;
   ```

3. Declare a private `String` attribute named name to store the name of the producer:

```
private String name;
```

4. Implement the constructor of the class to initialize its attributes:

```
public Producer(String name, LinkedTransferQueue<String> buffer){
    this.name=name;
    this.buffer=buffer;
}
```

5. Implement the `run()` method. Store `10,000` strings in the buffer using the `put()` method of the buffer object and write a message to the console indicating the end of the method:

```
@Override
public void run() {
    for (int i=0; i<10000; i++) {
        buffer.put(name+": Element "+i);
    }
    System.out.printf("Producer: %s: Producer done\n",name);
}
```

6. Implement a class named `Consumer` and specify that it implements the `Runnable` interface:

```
public class Consumer implements Runnable {
```

7. Declare a private `LinkedTransferQueue` attribute parameterized with the `String` class named buffer:

```
private LinkedTransferQueue<String> buffer;
```

8. Declare a private `String` attribute named name to store the name of the consumer:

```
private String name;
```

9. Implement the constructor of the class to initialize its attributes:

```
public Consumer(String name, LinkedTransferQueue<String> buffer){
    this.name=name;
    this.buffer=buffer;
}
```

10. Implement the `run()` method. Take out 10,000 strings from the buffer using the `take()` method of the buffer object and write a message to the console indicating the end of the method:

```
@Override
public void run() {
   for (int i=0; i<10000; i++){
     try {
       buffer.take();
     } catch (InterruptedException e) {
       e.printStackTrace();
     }
   }
   System.out.printf("Consumer: %s: Consumer done\n",name);
}
```

11. Implement the main class of the example. Create a class named `Main` and add to it the `main()` method:

```
public class Main {
   public static void main(String[] args) {
```

12. Declare a constant named `THREADS` and assign to it the value `100`. Create a `LinkedTransferQueue` object with the `String` class object and call it buffer:

```
final int THREADS=100;
LinkedTransferQueue<String> buffer=new LinkedTransferQueue<>();
```

13. Create an array of 100 Thread objects to execute 100 producer tasks:

```
Thread producerThreads[]=new Thread[THREADS];
```

14. Create an array of 100 Thread objects to execute 100 consumer tasks:

```
Thread consumerThreads[]=new Thread[THREADS];
```

15. Create and launch 100 `Consumer` objects and store the threads in the array created earlier:

```
for (int i=0; i<THREADS; i++){
   Consumer consumer=new Consumer("Consumer "+i,buffer);
   consumerThreads[i]=new Thread(consumer);
   consumerThreads[i].start();
}
```

16. Create and launch 100 `Producer` objects and store the threads in the array created earlier:

```
for (int i=0; i<THREADS; i++) {
    Producer producer=new Producer("Producer: "+ i , buffer);
    producerThreads[i]=new Thread(producer);
    producerThreads[i].start();
}
```

17. Wait for the finalization of the threads using the `join()` method:

```
for (int i=0; i<THREADS; i++){
    try {
        producerThreads[i].join();
        consumerThreads[i].join();
    } catch (InterruptedException e) {
        e.printStackTrace();
    }
}
```

18. Write a message to the console with the size of the buffer:

```
System.out.printf("Main: Size of the buffer: %d\n",
                  buffer.size());
System.out.printf("Main: End of the example\n");
```

How it works...

In this recipe, you have used the `LinkedTransferQueue` class parameterized with the String class to implement the producer/consumer problem. This `LinkedTransferQueue` class is used as a buffer to share the data between producers and consumers.

You have implemented a `Producer` class that adds strings to the buffer using the `put()` method. You have executed 100 producers and every producer inserts in the buffer 10,000 strings, so you insert 1,000,000 strings in the buffer. The `put()` method adds the element at the end of the buffer.

You also have implemented a `Consumer` class, which gets a string from the buffer using the `take()` method. This method returns and deletes the first element of the buffer. If the buffer is empty, the method blocks the thread that makes the call until there are strings in the buffer to consume. You have executed 100 consumers, and every consumer gets 10,000 strings from the buffer.

In the example, first, you have launched the consumers and then the producers, so, as the buffer is empty, all the consumers will be blocked until the producers begin their execution and stores strings in the list.

The following screenshot shows part of the output of an execution of this example:

```
Problems   Javadoc   Declaration   Console ⅔
<terminated> Main (71) [Java Application] C:\Program Files\Java\jdk-9\bin\javaw.exe (20 nov. 2016 1:22:08)
Producer: Producer: 62: Producer done
Producer: Producer: 60: Producer done
Producer: Producer: 57: Producer done
Main: Size of the buffer: 0
Main: End of the example
```

To write the number of elements of the buffer, you have used the `size()` method. You have to take into account that this method can return a value that is not real, if you use them when there are threads adding or deleting data in the list. The method has to traverse the entire list to count the elements and the contents of the list can change for this operation. Only if you use them when there aren't any threads modifying the list, you will have the guarantee that the returned result is correct.

There's more...

The `LinkedTransferQueue` class provides other useful methods. The following are some of them:

- `getWaitingConsumerCount()`: This method returns the number of consumers that are blocked in the `take()` method or `poll (long timeout, TimeUnit unit)` because the `LinkedTransferQueue` object is empty.
- `hasWaitingConsumer()`: This method returns `true` if the `LinkedTransferQueue` object has consumers waiting, or false otherwise.
- `offer(E e)`: This method adds the element passed as a parameter at the end of the `LinkedTransferQueue` object and returns the true value. E represents the class used to parameterize the declaration of the `LinkedTransferQueue` class or a subclass of it.

- `peek()`: This method returns the first element in the `LinkedTransferQueue` object, but it doesn't delete it from the list. If the queue is empty, the method returns the null value.
- `poll(long timeout, TimeUnit unit)`: This version of the poll method, if the `LinkedTransferQueue` buffer is empty, waits for it for a specified period of time. If the specified period of time passes and the buffer is still empty, the method returns a `null` value. The `TimeUnit` class is an enumeration with the following constants-DAYS, HOURS, MICROSECONDS, MILLISECONDS, MINUTES, NANOSECONDS, and SECONDS.

See also

- The *Using conditions in synchronized code* recipe in `Chapter 2`, *Basic Thread Synchronization*
- The *Exchanging data between concurrent tasks* recipe in `Chapter 3`, *Thread Synchronization Utilities*

Monitoring a Thread class

Threads are the most basic element of the Java Concurrency API. Every Java program has at least one thread that executes the `main()` method, which, in turn, starts the execution of the application. When you launch a new `Thread` class, it's executed in parallel with the other threads of the application and with the other processes on an operating system. There is a critical difference between process and thread. A process is an instance of an application that is running (for example, you're editing a document in a text processor). This process has one or more threads that execute the tasks that make the process. You can be running more than one process of the same application, for example, two instances of the text processor. Threads inside a process share the memory while processes of the same OS don't.

All the kinds of Java tasks that you can execute (`Runnable`, `Callable`, or fork/join tasks) are executed in threads, and all the advanced Java concurrency mechanisms, such as the `Executor` framework and the fork/join framework, are based on pools of threads.

In this recipe, you will learn what information you can obtain about the status of a `Thread` class and how to obtain it.

Getting ready

The example of this recipe has been implemented using the Eclipse IDE. If you use Eclipse or any other IDE such as NetBeans, open it and create a new Java project.

How to do it...

Perform the following steps to implement the example:

1. Create a class named `Task` that implements the `Runnable` interface:

    ```
    public class Task implements Runnable {
    ```

2. Implement the `run()` method of the task:

    ```
    @Override
    public void run() {
    ```

3. Create a loop with 100 steps:

    ```
    for (int i=0; i<100; i++) {
    ```

4. In each step, put the thread to sleep for 100 milliseconds:

    ```
    try {
       TimeUnit.MILLISECONDS.sleep(100);
    } catch (InterruptedException e) {
       e.printStackTrace();
    }
    ```

5. Write a message in the console with the name of the thread and the step number:

    ```
    System.out.printf("%s: %d\n",Thread.currentThread()
                                    .getName(),i);
            }
        }
    }
    ```

6. Create the main class of the example. Create a class named `Main` with a `main()` method:

    ```
    public class Main {
       public static void main(String[] args) throws Exception{
    ```

7. Create a `Task` object named task:

```
Task task = new Task();
```

8. Create a `Thread` array with five elements:

```
Thread threads[] = new Thread[5];
```

9. Create and start five threads to execute the `Task` object created earlier:

```
for (int i = 0; i < 5; i++) {
    threads[i] = new Thread(task);
    threads[i].setPriority(i + 1);
    threads[i].start();
}
```

10. Create a loop with ten steps to write information about the threads launched before. Inside it, create another loop with five steps:

```
for (int j = 0; j < 10; j++) {
    System.out.printf("Main: Logging threads\n");
    for (int i = 0; i < threads.length; i++) {
```

11. For each thread, write its name, its status, its group, and the length of its stack trace in the console:

```
System.out.printf("**********************\n");
System.out.printf("Main: %d: Id: %d Name: %s: Priority: %d\n",i,
                threads[i].getId(),threads[i].getName(),
                threads[i].getPriority());
System.out.printf("Main: Status: %s\n",threads[i].getState());
System.out.printf("Main: Thread Group: %s\n",
                threads[i].getThreadGroup());
System.out.printf("Main: Stack Trace: \n");
```

12. Write a loop to write the stack trace of the thread:

```
for (int t=0; t<threads[i].getStackTrace().length; t++) {
    System.out.printf("Main: %s\n",threads[i].getStackTrace()
                [t]);
}
System.out.printf("**********************\n");
}
```

13. Put the thread to sleep for one second and close the loop and the class:

```
TimeUnit.SECONDS.sleep(1);
        }
    }
}
```

How it works...

In this recipe, you have used the following methods to get information about a `Thread` class:

- `getId()`: This method returns the ID of a thread. It's a unique long number and it can't be changed.
- `getName()`: This method returns the name of a thread. If you don't establish the name of the thread, Java gives it a default name.
- `getPriority()`: This method returns the priority of execution of a thread. Threads with higher priority are executed in preference to threads with lower priority. It's an int value that has a value between the MIN_PRIORITY and MAX_PRIORITY constants of the `Thread` class. By default, threads are created with the same priority that specified by the constant NORM_PRIORITY of the `Thread` class.
- `getState()`: This method returns the status of a thread. It's a `Thread.State` object. The `Thread.State` enumeration has all the possible states of a thread.
- `getThreadGroup()`: This method returns the `ThreadGroup` object of a thread. By default, threads belong to the same thread group, but you can establish a different one in the constructor of a thread.
- `getStackTrace()`: This method returns an array of `StackTraceElement` objects. Each of these objects represent a call to a method that begins with the `run()` method of a thread and includes all the methods that have been called until the actual execution point. When a new method is called, a new stack trace element is added to the array. When a method finishes its execution, its stack trace element is removed from the array.

There's more...

The Thread class includes other methods that provide information about it that can be useful. These methods are as follows:

- activeCount(): This method returns the number of active threads in a group of threads.
- dumpStack(): This method prints the stack trace of a thread to the standard error output.

See also

- The *Creating, running, and setting the characteristics of a thread* recipe in Chapter 1, *Thread Management*
- The *Using a ThreadFactory interface in an Executor framework* and *Implementing a ThreadFactory interface to generate custom threads for the fork/join framework* recipes in Chapter 8, *Customizing Concurrency Classes*

Monitoring a Semaphore class

A semaphore is a counter that protects the access to one or more shared resources.

The concept of semaphore was introduced by Edsgar Dijkstra in 1965 and was used for the first time in the THEOS operating system.

When a thread wants to use shared resources, it must acquire a semaphore. If the internal counter of the semaphore is greater than 0, the semaphore decrements the counter and allows the access to the shared resource. If the counter of the semaphore is 0, the semaphore blocks the thread until the counter is greater than 0. When the thread has finished using the shared resource, it must release the semaphore. That operation increases the internal counter of the semaphore.

In Java, semaphores are implemented in the Semaphore class.

In this recipe, you will learn what information you can obtain about the status of a semaphore and how to obtain it.

Getting ready

The example of this recipe has been implemented using the Eclipse IDE. If you use Eclipse or any other IDE such as NetBeans, open it and create a new Java project.

How to do it...

Perform the following steps to implement the example:

1. Create a class named `Task` that implements the `Runnable` interface:

```
public class Task implements Runnable {
```

2. Declare a private `Semaphore` attribute named `semaphore`:

```
private final Semaphore semaphore;
```

3. Implement the constructor of the class to initialize its attribute:

```
public Task(Semaphore semaphore){
    this.semaphore=semaphore;
}
```

4. Implement the `run()` method. First, acquire permit for the `semaphore` attribute writing a message in the console to indicate that circumstance:

```
@Override
public void run() {
  try {
    semaphore.acquire();
    System.out.printf("%s: Get the semaphore.\n",
                    Thread.currentThread().getName());
```

5. Then, put the thread to sleep for two seconds using the `sleep()` method. Finally, release the permit and write a message in the console to indicate that circumstance:

```
    TimeUnit.SECONDS.sleep(2);
    System.out.println(Thread.currentThread().getName()+":
                    Release the semaphore.");
  } catch (InterruptedException e) {
    e.printStackTrace();
  } finally {
    semaphore.release();
  }
```

6. Implement the main class of the example. Create a class named `Main` with a `main()` method:

```
public class Main {
    public static void main(String[] args) throws Exception {
```

7. Create a `Semaphore` object named `semaphore` with three permits:

```
Semaphore semaphore=new Semaphore(3);
```

8. Create an array to store 10 `Thread` objects:

```
Thread threads[]=new Thread[10];
```

9. Create and start 10 `Thread` objects to execute 10 `Task` objects. After starting a thread, put the thread to sleep for 200 milliseconds and call the `showLog()` method to write information about the `Semaphore` class:

```
for (int i=0; i<threads.length; i++) {
    Task task=new Task(semaphore);
    threads[i]=new Thread(task);
    threads[i].start();

    TimeUnit.MILLISECONDS.sleep(200);

    showLog(semaphore);
}
```

10. Implement a loop with five steps to call the `showLog()` method to write information about the `semaphore` and put the thread to sleep for 1 second:

```
        for (int i=0; i<5; i++) {
            showLog(semaphore);
            TimeUnit.SECONDS.sleep(1);
        }
    }
```

11. Implement the `showLog()` method. It receives a `Semaphore` object as parameter. Write in the console information about the available permits, queued threads, and permits of the `semaphore`:

```
private static void showLog(Semaphore semaphore) {
    System.out.printf("********************\n");
    System.out.printf("Main: Semaphore Log\n");
    System.out.printf("Main: Semaphore: Avalaible Permits: %d\n",
                    semaphore.availablePermits());
```

```
System.out.printf("Main: Semaphore: Queued Threads: %s\n",
                  semaphore.hasQueuedThreads());
System.out.printf("Main: Semaphore: Queue Length: %d\n",
                  semaphore.getQueueLength());
System.out.printf("Main: Semaphore: Fairness: %s\n",
                  semaphore.isFair());
System.out.printf("********************\n");
}
```

How it works...

In this recipe, you have used the following methods to get information about a `semaphore`:

- `availablePermits()`: This method returns an `int` value, which is the number of available resources of a semaphore.
- `hasQueuedThreads()`: This method returns a Boolean value indicating if there are threads waiting for a resource protected by a semaphore.
- `getQueueLength()`: This method returns the number of threads that are waiting for a resource protected by a semaphore.
- `isFair()`: This method returns a Boolean value indicating if a semaphore has the fair mode activated. When the fair mode is active (this method returns the true value), and the lock has to select another thread to give to it the access to the shared resource, it selects the longest-waiting thread. If the fair mode is inactive (this method returns the false value), there is no guarantee about the order in which threads are selected to get the access to the shared resource.

See also

- The *Controlling concurrent access to one or more copies of a resource* recipes in Chapter 3, *Thread Synchronization Utilities*

Generating concurrent random numbers

The Java concurrency API provides a specific class to generate pseudorandom numbers in concurrent applications. It's the `ThreadLocalRandom` class and it's new in Java 7 version. It works as the thread's local variables. Every thread that wants to generate random numbers has a different generator, but all of them are managed from the same class, in a transparent way to the programmer. With this mechanism, you will get a better performance than using a shared Random object to generate the random numbers of all the threads.

In this recipe, you will learn how to use the `ThreadLocalRandom` class to generate random numbers in a concurrent application.

Getting ready

The example of this recipe has been implemented using the Eclipse IDE. If you use Eclipse or any other IDE such as NetBeans, open it and create a new Java project.

How to do it...

Follow these steps to implement the example:

1. Create a class named `TaskLocalRandom` and specify that it implements the `Runnable` interface:

   ```
   public class TaskLocalRandom implements Runnable {
   ```

2. Implement the `run()` method. Get the name of the thread that is executing this task and write 10 random integer numbers to the console using the `nextInt()` method:

   ```
   @Override
   public void run() {
     String name=Thread.currentThread().getName();
     for (int i=0; i<10; i++){
       System.out.printf("%s: %d\n",name,
                       ThreadLocalRandom.current().nextInt(10));
     }
   }
   ```

3. Implement the main class of the example by creating a class named `Main` and add the `main()` method to it:

```
public class Main {
    public static void main(String[] args) {
```

4. Create an array for three `Thread` objects:

```
Thread threads[]=new Thread[3];
```

5. Create and launch three `TaskLocalRandom` tasks. Store the threads in the array created earlier:

```
for (int i=0; i<3; i++) {
  TaskLocalRandom task=new TaskLocalRandom();
  threads[i]=new Thread(task);
  threads[i].start();
}
```

How it works...

The key of this example is in the `TaskLocalRandom` class. In the constructor of the class, we make a call to the `current()` method of the `ThreadLocalRandom` class. This is a static method that returns the `ThreadLocalRandom` object associated with the current thread, so you can generate random numbers using that object. If the thread that makes the call does not have any object associated yet, the class creates a new one. In this case, you use this method to initialize the random generator associated with this task, so it will be created in the next call to the method.

In the `run()` method of the `TaskLocalRandom` class, make a call to the `current()` method to get the random generator associated with this thread, also you make a call to the `nextInt()` method passing the number 10 as the parameter. This method will return a pseudo random number between 0 and 10. Each task generates 10 random numbers.

There's more...

The `ThreadLocalRandom` class also provides methods to generate long, float, and double numbers, and Boolean values. There are methods that allow you to provide a number as a parameter to generate random numbers between zero and that number. The other methods allow you to provide two parameters to generate random numbers between these numbers.

See also

The *Using local thread variables* recipe in `Chapter 1`, *Thread management*

11

Concurrent Programming Design

In this chapter, we will cover the following topics:

- Using immutable objects when possible
- Avoiding deadlocks by ordering locks
- Using atomic variables instead of synchronization
- Holding locks for as short time as possible
- Delegating the management of threads to executors
- Using concurrent data structures instead of programming yourselves
- Taking precautions using lazy initialization
- Using the fork/join framework instead of executors
- Avoiding the use of blocking operations inside a lock
- Avoiding the use of deprecated methods
- Using executors instead of thread groups
- Using streams to process big data sets
- Other tips and tricks

Introduction

Implementing a concurrent application is a difficult task. You have more than one thread in an execution at a time and all of them share resources, such as files, memory, objects, and so on. You have to be very careful with the design decisions you take. A bad decision can affect your program in a way that it would lead to poor performance or simply provoke data inconsistency situations.

In this chapter, I've included some suggestions to help you take correct design decisions, which would make your concurrent application better.

Using immutable objects when possible

When you develop an application in Java using object-oriented programming, you create some classes formed by attributes and methods. The methods of a class determine the operations that you can do with the class. Attributes store the data that defines the object. Normally, in each class, you implement some methods to establish the value of the attributes. Also, objects change as the application runs, and you use those methods to change the value of their attributes.

When you develop a concurrent application, you have to pay special attention to the objects shared by more than one thread. You must use a synchronization mechanism to protect access to such objects. If you don't use it, you may have data inconsistency problems in your application.

There are special kinds of objects that you can implement when you work with concurrent applications. They are called **immutable objects**; their main characteristic is that they can't be modified after they are created. If you need to change an immutable object, you must create a new one instead of changing the values of the attributes of the object.

This mechanism presents the following advantages when you use them in concurrent applications:

- These objects cannot be modified by any thread once they are created, so you won't need to use any synchronization mechanism to protect access to their attributes.
- You won't have any data inconsistency problems. As the attributes of these objects cannot be modified, you will always have access to a coherent copy of the data.

The only drawback of this approach is the overhead: creating new objects instead of modifying existing ones.

Java provides some immutable classes, such as the String class. When you have a String object and you try to assign a new value to it, you are creating a new String object instead of modifying the old value of the object. For example, check out the following code:

```
String var = "hello";
var = "new";
```

In the second line, JVM creates a new `String` object.

Getting ready

The example of this recipe has been implemented using the Eclipse IDE. If you use Eclipse or a different IDE, such as NetBeans, open it and create a new Java project.

How to do it...

Follow these steps to implement an immutable class:

1. Mark the class as `final`. It should not be extended by another class.
2. All the attributes must be `final` and `private`. You can assign a value to an attribute only once.
3. Don't provide methods that can assign a value to an attribute. Attributes must be initialized in the constructor of the class.
4. If any field value object is mutable (for example, `java.util.Date`), always return a defensive copy in the getter field.
5. Don't leak the `this` reference from the immutable class constructor (for example, the following code that leaks the `this` reference before the constructor is complete):

```
public final NotSoImmutable implements Listener {
  private final int x;
  public NotSoImmutable(int x, Observable o) {
    this.x = x;
    o.registerListener(this);
  }
}
```

How it works...

If you want to implement a class that stores the first and last name of a person, you would normally implement something like this:

```
public class PersonMutable {
  private String firstName;
  private String lastName;
  private Date birthDate;
```

```
      public String getFirstName() {
        return firstName;
      }

      public void setFirstName(String firstName) {
        this.firstName = firstName;
      }

      public String getLastName() {
        return lastName;
      }

      public void setLastName(String lastName) {
        this.lastName = lastName;
      }
      public Date getBirthDate() {
        return birthDate;
      }

      public void setBirthDate(Date birthDate) {
        this.birthDate = birthDate;
      }


}
```

You can convert this class into an immutable class by following the rules explained earlier. The following is the result:

```
public final class PersonImmutable {

    final private String firstName;
    final private String lastName;
    final private Date birthDate;

    public PersonImmutable (String firstName, String lastName,
                            String address, Date birthDate) {
      this.firstName=firstName;
      this.lastName=lastName;
      this.birthDate=birthDate;
    }

    public String getFirstName() {
      return firstName;
    }

    public String getLastName() {
      return lastName;
    }
```

```
public Date getBirthDate() {
  return new Date(birthDate.getTime());
}

}
```

Essentially, you followed the basic principles of an immutable class, which are as follows:

- The class is marked as `final`.
- The attributes are marked as `final` and `private`.
- The value of the attributes can only be established in the constructor of the class. Its methods return the value of an attribute, but they don't modify them.
- For mutable attributes (the `birthDate` attribute in our case), we return a defensive copy of the `get()` method by creating a new object.

There's more...

Immutable objects can't always be used. Analyze each class of your application to decide whether you can implement them as immutable objects or not. If you can't implement a class as an immutable class and its objects are shared by more than one thread, you must use a synchronization mechanism to protect access to the attributes of the class.

See also

- The *Using atomic variables instead of synchronization* recipe in this chapter

Avoiding deadlocks by ordering locks

When you need to acquire more than one lock in the methods of your application, you must be very careful with the order in which you get control of your locks. A bad choice can lead to a deadlock situation.

In this recipe, you will implement an example of a deadlock situation, then learn how to solve it.

How to do it...

Follow these steps to implement the example:

1. Create a class named `BadLocks` with two methods, named `operation1()` and `operation2()`:

```java
public class BadLocks {

    private Lock lock1, lock2;

    public BadLocks(Lock lock1, Lock lock2) {
        this.lock1=lock1;
        this.lock2=lock2;
    }

    public void operation1(){
        lock1.lock();
        lock2.lock();

        try {
            TimeUnit.SECONDS.sleep(2);
        } catch (InterruptedException e) {
            e.printStackTrace();
        } finally {
            lock2.unlock();
            lock1.unlock();
        }
    }

    public void operation2(){
        lock2.lock();
        lock1.lock();

        try {
            TimeUnit.SECONDS.sleep(2);
        } catch (InterruptedException e) {
            e.printStackTrace();
        } finally {
            lock1.unlock();
            lock2.unlock();
        }
    }

}
```

2. Let's analyze the preceding code. If a thread calls the `operation1()` method and another thread calls the `operation2()` method, you can have a deadlock. If both `operation1()` and `operation2()` execute their respective first sentences at the same time, you will have the `operation1()` method waiting to get control of `lock2` and the `operation2()` method waiting to get control of `lock1`. Now you have a deadlock situation.

3. To solve this situation, you can follow this rule:

   - If you have to get control of more than one lock in different operations, try to lock them in the same order in all methods.
   - Then, release them in inverse order and encapsulate the locks and their unlocks in a single class. This is so that you don't have synchronization-related code distributed throughout the code.

How it works...

Using this rule, you will avoid deadlock situations. For example, in the case presented earlier, you can change `operation2()` to first get `lock1` and then `lock2`. Now if both `operation1()` and `operation2()` execute their respective first sentences, one of them will be blocked waiting for `lock1` and the other will get `lock1` and `lock2` and they will do their operations. After this, the blocked thread will get the `lock1` and `lock2` locks and it will do its operation.

There's more...

You can find a situation where a requirement prevents you from getting the locks in the same order in all the operations. In this situation, you can use the `tryLock()` method of the `Lock` class. This method returns a `Boolean` value to indicate whether you have control of the lock. You can try to get all the locks that you need to do the operation using the `tryLock()` method. If you can't get control of one of the locks, you must release all the locks that you may have had and start the operation again.

See also

- The *Holding locks for as short a time period as possible* recipe in this chapter

Using atomic variables instead of synchronization

When you have to share data between multiple threads, you have to protect access to that piece of data using a synchronization mechanism. You can use the `synchronized` keyword in the declaration of the method that modifies the data so that only one thread can modify data at a time. Another possibility is the utilization of a `Lock` class to create a critical section with instructions that modify data.

Since version 5, Java includes atomic variables. When a thread is doing an operation with an atomic variable, the implementation of the class includes a mechanism to check that the operation is done in one step. Basically, the operation gets the value of the variable, changes the value in a local variable, and then tries to change the old value with the new one. If the old value is still the same, it does the change. If not, the method begins the operation again. Java provides the following types of atomic variables:

- AtomicBoolean
- AtomicInteger
- AtomicLong
- AtomicReference

In some cases, Java's atomic variables offer a better performance than solutions based on synchronization mechanisms (specially when we care about atomicity within each separate variable). Some classes of the `java.util.concurrent` package use atomic variables instead of synchronization. In this recipe, you will develop an example that shows how an atomic attribute provides better performance than synchronization.

Getting ready

The example of this recipe has been implemented using the Eclipse IDE. If you use Eclipse or a different IDE, such as NetBeans, open it and create a new Java project.

How to do it...

Follow these steps to implement the example:

1. Create a class named `TaskAtomic` and specify that it implements the `Runnable` interface:

   ```
   public class TaskAtomic implements Runnable {
   ```

2. Declare a private `AtomicInteger` attribute named `number`:

   ```
   private final AtomicInteger number;
   ```

3. Implement the constructor of the class to initialize its attributes:

   ```
   public TaskAtomic () {
      this.number=new AtomicInteger();
   }
   ```

4. Implement the `run()` method. In a loop with 1,000,000 steps, assign the number of steps to the atomic attribute as a value, using the `set()` method:

   ```
   @Override
   public void run() {
      for (int i=0; i<1000000; i++) {
        number.set(i);
      }
   }
   ```

5. Create a class named `TaskLock` and specify that it implements the `Runnable` interface:

   ```
   public class TaskLock implements Runnable {
   ```

6. Declare a private `int` attribute named `number` and a private `Lock` attribute named `lock`:

   ```
   private Lock lock;
   private int number;
   ```

7. Implement the constructor of the class to initialize its attributes:

   ```
   public TaskLock() {
      this.lock=new ReentrantLock();
   }
   ```

8. Implement the `run()` method. In a loop with 1,000,000 steps, assign the number of the steps to the integer attribute. You have to get the lock before the assignment and release it after:

```
@Override
public void run() {
    for (int i=0; i<1000000; i++) {
        lock.lock();
        number=i;
        lock.unlock();
    }

}
```

9. Implement the main class of the example by creating a class named `Main` and adding the `main()` method to it:

```
public class Main {
    public static void main(String[] args) {
```

10. Create a `TaskAtomic` object named `atomicTask`:

```
TaskAtomic atomicTask=new TaskAtomic();
```

11. Create a `TaskLock` object named `lockTask`:

```
TaskLock lockTask=new TaskLock();
```

12. Declare the number of threads and create an array of `Thread` objects to store the threads:

```
int numberThreads=50;
Thread threads[]=new Thread[numberThreads];
Date begin, end;
```

13. Launch the specified number of threads to execute the `TaskLock` object. Calculate and write its execution time in the console:

```
begin=new Date();
for (int i=0; i<numberThreads; i++) {
    threads[i]=new Thread(lockTask);
    threads[i].start();
}
```

```
for (int i=0; i<numberThreads; i++) {
  try {
    threads[i].join();
  } catch (InterruptedException e) {
    e.printStackTrace();
  }
}
end=new Date();

System.out.printf("Main: Lock results: %d\n",
                  (end.getTime()-begin.getTime()));
```

14. Launch the specified number of threads to execute the `TaskAtomic` object. Calculate and write its execution time in the console:

```
begin=new Date();
for (int i=0; i<numberThreads; i++) {
  threads[i]=new Thread(atomicTask);
  threads[i].start();
}

for (int i=0; i<numberThreads; i++) {
  try {
    threads[i].join();
  } catch (InterruptedException e) {
    e.printStackTrace();
  }
}
end=new Date();

System.out.printf("Main: Atomic results: %d\n",
                  (end.getTime()-begin.getTime()));
```

How it works...

When you execute the example, you will see how the execution time of the `TaskAtomic` tasks that use atomic variables are always better than the `TaskLock` tasks that use locks. You will obtain a similar result if you use the `synchronized` keyword instead of locks.

The conclusion of this recipe is that utilization of atomic variables will give you better performance than other synchronization methods. If you don't have an atomic type that fits your needs, maybe you can try to implement your own atomic type.

See also

- The *Implementing your own atomic object* recipe in Chapter 8, *Customizing Concurrency Classes*

Holding locks for as short time as possible

Locks, just like other synchronization mechanisms, allow the definition of a critical section that only one thread can execute at a time. You must be very careful to define the critical section. It must only include those instructions that really need mutual exclusion. This is especially true if the critical section includes long operations. If the critical section includes lengthy operations that do not use shared resources, application performance will be worse than it could be.

In this recipe, you will implement an example to see the difference in the performance of a task with a long operation inside the critical section and a task with a long operation outside the critical section.

Getting ready

The example of this recipe has been implemented using the Eclipse IDE. If you use Eclipse or a different IDE, such as NetBeans, open it and create a new Java project.

How to do it...

Follow these steps to implement the example:

1. Create a class named `Operations`:

   ```
   public class Operations {
   ```

2. Implement a `public static` method named `readData()`. It puts the current thread to sleep for 500 milliseconds:

   ```
   public static void readData(){
     try {
       TimeUnit.MILLISECONDS.sleep(500);
     } catch (InterruptedException e) {
       e.printStackTrace();
   ```

```
    }
  }
```

3. Implement a `public static` method named `writeData()`. It puts the current thread to sleep for 500 milliseconds:

```
public static void writeData(){
  try {
    TimeUnit.MILLISECONDS.sleep(500);
  } catch (InterruptedException e) {
    e.printStackTrace();
  }
}
```

4. Implement a `public static` method named `processData()`. It puts the current thread to sleep for 2,000 milliseconds:

```
public static void processData(){
  try {
    TimeUnit.SECONDS.sleep(2);
  } catch (InterruptedException e) {
    e.printStackTrace();
  }
}
```

5. Implement a class named `Task1` and specify that it implements the `Runnable` interface:

```
public class Task1 implements Runnable {
```

6. Declare a private `Lock` attribute named `lock`:

```
private final Lock lock;
```

7. Implement the constructor of the class to initialize its attributes:

```
public Task1 (Lock lock) {
  this.lock=lock;
}
```

8. Implement the `run()` method. Acquire the lock, call the three operations of the `Operations` class, and release the lock:

```
@Override
public void run() {
  lock.lock();
  Operations.readData();
```

```
       Operations.processData();
       Operations.writeData();
       lock.unlock();
    }
```

9. Implement a class named `Task2` and specify that it implements the `Runnable` interface:

```
public class Task2 implements Runnable {
```

10. Declare a private `Lock` attribute named `lock`:

```
private final Lock lock;
```

11. Implement the constructor of the class to initialize its attributes:

```
public Task2 (Lock lock) {
    this.lock=lock;
}
```

12. Implement the `run()` method. Acquire the lock, call the `readData()` operation, and release the lock. Then, call the `processData()` method, acquire the lock, call the `writeData()` operation, and release the lock:

```
@Override
public void run() {
    lock.lock();
    Operations.readData();
    lock.unlock();
    Operations.processData();
    lock.lock();
    Operations.writeData();
    lock.unlock();
}
```

13. Implement the main class of the example by creating a class named `Main` and adding the `main()` method to it:

```
public class Main {

    public static void main(String[] args) {
```

14. Create a `Lock` object named `lock`, a `Task1` object named `task1`, a `Task2` object named `task2`, and an array of 10 threads:

```
Lock lock=new ReentrantLock();
Task1 task1=new Task1(lock);
Task2 task2=new Task2(lock);
Thread threads[]=new Thread[10];
```

15. Launch 10 threads to execute the first task by controlling its execution time:

```
Date begin, end;

begin=new Date();
for (int i=0; i<threads.length; i++) {
  threads[i]=new Thread(task1);
  threads[i].start();
}

for (int i=0; i<threads.length; i++) {
  try {
    threads[i].join();
  } catch (InterruptedException e) {
    e.printStackTrace();
  }
}
end=new Date();
System.out.printf("Main: First Approach: %d\n",
                  (end.getTime()-begin.getTime()));
```

16. Launch 10 threads to execute the second task by controlling its execution time:

```
begin=new Date();
for (int i=0; i<threads.length; i++) {
  threads[i]=new Thread(task2);
  threads[i].start();
}

for (int i=0; i<threads.length; i++) {
  try {
    threads[i].join();
  } catch (InterruptedException e) {
    e.printStackTrace();
  }
}
end=new Date();
System.out.printf("Main: Second Approach: %d\n",
                  (end.getTime()-begin.getTime()));
```

How it works...

If you execute the example, you will see a big difference between the execution time of the two approaches. The task that has all the operations inside the critical section takes longer than the other task.

When you need to implement a block of code protected by a lock, analyze it carefully to only include necessary instructions. Split the method into various critical sections, and use more than one lock if necessary to get the best performance of your application.

See also

- The *Avoiding deadlocks by ordering locks* recipe in this chapter

Delegating the management of threads to executors

Before Java 5, the Java Concurrency API, when we wanted to implement a concurrent application, we had to manage the threads by ourselves. First we used to implement the `Runnable` interface or an extension of the `Thread` class. Then, we used to create a `thread` object and start its execution using its `start()` method. We also had to control its status to know whether the thread had finished its execution or was still running.

In Java version 5, the concept of executor as a provider of a pool of execution threads appeared. This mechanism, implemented by the `Executor` and `ExecutorService` interfaces and the `ThreadPoolExecutor` and `ScheduledThreadPoolExecutor` classes, allows you to concentrate only on the implementation of the logic of the task. You implement the task and send it to the executor. It has a pool of threads, and it is this pool that is responsible for the creation, management, and finalization of the threads. In Java version 7, another implementation of the executor mechanism in the fork/join framework, specialized in problems that can be broken down into smaller subproblems, appeared. This approach has numerous advantages, which are as follows:

- We don't have to create threads for all the tasks. When we send a task to the executor and it's executed by a thread of the pool, we save the time used in creating a new thread. If our application has to execute a lot of tasks, the total saved time will be significant and the performance of the application will be better.

- If we create fewer threads, our application will use less memory as well. This can also extract better performance from our application.
- We can build concurrent tasks executed in the executor by implementing either the `Runnable` or `Callable` interface. The `Callable` interface allows us to implement tasks that return a result, which provide a big advantage over traditional tasks.
- When we send a task to an executor, it returns a `Future` object that allows us to know the status of the task and the returned result, whether it has finished its execution easily.
- We can schedule our tasks and execute them repeatedly with the special executor implemented by the `ScheduledThreadPoolExecutor` class.
- We can easily control the resources used by an executor. We can establish the maximum number of threads in the pool, so our executor will never have more than that number of tasks running at a time.

The use of executors has a lot of advantages over direct utilization of threads. In this recipe, you are going to implement an example that shows how you can obtain better performance using an executor than creating the threads yourself.

Getting ready

The example of this recipe has been implemented using the Eclipse IDE. If you use Eclipse or a different IDE, such as NetBeans, open it and create a new Java project.

How to do it...

Follow these steps to implement the example:

1. Create a class named `Task` and specify that it implements the `Runnable` interface:

   ```
   public class Task implements Runnable {
   ```

2. Implement the `run()` method. Create a loop with 1,000,000 steps, and in each step, do some mathematical operations with an integer variable:

   ```
   @Override
   public void run() {
      int r;
      for (int i=0; i<1000000; i++) {
   ```

```
    r=0;
    r++;
    r++;
    r*=r;
  }
}
```

3. Implement the main class of the example by creating a class named `Main` and adding the `main()` method to it:

```
public class Main {

  public static void main(String[] args) {
```

4. Create 1,000 threads to execute 1,000 task objects and wait for their finalization, controlling the total execution time:

```
Thread threads[]=new Thread[1000];
Date start,end;

start=new Date();
for (int i=0; i<threads.length; i++) {
  Task task=new Task();
  threads[i]=new Thread(task);
  threads[i].start();
}

for (int i=0; i<threads.length; i++) {
  try {
    threads[i].join();
  } catch (InterruptedException e) {
    e.printStackTrace();
  }
}
end=new Date();
System.out.printf("Main: Threads: %d\n",
                  (end.getTime()-start.getTime()));
```

5. Create an `Executor` object, send 1,000 `Task` objects to it, and wait for their finalization. Measure the total execution time:

```
ThreadPoolExecutor executor=(ThreadPoolExecutor)Executors
                                .newCachedThreadPool();

start=new Date();
```

```
for (int i=0; i<threads.length; i++) {
  Task task=new Task();
  executor.execute(task);
}
executor.shutdown();
try {
  executor.awaitTermination(1, TimeUnit.DAYS);
} catch (InterruptedException e) {
  e.printStackTrace();
}
end=new Date();
System.out.printf("Main: Executor: %d\n",
                  (end.getTime()-start.getTime()));
```

How it works...

In the entire execution of this example, we always obtained a smaller execution time for the executor than creating the thread directly. If your application has to execute a lot of tasks, better employ an executor.

See also

- The *Using executors instead of thread groups* and *Using the fork/join framework instead of executors* recipes in this chapter

Using concurrent data structures instead of programming yourself

Data structures are an essential part of every program. You always have to manage the data that you store in a data structure. Arrays, lists, or trees are examples of common data structures. The Java API provides a lot of ready-to-use data structures, but when you work with concurrent applications, you have to be careful because not all structures provided by the Java API are **thread-safe**. If you choose a data structure that is not thread-safe, you can have inconsistent data in your applications.

When you want to use a data structure in your concurrent application, you have to review the documentation of the class that implements that data structure to check that it supports concurrent operations. Java provides the following two kinds of concurrent data structures:

- **Non-blocking data structures**: All the operations provided by these data structures to either insert in or take off elements from the data structure return a null value if they can't be done currently because the data structure is full or empty respectively.
- **Blocking data structures**: These data structures provide the same operations that are provided by non-blocking data structures. However, they also provide operations to insert and take off data that, if not done immediately, would block the thread until you're able to do the operations.

These are some data structures provided by the Java API that you can use in your concurrent applications:

- `ConcurrentLinkedDeque`: This is a non-blocking data structure based on linked nodes that allow you to insert data at the beginning or end of the structure.
- `LinkedBlockingDeque`: This is a blocking data structure based on linked nodes. It can have fixed capacity. You can insert elements at the beginning or end of the structure. It provides operations that, if not done immediately, block the thread until you're able to do the operation.
- `ConcurrentLinkedQueue`: This is a non-blocking queue that allows you to insert elements at the end of the queue and take elements from its beginning.
- `ArrayBlockingQueue`: This is a blocking queue with fixed size. You insert elements at the end of the queue and take elements from its beginning. It provides operations that, if not done because the queue is either full or empty, puts the thread to sleep until you're able to do the operation.
- `LinkedBlockingQueue`: This is a blocking queue that allows you to insert elements at the end of the queue and take off elements from its beginning. It provides operations that, if not done because the queue is either full or empty, puts the thread to sleep until you're able to do the operation.
- `DelayQueue`: This is a `LinkedBlockingQueue` queue with delayed elements. Every element inserted in this queue must implement the `Delayed` interface. An element can't be taken off the list until its delay is 0.

- LinkedTransferQueue: This is a blocking queue that provides operations to work in situations that can be implemented as a producer/consumer problem. It provides operations that, if not done because the queue is either full or empty, puts the thread to sleep until you're able to do the operation.
- PriorityBlockingQueue: This is a blocking queue that orders its elements based on priority. All the elements inserted in this queue must implement the Comparable interface. The value returned by the compareTo() method will determine the position of the element in the queue. Just like all the blocking data structures, it provides operations that, if done immediately, puts the thread to sleep until you're able to do the operation.
- SynchronousQueue: This is a blocking queue where every insert operation must wait for a remove operation for the other thread. The two operations must be done at the same time.
- ConcurrentHashMap: This is a HashMap that allows concurrent operations. It's a non-blocking data structure.
- ConcurrentSkipListMap: This data structure associates keys with values. Every key can have only one value. It stores the keys in an ordered way and provides a method to find elements and get some elements from the map. It's a non-blocking data structure.

There's more...

If you need to use a data structure in your concurrent application, look in the Java API documentation to find the data structure that best fits your needs. Implement your own concurrent data structure that has some problems, which are as follows:

- They have a complex internal structure
- You have to take into account a lot of different situations
- You have to design a lot of tests to guarantee that it works correctly

If you don't find a data structure that fits your needs completely, try to extend one of the existing concurrent data structures to implement one adequately to your problem.

See also

- The recipes in Chapter 7, *Concurrent Collections*

Taking precautions using lazy initialization

Lazy initialization is a common programming technique that delays object creation until it is needed for the first time. This normally causes the initialization of the objects to be made in the implementation of the operations, instead of the constructor of the classes. The main advantage of this technique is that you can save memory. This is because you only create the indispensable objects needed for the execution of your applications. You could have declared a lot of objects in one class, but you don't use every object in every execution of your program; therefore, your application doesn't use the memory needed for the objects that you don't use in an execution of the program. This advantage can be very useful for applications that run in environments with limited resources.

By contrast, this technique has the disadvantage of having performance issues in your application, as you create objects the first time they are used inside an operation.

This technique can also provoke problems if you use it in concurrent applications. As more than one thread can be executing an operation at a time, they can be creating an object at the same time, and this situation can be problematic. This has a special importance with **singleton** classes. An application has only one object of these classes and, as mentioned earlier, a concurrent application can create more than one object. Consider the following code:

```
public static DBConnection getConnection(){
  if (connection==null) {
    connection=new DBConnection();
  }
  return connection;
}
```

This is the typical method in a singleton class to obtain the reference of the unique object of that class existing in the application, using lazy initialization. If the object hasn't been created yet, it creates the object. Finally, it always returns it.

If two or more threads executes at the same time the comparison of the first sentence (`connection == null`), all of them will create a `Connection` object. This isn't a desirable situation.

In this recipe, you will implement an elegant solution to the lazy initialization problem.

Getting ready

The example of this recipe has been implemented using the Eclipse IDE. If you use Eclipse or a different IDE, such as NetBeans, open it and create a new Java project.

How to do it...

Follow these steps to implement the example:

1. Create a class named DBConnectionOK:

   ```
   public class DBConnectionOK {
   ```

2. Declare a private constructor. Write the name of the thread that executes it:

   ```
   private DBConnectionOK() {
     System.out.printf("%s: Connection created.\n",
                      Thread.currentThread().getName());
   }
   ```

3. Declare a private static class named LazyDBConnectionOK. It has a private static final DBConnectionOK instance named INSTANCE:

   ```
   private static class LazyDBConnection {
     private static final DBConnectionOK INSTANCE = new
                                        DBConnectionOK();
   }
   ```

4. Implement the getConnection() method. It doesn't receive any parameter and returns a DBConnectionOK object. It returns the INSTANCE object:

   ```
   public static DBConnectionOK getConnection() {
     return LazyDBConnection.INSTANCE;
   }
   ```

5. Create a class named `Task` and specify that it implements the `Runnable` interface. Implement the `run()` method. Call the `getConnection()` method of the `DBConnectionOK()` method:

```
public class Task implements Runnable {

    @Override
    public void run() {

        System.out.printf("%s: Getting the connection...\n",
                        Thread.currentThread().getName());
        DBConnectionOK connection=DBConnectionOK.getConnection();
        System.out.printf("%s: End\n",
                        Thread.currentThread().getName());

    }


}
```

6. Implement the main class of the example by creating a class named `Main` and adding the `main()` method to it:

```
public class Main {
    public static void main(String[] args) {
```

7. Create 20 `Task` objects and 20 threads to execute them:

```
        for (int i=0; i<20; i++){
            Task task=new Task();
            Thread thread=new Thread(task);
            thread.start();
        }
    }
```

How it works...

The key of the example is the `getConnection()` method and the `private static class` `LazyDBConnection` instance. When the first thread calls the `getConnection()` method, the `LazyDBConnection` class initializes the `INSTANCE` object by calling the constructor of the `DBConnection` class. This object is returned by the `getConnection()` method. When the rest of the threads call the `getConnection()` method, the object is already created, so all the threads use the same object that is created only once.

When you run the example, you will see the start and end messages of 20 tasks, but only one creation message.

Using the fork/join framework instead of executors

Executors allow you to avoid the creation and management of threads. You implement tasks by implementing `Runnable` or `Callable` interfaces and sending them to the executor. It has a pool of threads and uses one of them to execute the tasks.

Java 7 provides a new kind of executor with the fork/join framework. This executor, implemented in the `ForkJoinPool` class, is designed for problems that can be split into smaller parts using the divide and conquer technique. When you implement a task for the fork/join framework, you have to check the size of the problem you have to resolve. If it's bigger than a predefined size, you divide the problem into two or more subcategories and create as many subtasks as the number of divisions you have made. The task sends these subtasks to the `ForkJoinPool` class using the `fork()` operation and waits for its finalization using the `join()` operation.

For these kinds of problems, fork/join pools get better performance than classical executors. In this recipe, you are going to implement an example where you can check this point.

Getting ready

The example of this recipe has been implemented using the Eclipse IDE. If you use Eclipse or a different IDE, such as NetBeans, open it and create a new Java project.

How to do it...

Follow these steps to implement the example:

1. Create a class named `TaskFJ` and specify that it extends the `RecursiveAction` class:

   ```
   public class TaskFJ extends RecursiveAction {
   ```

2. Declare a private array of `int` numbers named `array`:

   ```
   private final int array[];
   ```

3. Declare two private `int` attributes, named `start` and `end`:

   ```
   private final int start, end;
   ```

4. Implement the constructor of the class to initialize its attributes:

```
public TaskFJ(int array[], int start, int end) {
   this.array=array;
   this.start=start;
   this.end=end;
}
```

5. Implement the `compute()` method. If this task has to process a block of more than 1,000 elements (determined by the `start` and `end` attributes), create two `TaskFJ` objects, send them to the `ForkJoinPool` class using the `fork()` method, and wait for their finalization using the `join()` method:

```
@Override
protected void compute() {
   if (end-start>1000) {
      int mid=(start+end)/2;
      TaskFJ task1=new TaskFJ(array,start,mid);
      TaskFJ task2=new TaskFJ(array,mid,end);
      task1.fork();
      task2.fork();
      task1.join();
      task2.join();
```

6. Otherwise, increment the elements that this task has to process. After every increment operation, put the thread to sleep for 1 millisecond:

```
} else {
   for (int i=start; i<end; i++) {
      array[i]++;
      try {
         TimeUnit.MILLISECONDS.sleep(1);
      } catch (InterruptedException e) {
         e.printStackTrace();
      }
   }
}
```

7. Create a class named `Task` and specify that it implements the `Runnable` interface:

```
public class Task implements Runnable {
```

8. Declare a private array of `int` number named `array`:

```
private final int array[];
```

9. Implement the constructor of the class to initialize its attribute:

```
public Task(int array[]) {
   this.array=array;
}
```

10. Implement the `run()` method. Increment all the elements of the array. After every increment operation, put the thread to sleep for 1 millisecond:

```
@Override
public void run() {
   for (int i=0; i<array.length; i++ ){
     array[i]++;
     try {
       TimeUnit.MILLISECONDS.sleep(1);
     } catch (InterruptedException e) {
       e.printStackTrace();
     }
   }
}
```

11. Implement the main class of the example by creating a class named `Main` and adding the `main()` method to it:

```
public class Main {

   public static void main(String[] args) {
```

12. Create an `int` array with 100,000 elements:

```
int array[]=new int[100000];
```

13. Create a `Task` object and a `ThreadPoolExecutor` object and execute them. Execute the task by controlling the time during which the task is running:

```
Task task=new Task(array);
ExecutorService executor=Executors.newCachedThreadPool();

Date start,end;
start=new Date();
executor.execute(task);
executor.shutdown();
try {
   executor.awaitTermination(1, TimeUnit.DAYS);
} catch (InterruptedException e) {
   e.printStackTrace();
}
```

```
       end=new Date();
       System.out.printf("Main: Executor: %d\n",
                        (end.getTime()-start.getTime()));
```

14. Create a `TaskFJ` object and a `ForkJoinPool` object and execute them. Execute the task by controlling the time during which the task is running:

```
       TaskFJ taskFJ=new TaskFJ(array,1,100000);
       ForkJoinPool pool=new ForkJoinPool();
       start=new Date();
       pool.execute(taskFJ);
       pool.shutdown();
       try {
          pool.awaitTermination(1, TimeUnit.DAYS);
       } catch (InterruptedException e) {
          e.printStackTrace();
       }
       end=new Date();
       System.out.printf("Core: Fork/Join: %d\n",
                        (end.getTime()-start.getTime()));
    }
```

How it works...

When you execute the example, you will see how the `ForkJoinPool` and `TaskFJ` classes get better performance than the `ThreadPoolExecutor` and `Task` classes.

If you have to solve a problem that can be split using the divide and conquer technique, use a `ForkJoinPool` class instead of a `ThreadPoolExecutor` class. You will get better performance.

See also

- The *Delegating the management of threads to executors* recipe of this chapter

Avoiding the use of blocking operations inside a lock

Blocking operations are operations that block the execution of the current thread until an event occurs. Typical blocking operations are those that involve input or output operations with the console, a file, or network.

If you use a blocking operation inside the critical section of a lock, you're deteriorating the performance of the application. While a thread is waiting for the event that would finish the blocking operation, the rest of the application might be waiting for the same event as well; however, none of the other threads will have access to the critical section and execute its code (the code of the critical section).

In this recipe, you will implement an example of this situation. The threads read a line from the console inside the critical section. This instruction makes the rest of the threads of the application will be blocked until the user introduces the line.

Getting ready

The example of this recipe has been implemented using the Eclipse IDE. If you use Eclipse or a different IDE, such as NetBeans, open it and create a new Java project.

How to do it...

Follow these steps to implement the example:

1. Create a class named `Task` and specify that it implements the `Runnable` interface:

```
public class Task implements Runnable {
```

2. Declare a private `Lock` attribute named `lock`:

```
private final Lock lock;
```

3. Implement the constructor of the class to initialize its attribute:

```
public Task (Lock lock) {
  this.lock=lock;
}
```

4. Implement the `run()` method:

```
@Override
public void run() {
    System.out.printf("%s: Starting\n",
                    Thread.currentThread().getName());
```

5. Acquire the lock using the `lock()` method:

```
lock.lock();
```

6. Call the `criticalSection()` method:

```
try {
    criticalSection();
```

7. Read a line from the console:

```
System.out.printf("%s: Press a key to continue: \n",
                Thread.currentThread().getName());
InputStreamReader converter = new InputStreamReader
                                    (System.in);
BufferedReader in = new BufferedReader(converter);
String line=in.readLine();
} catch (IOException e) {
e.printStackTrace();
```

8. Free the lock using the `unlock()` method in the finally section:

```
} finally {
    lock.unlock();
}
}
```

9. Implement the `criticalSection()` method. Wait for a random period of time:

```
private void criticalSection() {
    Random random=new Random();
    int wait=random.nextInt(10);
    System.out.printf("%s: Wait for %d seconds\n",
                    Thread.currentThread().getName(),wait);
    try {
        TimeUnit.SECONDS.sleep(wait);
    } catch (InterruptedException e) {
        e.printStackTrace();
    }
}
```

10. Implement the main class of the application by creating a class named `Main` and adding the `main()` method to it:

```
public class Main {
    public static void main(String[] args) {
```

11. Create a new `ReentrantLock` object named `lock`. Create 10 `Task` objects and 10 threads to execute them:

```
ReentrantLock lock=new ReentrantLock();
for (int i=0; i<10; i++) {
  Task task=new Task(lock);
  Thread thread=new Thread(task);
  thread.start();
}
```

How it works...

When you execute this example, 10 threads start their execution, but only one enters in the critical section, which gets implemented in the `run()` method. As every task reads a line from the console before releasing the lock, all the applications will be blocked until you introduce text in the console.

See also

- The *Holding locks for as short a time period as possible* recipe

Avoiding the use of deprecated methods

The Java concurrency API also has deprecated operations. These are operations that were included in the first versions of the API, but now you shouldn't use them. They have been replaced by other operations that implement better practices than the original ones.

The more critical deprecated operations are those that are provided by the Thread class. These operations are:

- destroy(): In the past, this method destroyed the thread. Actually, it throws a NoSuchMethodError exception.
- suspend(): This method suspends the execution of the thread until it's resumed.
- stop(): This method forces the thread to finish its execution.
- resume(): This method resumes the execution of the thread.

The ThreadGroup class also has some deprecated methods, which are as follows:

- suspend(): This method suspends the execution of all the threads that belong to this thread group until they resume
- stop(): This method forces the execution of all the threads of this thread group to finish
- resume(): This method resumes the execution of all the threads of this thread group

The stop() operation has been deprecated because it can provoke inconsistent errors. As it forces the thread to finish its execution, you can have a thread that finishes its execution before the completion of an operation and can leave the data in an inconsistent status. For example, if you have a thread that is modifying a bank account and it's stopped before it is finished, the bank account will probably have erroneous data.

The stop() operation can also cause a deadlock situation. If this operation is called when the thread is executing a critical section protected by a synchronization mechanism (for example, a lock), this synchronization mechanism will continue to block and no thread will be able to enter the critical section. This is the reason why the suspend() and resume() operations have been deprecated.

If you need an alternative to these operations, you can use an internal attribute to store the status of the thread. This attribute must be protected with synchronized access, or use an atomic variable. You must check the value of this attribute and take actions according to it. Take into account that you have to avoid data inconsistency and deadlock situations to guarantee the correct operation of your application.

Using executors instead of thread groups

The `ThreadGroup` class provides a mechanism to group threads in a hierarchical structure so you can do operations with all the threads that belong to a thread group with only one call. By default, all the threads belong to the same group, but you can specify a different one when you create the thread.

Anyway, thread groups don't provide any features that make their use interesting:

- You have to create the threads and manage their status
- The methods that control the status of all the threads of the thread group have been deprecated and their use is discouraged

If you need to group threads under a common structure, it is better to use an `Executor` implementation, such as `ThreadPoolExecutor`. It provides more functionalities, which are as follows:

- You don't have to worry about the management of the threads. The executor creates and reuses them to save execution resources.
- You can implement your concurrent tasks by implementing either the `Runnable` or `Callable` interface. The `Callable` interface allows you to implement tasks that return a result, which provides a big advantage over traditional tasks.
- When you send a task to an executor, it returns a `Future` object that allows you to know the status of the task and the returned result if it has finished its execution easily.
- You can schedule your tasks and execute them repeatedly with the special executor implemented by the `ScheduledThreadPoolExecutor` class.
- You can easily control the resources used by an executor. You can establish the maximum number of threads in the pool so your executor will never have more than that number of tasks running at a time.

For these reasons, it is better that you don't use thread groups and use executors instead.

See also

- The *Delegating the management of threads to executors* recipe in this chapter

Using streams to process big data sets

A `Stream` interface is a sequence of elements that can be filtered and transformed to get a final result sequentially or in parallel. This final result can be a primitive data type (an integer, a long ...), an object or a data structure. These are the characteristics that better define `Stream`:

- A stream is a sequence of data, not a data structure.
- You can create streams from different sources as collections (lists, arrays...), files, strings, or a class that provides the elements of the stream.
- You can't access an individual element of the streams.
- You can't modify the source of the stream.
- Streams define two kinds of operations: intermediate operations that produce a new `Stream` interface that allows you to transform, filter, map, or sort the elements of the stream and terminal operations that generate the final result of the operation. A stream pipeline is formed by zero or more intermediate operations and a final operation.
- Intermediate operations are lazy. They're not executed until the terminal operation begins its execution. Java can avoid the execution of an intermediate operation over an element or a set of elements of the stream if it detects that it doesn't affect the final result of the operation.

When you need to implement an operation that processes a big set of data in a concurrent way, you can use different elements of the **Java Concurrency API** to implement it. Java threads to either the **fork/join framework** or the **Executor framework**, but I think parallel streams are the best option. In this recipe, we will implement an example to explain the advantages that are provided by the use of parallel streams.

Getting ready

The example of this recipe has been implemented using the Eclipse IDE. If you use Eclipse or a different IDE, such as NetBeans, open it and create a new Java project.

How to do it...

Follow these steps to implement the example:

1. Create a class named `Person`. This class will have six attributes to define some basic characteristics of a person. We will implement the methods to `get()` and `set()` the values of the attributes, but they won't be included here:

```java
public class Person {
    private int id;
    private String firstName;
    private String lastName;
    private Date birthDate;
    private int salary;
    private double coeficient;
```

2. Now, implement a class named `PersonGenerator`. This class will only have a method named `generatedPersonList()` to generate a list of `Person` objects with random values with the size specified in parameters. This is the source code of this class:

```java
public class PersonGenerator {
    public static List<Person> generatePersonList (int size) {
        List<Person> ret = new ArrayList<>();

        String firstNames[] = {"Mary","Patricia","Linda",
                               "Barbara","Elizabeth","James",
                               "John","Robert","Michael","William"};
        String lastNames[] = {"Smith","Jones","Taylor",
                              "Williams","Brown","Davies",
                              "Evans","Wilson","Thomas","Roberts"};

        Random randomGenerator=new Random();
        for (int i=0; i<size; i++) {
            Person person=new Person();
            person.setId(i);
            person.setFirstName(firstNames
                                [randomGenerator.nextInt(10)]);
            person.setLastName(lastNames
                               [randomGenerator.nextInt(10)]);
            person.setSalary(randomGenerator.nextInt(100000));
            person.setCoeficient(randomGenerator.nextDouble()*10);
            Calendar calendar=Calendar.getInstance();
            calendar.add(Calendar.YEAR, -randomGenerator
                                        .nextInt(30));
            Date birthDate=calendar.getTime();
```

```
                person.setBirthDate(birthDate);

                ret.add(person);
            }
            return ret;
        }
    }
```

3. Now, implement a task named `PersonMapTask`. The main purpose of this task will be to convert a list of persons on a map, where the keys will be the name of the persons and the values will be a list with `Person` objects whose name is equal to the key. We will use the fork/join framework to implement this transformation, so the `PersonMapTask` will extend the `RecursiveAction` class:

```
public class PersonMapTask extends RecursiveAction {
```

4. The `PersonMapTask` class will have two private attributes: `List` of `Person` objects to process and `ConcurrentHashMap` to store results. We will use the constructor of the class to initialize both the attributes:

```
private List<Person> persons;
private ConcurrentHashMap<String, ConcurrentLinkedDeque
                                <Person>> personMap;

public PersonMapTask(List<Person> persons, ConcurrentHashMap
        <String, ConcurrentLinkedDeque<Person>> personMap) {
    this.persons = persons;
    this.personMap = personMap;
}
```

5. Now it's time to implement the `compute()` method. If the list has less than 1,000 elements, we will process the elements and insert them in `ConcurrentHashMap`. We will use the `computeIfAbsent()` method to get `List` associated with a key or generate a new `ConcurrentMapedDeque` object if the key doesn't exist in the map:

```
protected void compute() {

    if (persons.size() < 1000) {

        for (Person person: persons) {
            ConcurrentLinkedDeque<Person> personList=personMap
                    .computeIfAbsent(person.getFirstName(), name -> {
            return new ConcurrentLinkedDeque<>();
            });
```

```
            personList.add(person);
        }
        return;
    }
}
```

6. If `List` has more than 1,000 elements, we will create two child tasks and delegate the process of a part of the list to them:

```
PersonMapTask child1, child2;

child1=new PersonMapTask(persons.subList(0,persons.size()/2),
                         personMap);
child2=new PersonMapTask(persons.subList(persons.size()/2,
                                         persons.size()),
                         personMap);

    invokeAll(child1,child2);
    }
}
```

7. Finally, implement the `Main` class with the `main()` method. First, generate a list with 100,000 random `Person` objects:

```
public class Main {

    public static void main (String[] args) {
        List<Person> persons=PersonGenerator
                                    .generatePersonList(100000);
```

8. Then, compare two methods to generate `Map` with the names as keys, which are part of `List`, and `Person` as value. List will use a parallel `Stream` function and the `collect()` method using the `groupingByConcurrent()` collector:

```
Date start, end;

start =  new Date();
Map<String, List<Person>> personsByName = persons
                                        .parallelStream()
.collect(Collectors.groupingByConcurrent(p -> p
                                        .getFirstName()));
end = new Date();
System.out.printf("Collect: %d - %d\n", personsByName.size(),
                  end.getTime()-start.getTime());
```

9. The second option is using the fork/join framework and the `PersonMapTask` class:

```
start = new Date();
ConcurrentHashMap<String, ConcurrentLinkedDeque<Person>>
                forkJoinMap=new ConcurrentHashMap<>();
PersonMapTask personMapTask=new PersonMapTask
                                (persons,forkJoinMap);
ForkJoinPool.commonPool().invoke(personMapTask);
end = new Date();

System.out.printf("Collect ForkJoinPool: %d - %d\n",
                forkJoinMap.size(),
                end.getTime()-start.getTime());
    }
}
```

How it works...

In this recipe, we implemented two different versions of the same algorithm to obtain Map from List. If you execute it, you will obtain the same results and a similar execution time (at least the latter is true in my case when I executed the example in a four core computer). The biggest advantage we obtained using streams is the simplicity of the solution and its development time. With only one line of code, we implemented the solution. While in the other case, we implemented a new class (the `PersonMapTask`) using concurrent data structures and then executed it in the fork/join framework.

With Streams, you can divide your algorithm into simple steps that can be expressed in an elegant way, be easy to program and understand.

See also

- The *Creating streams from different sources, Reducing the elements of a stream* and *Sorting the elements of a stream* recipes in Chapter 6, *Parallel and reactive streams*

Other tips and tricks

In this final recipe, we have included other tips and tricks that haven't been included in other recipes of the chapter:

- Whenever possible, use concurrent design patterns: In software engineering, a design pattern is a solution to a common problem. They are commonly used in software development and concurrency applications and are not an exception. Patterns such as signaling, rendezvous, and mutex define how to implement concurrent applications in concrete situations, and they have been used to implement concurrent utilities.

- Implement concurrency at the highest possible level: Rich threading APIs, such as the Java concurrency API, offer you different classes to implement concurrency in your applications. Try to use the ones that provide you a higher level of abstraction. It will make it easier for you to implement your algorithm, and they are optimized to give better performance than using threads directly. Therefore, performance won't be a problem.

- Take scalability into account: One of the main objectives when you implement a concurrent algorithm is to take advantage of all the resources of your computer, especially the number of processors or cores. But this number may change over time. When you design a concurrent algorithm, don't presuppose the number of cores or processors that your application will execute on. Get information about the system dynamically. For example, in Java, you can get it with the `Runtime.getRuntime().availableProcessors()` method and make your algorithm use this information to calculate the number of tasks it's going to execute.

- Prefer local thread variables over static and shared when possible: Thread local variables are a special kind of variable. Every task will have an independent value for this variable, so you don't need any synchronization mechanism to protect access to it.

See also

- All the recipes in this chapter

Index

Lightning Source UK Ltd.
Milton Keynes UK
UKOW04f2033280417
300152UK00001B/36/P